AREA HANDBOOK for MOROCCO

Co-Authors

Richard F. Nyrop

Beryl Lieff Benderly
William W. Cover
Hany H. Makhlouf
Newton B. Parker
Suzanne Teleki

Research and writing were completed October 19/1

Published 1972

(This handbook supersedes DA Pam 550-49, November 1965)

WILDSIDE PRESS

DA PAM 550-49

FOREWORD

This volume is one of a series of handbooks prepared by Foreign Area Studies (FAS) of The American University, designed to be useful to military and other personnel who need a convenient compilation of basic facts about the social, economic, political, and military institutions and practices of various countries. The emphasis is on objective description of the nation's present society and the kinds of possible or probable changes that might be expected in the future. The handbook seeks to present as full and as balanced an integrated exposition as limitations on space and research time permit. It was compiled from information available in openly published material. An extensive bibliography is provided to permit recourse to other published sources for more detailed information. There has been no attempt to express any specific point of view or to make policy recommendations. The contents of the handbook represent the work of the authors and FAS and do not represent the official view of the United States government.

An effort has been made to make the handbook as comprehensive as possible. It can be expected, however, that the material, interpretations, and conclusions are subject to modification in the light of new information and developments. Such corrections, additions, and suggestions for factual, interpretive, or other change as readers may have will be welcomed for use in future revisions. Comments may be addressed to:

> The Director
> Foreign Area Studies
> The American University
> 5010 Wisconsin Avenue, N.W.
> Washington, D.C. 20016

PREFACE

In late 1971 Morocco continued to be strategically important, in part because of its location in the northwest corner of Africa and its proximity to the Strait of Gibraltar and in part because of its role as an Arabic and African state with close historic ties to France and Spain. In addition, during the late 1960s and early 1970s Morocco successfully maintained cordial economic and diplomatic relations with the United States, the Soviet Union, and the People's Republic of China.

In 1970 King Hassan II promulgated a new constitution, pursuant to which a single chamber legislature was elected and assumed its duties. Despite an attempted coup d'etat in July 1971, the king in late 1971 was continuing to delegate increased responsibility to the legislature and to his Council of Ministers, but the limits on royal power were largely self-imposed and could therefore be removed at any time.

The present *Area Handbook for Morocco* is the second revision of a 1958 study. The first revision was researched and written in 1965 by a team composed of Frederick R. Eisele, Allison Butler Herrick, Howard J. John, Dennis H. Morrissey, and Suzanne Teleki, under the chairmanship of Norman C. Walpole. Although the present handbook incorporates some of the material in the earlier studies, it is a substantial revision, and most of the chapters were totally rewritten.

The handbook is an attempt to provide a comprehensive study of the dominant social, economic, and political aspects of Moroccan society. Sources of information used included scholarly studies, official reports of governments and international organizations, and newspapers, periodicals, and journals. Relatively up-to-date economic data were available; the demographic statistics used were, for the most part, estimates used by the Population Reference Bureau, the International Bank for Reconstruction and Development; the United Nations; and various official publications of the governments of Morocco and the United States.

Two weeks after research and writing were completed on October 15, 1971, the Moroccan government released some preliminary data from a census reportedly completed on July 20, 1971. According to these data, the population as of July 20, 1971, was 15,379,359, and the annual growth rate was between 2.6 and 2.7 percent. These figures vary sharply from the estimates used by the sources cited above that as of mid-1971 the population was about 16.2 million, and the growth rate was about 3.2 or 3.3 percent a year. The Moroccan census report contained neither an explanation for the discrepancy between these figures and earlier government estimates nor a description of the methodology of the census. As of early 1972, it seems probable that both the Moroccan census figures and the estimates used in this book should be viewed as provisional and subject to revision.

The authors wish to express their gratitude to persons in various agencies of the United States government who gave of their time, documentary possessions, and special knowledge to provide data and perspective. In addition, the staff of the Joint Library of the International Monetary Fund and the International Bank for Reconstruction and Development were particularly helpful.

The literature on Morocco—academic and popular alike—is frequently confusing because of the indiscriminate mixing of English and French transliterations of Arabic words and phrases. For example, the more common transliterations of the Arabic words for *stream* and *troops* are, respectively, *oued* and *guich*, whereas a transliteration of those words according to the system recommended by the Library of Congress is *wadi* and *jaysh*. In an effort to reduce this confusion, the authors adhered to the Library of Congress system, but without diacritical markings, and indicated in the Glossary the more common French transliterations that a reader may encounter in other works. The place names used are those established for Morocco by the United States Board on Geographic Names in June 1970.

COUNTRY SUMMARY

1. COUNTRY: Kingdom of Morocco. Located at the northwest corner of Africa, separated from Europe by the Strait of Gibraltar. Regained independence on March 3, 1956, after forty-four years of French and Spanish rule. Capital, Rabat.
2. POPULATION: About 16.2 million in mid-1971, with Moroccan Muslims accounting for over 98 percent of the population. Estimated annual population growth rate, 3.3 percent. Population is densest in the coastal plains north and west of the Atlas ranges (more than 100 per square mile; overall density, eighty-eight per square mile).
3. SIZE AND TOPOGRAPHY: About 174,000 square miles of mountains, plains, and desert. Topographically the country divides into an open, agriculturally rich plains area in the northwest and economically poor mountains and plateaus in the eastern and southern portions.
4. LANGUAGES: Arabic is the official language and the native language of about 60 percent of the population. Estimated 40 percent of the population speaks one of several dialects of Berber; French widely used in government and modern sector. Bilingualism and trilingualism common.
5. RELIGION: Observance of Sunni Islam nearly universal. Islam is official religion, with king known as commander of the faithful (*amir al muaminin*).
6. EDUCATION: Enrollment levels rising, but public demand continues for more facilities and government scholarships. School system, adapted from French models, consists of a five-year primary, a four-year lower secondary, and a three-year upper secondary (academic or vocational) education. Five-year primary cycle compulsory by law, but in 1970 only 53 percent of school age children enrolled. Severe shortage of secondary school teachers. Main official efforts aimed at strengthening technical education on secondary and higher levels to meet manpower demands. In 1970 literacy estimated to be between 15 and 20 percent.
7. HEALTH: Gastrointestinal infections, tuberculosis, trachoma, typhoid, and malaria are widespread. Major contagious diseases (smallpox, cholera, and bubonic plague) controlled. Severe shortage of medical and paramedical personnel. Physician to population ratio one to 7,000 in cities, one to 60,000 in rural areas.

8. GOVERNMENT: A monarchy since independence in 1956. Constitution of 1970 reserves paramount power to king but provides for elected 240-member House of Representatives. Prime minister and the Council of Ministers appointed and dismissed by king.

9. JUSTICE: Civil and criminal codes adopted in 1958 and 1959 combine French and traditional Islamic law. Judiciary, appointed by king, constitutionally separate from executive and legislature. Supreme Court located at Rabat; four courts of appeal and numerous courts of first instance. Military justice, under separate code, revised July 25, 1971.

10. ADMINISTRATIVE DIVISIONS: Local government organized under nineteen provinces and two urban prefectures (Rabat and Casablanca) having status of provinces. Basic unit is urban or rural constituency of one or more communes; above the constituency is the circle, then the province. In 1971 seven higher entities called administrative regions, encompassing two or more provinces each, were being formed. All governors and lower executive heads appointed by royal authority; whole system administered under minister of interior. Elected provincial and communal councils since 1963 have had advisory role.

11. ECONOMY: Gross domestic product (GDP) increased at better than 5 percent annually (at constant prices) between 1967 and 1970. Throughout period largest contributions to the gross domestic product were made by agriculture (28 percent) and commerce (20 percent); manufacturing industry contributed about 12 percent per year.

12. EXPORTS: Export earnings increased at an average rate of over 3.5 percent per year from 1967 to 1970. Major exports (1970) were phosphate rock, citrus fruits, fresh vegetables, and canned fish.

13.' IMPORTS: Imports (cost, insurance, freight) increased at an average rate of over 9 percent from 1967 to 1970. Major imports (1970) were industrial equipment, automotive vehicles and parts, nonelectrical metal products, petroleum products, sugar, and soft wheat.

14. INDUSTRY: Industry represented about 20 percent of gross domestic product in 1969–70 period. Mining accounted for about 3 percent; energy, about 5 percent; and manufacturing, about 12 percent. The relative importance of the sector in the gross domestic product remained essentially static throughout the decade. Among manufactures the most important categories were foodstuffs and beverages, metal transformation, textiles, chemicals, and construction materials.

15. FINANCE: *Public.* Expenditures (budgeted) of the central government increased about 9 percent per year from 1967 to 1970. In 1970 they represented around 24 percent of gross domestic product— about 17.5 percent for current expenditures and 6.5 percent for investment. *Private.* Money supply increased about 9.8 percent per

year from 1967 to 1970. The major contribution to the increase was made by the central government.

16. LABOR: Work force estimated at over 5.5 million out of a total population of about 14.5 million in 1968. About 70 percent engaged in agriculture; 8.9 percent, in industry and handicrafts; 5.9 percent, in commerce; 4.6 percent, in services; 4.4 percent, in public sector; 2.2 percent, in transportation; and 4.3 percent, in other occupations. Unemployment, estimated at 12.4 percent in 1968, was rising rapidly. Severe shortage of skilled laborers, technicians, and managerial and professional personnel.

17. COMMUNICATIONS: Nine dailies in 1970; one a government newspaper, the rest published privately by Moroccans and foreign publishers. No prepublication censorship, but frequent bans and seizures of newspapers critical of government. Radio and television government owned and controlled. Radio most important medium. About 1 million radio receivers and some 173,000 television sets in 1970.

18. RAILROADS: Government-owned system of over 1,000 miles. Modernization program scheduled for completion during 1970s.

19. ROADS: Well-developed network in 1971 of about 31,000 miles, of which nearly 15,000 miles paved.

20. AIR TRANSPORT: Two national airlines—Royal Air Maroc (RAM) and Royal Air Inter (RAI). Majority of stock in both companies either directly or indirectly state owned. Over fifty civil airports, of which eight can handle international flights. In 1970 sixteen foreign airlines had regularly scheduled flights into and out of the country.

21. PORTS: Four major and thirteen lesser ports. Casablanca by far the largest, accounting for 75 percent of freight handled by all ports in 1969.

22. INTERNATIONAL AGREEMENTS AND MEMBERSHIPS: Member of the United Nations and its specialized agencies, the Organization of African Unity, and the League of Arab States.

23. AID PROGRAMS: During late 1960s Morocco received about DH2,500 million (5.06 dirham equal US$1) in grants and loans (grants about 25 percent) from the United States, France, West Germany, the International Bank for Reconstruction and Development, and other groups. In addition, substantial amounts of training and technical assistance secured from a number of the specialized agencies of the United Nations.

24. NATIONAL DEFENSE: Royal Armed Forces (Forces Armées Royales—FAR) composed of a nearly 50,000-man army, a small air force and navy, and small special detachments. Sûreté Nationale (16,000-man police force) has primary responsibility for internal security. In addition, Auxiliary Forces and Royal Gendarmerie perform police work. All forces responsible to the king.

MOROCCO

TABLE OF CONTENTS

	Page
FOREWORD	iii
PREFACE	v
COUNTRY SUMMARY	vii

SECTION I. SOCIAL

Chapter 1. General Character of the Society 1

            2. Geography and Population 7
               Geography—Population—Living Conditions

            3. Historical Setting 31
               Early History—The Coming of Islam and the Arabs—The Medieval Berber Empires—The Sharifian Dynasties— Morocco in European Diplomacy—Colonialism: The French and Spanish Protectorates—The Struggle for Independence—The First Years of Independence, 1956–65—The Emergency Period: 1965–70

            4. Ethnic Groups and Languages 71
               The Peoples of Morocco—Language and Society

            5. Religious Life 85
               Islam—Folk Beliefs and Folk Religion—Minority Religions

            6. Social Structure 99
               Structure of Society—The Individual, the Family, and the Sexes

            7. Education, Communication, and the Arts and Sciences
               Education—The Arts and Sciences—Communication 119

SECTION II. POLITICAL

Chapter 8. The Governmental System and Political Dynamics
               Constitutional System—The Monarchy—Government and Executive Agencies—Legal System, Judiciary, and Courts—Legislative Arm and the Electoral System—Local Government—Parties, Interest Groups, and Elections—Political Stress and Crisis—National Goals 157

		Page
9.	Foreign Relations	195
	Relations with the States of the Maghrib—Relations with Other African States—Relations with Other Arab States—Relations with West European States—Relations with the United States—Relations with the Communist States—The United Nations and Other International Organizations—Mechanics of Foreign Policy	
10.	Political Values	213

SECTION III. ECONOMIC

Chapter			
	11.	Character and Structure of the Economy	217
		Resources and Problems—Gross Domestic Product—Consumption and Investment—Role of the Government—Development Planning—Public Sector Finances—Banking and Currency	
	12.	Agriculture and Industry	245
		Agriculture—Industry—Labor	
	13.	Trade and Transportation	277
		Domestic Trade—Transportation and Telecommunication—Tourism—Balance of Payments—Foreign Trade—Foreign Investment—Foreign Aid	

SECTION IV. NATIONAL SECURITY

Chapter	14.	National Defense and Internal Security	307
		The Armed Forces—The Place of the Military in National Life—Weapons and Equipment—Organization of the Armed Forces—Internal Security Forces—Prisons	

	Page
BIBLIOGRAPHY FOR THE NOVEMBER 1965 EDITION	327
BIBLIOGRAPHY FOR REVISED EDITION	357
GLOSSARY	383
INDEX	387

LIST OF ILLUSTRATIONS

Figure		Page
1	Morocco	xiv
2	Geographic Regions of Morocco, 1971	8
3	Rivers, Dams, and Irrigated Areas of Morocco, 1971	17
4	Rainfall and Temperature in Morocco	19
5	Mineral Resources of Morocco, 1971	22
6	Languages of Morocco	72
7	Jewish Population of Morocco, Selected Years, 1948–70	78
8	Schematic Representation of a Typical Segmentary System in Morocco	103
9	Railroads, Principal Highways, Ports, and Airports of Morocco, 1970	282
10	Defense and Security Forces of Morocco, 1971	308
11	Organization of the Moroccan Sûreté Nationale	322
12	Organization of a Police Region in Morocco	324

LIST OF TABLES

Table		Page
1	Administrative Regions, Provinces, and Prefectures of Morocco, 1971	177
2	Gross Domestic Product of Morocco, by Industrial Origin at 1960 Market Prices, Selected Years, 1960–69	221
3	Morocco's Five Year Development Plan, 1968–72, at Constant (1967) Prices, by Sectors and Investing Agencies	226
4	Budget Estimates of the Current Expenditures of the Central Government of Morocco, 1966–71	231
5	Budget Estimates of the Investment Outlays of the Central Government of Morocco, 1966–71	232
6	Budget Estimates for Financing of Current and Investment Outlays of Morocco, 1966–71	234
7	Changes in and Sources of Money Supply in Morocco, 1965–70	241
8	Estimated Land Utilization in Morocco, Mid-1960s	247
9	Estimated Distribution of Agricultural Land in Morocco, by Ownership, Mid-1960s	249
10	Output of Principal Agricultural Commodities in Morocco, Average 1961–65, Annual 1966–70	252
11	Index of Industrial Production in Morocco, by Sector, Selected Years, 1963–69	260
12	Mineral Production in Morocco, Selected Years, 1964–70	263
13	Manufacturing Production in Morocco, Selected Commodities, 1965–69	267
14	Distribution of Work Force in Morocco, 1964, 1968, and 1973	268
15	Balance of Payments of Morocco, 1969	291
16	Foreign Trade of Morocco, 1966–69	294
17	Principal Suppliers and Customers of Morocco, 1969	296

Rain in summer occurs only in the mountains, where in June and July there may be violent storms. The heat and dryness that pervade the country in summer are largely the results of the anticyclone from the Azores and the winds from the northeast (*levante*). The heat is intensified by the occasional Saharan winds, such as the sirocco, which howl in off the desert in midsummer and make even the Rifian seaports almost unbearable for days at a time.

In spring and fall precipitation is slight and irregular. For at least two months but generally four, and sometimes five or six, the mean temperature is above 68°F. In winter it is nowhere colder than 46°F except in the Middle Atlas, which often has registered temperatures below zero. August is generally the hottest month, and January, the coldest.

The coast in general has a more stable climate than the interior, and on the Atlantic side, particularly around Casablanca, it is fresher and less humid than on the Mediterranean. Nowhere, except in Tangier, in parts of the Rif, and in parts of the Middle Atlas, does annual rain exceed thirty-two inches. Tangier, because of its location at the entrance to the straits, has a freakish climate and is subjected to local winds and rains but to no snow. The cedar forests of the Middle Atlas and the Rif are the wettest spots in the country. Elsewhere, annual means are usually less than twenty inches. Summer rainfall is never more than 20 percent of the total anywhere, even in the mountains, and elsewhere it is less than 10 percent.

Soils, Flora, and Fauna

Some soils of good quality with satisfactory humus content are found between the Atlas and Rif ranges and in the valleys of the Atlas. The soils, however, are thin and calcareous, causing decrease of the humus content under intensive cultivation. Alluvial plains are scarce; the principal ones are located in the Rharb Plain and the Sous Valley. Other soils of good quality are found in the Chaouia and Doukkala plains. Elsewhere, as on the plateau east of Midelt or on the eastern High Plateau near the Algerian border, the soils are poor, with considerable acidity and much leaching of nutrients.

The dominant vegetation of the Atlantic plains and the plateaus include asphodels, fennels, and dwarf palm. The plateau is dominated by grasses, such as esparto or alfa grass, not found on the Atlantic plain. Vegetation in the desert region is limited to date palms in the oases; these also exist to an extent north of the Atlas, and the palm trees of Marrakech are famous. The pre-Saharan plateaus are almost completely bare of plants.

It is only in the mountains that there is any real floral diversification. There are fewer forests on the mountains than before, as a result of soil erosion, woodcutting, and the destructive influence of wild goats. The vegetation in the Rif, more denuded than in the Middle Atlas, consists primarily of tough, low bushes. Along the riverbeds in the western part of the Rif, oleanders predominate, and in the central part there are canebrakes. Cedars are restricted to the middle slopes of the highest mountains of the Middle Atlas. To the west, cork oak predominates, and the wild olive is found throughout the chain. Aleppo pine and evergreen oak occur in the central Rif.

In the Atlas chains are the thuja (a tree related to the cypress) forests of the High Atlas, the argan trees of the Sous Valley, and the cork oak forests of the Mamora. The most beautiful Moroccan forests are those of the evergreen oaks and conifers that cover the Middle Atlas. The cedar forests of this region are particularly impressive, especially those of the region around Ifrane, south of Meknès.

Outside the actual forest area isolated trees are found, and hardwoods—poplars, elms, and ash—as well as tamarisk and oleander adorn the riverbanks. In the less watered regions, as in the Rif, lentiscus and rockrose thickets are fairly common.

There are few species of large animals in Morocco. The striped hyena roams the eastern steppes, jackals and foxes are everywhere, and mountain cats live in the Atlas ranges. Ferrets are used in the Rif to hunt rabbits. Wild boar abound in all the higher mountains. They are hunted by the Berbers because of the damage they do to cultivated plots of land and because their hides may be sold and their tusks can be used for magical purposes.

Rabbits and hares are everywhere. Barbary apes live in the northern foothills of the Rif but not in the Rif proper or in the Atlas ranges. The porcupine and the hedgehog are abundant. The Barbary sheep live in the Atlas, and gazelle inhabit the pre-Saharan steppes.

Hawks, small eagles, and owls abound in the Rif, as they do in the Atlas ranges, where the white vulture is also found. Partridges and doves are found in great numbers in the mountains. Ravens are everywhere, as are cowbirds and sparrows.

Snakes are not common, but some poisonous varieties, such as vipers, puff adders, and Egyptian cobras, exist in the south.

Mineral Resources

Mineral resources are varied, and some of them are of major importance (see fig. 5). In addition to phosphates, other important mineral deposits include anthracite, iron, manganese, lead, zinc, and cobalt, and there are minor deposits of petroleum, antimony, copper, silver, barite, asbestos, tungsten, gypsum, fluorite, beryl, mica, and graphite. The country is self-sufficient in salt; potash has been discovered near Khemisset, about thirty-five miles south of Rabat.

Phosphate reserves, of undetermined size but estimated at several billion tons, are among the largest in the world. The highest grade of

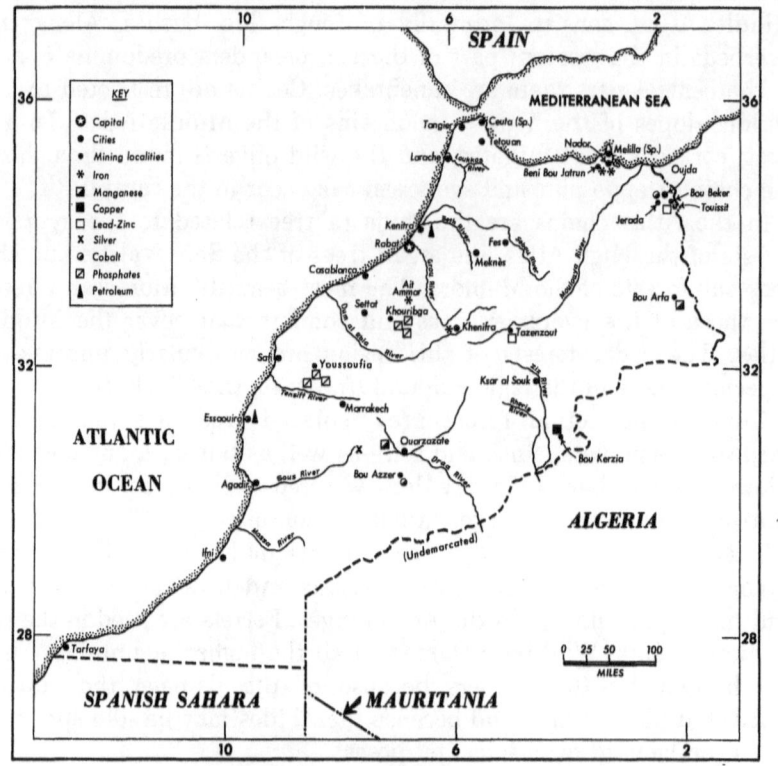

Source: Adapted from "Maroc," *Monde Diplomatique* (Supplement) [Paris], XVII, No. 192, March 25, 1970, p. 34.

Figure 5. Mineral Resources of Morocco, 1971.

phosphate rock comes from Khouribga, but the second major producing area at Youssoufia, fifty miles east of the port of Safi, has much larger reserves (see ch. 12, Agriculture and Industry).

The Jerada mine, in the Oujda region near the eastern border with Algeria, is the only anthracite field in the Mediterranean area. The coal is generally of high quality but is fragile and occurs in thin seams. Iron deposits and mines are spread throughout the country, but few of them are located near existing transportation facilities. The principal mines are the two near Nador on the Mediterranean coast; others are near Ait Ammar, about seventy miles inland from Casablanca. A large deposit, but with a low iron content, is located at Khenifra in the Middle Atlas.

There are two principal manganese fields with high-grade reserves: one at Bou Arfa in Eastern Morocco and another on the Imini River in the High Atlas southeast of Marrakech. Lead and zinc are mined at Bou Beker and Touissit near the Algerian border but, according to information in 1965, reserves in this area were nearly exhausted.

There is another lead-zinc mine near Tazenzout, in the upper Moulouya Valley. Cobalt is found at Bou Azzer, about twenty miles south of Ouarzazate. According to information published in 1965, the quality of the ore from the principal mines has declined, but surveying for new and apparently rich reserves was in progress in 1970. In 1971 prospecting for silver was underway fifty miles west of Ouarzazate, and prospecting for copper was being conducted in the region between Casablanca and Khouribga and at Bou Kerzia.

Limited oil and natural gas resources are located along the Atlantic shore and on the Rharb Plain about twenty miles east of Kenitra. Wells in the Kenitra area were near exhaustion during the late 1960s, but those near Essaouira on the southern shore yielded significant quantities. In 1970 intensive offshore prospecting for oil, mostly by foreign companies, was in progress in several places (see ch. 12, Agriculture and Industry).

POPULATION

According to Moroccan and foreign demographers, the country's population is increasing at an annual rate in excess of 3 percent. Assuming a growth rate of about 3.3 percent annually, experts estimated the population in mid-1970 at 15.7 million and, in mid-1971, at 16.2 million. Increasing at this rate, the population is expected to reach almost 22 million by 1980 and to double by 1991.

Fluctuations in the number of people in the country at any given time are related to tourist traffic and to the emigration of Moroccan workers to European countries and Libya. Workers' emigration has been officially encouraged and supported by the government. During the mid-1960s an estimated average of 10,000 workers emigrated each year, mostly to France and Libya (see ch. 12, Agriculture and Industry).

Since the mid-1960s the government has officially advocated birth control. In 1965 King Hassan publicly urged the adoption of policies to check the rapid population growth. In 1966 the High Commission on Population was created to disseminate family planning information and publicity, and a birth control program was launched with financial assistance from the Ford Foundation. Earlier legislation that prohibited the use of contraceptive devices was abolished in 1968. In 1970, however, many population experts expressed doubts regarding the practicability of birth control in the country. Opposition was forthcoming from conservative Islamic leaders, and members of the political opposition attacked the program in the context of general criticism of official social policies.

Birth control has found response mostly among urban groups. A limited survey conducted in 1966 among urban women showed that a majority, especially the wives of middle-level government functionaries and skilled workers, were interested in acquiring more birth control information and in limiting the size of their families to four children. According to reports published in 1970, birth control information reached only about 5 percent of the population in 1968, and about 114,500 women used contraceptive devices.

Characteristics

According to the census of June 1960—the country's first and, as of mid-1971, only unified population count—the population was 11,627,000, of which 11,071,000, or slightly over 95 percent, were Moroccan Muslims. Also included as Moroccans were about 160,000 Moroccan Jews. The non-Moroccan minority of about 396,000 included 173,000 French, 97,000 Spanish, 95,000 Algerian refugees, and 31,000 others. Comparable estimated figures for early 1970 show Muslims accounting for 98.6 percent of the total. The policy of Moroccanization and the Jewish exodus had markedly diminished the number of the Moroccan Jews and of the foreign community; in 1971 there were 40,000 Jewish Moroccans and some 170,000 non-Moroccan foreign residents (see ch. 4, Ethnic Groups and Languages). The latter group included 90,000 French, 45,000 Spanish, and 35,000 others.

Age, Sex, and Vital Statistics

The country's high growth rate is reflected in the overwhelming youthfulness of its population. According to a Moroccan official source, children under fifteen years of age accounted for nearly half of the total population in 1970. A population survey of the city and prefecture of Casablanca in 1968 showed that 60 percent of the residents were less than twenty years old.

Estimates published by the United Nations, based on a total population of 15,050,000 in 1969, show that there were about 14,000 more women than men. Men constituted a slight majority in the age groups from one to twenty, but there was some excess of women in the age group from twenty to twenty-nine and among persons fifty years and older.

The absence of earlier data prevents the establishment of a trend in vital statistics, but demographers generally agree that during the late 1960s, as environmental health conditions improved and medical facilities became available in some rural areas, the birth rate remained high and the death rate fell. In 1969 the United Nations estimated the birth rate among Moroccan Muslims at 46.1 per 1,000 and the death rate at 18.7 per 1,000. Other population experts calculated the death rate at 19 per 1,000 in 1968 and predicted that the rate would decrease to 10 per 1,000 by 1972. The minister of public health reported in 1971 that the birth rate was 50 per 1,000 and the death rate was 17 per 1,000. He urged an intensification of family planning efforts to achieve a reduction of the birth rate to 45 per 1,000 by the end of the Five Year Plan.

Density, Settlement, and Mobility

Because of the country's relatively broad and adequately watered coastal plains and plateaus, the population is spread over a larger portion of the country than is the case in the rest of North Africa, where it is concentrated in a narrow strip along the coast. According to United Nations estimates, the country's overall population density in 1969 was 88 per square mile, but there were wide regional variations. The major portion of the population is concentrated north and west of the Atlas ranges; throughout much of this area the density exceeds 100 per square mile, and it reaches more than 1,000 in the highly urbanized, intensively farmed coastal strip centering on Casablanca. These areas are in sharp contrast with the sparsely populated region south of the High Atlas (where the population is concentrated in oases lining the Draa River Valley southeast of Ouarzazate) and the Tafilalt Plain south of Ksar al Souk.

The settled agricultural population lives mainly in the relatively well watered northern portion of the Atlantic lowlands, southward along the coast, and inland at the foot of the Atlas mountains where irrigation is practiced. In the late fall families in the Middle Atlas in search of pasture move to the plains surrounding Fes and Meknès, to the Tadla Plain of the upper Oum al Rbia, and to the steppe of the Moulouya River. In the spring they return to their mountain villages to resume sedentary cultivation. Similar localized movements in search of grazing land are also common in the semiarid steppe areas of the southeast.

The sedentary Arab, or Berber, population lives in one-room dwellings built of sun-baked clay, with roofs of clay tiles. In the mountainous areas the dwellings are staggered on the slopes, rising in tiers so that one family's rooftop becomes another's roadway. Traditional Berber military fortresses, called casbahs, are typical of the southern Atlas region where, together with the mosque, they constitute the core of many rural towns.

Market towns, scattered throughout the rural areas, serve as local centers of administration and trade. They are noted for the weekly market (*souk*), which serves as a gathering point for farmers and nomadic herders from the surrounding areas to buy, sell, conduct business with the government, and exchange news and gossip.

Rural-to-urban migration has been rapidly increasing since the nineteenth century. In 1900 urban residents accounted for 10 percent of the population; the comparable proportion in 1970 was about 30 percent. According to the census of 1960, 32 percent of the Muslims in urban areas were born in the countryside. An estimated 100,000 persons migrate to the cities each year. Urban populations have been growing at an average rate of more than 5 percent annually and, according to most projections, will total some 10 million by 1980. Casablanca, the country's largest city, receives between 25,000 and 40,000 immigrants each year. Its population is growing at a rate of almost 7 percent annually and is expected to reach nearly 4 million by 1980.

The majority of rural migrants are farmers or sharecroppers from the coastal and central plains and from the pre-Saharan region who come to the cities in search of employment and to ease family pressures on the land. To discourage this rural exodus the government has, on occasion, returned migrants to their places of origin; in other cases they were refused identity cards, a prerequisite for qualifying for the services of government labor exchanges. These measures, however, proved to be largely ineffective.

In 1968 one city, Casablanca, had a population of over 1.5 million (compared to 20,000 in 1900). In seven other cities, Rabat, Marrakech, Fes, Mèknes, Tangier, Oujda, and Tetouan, the population exceeded 100,000; twenty-five other cities had populations in excess of 25,000.

The coastal cities of Casablanca, Rabat, Tangier, Kenitra, and Safi, all of which were developed by the French and Spanish, are centers of industry and commerce. They have large foreign populations and are also the favorite destinations of rural migrants (see ch. 6, Social Structure). The modern sections of these cities are laid out on a rectangular plan with broad avenues, parks, and high buildings. The neighboring ancient Muslim and Jewish quarters (called, respectively, *madina* and *mallah*), are usually extremely crowded, with low, mud-brick stone houses along narrow, twisting alleys. The poor ventilation of dwellings and inadequate sewage and waste disposal facilities pose serious health hazards. In the *madina* of Casablanca, densities range between 3,000 and 3,700 persons per acre. Although originally there was some separation between the *madina* and the modern sector, the two have grown together in most cities, and frequently the modern city surrounds the *madina*.

Close around the modern cities are *bidonvilles*, agglomerations of makeshift shacks, frequently built of flattened oil drums, bits of lumber, and corrugated iron, in which are crowded the poorest and most recent migrants from the rural areas. Although sanitation facilities, electricity, and potable water are either entirely lacking or inadequate in the *bidonvilles*, their populations reportedly increased from 600,000 in 1965 to nearly 1 million in 1970. In Casablanca some 300,000 persons lived in *bidonvilles* in 1968, and the density in these areas was about 2,500 persons per acre.

LIVING CONDITIONS

Standards of Living and Health

Rapid population growth, low agricultural production, urban crowding, and widespread unemployment have kept the general living standard near or at subsistence level. The surge to the cities has aggravated the job shortage and has led to the disruption of traditional social patterns and forms of mutual assistance (see ch. 6, Social Structure). The scope of official social services is limited in relation to the needs of the large number of poor and destitute persons.

A small urban and rural minority, constituting some 5 to 10 percent of the population, derives its existence from the modern economic sector and receives more than half of the national income. The uneven distribution of wealth has been extensively criticized by leaders of the political opposition and by the press (see ch. 8, The Governmental System and Political Dynamics). The average per capita income increased from the equivalent of US$150 in 1964 to US$190 in 1968. The rural average per capita income, generally lower than the national average, was estimated at below the equivalent of US$150 in 1967. The figures, however, fail to show the large proportion of minimal incomes. During the late 1960s, for example, more than half of the urban population had annual incomes below the equivalent of US$100. Income differentials are most marked in the cities where many persons with high earnings or private wealth live in proximity with unemployed residents of *bidonvilles*. Disparities in wealth are less noticeable in the countryside, although a few rural families have been able to accumulate surplus products or cash.

The cost of living during the late 1960s rose despite government controls on some prices, notably on those of bread, cereals, and flour. At the same time wages and salaries remained stationary in accordance with official efforts to check inflation. Between September 1968 and March 1969 the cost of living index rose from 126 to 131, reflecting increases in rents and in the prices of services, recreation, and some food items.

The food supply is sufficient but, because of uneven distribution and varying availability, about 20 percent of the population, especially young children and pregnant women, are inadequately fed. Most affected by shortages are people in poorly irrigated rural areas and in the *bidonvilles*. Many foods are not available because they are exported or because they deteriorate through inadequate preservation and storage.

Caloric intake varies from 800 calories per day among the poor rural population to more than 3,500 calories among wealthy groups. Nutritional deficiency diseases are widespread: in 1967 approximately

2 million people suffered from diseases related to shortages of calcium, vitamin D, and protein in the diet. Rickets and kwashiorkor (a serious form of malnutrition caused by a shortage of protein) were especially common among infants and young children.

The diet is based on cereals—barley, wheat and, to a lesser extent, corn—and oil. Vegetables and fruit are consumed for variation. Legumes are consumed in minimal amounts, and about half of the population does not eat meat. Milk production and consumption are low; when available, it is taken in the form of yogurt and, less frequently, as cheese.

Contagious diseases, such as smallpox, bubonic plague, and cholera, have been controlled and no longer reach epidemic proportions, but intestinal infections, tuberculosis, trachoma, typhoid, and malaria remained widespread in 1971. Parasitic ailments and infectious diseases of childhood were the principal causes of death in 1970, according to the Ministry of Public Health. Lack of sanitation, poor personal hygiene, and the prevalence of disease-carrying insects contribute to their high incidence. Curative and preventive medical services are offered by the Ministry of Public Health free of charge. In 1968 public health physicians examined more than 5 million persons visiting health centers operated by the ministry; during the same year 330,000 persons were treated in government hospitals, 2.6 million children were vaccinated, and more than 5 million tubes of ophthalmic ointment were distributed. The minister of public health stated in 1970 that there were 650 public health physicians and 632 physicians in private practice. The physician-to-population ratio was 1 to 7,000 in the cities and 1 to 60,000 in the rural areas. The Medical School of the University of Rabat (also known as Mohammed V University) graduates about 50 physicians annually.

Government Welfare Activities

In 1971 welfare and social services were administered by the Ministry of Labor and Social Affairs, the Ministry of Youth and Recreation, and the Ministry of Public Health. Official agencies dealing with public housing were under the jurisdiction of the Ministry of Interior. These included the Office of Urban Planning and Housing with regional offices in Rabat, Casablanca, Fes, and Marrakech. The office conducted studies of crowded urban areas, directed low-interest housing loan programs, and supervised the preparation of lots. The Center of Experimentation, Research and Training, also within the Ministry of Interior, encouraged and coordinated research in areas earmarked for physical and social development.

The Ministry of Labor and Social Affairs directed two major public welfare programs: social security and the National Development

Program (Promotion Nationale). The latter was created in 1961 to provide temporary jobs to the unemployed on public work projects for food rations and a small cash wage (see ch. 12, Agriculture and Industry). The ministry also operated day care centers, maternal and child clinics, and homes and centers for orphaned children, the aged, and handicapped persons and administered vacation centers.

Social security was introduced in 1961; in 1971 it was operated by the National Social Security Bank under the supervision of the ministry. The scope of the system was modest, extending coverage only to regularly employed salary and wage earners in industry and commerce. In 1965 these workers accounted for about 15 percent of the labor force. Farmers, farmworkers, and domestic workers were not covered. Artisans, public servants, and self-employed professionals and businessmen were also ineligible, but some of these groups, notably public servants, have pension plans that pay appreciably higher benefits than social security.

Allowances and pensions under the social security system in 1970 offered benefits in minimal amounts for old age, sickness, accident, maternity, and death; family allowances were paid at the rate of DH24 (5.06 dirham equal US$1—see Glossary) for each child. Employers contributed 13 percent of each worker's salary, and workers, 2.5 percent of their wages. Information on the number of workers covered by social security in 1971 was not available. According to data published in 1968 the monthly average during that year of workers contributing social security payments was 242,884; other data for the same year indicated that the majority of persons benefiting from social security were recipients of family allowances (see ch. 12, Agriculture and Industry).

Most of the country's voluntary social welfare societies were subsidized by the government and coordinated by the central and regional offices of the National Mutual Aid (Entr'Aide Nationale—EAN), which was organized in 1957. Its central office, located in Rabat, was headed by King Hassan's sister, Princess Lala Aisha. The primary activity of EAN was the distribution of food and clothing and fuel to the needy on religious holidays and royal birthdays. To be eligible for aid, men must be over sixty years old, and women must be widowed or divorced with children.

Private charitable organizations affiliated with EAN included the Moroccan League for the Protection of Children and the Red Crescent. The latter was an affiliate of the International Red Cross and provided service in all spheres of social service governed by international conventions, notably in the assistance to soldiers and their dependents, the sick, and victims of disaster.

Government initiative in public housing between 1956 and 1965 took the form of direct construction of low-cost dwellings; some 13,000 housing units were built during the period under official auspices. A major shift in public housing policies occurred during the mid-1960s when the focus of government development activities changed from social programs to agricultural and industrial development, and public housing funds were substantially reduced (see ch. 12, Agriculture and Industry). Government-owned land in urban areas, however, was divided into lots, cleared, and supplied with roads, water pipes, and sewers. More than 1,000 such lots were developed during 1966 and 1967, and 850 were sold at modest prices to individuals in need of housing; the recipients were also granted low-interest building loans. In selecting recipients for lots and loans, priority was given to residents of *bidonvilles* and to families with many children. In the course of the Five Year Plan the government has planned to make available some 20,000 developed lots. Loans for housing construction have been granted to private builders and to industrial enterprises prepared to use the lots to build workers' housing.

CHAPTER 3
HISTORICAL SETTING

In July 1970 King Hassan II promulgated and secured electoral endorsement of a new constitution. Elections were held in August for a new legislature, and limited parliamentary government was restored after a five-year emergency period of direct royal rule. The position of the king, however, remained paramount. The traditional dual and patriarchal role of the monarch as both temporal ruler and as Muslim religious leader (*amir al muaminin*, or commander of the faithful) was strengthened by King Mohammed V (before 1957, titled Sultan Mohammed; also known as Sidi Mohammed), the venerated hero of post-World War II independence. His son, King Hassan II, maintained this role after his accession in 1961, pursuing the goals of modernization in a constitutional monarchy visualized by his father.

Moroccans take pride in their country's distinctiveness and its role as the center of several medieval empires that at various times controlled much of North Africa and Spain. Unlike the rest of North Africa, the country did not fall under Ottoman Turkish sovereignty in the sixteenth century. In perspective, the relatively brief period of the French and Spanish protectorates (1912–56), during which tribal resistance was succeeded by Moroccan nationalism generated by such leaders as Allal al Fassi, may be seen simply as a hiatus in the long history of independent Morocco. The country's ethnic and cultural identification with North Africa and the Arab and Islamic world areas antedated the European protectorates by thirteen centuries or more.

The effects of the colonial protectorate period, however, were profound. During this time the country was unified under central control, industrial and economic development was initiated, government administration was reorganized, and notable improvements were made in transportation and communications. The colonial legacy, however, left severe postindependence problems in regard to language and education and the replacement of the French bureaucracy in government and commerce (see ch. 4, Ethnic Groups and Languages; ch. 7, Education, Communication, and the Arts and Sciences).

In world affairs Morocco after 1956 followed a policy of nonalignment in the bipolar confrontations of the post-World War II era, but its foreign association, by custom and experience, was oriented mainly to the West. In regional African and Arab affairs

Morocco played an important, moderate role and strengthened its position by several diplomatic successes in the 1969-70 period, notably, in reaching agreement with Algeria on their longstanding border dispute. Foreign policy questions in late 1970 thus appeared to be less significant than domestic problems of the economy, political factionalism, runaway population growth, effectiveness of government machinery, and education.

EARLY HISTORY

Indigenous tribal peoples of Mediterranean stock, speaking a language belonging to the broad Afro-Asiatic classification, have inhabited North Africa from before the recorded history of the area. Eventually, they became known to Europe and the Middle East as Berbers. Except for the Tuareg peoples in the southern Sahara, they had no separate alphabet and no written language; apparently, they also had no specific name either for the geographical region they inhabited or for their society and identified themselves primarily in local terms of tribe and family. Collectively, they referred to themselves simply as *imazighan*, or "free men" (see ch. 4, Ethnic Groups and Languages).

In the region of present-day Morocco, independent tribes roved the Rif and Atlas mountains or settled in the plains, struggling with each other for control of limited, local areas. Phoenician traders, who reached the western Mediterranean as early as the twelfth century B.C., founded seaports at Tangier, Ceuta, and other points. Carthage, founded in what is now Tunisia by Phoenician colonists probably in the eighth century B.C., extended its dominion over the North African coast. Neither the Phoenicians nor the Carthaginians colonized the hinterland but traded with the Berber herders and farmers at coastal points.

After the defeat of Carthage in 146 B.C., Rome gained a firm foothold on the southern shore of the Mediterranean and pushed the boundaries of Roman Africa westward, bringing northern Morocco securely under its administration in the first century A.D. For the next two centuries Rome administered the area generally north of a line through present-day Rabat, Fes, and Taza, calling it the province of Mauretania Tingitana, with its capital at Tingis (Tangier). The Latin word *Mauretania* meant the land of the Maures, or Moors, and from this designation the name Morocco derived.

Beginning in the third century the Roman Empire, gradually eroded by political crises at home, also encountered increasing pressure from the peoples along the imperial frontiers. In the face of increasing Berber encroachment, Rome withdrew to a reduced province centered on Tangier and administered by the Roman authority in Spain. During this period Christianity gained a number of converts among the Berbers, who utilized the new religion as an organizational means for opposing the Romans. After the empire adopted Christianity as the state religion in the fourth century, schismatic and heretical movements among the Berbers continued as forms of protest and resistance.

Gothic Vandals, overrunning the crumbling empire's frontiers, crossed from Spain into North Africa in 429. Although they destroyed Roman authority, they did not eliminate the Roman cultural influence or Christianity. In 534 the Byzantine successors to the Roman empire drove out the Vandals and attempted to reestablish imperial dominion, but with only limited success. Neo-Latin influence returned weakly to North Africa for about a century. The independent Berber tribes, some having a well-developed political organization, successfully resisted reassimilation into an imperial system whose authority was restricted to scattered cities and fortified outposts. By the seventh century, as European political ties loosened and attenuated, North Africa in effect turned away from primary identification with the neo-Latin European world. The determinant synthesis that then took place was that of the meeting of the native Berber peoples with the culture of Islam and the Arabs from the east.

THE COMING OF ISLAM AND THE ARABS

By the time of his death in 632 the Prophet Muhammad and his followers had brought most of the tribes of the Arabian Peninsula under the banner of the new monotheistic religion of Islam ("submission"), uniting the individual, state, and society under the all-powerful will of God. True Islamic rulers therefore exercised both temporal and religious authority; conversely, to them the much later Western idea of separation of church and state would have appeared not only heretical but fundamentally illogical. Adherents of Islam, called Muslims, collectively formed the Dar al Islam (House of Islam); all others lay outside, awaiting their opportunity to choose enlightenment (see ch. 5, Religious Life).

By the middle of the seventh century the Prophet's successors carried the conquests of Islam north and east from the Arabian Peninsula and also westward into North Africa. There, stubborn Berber resistance prevented them from pressing into the area in force until the last quarter of the century. The first Arab raids through the Taza Gap and into the Moroccan plains are traditionally dated from 684, but firm Arab control and permanent conversion to Islam did not occur until later.

In 710 Arab armies under the leadership of Musa Ibn Nusayr, the governor of Islamized Ifriquiya (present-day Tunisia), conquered the

Moroccan area and succeeded in converting the Berbers of the plains and northern cities. New converts to Islam formed the bulk of the forces sent into Spain beginning in 711. So successful were the Muslim Moorish armies that within a few years most of the Iberian Peninsula (known as the province of Andalusia) was under Muslim control, with allegiance to the Umayyad dynasty, whose capital was Damascus.

Although Islam as a religion was firmly implanted in large areas of Morocco, assimilation to Arab rule and language was slower. The Berbers found the Arabs' way of life compatible and respected the effective organization and mobility of their forces but became dissatisfied with the treatment accorded by them after Berber acceptance of Islam. Contrary to the tenets of the Quran, the Islamic scripture, which prescribed preferential treatment for all Muslims, Arab rulers continued to levy heavy taxes on the Berber converts and treated them as conquered inferiors.

The Berbers utilized an early schism in Islam as a rallying point for resistance to Arab domination, as they had earlier used Christianity against the Romans. The Islamic Kharidjite heresy had arisen in the mid-seventh century over the question of the choice of caliph, or the successor of Muhammad as supreme earthly leader of Islam. This conflict between the supporters of rival claimants split Islam into two great branches—the Sunni and the Shia—which continued thereafter as the basic division among Muslims. The Shia supported the claim of the descendants of Ali, son-in-law of Muhammad and fourth caliph, whereas the Sunni supported that of Ali's rival, Muawiya, a leader of a collateral branch of Muhammad's tribe, the Quraysh of Mecca. The Kharidjites refused to accept either choice, insisting that the caliph should be elected from among any suitable Muslim candidates without regard to race, station, or direct descent from, or tribal connection with, the Prophet.

The reduction of the Arab monopoly on the supreme leadership of Islam inherent in the Kharidjite position appealed to the independence-minded Berbers; and in 740 Berbers across North Africa revolted in the name of this heresy against Arab political and religious domination. In Morocco and elsewhere in North Africa the intensity of commitment to doctrinal or ideological quarrels for their own sake was less than in the central Middle East. The Berber revolt, although utilizing the Kharidjite heresy of the great Islamic dynastic wars, was animated pragmatically by local motivations rather than abstract ideas and aimed primarily at relief from the onerous constraints of Arab rule.

The revolt was suppressed, but the Arab caliphate was unable to sustain its temporal authority. During the period of autonomy that followed, several small Berber kingdoms of Kharidjite sectarians arose. In the mid-eighth century a second struggle among rival claimants to the central caliphate in Damascus had important consequences for Morocco. When the Abbasid faction overthrew the Umayyads of Damascus in 750, the only surviving scion of the Umayyad line fled to Morocco, where he gained support for a new incursion into Spain. In 756 he succeeded in establishing an independent kingdom at Cordova, often called the Umayyad caliphate of the West. This western caliphate became a cultural island during the European Dark Ages, as scholars from Europe and the Middle East illuminated the court at Cordova.

In 785 further wars between Shia and Sunni in the east led to the establishment of Morocco's first independent Arab dynasty. Idris Ibn Abdullah, a great-great-grandson of Ali, fled to Morocco after defeat by the Sunni Abbasids in Arabia. Idris succeeded in gaining acceptance as ruler by the tribes of northern Morocco and in 808 founded the city of Fes. Idris was a *sharif* because he was a descendant of the Prophet. His line, from about 788 to 974, was thus the first sharifian dynasty; it was also the first and only Shia rule. An identifiable central government structure was introduced, and the conversion of northern Morocco's Berbers was virtually completed. Idris and his son, Idris II, continue in modern times to be among the most revered of the country's rulers. In the city of Fes, many of the old aristocratic families trace their descent from the Idrisids.

Although weakened by struggles over succession, Idrisid hegemony over most of northern Morocco continued into the tenth century. Supported by Sanhaja Berbers of Kabylia (in present-day Algeria), the Shia Fatimid dynasty, originating in Qairwan in present-day Tunisia, destroyed the Kharidjite kingdom in 958 and threatened the Idrisids. They established their authority over western North Africa to the east of Fes but turned their primary attention eastward toward Egypt. The Sunni Umayyads of Cordova, at the height of their power, moved into northern Morocco to oppose the Fatimids. They established themselves at Ceuta, gained suzerainty of most of northern Morocco, and overthrew the remnant Idrisid dynasty in 974.

Until the tenth and eleventh centuries one major group or "family" of Berber tribes, the Masmuda, had formed the dominant population, particularly in the more densely settled plains of northwest Morocco. The Sanhaja group, the western mainstay of Fatimid forces, settled the eastern frontiers of Morocco along the Moulouya River and the southern oases. In opposing the Fatimids, the Umayyads allied themselves to a third major Berber group, the Zanata confederations of Bani Ifran and Maghrawa, who were traditional enemies of the Sanhaja and encouraged them to move into the northern plains. Rivalry among the small kingdoms of these Berber confederations colored the entire early medieval period of Moroccan history. The Zanata were Sunni and initiated the return to this branch of Islam.

Even more important to the future of Morocco was the large-scale Arab immigration that began in the eleventh century. Before that time the Arabs in Morocco consisted mainly of the descendants of the relatively small numbers of initial invaders and of the Idrisids, who had married Berber women. Many of these early arrivals had been aristocrats from Arabia who settled in the cities. The character of the Arab migrations of the eleventh century was distinctly different. The Fatimids, at this time ruling from their capital in Cairo and infuriated by Berber refusal to acknowledge their hegemony, encouraged masses of beduin Arabs of the Beni Hilal and Beni Salim tribes to migrate into North Africa. Over a long period, they displaced the Berbers from some of the best lands or settled among them. This immigration introduced for the first time comparatively large numbers of Arabs into the Moroccan population and quickly spread use of the Arabic language.

THE MEDIEVAL BERBER EMPIRES

The Almoravids

While the northern rim of the Maghrib was being subjected to these Arab invasions, veiled nomadic Sanhaja Berber tribes of the Sahara were being united under the banner of an Islamic religious brotherhood, which had originated early in the eleventh century and matured, according to older references, in a *ribat* (Berber religious retreat) along the Senegalese coast. Recent historians have increasingly discounted the notion of the island fortress or coastal enclave. The region centered in the present-day junction of Mauritania, Algeria, and Morocco seems more likely as the area of maturation of this movement. About 1050 the warrior monks, who came to be known as the Almoravids (a Spanish corruption of *al murabitun*—men of the *ribat*), began to push northward and northeastward, conquering in the name of their Sunni form of Islam. Their crusade was directed also against the Zanata, who had encroached on Sanhaja control of Saharan oases and trade routes.

They moved into Morocco through the Tafilalt south-central area and founded Marrakech in 1062 as their capital. Forcibly converting Moroccan Jews and the remaining Christians, the Almoravids swept north to the Mediterranean; by 1082 they had conquered the whole of the Maghrib as far east as Algiers. For the first time, under the Almoravid sultan Yusif Ibn Tashfin, all of present-day Morocco was unified. The conservative interpretation of the Sunni Malikite rite was adopted and endured as the official form of Islam in Morocco.

In 1085 the Almoravids responded to a request for assistance from the petty Muslim princes of southern Spain, who earlier in the century had succeeded to the ruins of the Umayyad dynasty and were being threatened by the Christians in the Iberian Peninsula. They pushed back the Christians and in 1090 conquered their erstwhile allies and established their empire north as far as the Tagus River. The leaders of the Almoravids settled in Seville and came greatly to admire the good life of Andalusia. Under their aegis, this mixture of Berber, Arab, and Spanish culture was introduced into Morocco. Marrakech became one of North Africa's largest cities and a widely admired center of Islamic art and learning. Under the Almoravids, Morocco and Spain acknowledged the spiritual authority of the Abbasid caliphate in Baghdad, reuniting Morocco temporarily with the Islam of the Middle East.

The Almohads

As the initial puritanism of the Almoravids quickly dissolved in the sophistication of the Andalusian culture, the military power on which their authority rested was dissipated. As a result, a new Islamic reform movement, based on a tribal confederation of the Masmuda Berbers centered in the Atlas, was able to defeat the Almoravids before the middle of the twelfth century, finally taking Marrakech in 1147. The new rulers were known as Almohads (a Spanish corruption of *al muwahidin*—unitarians) because of their strict monotheistic belief in the unity of a nonanthropomorphic god.

The founder of the Almohad movement, Muhammad bin Tumart, was a personality cult leader, recognized by his disciples in 1121 as the *mahdi*, or lord of the end of time. He died in 1130, but under him and his successors the empire in Spain and North Africa pushed its borders as far north as Castile and as far east as Tripoli. These early rulers established a strong central government, or *makhzan* (see Glossary) that lasted for about half a century.

The Almohad empire lasted little longer than had that of the Almoravids, however. The Almohad leaders accepted beduin Arabs into their army and settled the beduins in the plains of northern Morocco, seriously weakening the internal fabric of the empire. The disastrous defeat of Almohad forces by the Christian king of Castile in 1212 began the drawn-out final ebb of Muslim power in Spain. Almohad religious reforms did not take hold, and the Malikite orthodoxy of the Almoravids persisted in the *makhzan*, whereas emotional Islamic Sufi mysticism, the veneration of saints, and the power of the *marabouts* (Islamic holy men) grew among the masses. The growth of folk religion, the revival of the Malikite rite among the elite, and the flowering of North African Arab art and literature that occurred in the middle and late Almohad era, while seeming paradoxes, were antidotal to the dry severity of early Almohad ways.

The Marinids

The third great Berber empire was based on the Zanata tribes led by the Bani Marin. Called upon by the Almohads to help defend the eastern frontier against Arab incursions, the Bani Marin took advantage of waning Almohad power to migrate westward through the Taza Gap into Morocco proper in 1216. In 1269 they captured Marrakech and ended the Almohad empire. Basing their power on tribal unity rather than on religious reform as their predecessors had done, the Marinid dynasty lasted until the middle of the fifteenth century. Of necessity, the Marinids compromised with the widespread cults of Sufi folk mysticism. Moroccan Islam thus took shape as a coexistent and partial blend of the scrupulous intellectualism of the *ulama* (religious scholars) of Fes and the sometimes frenzied emotionalism of the masses.

The Marinids never succeeded in reestablishing the frontiers of the Almohad empire; in Spain they were forced to withdraw to the area around Granada, while their eastern frontier in North Africa was withdrawn to approximately the position of the present Moroccan-Algerian frontier. Gradually, the unsettling influence of the beduin Arabs in the plains undermined traditional sedentary Berber agriculture. City life also deteriorated, and the previous high cultural level sharply declined. Increasingly, the more remote tribes refused to acknowledge the authority of the *makhzan* and looked to the *marabouts* as sources of political power.

By the middle of the fifteenth century, the Marinids had spent their strength in efforts to rebuild the empire and in internal struggles. They were replaced by a related Zanata tribe, the Bani Wattas, who assumed control of the government in Fes in 1465 and, until the end of their dynasty in 1549, prevented the growing anarchy of the countryside from destroying a semblance of central authority.

As Muslim power declined, the Christian kingdoms of northern Spain and Portugal were growing steadily stronger. Although the Marinids and the Bani Wattas were able to prolong Muslim control over the reduced province of Granada, this last foothold was overrun by the armies of Ferdinand and Isabella in 1492, and the Spanish and Portuguese then looked toward the north coast of Africa. The triumph of Christianity in Spain was accompanied by the persecution of Muslims and the expulsion of Jews. Thousands of Muslims (also known as Moriscos) and Sephardic (Spanish-Oriental) Jews fled to North Africa, where they gained great influence in government, commerce, and urban culture. Settled in Rabat and Salé, the Moriscos for a time in the seventeenth century formed an independent republic. The pirates of the North African coastal states and enclaves, who became known as Barbary pirates, included some of these seagoing Moriscos (see ch. 4, Ethnic Groups and Languages).

Loss of effective political control by the *makhzan*, the growth of piracy off the Moroccan coasts, and the increasing tensions in Muslim-Christian relations provided the Europeans with pretexts for intervention in Morocco. The Spanish occupied Tetuán (in modern times known as Tetouan) in 1399 but shortly thereafter recognized Portugal's sole right to occupy the Moroccan coasts west of Peñon de Velez. The Portuguese occupied Ceuta in 1415 and by 1471 were in control of Tangier and other northern Moroccan ports. In the early sixteenth century they established a number of fortified ports along the Atlantic coasts, including Agadir (1505), Safi (1508), Azemmour (1513), and Mazagan (1514). The Spanish occupied Melilla in 1471.

Neither the Portuguese nor the Spaniards were able permanently to occupy the hinterland around their ports, however, because of stubborn resistance by the population. Moroccan forces drove the Portuguese out of some of their coastal holdings, including Agadir, by 1550. The Portuguese, however, retained control of some locations, including Tangier and Ceuta. They ceded the latter port to the Spaniards in 1668 and Tangier to the English, who in turn ceded it back to the Moroccans in 1684. The Spanish ports of Ceuta and Melilla were under recurring attack until the twentieth century. The reason that the European powers did not more actively press the occupation of Morocco in the sixteenth century is not certain. Historians have observed that the effort was probably limited by the appearance elsewhere of richer targets for colonial expansion.

THE SHARIFIAN DYNASTIES

Popular adherence to strict Sunni Islam had declined in step with the decadence of the *makhzan* during the fourteenth and fifteenth centuries. Sufic mysticism and the cult of saints was prevalent. The rise of the power of the *marabouts* and the religious brotherhoods (*zawiyiin*) was associated with the spread of a belief in *baraka* (spiritual power), which was considered to stem from God and to reside in its strongest form in saints, holy men, and descendants of Muhammad (see ch. 5, Religious Life). Several Arab tribes that had settled in the twelfth and thirteenth centuries in the oases of the Tafilalt and the sub-Saharan steppes along the Draa River claimed direct descent from Muhammad. Called *shurfa* (noble) tribes, they were accepted by many Moroccans as possessing *baraka*. When the Marinids and Bani Wattas proved impotent to oust the infidel Portuguese, the *marabouts* of the Sous plains south of Agadir called upon the *shaykh* (tribal leader) of the *shurfa* tribe of Saad, from the present-day Zagora region along the Draa River, to lead a holy war in 1511 against the Portuguese.

The Saads

Although initially unsuccessful, the Saadian *sharif* and his successors led the southern tribes against the cities of Marrakech, Meknès, and Fes, still held by the Bani Wattas. The capture of Fes in 1549 is considered to mark the beginning of the Saad dynasty. Thenceforth, the period of this line and its successor, the Alawis, is often called that of the Sharifian dynasties. In 1550 Saadian forces succeeded in forcing the Portuguese to relinquish most of their Moroccan strongholds.

Subsequent Portuguese attempts to exploit rivalries among Saadian claimants to the throne resulted in the deaths in battle in 1578 of the leaders of the warring factions and the rise of Sultan Mulay Ahmad al Mansur, who is regarded as the greatest of the Saadian sultans. The title-name of *Mulay* is reserved for Islamic nobility who are descendants of the Prophet in the male line. Mansur prevented the Ottoman Turks, who were firmly established as far west as Tlemcen, from expanding into Morocco—a notable achievement for Moroccan history. Successful but costly expeditions to Timbuktu and the surrounding region in what is now Mali and Mauritania established Morocco as a leading slave-trading power and laid the basis of later Moroccan claims to the south. Morocco's prestige in European courts was high, and Mansur was treated with great respect by the European powers.

Much is owed to Sultan Mansur for the basic structure of the *makhzan* in the twentieth century. He reactivated many of the forms developed under the Berber dynasties and added elements borrowed from Ottoman practice, particularly in his rule of holdings to the south through *pashas*, or local governors. His policy of relying for military support on certain tribes, which in return were exempted from taxation, was followed by all his successors. These were called *jaysh* (see Glossary) tribes. He placed a *caid*, or local administrator, as tax collector and general representative of the *makhzan* in all tribes that submitted to his power.

Although the concept of the universal Islamic state persisted in theory, the Islamic world of North Africa and the Middle East early divided into political societies essentially tribal-military-authoritarian in nature. Fixed rules of succession were not firmly established, and the Islamic polities, veering between hereditary and consensus-electoral monarchies, became characterized by frequent and violent successional struggles. On Mansur's death the question of succession again divided the country, and the power and authority of the Saadians waned. Outside the limited areas in which the authority of the rival cities of Fes and Marrakech was recognized, a large number of *marabouts* held local power. Amid the chaos, another *shurfa* Arab tribe from the southern oases around Tafilalt was gaining a commanding position. This tribe, known both as the Alawi and the Filali, had come to Morocco from the Arabian Peninsula in Marinid times.

The Alawis

The new Alawite dynasty rode to power on the cause of unity, reform, and orthodoxy about 1660. Mulay Rashid, the first strong ruler, became sultan in 1664 and by 1670 brought all of Morocco under his control. Everywhere, he sought to suppress the *marabouts* and to enforce the will of the *makhzan*. His successor, Mulay Ismail, who came to the throne in 1672, struggled for eighteen years to consolidate his power and put down tribal revolts. Although he succeeded in restoring Moroccan sovereignty over Larache and Tangier, as well as in pacifying the plains and isolating the dissident Berber tribes of the Atlas, he was unable to unite the whole country.

Ismail added to the Moroccan army further contingents of slaves brought from the Sudan. When not involved in war the *abid* (slave) troops, numbering at least 50,000 by the end of his reign, were used in constructing the many *casbahs* (fortresses) from which the troops maintained peace in the countryside. Ismail brought Morocco into closer commercial contact with the European powers, and various embassies were exchanged. He sent envoys to Louis XIV of France, whose court he admired, and sought to be recognized on an equal footing with his rival, the Ottoman sultan in Istanbul.

Wars of succession raged for thirty years after Ismail's death. Finally, in 1757 Sultan Mohammed was able to suppress the Berber revolts and gain acceptance by the tribes. He wished to establish diplomatic relations with European powers, and a treaty in 1767 gave the French freedom of commerce, the right to open a consulate at Salé, and concessions in favor of French nationals. Treaties of amity and commerce were also signed with Denmark, Sweden, and, toward the end of his reign, with the United States.

In 1787 Morocco and the United States signed the Treaty of Marrakech, which settled outstanding difficulties resulting from the seizure by Moroccan pirates of American ships and seamen and established commercial relations favorable to the United States. The United States agreed to pay Morocco an annual tribute of US$10,000, a common term of relationship between the North African, or Barbary, states and European powers at the time. Mohammed's immediate successors were involved in further Berber revolts in central Morocco that the central power never succeeded in putting down completely. The division of the country into the *bilad al makhzan* (land under the central government—see Glossary) and the *bilad al siba* (land of dissidence—see Glossary) became a long-lasting feature.

A new treaty, the Treaty of Meknès, signed in 1836, modified earlier commercial agreements to give the United States certain economic advantages in addition to the most-favored-nation treatment agreed to in 1824. It also accorded to United States citizens certain capitulatory rights, such as the right to be tried only by courts established by United States consulates in Morocco, similar to privileges assumed by other Western governments in the country and elsewhere in North Africa and the Middle East.

MOROCCO IN EUROPEAN DIPLOMACY

European Interests in Morocco

The latter part of the nineteenth century saw the acceleration of colonialist expansion by Great Britain, France, and Germany. Morocco, isolated from the social, political, and economic upheavals that were reshaping European society, was seen by each of the European powers as a threat in the hands of any of the others, as a prize to be added to empire, and as an area that held possibilities for profitable economic penetration.

Although Great Britain had some economic interest in Morocco, its main concern since obtaining Gibraltar in 1704 had been to protect the strait, a key point on the route to the Levant. Great Britain therefore regarded Morocco as an area that must remain out of the hands of rival powers.

France and Morocco came into direct conflict over the French seizure of Algeria in 1830, a date that marks the beginning of a long period during which the threat of French intervention was added to the internal troubles of the country. For years Moroccan sultans had sought to control the Tlemcen area, which was sometimes under Moroccan hegemony but nominally part of the enfeebled Ottoman Empire. When the French first entered the area, the people of Tlemcen appealed to Moroccan Sultan Mulay Abdul Rahman for aid, but though he sent an envoy to Tlemcen to rule in his name, he agreed under French pressure not to use armed force.

The situation became more confused when the Algerian leader, Abdul Qadr, claiming to be the agent of Abdul Rahman, led the Berber tribes in a holy war against the French. When driven back by the French, Abdul Qadr took refuge in eastern Morocco. Accused of harboring the rebel, the Moroccan sultan contended accurately that his control of northeastern Morocco was insufficient for him to enforce his will in the matter. After French attacks on Morocco involving the bombardment of Tangier, the occupation of Mogador, and a Moroccan military defeat at Isly, Abdul Rahman in 1844 agreed to cooperate with the French in hunting down Abdul Qadr. The following year the Convention of Lalla Marhnia defined the northern part of the Moroccan-Algerian frontier (see ch. 2, Geography and Population).

Spanish interest derived from geographical propinquity and the long historical connection between the two countries. The only power that directly controlled territory in Morocco at the end of the nineteenth century, Spain held the presidios of Ceuta, Melilla, Al Hoceima, and Peñon de Velez and had established a claim to the Atlantic coastal enclave of Ifni. Until the last quarter of the century, Spain had enjoyed a limited success in keeping scattered footholds in Morocco, but a continued power decline in relation to the rest of Europe made it difficult to press these interests.

French policy rested on a desire to protect France's Mediterranean trade, increase economic and political interest in North Africa, and control border raids from Morocco into Algeria. When in 1881 France established a protectorate over Tunisia, Morocco was already accepted by French imperialists as the next objective of empire and as part of their self-assumed task of spreading French culture and its benefits under the French concept of *mission civilisatrice* (civilizing mission).

Spain and Great Britain, fearful that France would press its interests in Morocco, discussed means of preserving the status quo. Spain then called the Madrid Conference of 1880. At the conference, twelve European nations, the United States, and Morocco agreed that Morocco should remain independent. An agreement to limit the longstanding capitulatory rights exercised by European consuls to interfere in internal Moroccan affairs had little effect, however. Foreign intervention continued to weaken the power of the *makhzan* and to present the threat of international conflict in Morocco.

The Madrid Conference was the first of several instances in which the European powers considered jointly the problem of Morocco and agreed not to intervene. It was important as the precedent for the guarantee of Morocco's status by international treaty, but it acted as a check on French interests for only a short time.

The Late Nineteenth and Early Twentieth Centuries

Morocco in 1900 was little different from the Morocco of 1700. Because of no fixed rule of succession, the death of a sultan usually led to long periods of instability. The country was not a unitary political community; the government's influence over the tribes varied according to the strength of its army and the accessibility of the tribe. To finance the government, the sultan had each year to call out his army, drawn from the *jaysh* tribes, and to travel with them throughout the kingdom, extracting levies from each tribe. Often force was necessary; many of the tribes denied the sultan's right to tax them and resented having to support his huge entourage in their territory. Still, a sultan with a strong personality could create a relatively strong government during his reign, though he could not ensure that his successor would be able to keep it.

The government, composed initially of a small group of palace officials, became by the nineteenth century a highly centralized machine. Absolute power was vested in the sultan, and all legislation was embodied in his *dahirs* (decrees). The grand *wazir*, as the sultan's highest executive official, was in effect premier and minister of interior. He held the responsibility for tax collection and the maintenance of order, and under him the *pashas* (governors of the cities) and *caids* (governors of the tribes) exercised their authority. At the end of the nineteenth century, the government comprised five ministries—interior, justice, finance, war, and foreign affairs—and various other high offices of the sultan's court. The offices of *pasha* and *caid* were more or less hereditary and were restricted to families powerful in a given locality. As long as revenues continued to come in and order prevailed, the sultan placed no restrictions on their actions.

The sharifian *makhzan* relied on personal relationships rather than rigid procedures and was organized on the basis of tribal, rather than territorial, divisions. The traditional differences between the *bilad al makhzan* and the *bilad al siba* did not alter the existing social and political structure; the people continued to live within the traditional framework—family, village, and tribe—and these institutions and attitudes are still important in the framework of the modern state (see ch. 6, Social Structure; ch. 8, The Governmental System and Political Dynamics).

Sultan Hassan developed a strong, stable government during the last quarter of the nineteenth century and tried, with little success, to introduce modernizing reforms. On his death in 1894 he was succeeded by fourteen-year-old Abdul Aziz. For six years Morocco was ruled by a regent who maintained an iron rule but made no effort to continue Hassan's modernization program. When Abdul Aziz took the throne in his own name, he proved to be anxious to modernize the country but, under a variety of pressures, was easy prey to unscrupulous adventurers.

During the critical first decade of the twentieth century, Morocco was practically without a government; the country's financial position deteriorated to the point where the country was in bondage to foreign lenders. The sultan's popularity plummeted and with it the central government's authority. The government's impotence to put down two outlaws—an adventurer, Raisuli, and a pretender to the throne, Bou Hamara—had serious international repercussions.

In 1904 the bandit Raisuli boldly penetrated Tangier and kidnapped a United States citizen, and the event quickly became a lively international incident. The Moroccan government was powerless to act, however, and was forced to conciliate Raisuli with a large ransom and an appointment as governor of the districts surrounding Tangier. Raisuli continued his extortions even after he had helped overthrow Abdul Aziz in 1908 and placed Aziz's brother, Mulay Hafid, on the throne. Bou Hamara established a fiefdom in the Rif Massif early in the century and gathered a sizable body of supporters behind his claim to the sharifian throne. Although he was unsuccessful in pressing his claim, Bou Hamara contributed to the growth of anarchy, which became the major pretext for European intervention.

The Diplomacy of Protection

After 1880 Morocco received constant European attention in the form of treaties between the European powers and Morocco, and among the powers concerning Morocco, in which the Europeans reiterated their intent to guarantee its independence and territorial integrity. The early years of the twentieth century witnessed a rush of open and secret diplomatic maneuvers through which the European states, and particularly France, furthered their interests in North Africa. In 1901 France secretly agreed to allow Italy a free hand in Tripolitania (present-day Libya) in return for the same freedom in Morocco. In 1904 a major part of the basic agreement between France and Great Britain—the Entente Cordiale—dealt with Morocco. The published agreement stated once more the intention to respect the territorial and economic integrity of Morocco. In settlement of their century-long differences, however, the primacy of Great Britain's influence in Egypt was recognized in exchange for recognition of France's primary influence in Morocco. A secret clause provided that if Morocco were occupied, the Mediterranean ports of Morocco would go to Spain. Later in 1904, France and Spain reached a secret agreement that incorporated the principles of the entente and outlined the territory to be under Spanish administration.

Proceeding along the partially cleared path, France in 1905 presented Morocco with a series of reform proposals to be carried out under French tutelage. Angered by France's failure to consult Germany, Kaiser Wilhelm II made a dramatic appearance in Tangier during which he publicly endorsed the internationally agreed policies of territorial integrity and equal access to trade, and referred pointedly to the sultan as an independent sovereign. Two months after the kaiser's visit, the sultan answered the French demands by saying that the reforms should be carried out not solely with French help, but with the aid of all the nations that were parties to the Madrid Conference of 1880. With United States and German backing, he called for an international meeting.

At the Algeciras Conference in Spain, which followed in early 1906, the major European powers and the United States reaffirmed the principle that Morocco's sovereignty and independence should be respected and that all foreign states should have equal rights in the country. Working to preserve equal commercial access by all countries to Morocco, the United States ambassador effectively mediated the differences between France and Germany.

The Act of Algeciras granted to France and Spain the right to help develop Morocco's police force in order to strengthen the authority of the government; and, to France the right to help create a state bank of Morocco. No single country was granted any special privileges, and all were guaranteed equal access to Morocco. Conclusion of an international agreement could not, however, alter the realities of France's and, to a lesser extent, Spain's active influence in the country.

In 1904 French forces had occupied several oases in the Figuig area along the Moroccan-Algerian frontiers about 180 miles south of Oujda. In the absence of an agreed boundary with Algeria these oases had been included nominally in the Moroccan realm; at the same time, France assumed responsibility for policing the Moroccan-Algerian frontier. Also in 1904 Morocco's debt of £800,000 to British, French, and Spanish interests was assumed by France; France then took control of Moroccan customs administration. Further loans from France in 1905 and 1906 were used to purchase arms in France, and after 1910 the entire customs income was collected by France. The murder of a French citizen in Marrakech led to reprisal in the occupation of Oujda in 1907. After similar incidents, Casablanca and Rabat were occupied. In these actions, and even more in the occupation of Fes in 1911, the Committee of Morocco (Comité du Maroc), an organization of French economic interests, constituted the major pressure group urging the Paris government to take strong measures.

Hafid, who in 1908 obtained recognition as sultan by the powers of Algeciras, was unable to fulfill his obligation and his desire to enforce order; local revolts increased in frequency and intensity, and finally, in 1911, when the sultan was besieged in Fes itself, he appealed to France for military assistance. French troops occupied Fes; the Spanish countered by seizing Alcazarquivir and Larache in northern Morocco, south of Tangier. Germany, having obtained little from Algeciras, reacted against the French presence in Fes by dispatching a gunboat to Agadir, ostensibly to protect German interests, but withdrew the gunboat in exchange for a gift of French territory in the Congo. The establishment of a French protectorate over Morocco was agreed upon by all of the signatories to the Act of Algeciras except the United States, which did not recognize the French Protectorate until it entered World War I in 1917.

The Franco-Moroccan Protectorate Treaty of Fes of March 30, 1912, provided that the French government would establish in cooperation with the sultan "a new regime comprising the administrative, judicial, educational, economic, financial and military reforms which the French government may see fit to introduce within the Moroccan territory." While preserving the religious status and traditional prestige of the sultan, the French would organize a reformed sharifian *makhzan*. Measures of the new regime would be established by decree of the sultan upon the proposal of the French government, represented by a resident general, who was empowered to act as the sole intermediary between the sultan and foreign representatives. France would thus control Morocco's foreign relations and, specifically, its foreign borrowing. France was permitted to station troops in Morocco, to exercise police powers, and to reorganize with the sultan's approval the finances of the central government.

Sultan Hafid was caught between accepting foreign intervention or facing increasing chaos within his country. He signed the treaty but tried to refuse to put it into effect. The French forced him to abdicate in favor of his younger brother, Mulay Yusif, who had been selected by the French but ratified in the traditional manner by a consensus of the *ulama* of Fes.

The treaty specified that Spanish interests and possessions in Morocco would be recognized in special Franco-Spanish negotiations, without Moroccan participation, and accepted the existing special international status of Tangier. The Franco-Spanish Treaty of November 27, 1912, established the Spanish Protectorate in a northern, coastal zone and over a desert area south of the Draa River. The sultan remained nominally sovereign and was represented in the zone by a *khalifa* (agent) under the control of a Spanish high commissioner. The Spanish zone of Morocco was recognized as an independent protectorate, though in fact it was "sublet" to Spain by France as a recognition of the validity of Spanish claims in the area of the Strait of Gibraltar. The Atlantic coastal enclave of Ifni, where Spain had established treaty rights with Morocco in 1860 and 1883, was recognized in the 1912 Franco-Spanish Treaty as sovereign Spanish territory distinct from the protectorate zones. Spain also claimed exclusive sovereignty over several coastal towns—Ceuta, Melilla, Villa Sanjurjo (Al Hoceima), and Peñon de Velez—where Spanish presidios had been established as early as the sixteenth century.

The special status of the city of Tangier was recognized by the Fes treaty and by the Franco-Spanish Treaty of 1912. Tangier became an international zone under a regime of permanent neutrality in 1923; in 1924 it was placed under an international administration in which foreign relations were reserved to the French and religious authority over Moroccan subjects was reserved to the *mandub*, or sultan's delegate.

COLONIALISM: THE FRENCH AND SPANISH PROTECTORATES

From a strictly legal point of view, the Treaty of Fes did not deprive Morocco of its status as a sovereign state, even though all external prerogatives and most of the internal jurisdiction had been transferred to the French. Theoretically, the sultan remained the sole source of sovereignty in the three separate zones of Morocco. He reigned but did not rule; in the respective zones the real authority and the source of legislative, executive, and judicial powers (in matters other than religious) rested with the French resident general in Rabat, the Spanish high commissioner in Tetuán, and the International Committee of Control in Tangier.

Pacification

The first French resident general, Marshal Louis Lyautey (1912–25), attempted to implement a limited interpretation of the role of France in its protectorate. His view was that France had undertaken to act in the name of the sultan in order to modernize the government while respecting the sultan's sovereignty and the Moroccan culture. In pursuit of this goal, his first task was the pacification of the dissident tribes and the assertion of central government authority throughout the country.

Within weeks of the promulgation of the protectorate treaty, riots broke out in Fes protesting the sultan's surrender to what were termed foreign infidels, Marrakech was seized by a *marabout*, and other large areas escaped from the control of the sultan. In the first two years of the protectorate, Lyautey succeeded in establishing a working relationship with the *makhzan*, reorganizing the Moroccan army and pacifying central Morocco between Fes and Marrakech and the High Atlas and the Taza Gap. During this period he won over the Berber leaders of the Atlas, including the important Thami al Glaoui, *pasha* of Marrakech.

In 1919, after World War I, Lyautey resumed his pacification campaign only to be interrupted again in 1924 by the threat to French Morocco of a revolt of Berber tribes in the Rif Massif in the Spanish zone under Abdul Karim. For three years the Berber rebel leader steadily undermined Spanish rule in its protectorate. By the end of 1924, Lyautey was convinced that French forces would have to be used to put down the rebellion. During the last year of his residency, therefore, Lyautey was forced to devote himself largely to the problem of the Rif War, which was not finally put down until a year after he had been replaced. It required a combined French-Spanish military force of over 300,000 men, with tanks and aircraft, to pacify the Rif conflict. Between 1926 and 1932 the French forces gradually subdued the Middle Atlas, the Sous and Draa valleys, the Anti-Atlas, and the sub-Saharan plateaus. Thus, by 1934 all the area within the present-day state of Morocco was brought under central control for the first time in centuries.

Administration Under the Protectorates

Under the terms of the Treaty of Fes, the resident general acted in a dual role; he was the supreme representative of the French Republic; also, he was the sultan's minister of war and foreign affairs and his supreme representative in control and supervision of the government. Lyautey's policy was to preserve the traditional institutions and provide guidance for Morocco in the economic and political spheres. "Govern," he said, "with the *makhzan*, not against it. Do not offend a single tradition, do not change a single habit."

Even in Lyautey's time, however, official French circles were beginning to favor the policy of assimilation rather than tutelage, and the drive toward direct administration proved impossible to check. Lyautey's dual position as both resident general and commander in chief of the French forces in Morocco opened him to attack from both left and right in the French political spectrum. The liberals opposed his combination of civil and military leadership; the nationalists resented his resistance to colonization. By July 1925 the French government agreed, under heavy pressure, to replace him. In September Lyautey resigned as resident general, and during the next two decades Morocco was reduced, for all practical purposes, to the status of a French colony.

Under Lyautey's successors, direct French administration was progressively introduced. Although care was taken to preserve the paraphernalia of authority, the sultan became a mere figurehead. The *makhzan* had no real powers, and the *caids* and *pashas* became merely the executive officials of the French regional administrators. The influx of French officials into Morocco started on a large scale under Lyautey's successor.

The bureaucracy became a political power when protectorate officials allied themselves with the *colons* (French settlers) in Morocco and with their supporters in France to prevent any moves in the direction of Moroccan autonomy. The process of legislation passed fully into the hands of the resident general and his staff. *Dahirs*, or decree laws, were drawn up and approved by the resident general and submitted in final form for the sultan's seal. The French administration promulgated and executed the new laws. Decrees issued by the resident general in administrative matters did not need the sultan's approval and were widely used in times of strained relations between the palace and the residency.

The central government was composed of the grand *wazir*, who was nominally the sultan's premier and minister of interior insofar as he had de jure supervision over *pashas* and *caids*; the minister of Muslim justice, who supervised the *sharia* (Islamic law) courts; and the minister of the religious endowments, or *habus*. The French-staffed residency services were divided into the directorates of sharifian affairs, the interior, and public security. In addition, the residency had a number of other regulatory and supervisory agencies: political, economic, administrative, and military.

The regional administration divided the country into civil regions under appointees of the French foreign ministry and military regions under military officers from the Bureau of Native Affairs. Cities were controlled by French chiefs of municipal services. The *pashas* and *caids* were retained as collectors of taxes, supervisors of public order, and judges in civil and criminal cases. All their regulations, however, required the countersignature of an appropriate French official, and all their reports and communications to the *makhzan* were routed through French regional offices. After World War II the sultan was forbidden to initiate informal meetings with the *pashas* and *caids*. The most important representative of the residency in the rural areas was the district officer, who was the chief contact between the French administration and the local Moroccan population, represented by the *caid*.

In reorganizing the judicial system, the French asserted the right to administer justice in cases involving non-Moroccans. By 1916 all foreign states except the United States and Great Britain renounced their longstanding capitulatory rights. Great Britain renounced its rights in 1937, but the United States retained its rights until 1959 (see ch. 9, Foreign Relations).

Local consultative bodies were established under the protectorate, ostensibly to voice popular interests and demands but in fact to act as sounding boards for French policies. The highest of these was the Council of Government with French and Moroccan sections, each composed of representatives of the local consultative bodies and administration officials who belonged ex officio. The major task of the council was the discussion of the proposed budget, but members had no vote. After 1945 the French tried to develop consultative bodies on a wider basis, but since all attempts were made on the premise that the French minority should have representation equal to that of the Moroccan majority, Sultan Mohammad V, and the growing nationalist movement with which he was allied, refused to cooperate.

The French gave support to the secret, mystical religious brotherhoods and the antisultan *pashas* and *caids*. The Glaoui family in the south, as well as several other tribal chiefs, having become enemies of the ruling family by supporting rebellions against it, allied early with the French. In return for his assurance of peace in a large area around Marrakech, the French authorities left the Glaoui chief alone to multiply his landholdings and to exercise a nearly absolute control over administration, commerce, and agriculture in southwestern Morocco. Some of the religious brotherhoods cooperated with the French for their own protection. They had earlier opposed any contact with the Europeans, whom they regarded as infidels. The French allowed considerable freedom of operation to cooperative *marabouts* and brotherhoods, since they seemed to represent a religious counterweight against extension of the orthodox Malikite sultan's authority through his role as religious leader.

The government and power relationship in the Spanish zone developed on much the same patterns as in the French zone. Nominally, executive power in the zone resided in the appointed representative of the sultan. In practice, the highest authority was exercised by the Spanish high commissioner and the Spanish administration. Ifni was governed as a Spanish colony, and the high commissioner in Tetuán was the highest civil and military authority. In 1946 the administration of Ifni and the Spanish Sahara was integrated with that of Spanish West Africa and placed under a military governor.

The sovereignty of the sultan in Tangier was recognized by all the treaties regulating the special status of the city, and the international administration was legally based on delegated powers. The *mandub*, a personal representative of the sultan, had powers similar to those of a *pasha* with respect to the Moroccan population of Tangier but was subject to the same limitations in the discharge of his duties as was his sovereign. The highest supervisory body of the international administration of Tangier was the Committee of Control, composed of the consular representatives of the signatory powers of the Algeciras Conference.

Economic and Social Developments

European, and particularly French, private commercial interests were active in Morocco long before the establishment of the protectorate. As pacification proceeded, the French government pushed economic development, particularly the exploitation of Morocco's mineral wealth, the creation of a modern transportation system, and the creation of a modern agricultural sector geared to the export market. Under Lyautey's administration, Casablanca was converted into a great seaport, and work was begun on several other ports. A railroad system, begun before the protectorate, was extended initially for military purposes but also with a view to opening the interior to economic exploitation; an extensive road network was also begun. Agricultural timber surveys were undertaken, mineral prospecting was encouraged and regulated, industrialization was stimulated, an electrification program and irrigation projects were initiated, chambers of commerce were opened, and a start was made toward modernizing the tax system.

Lyautey opposed, but could not stem, the influx of French settlers and exploitative commercial interests. Thousands of *colons* entered Morocco and bought up large acreages of the rich agricultural lands of the plains (see ch. 12, Agriculture and Industry). Under his successor, private and officially sponsored colonization doubled in three years, and by the late 1930s, *colons* owned about 2.5 million acres of the best agricultural land. In 1936 about 200,000 non-Moroccans, including about 150,000 French, lived in Morocco and controlled the economy. Interest groups formed among these elements continually pressured the residency to increase its controls over Morocco and promote French economic penetration.

Beginning in the 1920s, modern European cities mushroomed. Modern sanitation, hygiene, and medical facilities were introduced for the French population and gradually extended to the Moroccan population as well. This development was hastened by the growth of shantytowns (*bidonvilles*) around the European cities as Moroccans migrated to the industrialized urban areas in search of work (see ch. 6, Social Structure; ch. 12, Agriculture and Industry).

The French educational system was introduced intact for the children of the *colons*. As the educational facilities expanded, the number of Moroccan children attending the French-administered schools steadily increased. These developments were to have serious future consequences. The French colonials used and promoted their own language. Arabic became relegated to classical studies, religion, ceremonial use, and the common dialectical speech of the people. A modernized school system in Arabic was not developed. The educational system and the practical operations of government and the larger economy were thus tied to French (see ch. 4, Ethnic Groups and Languages). Although relatively few Moroccans achieved university educations, a small Western-educated elite, oriented toward the French culture, came into existence (see ch. 7, Education, Communication, and the Arts and Sciences). It was among this group, however, that the nationalist movement first took root in the mid-1920s.

Origins of the Nationalist Movement

Moroccan nationalism stemmed from the merger of two reform movements that had appeared in the early 1920s and whose aims, originally unrelated, later became blended. The first was a religious purification reform movement, known as Salafiya, which grew up among the *ulama* and students associated with the ancient Karaouine University at Fes and was imbued with the fundamentalist ideals originally preached by Islamic reformers in the late nineteenth century. The Salafiya sought the spiritual and intellectual revival of an independent Islam stripped of its mystical accretions and adapted to the requirements of the modern world by using the tools of Western technology while retaining the essential spiritual and moral values of Islam. Its main attacks were aimed at the *marabouts* and the religious brotherhoods. By 1925 Salafiya schools were operating in several cities to spread knowledge of Arabic and Islamic culture, which were ignored by the French schools.

The first truly nationalist movement arose in 1925 among French-educated students in Rabat who founded secret societies to spread opposition to the growing intervention of the French administration. By 1927 these two movements were in contact. Societies combining the aims of religious reform and the assertion of Morocco's political independence formed throughout the country. In Paris the Association of North African Muslim Students was formed. By 1930 the future leaders of the nationalist movement were already becoming well known. Allal al Fassi had assumed leadership of the Salafiya movement; Ahmed Balafrej, one of the founders of the Rabat group, was in Paris where he was gaining support by French Socialists. Mohammed Hassan Ouezzani was a university student in Paris and in contact with Shakib Arslan, the mentor of Arab nationalists throughout North Africa and the Middle East.

The French promulgation in 1930 of the so-called Berber *dahir* converted what had been an isolated elite-based movement into a popular force strongly opposed to continued French rule. The French claimed that the *dahir* was intended to help modernize the complex Moroccan legal system by ending the judicial powers formerly exercised over the Berber tribes by the *caids* and *pashas* appointed by the *makhzan* and granting these powers to the traditional representative Berber community councils. The effect of this step, however, would have been to reduce further the authority of the *makhzan* and to strengthen the autonomy of the Berber tribes. Nationalists saw in it still another, and particularly odious, attempt by the French to divide the Berber and Arab elements of the population in order more easily to impose French control through deliberately reviving the old divisions of *bilad al makhzan* and *bilad al siba* under French overall authority. The supporters of Islamic orthodoxy were incensed by what they took to be a threat to Islam in the strengthening of Berber customary law at the expense of *sharia* law. Public demonstrations against the *dahir* rapidly spread through all Moroccan cities and were suppressed by the arrest of nationalist leaders.

In the Berber *dahir* of 1930 the French managed to bring together in a unity of opposition all diverse strands of Moroccan politics at the time. Indignant protests against the measure were manifested all over the Muslim world in response to the publicity given the *dahir* by Arslan and the Moroccan nationalists in Paris. The French government reacted by instructing the resident general not to enforce it.

Although the *dahir* protest movement then quickly subsided, the proof it had given of the breadth and depth of potential Moroccan national unity against the French encouraged the nationalists to organize on a more ambitious scale. In 1932 the anti-French Spanish-Muslim Association was formed in Madrid. Two nationalist newspapers were suppressed by the French in mid-1934 after a wild demonstration in honor of Sultan Mohammed during his visit to Fes. From that time, the young sultan, who had taken the throne in 1927 at the age of sixteen, became the symbol of the nationalist movement and increasingly supported its aims.

In December 1934 a small group of nationalist leaders issued in the name of the newly formed Moroccan Action Committee (Comité d'Action Marocaine—CAM) the long, detailed Plan of Reforms, which they submitted simultaneously to the sultan, the resident general, and the French foreign ministry. The plan called for a return to indirect rule as envisaged by the Treaty of Fes, unification of the judicial systems of Morocco, the admission of Moroccans to government positions, the elimination of the judicial functions of *caids* and *pashas*, and the establishment of representative councils. The signatories included the recognized leaders of Moroccan nationalism: Allal al Fassi, Ahmed Balafrej, Mohammed Lyazidi, Mohammed Ouezzani, Mekki Naciri, Mohammed Douiri, Abdelaziz ben Driss, Ahmed Cherkaoui, and Ahmed Mekouar.

The means used by the CAM to obtain reforms—petitions, letters, newspaper editorials, and individual pressure—proved inadequate. The Plan of Reforms created a stir in Morocco but was rejected by the French government. The tensions created in the CAM caused it to split; Ouezzani withdrew from the movement and took with him most of the traditionalists, that is, those who had originally pursued religious reforms. The rump CAM led by Fassi was reconstituted as a political party—the National Party—to gain mass support for its radical demands. A number of violent incidents occurred in September 1937 that led the French administration to suppress the party. Fassi and several of his supporters were placed under arrest; he was exiled to Gabon until 1946. Ouezzani's splinter Popular Movement was also proscribed, and Ouezzani was sent into exile.

In the Spanish zone, the creation of a nationalist movement more or less paralleled events in the French Protectorate. Groups similar to the Rabat nationalist movement were formed in Tetouan in 1926 and in Tangier in 1927. After the suppression by the French of nationalist demonstrations in 1930, Tetouan became a nationalist center. Shortly after the Spanish Republic was formed in late 1930, Abdel Torres founded a nationalist movement in Tetouan. Nationalists in the northern zone followed the reactions of their allies in the south to the

Berber *dahir* and the Plan of Reforms. Torres and Mekki Naciri formed a branch of the CAM in the north. In 1937 the northern nationalist movement split, as Torres founded the National Reform Party and Naciri, the Moroccan Unity Party.

World War II

During World War II the badly split Moroccan nationalist movement regained cohesion and new hope. The French defeat, the Atlantic Charter, and the promises of independence to Syria and Lebanon led a wide segment of the Moroccan educated population to consider the feasibility of political change. At the outbreak of war, Sultan Mohammed pledged Moroccan support to France and the Allies. Gradually, however, he began to express his views more independently. After the fall of France, he continued to give his personal loyalty to the Allies and refused to see the German representatives in Morocco. He declined to issue a Vichy-initiated decree aimed at persecution of Jews and refused to join the pro-Vichy resident general in his attempted resistance to the American landings in November 1942.

The French community was divided in its loyalties, the majority of the French administration supporting the Vichy regime; the majority of the Moroccans, however, followed the sultan in his loyalty to the Allies. During the Casablanca Conference in January 1943, President Franklin D. Roosevelt and Prime Minister Winston Churchill met with the sultan separately from the French. Two letters from Roosevelt after the conference strengthened the sultan's belief that the United States would support Moroccan demands for independence.

Although the nationalists had assumed that the Allied landings would lead to a modification of French rule in Morocco, this was not the case. The continued suppression of their activities led the nationalists to the conviction that independence must precede political reform. Balafrej and Lyazidi led a group of veteran nationalists joined by young urban intellectuals and middle-class Moroccans in forming the Istiqlal (Independence) Party. At its first conference in Rabat in January 1944, the Istiqlal issued a manifesto demanding full independence, national reunification, and a democratic constitution. The sultan had received and approved the manifesto prior to its submission to the resident general and the Allied government. The resident general answered that while political and social reforms would be granted, no basic change in the protectorate status would be considered. The general principles of reform that he voiced were categorically rejected by the Istiqlal. When, a few days later, eighteen Istiqlal leaders, including Balafrej and Lyazidi, were arrested on a slim charge of collaboration with the Germans, violent demonstrations broke out against the French.

Other nationalist parties were formed during this period and immediately after the end of the war. On his return from exile, Ouezzani formed the Democratic Independence Party (Parti Démocratique de l'Indépendance—PDI), thus preserving the split in the nationalist movement created in the mid-1930s.

THE STRUGGLE FOR INDEPENDENCE

By the end of World War II, some 300,000 Moroccans had fought with the Allies in the North African campaigns, the invasions of Italy, and the liberation of France. The general sympathy of the sultan with the nationalists had become evident, although he still hoped to see independence reached gradually. Public opinion was much more aware of and behind the nationalists than in 1939. On the other hand, the residency, supported by the French economic interests and vigorously backed by most of the *colons*, defended a concept of permanent French right to the position in Morocco and refused all concessions.

Intransigence intensified the split between the nationalists and the *colons* and gradually between the sultan and the resident general. In 1946 a liberal resident general proposed a series of reforms aimed at improving living standards and giving Moroccans a greater voice in their government, but by then nothing short of independence would satisfy the nationalists. In deference to them the sultan withheld his signature from the *dahirs* that would implement the reforms. Each side accused the other of obstructing solutions to the conflict.

In this atmosphere the sultan's trip to Tangier, in the spring of 1947, an event of considerable importance since neither he nor his father had been permitted to visit the city, proved the final blow to hopes of cooperation. A riot in Casablanca during the visit brought French-Moroccan tension to a new high. Angered by the apparently unnecessary firing on Moroccans by the French police, the sultan in his major Tangier speech on April 10, 1947, called for national unity and eventual self-government, omitting his planned mention of Franco-Moroccan friendship and the benefits of French rule. French reaction to the Tangier visit was to designate General Alphonse Juin, the choice of the most conservative interests among the *colons*, as the new resident general.

Juin quickly decreed reorganization aimed at further weakening the *makhzan*, made statements intended to discredit the sultan, and encouraged the religious brotherhoods. He refused to promulgate a decree issued by the sultan limiting the activities of the brotherhoods. The sultan in turn refused to sign most of the decrees presented by

Juin, nearly all of which were intended to limit the sultan's authority. This veto power, established by the 1912 Treaty of Fes, proved to be the nationalists' major weapon as the Istiqlal intensified its public condemnation of the absence of basic liberties, the denial of union rights, and the tightening of press censorship.

Mounting Tensions, 1950–53

During the next four years, the French repeatedly proposed measures that would further reduce the power of the sultan, who doggedly refused to sign them. The nationalists boycotted the Council of Government in July 1950. In October 1950 the sultan went to Paris to discuss the growing Moroccan crisis directly with the French government. His proposals for greater Moroccan autonomy were ignored, but on his return the Moroccan population gave him a great show of support. In January 1951 Juin demanded that the sultan sign the *dahirs* and denounced the Istiqlal. Mohammed refused, and Juin threatened to depose him.

At the same time, Thami al Glaoui, *pasha* of Marrakech, who had supported the French from the early days of the protectorate, openly attacked the sultan for his support of the nationalists. After being exiled from the palace, Glaoui garnered support from some dissident Berber tribal *caids* with the help of the French administrators. Late in January 1951, on various pretexts, Glaoui and Juin called the tribes to move on Fes and Rabat. It is probable that few of the tribal leaders or their followers understood the crisis or the way they were being used in it. The result was, however, that the sultan agreed under duress to sign the *dahirs*, though making clear that he did not consider them to be valid.

Although the humiliation of the sultan and the accompanying arrests of the Istiqlal leaders ended one crisis, another was precipitated. Moroccans, particularly among the rural population who cared little about the Istiqlal, were furious at the insult to the sultan by the foreigners whose *mission civilisatrice* apparently had not, after all, changed Moroccans into Frenchmen. The various splintered nationalist parties joined with the Istiqlal in a Moroccan National Front to oppose the protectorates. The parties pledged to refuse to negotiate without a proclamation of independence, to keep Morocco out of the French Union, to remain loyal to Sultan Mohammed, to collaborate with the Arab League, and to refrain from forming any alliance with the new Moroccan Communist Party.

The Casablanca riots of December 1952, arising from proletarian nationalist reaction to the murder of a Tunisian labor leader, began a new era in Moroccan politics. In clashes between Moroccan rioters and police, hundreds were killed and wounded. After this the

Moroccan Communist Party and the Istiqlal were outlawed completely by the French.

Exile of Sultan Mohammed V

In early 1953 Glaoui, with the support of the resident general, once more mobilized his supporters among the Berber tribes against the sultan. In August 1953 the events of 1951 were repeated almost exactly, but this time overthrow, rather than temporary submission, was the object. When, after tribal horsemen were massed around Rabat and tanks around his palace, the sultan still refused to sign over his powers, the resident general deposed him, immediately arrested him, and sent him and his family into exile to Madagascar on August 20, 1953. A new sultan was installed in the traditional fashion. The French summoned the *ulama* to choose a new sultan, Mohammed Mulay Ben Arafa, an aged member of the Alawi house; two members of the *ulama* who failed to comply were arrested.

The deposition offended not only the nationalists but all those who recognized the sultan as the religious leader of the country. Never was the country so solidly united behind the sultan or was national sentiment so aroused. French attempts to bolster Ben Arafa by enacting reforms in his name only led to a further deterioration of the situation. Immediately after his accession on August 20, he not only signed over most of his powers to a French-appointed council but also signed a decree creating French-dominated municipal councils that Mohammed had refused to sign for six years.

By 1952 the Istiqlal had developed a mass organization of some 80,000 members. After December 1952 nearly all of the Istiqlal leaders were in exile or in prison. Control of the party passed into the hands of younger men more willing than the earlier leaders to use violent methods to attain their goals, and dispersal of the illegal party's organization left the chiefs of local sections free to determine local policy. In the cities many of them took to terrorist activity. Beginning in August 1953, incidents of terrorism occurred with increasing frequency. Unofficial French counterterrorist vigilantes operated virtually in the open. Both Moroccan and European terrorists chose victims largely from among their own communities. Moroccan shopkeepers who did not voluntarily abide by boycotts of European goods were often threatened with terrorist retribution. By mid-1955 the guerrillas were organized by a kinsman of Istiqlal leader Allal al Fassi into the Army of National Liberation (Armée de Liberation Nationale—ALN), numbering several thousand, and were openly active against French troops and settlers. It was estimated that during the two years of the sultan's exile 6,000 acts of terrorism were committed, and over 700 persons killed. Religious opposition also continued.

On August 20, 1955, the second anniversary of Ben Arafa's accession to the throne, Berber tribesmen of the Middle Atlas descended on a village and murdered every Frenchman present, thus shattering any remaining notion of Berber solidarity behind Glaoui. In addition, Berbers of the Rif Massif revolted against the French in sympathy with the growing rebellion in Algeria. As the French negotiated with various Moroccans in the hope of finding a solution in the form of a council of the throne, Berber attacks in the Middle Atlas and the Rif continued. Finally, Glaoui himself announced that Sultan Mohammed must return. Glaoui's supporters followed him in declaring their loyalty. Faced with the united Moroccan demand for the return of the sultan, the rising violence of the revolt, and the simultaneous deterioration of their situation in Algeria and Indochina, the French government decided to bring Mohammed back to Morocco.

In August 1955 French Premier Edgar Faure called a Franco-Moroccan conference at Aix-les-Bains at which it was decided that Ben Arafa should abdicate in favor of a four-man regency council. As a step toward a representative government, the Regency Council was instructed to form a cabinet, but the Istiqlal Party refused to participate, reiterating its demands for the return of Mohammed and the abrogation of the Treaty of Fes. On October 30 Ben Arafa renounced the throne, and on November 2 the Regency Council resigned to make way for the restoration of Mohammed V.

Attainment of Independence

A policy of Moroccan "independence with interdependence" was adopted by the French National Assembly in October 1955. At the same time the assembly affirmed that the Treaty of Fes should remain the basis of Franco-Moroccan relations; the principle of Moroccan sovereignty was restated, and it was agreed that Morocco should exercise fully all the powers and authority stipulated by the treaty. It was insisted, however, that France should continue its responsibility for Moroccan defense and foreign policy and that the French presence in Morocco should be permanent and acknowledged by a French settler-representation in Moroccan affairs.

Mohammed was received in Paris with full honors on October 31. He rejected the French position, and negotiations continued until agreement was reached on November 6. Although the Treaty of Fes still was not formally abrogated, provision was made for a gradual restoration of Moroccan independence within the framework of a guarantee of mutual rights and permanent ties of Franco-Moroccan interdependence. The sultan agreed to institute reforms to transform Morocco into a democratic state under a constitutional monarch. He reentered Morocco in triumph on November 16, 1955, and, after consultation with spokesmen of the several political parties, the labor movement, and other groups, entrusted a nonparty politician, Embarek Bekkai, with the task of forming a cabinet. The old ministerial system was abandoned, and a council of ministers was formed on the basis of the administrative structure created by the French. The new cabinet was sworn in on December 7, and government functions were transferred gradually from the French administration.

On February 11, 1956, limited home rule was restored to Morocco in a protocol implementing the November 6 declaration. Further negotiations for full independence culminated in the French-Moroccan Agreement signed in Paris on March 3, 1956. As of this date, Morocco again became an independent state and later that year, was admitted to the United Nations.

The French-Moroccan Agreement abrogated the 1912 Treaty of Fes. France recognized the independence and the territorial integrity of Morocco. Both governments undertook to conclude new agreements in order to define their interdependence on a free and equal basis in fields of common interest, especially in matters of defense, foreign relations, economy, and culture, and to guarantee the rights and liberties of Frenchmen in Morocco and Moroccans in France. A protocol annexed to the agreement defined the new relations between France and Morocco. The full exercise of legislative power reverted to the sultan. The sultan was empowered to create a national army with French assistance. The French resident general was replaced by a high commissioner who two months later became an ambassador.

Reunification Agreements

Spain did not participate in the Franco-Moroccan negotiations. During the reign of Ben Arafa, Spain had continued to recognize Mohammed as the rightful sultan and *imam* (spiritual leader—see Glossary) in the northern zone. Once France had accepted the principle of Moroccan independence, the nationalists expected Spain to follow suit. Spain hesitated, and when rumors circulated that a separate government under the *khalifa* might be established in the northern zone, Spain lost much of the popularity it had cultivated. In the northern zone the nationalists held that Spain had no right to adopt a policy toward independence different from that of France.

The abolition of the Spanish Protectorate and the recognition of Moroccan independence by Spain were negotiated separately in Madrid between the sultan and Generalissimo Francisco Franco and made final in a Joint Declaration of April 7, 1956. The declaration provided for "free collaboration" between Spain and Morocco, granted the sultan immediate legislative powers in the northern

Spanish zone, and provided for the stay of Spanish troops on Moroccan soil in the period of transition.

The Moroccan-Spanish agreement did not include the Tarfaya area south of the Draa River and the areas under exclusive Spanish sovereignty. A Spanish-Moroccan clash over Ifni in late 1957 raised the question of the transfer to Moroccan sovereignty of that enclave and the southern protectorate zone. Spain agreed to return the southern protectorate zone to Morocco, and the transfer became effective in April 1958. Spain continued to maintain at this time, however, that Ifni was ceded in perpetuity by the treaty of 1860. The sultan's sovereignty in Tangier was restored, and the international status of the city was officially ended at the Conference of Fedala in October 1956.

THE FIRST YEARS OF INDEPENDENCE, 1956-65

Policies, Problems, and Progress Under Mohammed V

In his first major speech following his restoration in November 1955, the sultan announced a policy for independent Morocco predicated on liberty and democracy for his people and recognition of the country's continued interdependence with France in terms of its needs for economic and technical support, while it trained its own citizens to assume administrative and technical positions formerly occupied by the French. The Bekkai government installed by the sultan in December 1956 included nine members of the most powerful nationalist party, the Istiqlal; six from the more conservative PDI; and six nonparty independents loyal to the sultan, including Prime Minister Bekkai himself. The Istiqlal leaders resented the sultan's failure to name a clearly predominant Istiqlal government but continued to support the sultan's basic policies while gradually moving into a role of "loyal opposition."

Mohammed's general popularity was high. He enjoyed the unusual position of being a royal figure who was hero of an independence struggle. Under him, the dual Moroccan monarchical role as simultaneous temporal head of state and *imam* was strengthened as it had not been for many centuries. In the latter capacity the monarch's title continued to include the ancient designation of *amir al muaminin*. The restored sultan's status and the popular veneration in which he was held gave him the balance of power among all institutions, factions, and parties. This enabled him to act in terms of consolidated loyalty to the crown rather than being dependent upon any particular party, including the Istiqlal—which, in essence, needed him more than he needed it.

In the months after independence, the sultan moved with deliberation to develop a modern governmental structure under a constitutional monarchy. His aim was to proceed cautiously in order to avoid loosing potentially uncontrollable forces seeking to divert or accelerate the course of development he had planned. Social and economic reforms were part of his program for independent Morocco, but he had no intention of permitting the more radical younger elements in the nationalist movement to overthrow the established social order and introduce a socialist system. He was also intent on preventing the Istiqlal from consolidating its control and establishing a single-party state.

The problems confronting the new regime were imposing. It was faced with the need to train people to head the ministries; fill the ranks of the civil service; assume judicial functions, establish central government control over localized, often recalcitrant tribes and rural localities; and form an independent foreign service, police, and national army. In addition, many of the local governors who had supported Ben Arafa fled their posts after Mohammed returned to Rabat.

On April 9, 1957, Mohammed named his son, Prince Mulay Hassan (later King Hassan II), as crown prince and chief of staff of the new Royal Armed Forces (Forces Armées Royales—FAR), which the French and Spanish agreed to support when they signed the treaty of independence. At the same time, the French army remained at stations in Morocco under the terms of the treaty. During the months following independence, the ALN resistance forces grew in strength, as it attracted Moroccans determined to push the French out of Morocco and all of North Africa. It became increasingly irresponsible, conducting a running terrorist campaign against the French and against former Moroccan collaborators with the French Protectorate.

In August 1956 the bulk of the ALN was incorporated into the Royal Moroccan Army, but dissident elements continued to operate independently, particularly around Oujda and Figuig along the Algerian border, where they supported the Algerian National Liberation Front, and in the south around Agadir. Units of these irregular forces attempted unsuccessfully to force the Spanish out of Ifni in late 1957. It was not until 1958 that combined French and Moroccan army operations succeeded in suppressing the remaining ALN units and imprisoning their leaders, including a number of former governors and officials who had opposed the sultan (see ch. 14, National Defense and Internal Security).

Another source of resistance to the independent government came from Berber tribes in the Rif and the Middle Atlas. With the foreigners' colonial rule abolished, ancient internal quarrels could be resumed. Several times during 1957 and 1958 tribes rose against local government officials to demonstrate their animosity toward what they considered the overly Arab-dominated central government. Whatever the cause, the Berber uprisings were readily put down and, by the beginning of 1959, the central government had successfully asserted its control throughout the state.

Suppression of these disturbances by no means solved the government's problems, however. New political parties and unions quickly formed to assert interests not directly served by the Istiqlal or the other nationalist parties. The first of these was the Popular Movement (Mouvement Populaire—MP), formed originally as a semiclandestine group in the Rif mountains among dissident Berber groups but, by 1959, established as a political party claiming to represent the rural population against the mainly urban nationalist parties. The Istiqlal itself became divided into radical and conservative wings by 1958. By early 1959 the radical wing broke away from the party, forming in September 1959 a separate political group, the National Union of Popular Forces (Union Nationale des Forces Populaires—UNFP) under a second-generation nationalist leader, Mehdi Ben Barka. This split, which was reflected in the governmental coalition, forced a crisis on the unstable government that led Mohammed, who had taken the title of king on August 15, 1957, to assume direct leadership of the government in May 1960 (see ch. 8, The Governmental System and Political Dynamics).

In order to assure his people that he was not instituting a dictatorial regime, King Mohammed promised to promulgate a written constitution by the end of 1962. Early efforts at representative government, attempted through the appointed Consultative Assembly, failed, largely because the bodies were given no real authority to legislate and the parties had little experience in parliamentary politics. Local communal councils were created in the new country's first national elections in 1960, but the effective power of these new councils in local government was slow in appearing.

In foreign relations Mohammed followed a mildly radical policy in his effort to establish Morocco's independent position. In October 1958 Morocco was admitted as a member of the Arab League and supported the general Arab causes but without excessive polemics. Mohammed insisted on renegotiating the 1950 treaty under which France had given to the United States the right to maintain airbases in Morocco for the defense of Europe. The whole question of French, Spanish, and United States military or quasi-military bases in Morocco formed a major political issue in the years following independence and by mid-1971, although diminished, had still not been finally resolved (see ch. 9, Foreign Relations).

In January 1961 Mohammed called a conference in Casablanca of several of the radical independent states of Africa, including Ghana, Guinea, the United Arab Republic (UAR), and the Provisional Government of the Algerian Republic in exile. At this conference he negotiated support for Morocco's claims to Mauritania in return for his support of the neutralist and anticolonialist policies of the other states. The so-called Casablanca group failed to attain its goals of close coordination in foreign policy, however, and gradually withered. Morocco's stand on Mauritania isolated the country from most of the newly independent countries of Africa and from the Arab states, since most of these had recognized Mauritania when it became independent of France in 1960.

Hassan II and the Constitution

Mohammed died suddenly and unexpectedly on February 26, 1961, following minor surgery, and the nation was plunged into deep mourning. Some initial doubts were expressed as to the ability of Prince Hassan, then thirty-two years old, to hold the country together; but he acted speedily and decisively to take command and to assure his people that he would follow the domestic policies of his father.

In foreign policies, however, Hassan did not show the same interest in militant neutralism as had Mohammed but turned increasingly toward the West (see ch. 9, Foreign Relations). Hassan took control of the government as prime minister and in June 1961 named a new cabinet. After an unsuccessful attempt at drafting a constitution by means of an appointed Constituent Assembly, the king drew up his own constitution, which he presented to the people in the form of a referendum in December 1962. The Istiqlal, the MP, and other governmental parties supported the constitution; the UNFP led a vehement, but ineffectual, campaign to boycott the referendum, complaining of undue government intervention in this and later electoral actions.

The results of the referendum on December 7, 1962, were overwhelmingly in favor of the draft constitution and it was promulgated. Under it the king remained the central figure in the executive branch of the government, but legislative power was vested in a two-house parliament, and an independent judiciary was guaranteed. Elections by universal suffrage to the parliament and to local governmental councils were held in 1963. In these elections substantial majorities were secured by the royalist government Front for the Defense of Constitutional Institutions (Front pour la Défense des Institutions Constitutionnelles—FDIC), formed in March 1963. On November 18, 1963, the king formally opened the first session of Parliament.

The Border War of 1963

The historical concept of unity among the North African states of the Maghrib revived after these states individually regained independence following World War II; political union, however, did not come about because there were extensive differences, as well as similarities, among them. Morocco supported the Algerian revolt against the French but soon thereafter was embroiled in a border dispute with Algeria. Under the French no border delineations had been made southwest of Bechar across some 600 miles of desert to Tindouf. Both countries had claims and maintained mobile military forces in this region.

As 1963 advanced, relations between the countries worsened. During the summer and early fall, Morocco charged Algeria with a sequence of unfriendly acts, chief of which was an allegation of support to a radical antigovernment conspiracy uncovered in Morocco in July. Starting October 1 and continuing throughout the month, Moroccan and Algerian forces fought a series of small-scale but sharp engagements in the disputed desert area. A cease-fire was arranged October 30, 1963, through the mediation of Emperor Haile Selassie of Ethiopia and President Modibo Keita of Mali (see ch. 9, Foreign Relations).

Strengthening Regional Relationships

During 1964 a number of important actions were taken to strengthen the country's regional relationships in the Arab and African worlds. The king attended a significant Arab summit meeting in January at Cairo, and on February 2 it was announced that diplomatic relations between Morocco and the UAR, broken because of the latter's support of Algeria in the border dispute, were being resumed. Prisoners were exchanged between Algeria and Morocco in April, and normal relations were resumed in May. Also in May, diplomatic connections were restored with Tunisia—broken because of Tunisian recognition of Mauritania in 1960 in the face of Moroccan claims in that area. In July an understanding was reached to end radio propaganda attacks between the last two, and the relationship became more amicable, although Moroccan recognition of Mauritania was not yet extended.

Western-Oriented Nonalignment

By the end of 1964 Morocco's relations with the Communist world were numerous, giving credence to the official policy of nonalignment between East and West. Recognition had been exchanged with the Soviet Union and the People's Republic of China in 1958, but these connections were not deep seated. Small numbers of Soviet military aircraft had been accepted in 1960, and Soviet tanks, trucks, and artillery arrived in 1962, but Morocco's primary economic and policy connections continued to be French and Western oriented. During a visit to the United States in 1963, Hassan observed, "Because I have relations with the Soviet Union does not mean I am a communist, any more than my relations with France mean I am a Catholic."

The Casablanca Riots of March 1965 and Their Aftermath

In August 1964 Hassan reorganized the government with Ahmad Bahnini, head of the Democratic Socialist Party (Parti Socialist Democrate—PSD), as prime minister and a cabinet mostly from the FDIC group of loyalist parties. This change was presented as a trend toward broadening the basis of government and allowing for easier cooperation by the opposition Istiqlal and UNFP parties.

Internal political tensions, however, dominated the first half of 1965. In March the Ministry of Education issued a directive requiring all students over seventeen years of age to include in their education some degree of technical training. Large numbers of students apparently believed that implementation of this directive would exclude them from certain professional and civil service jobs, and student demonstrations occurred in Casablanca on March 25.

Starting as a peaceful and apolitical protest against the curriculum change, the student movement soon attracted participation by laborers and other urban poor, among whom dissatisfaction had been growing for at least a year because of rising prices and increasing unemployment. For three days widespread rioting and looting spread out of control through Casablanca and, although in lesser degree, in other major cities. The police, assisted by the army, restored order but at high cost. According to reliable observers, about 400 were killed— some estimates were higher—and a chain of political actions was initiated.

During the riots, on March 27, fourteen antiregime Moroccan nationals previously convicted of subversively introducing arms into the country were executed as evidence of the government's determination to maintain public order. On March 29, in a broadcast to the nation, however, King Hassan dismissed rumors that the Casablanca riots had been caused by foreign provocation. He stated that the real cause lay in the internal economic and educational difficulties, and he placed chief blame on bickering politicians and factions which, he said, had paralyzed legislation. He then announced that he would immediately endeavor to form a government of national union.

In April the king declared an amnesty for political prisoners, including certain UNFP leaders who had earlier been condemned to death for participation in the conspiracy of July 1963. In addition, he consulted jointly with the leaders of all parties and unions and laid before them a proposed program of administrative, educational, economic, landholding, and social reforms (including birth-rate limitation) that covered almost all the current dissatisfactions and might have served as a basis for a new government. He reiterated these proposals in opening the Parliament on May 3, 1965.

These efforts, however, were unavailing. A consensus could not be reached because the counterproposals were unacceptable either to the king or to one or more of the parties; also, the king's plan did not allow for the dominance of any one party, and the FDIC government grouping had been divided since 1964. Prime Minister Bahnini resigned on June 4, 1965.

On June 7 King Hassan proclaimed a "state of exception," or national emergency, under his powers contained in Article 35 of the Constitution of 1962 and the precedent of royal control in the 1960-63 period. On the next day he assumed full legislative and executive powers and named a new government with himself as prime minister. He indicated that new elections would be held at an unspecified later date, after a new constitution had been drafted and submitted to a referendum. In the meantime, normal political and trade union activity was allowed, and government operations were resumed under the king and his cabinet of loyal technician-administrators.

THE EMERGENCY PERIOD: 1965-70

The Ben Barka Affair

The internal turbulence of mid-1965 was quieted by the king's decisive action in installing the emergency government. If no great changes were immediately forthcoming, the trend to political disintegration was, at least, arrested. Soon thereafter, however, severe strains developed in the relations between Morocco and France because of a cause celebre that became known as the Ben Barka affair.

On October 25, 1965, Mehdi Ben Barka, a leader of the UNFP who had been living in exile because of alleged complicity in the July 1963 conspiracy, was abducted in Paris and never appeared again to public view. This disappearance roused vehement protests and outcry among the left-wing opposition parties in Morocco. As the French authorities pursued their investigations, a tangled picture emerged, which was widely publicized but never fully clarified in public. A number of French as well as Moroccan nationals were involved. French authorities issued international warrants for the arrest of General Mohammed Oufkir—then the Moroccan minister of interior—and for Ahmad Dlimi, then chief of security services and, in 1971, director of the national police forces, or Sûreté National until September 1, when he became chief aide-de-camp to the king (see ch. 14, National Defense and Internal Security). The Moroccan government maintained that the warrants were in violation of the French-Moroccan judicial convention of 1957 and hence invalid. Each country withdrew its ambassador, although diplomatic relations were not broken.

At the trial, which opened in Paris on September 5, 1966, Oufkir and Dlimi were listed among those being tried in absentia. Later, Dlimi unexpectedly appeared in France and was arrested. The delayed trial ended June 5, 1967. The French court's action, approved by President Charles de Gaulle, acquitted Dlimi but sentenced two French officials to terms of imprisonment and Oufkir, in absentia, to life imprisonment for complicity in Ben Barka's abduction. Hassan subsequently made scores of changes in his cabinet but up to mid-1971 retained Oufkir as minister of interior without interruption until August 6, 1971, when he was made minister of defense (see ch. 8, The Governmental System and Political Dynamics).

The North African Arms Race

Moroccan-Algerian relations were disturbed again in 1966 and 1967 by what became known as the North African Arms Race. Alarmed by the mounting flow of Soviet arms into Algeria, some of which were alleged to have been deployed in the Tindouf desert border region, in November 1966 Hassan secured a number of new military aircraft from the United States; in addition, he visited Moscow in the fall of that year and the United States in February 1967. From both of these visits, new military and economic aid agreements resulted. In March 1967 the king urged Algeria to abandon the arms race and enter new discussions directly with Morocco or under the aegis of the United Nations. These developments had an ameliorating effect on relations between the two countries, and attention was soon attracted eastward.

The Arab-Israeli War of 1967

In the Arab-Israeli War of June 1967, Hassan placed three of his best battalions at the disposal of the United Arab Republic (Egypt); these forces were not committed and, in any case, probably could not have been committed because of the war's short duration. After the defeat of the Arab forces, some public demonstrations occurred in Morocco. An unofficial commercial boycott of the Moroccan Jewish community set in, and about 7,000 of the estimated 70,000 Jews remaining in Morocco quickly left the country. Others followed, so that by 1971 the total had declined to about 40,000 and was still falling.

The government proclaimed an anti-Zionist, anti-Israeli policy in support of the general Arab cause but condemned both the commercial boycott and acts of terrorism against Moroccan Jewish citizens. This attitude was not well received among the Moroccan trade unions, where radical Arab nationalist ideology has generally been stronger than elsewhere in the society, and the government was challenged on this issue by the secretary general of the Moroccan Labor Union (Union Marocain du Travail—UMT), Mahjub Ben Sadiq. He was promptly arrested and sentenced to eighteen months in jail for undermining respect due to the state.

Domestic Tranquillity Restored

In July 1967 the king took a major step in the direction of ending the emergency period by personally withdrawing from the post of prime minister, to which he designated Mohammed Benhima. During the balance of 1967 and in 1968 political party and union activity was gradually resumed although still under close royal scrutiny. In general, the internal political scene after mid-1967 to mid-1970, at least on the surface, was comparatively tranquil. Municipal and rural communal elections were conducted in October 1969. The opposition parties boycotted these local elections, and the successful candidates were mostly identified as of independent (nonparty) affiliation. Noteworthy disturbances or problems in the conduct of the elections, however, did not arise. Soon afterwards, the king again modified the cabinet, naming Ahmed Laraki, who as foreign minister had participated in various successful diplomatic ventures, to be prime minister in place of Benhima.

End of the Emergency Period

In mid-1970 the Istiqlal and UNFP continued to maintain a joint front of opposition to the government, and the economic questions of price and wage dissatisfactions were again coming to the fore. The national situation, however, particularly in view of the foreign policy successes of the two previous years, was such as to enable Hassan to move toward ending the "state of exception," or emergency period, which he had decreed in 1965. In a speech to the nation on May 18, 1970, on the occasion of the annual celebration of the birthday of the Prophet Muhammad, the king gave a strong indication that a change was imminent. This was confirmed in his speech of July 9, 1970, on the occasion of his forty-first birthday. He announced that a new constitution had been prepared and would be submitted to a popular referendum. This referendum was conducted July 24, 1970. Its results, by 98.7 percent, accepted the revised constitution; elections for a new unicameral legislature followed in August, and the emergency period ended (see ch. 8, The Governmental System and Political Dynamics). The role of the king, as in 1965, remained dominant, and internal, rather than external, stresses remained as the principal problem areas.

CHAPTER 4

ETHNIC GROUPS AND LANGUAGES

Modern Moroccans are, for the most part, descendants of indigenous tribal peoples who have lived in the area at least since Phoenician times. Beginning in the seventh century, successive waves of Arabic-speaking conquerors and settlers gradually but decisively replaced the local language and religion with their own; by modern times Arabic was predominant and Islam, nearly universal (see ch. 3, Historical Setting; ch. 5, Religious Life). A similar, though much less extensive, penetration by French culture began in the late nineteenth century and continues, in much attenuated form, to the present day.

Although they have no collective name for themselves, the indigenous tribesmen are known to others as Berbers, a term apparently derived from the Latin *barbarus*. Their unwritten language, composed of several substantially differing dialects, is widely spoken in the mountainous regions beyond the range of conquerors and colonizers and remains the native tongue of perhaps 40 percent of the people. Arabic, which has steadily gained ground at the expense of Berber, dominates the plains and the western coast (see fig. 6). More persons speak Arabic than any other language; it is the native tongue of some 60 percent of the total population and a second language of possibly as many as half the Berber speakers. It is the official language of the kingdom, and government policy ostensibly favors its exclusive use.

The vehicle of French penetration, the community of urban Europeans, has decreased in size since independence in 1956 but retains significant cultural and economic, if not political, influence. The resident Europeans, even those born in the country, are not considered Moroccan by the government, the only non-Muslim Moroccans being the small, but significant and very ancient, Jewish community. At present concentrated in Casablanca and other cities, the Jews previously lived in many rural places as well. Since the founding of Israel in 1948, however, and especially since the June 1967 Arab-Israeli War, in which Moroccan forces were not engaged, large numbers of Jews have emigrated. Most observers agree that members of the Jewish community will continue to leave the country, as did many in the aftermath of the attempted coup in July 1971 (see ch. 8, The Governmental System and Political Dynamics).

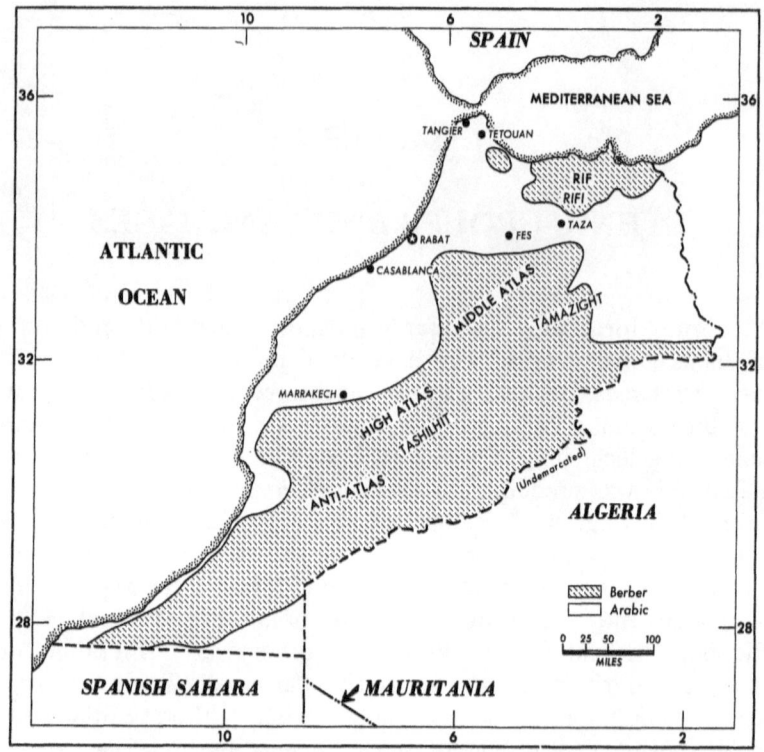

Source: Adapted from Marvin W. Mikesell, *Northern Morocco: A Cultural Geography*, Berkeley, 1961; and Bernard G. Hoffman, *The Structure of Traditional Moroccan Rural Society*, The Hague, 1967.

Figure 6. *Languages of Morocco.*

Despite the relatively short duration of the French Protectorate (1912–56), the French language made important inroads. France's colonial policy, based on the concept of the *mission civilisatrice* (civilizing mission), resulted in the formation of a French-educated native elite which, in 1971, dominated all aspects of the modern sector of society—government, economic life, education, and most other positions of importance (see ch. 7, Education, Communication, and the Arts and Sciences). As a consequence, access to higher education, to the government, and to important avenues of social mobility has been severely limited for persons of modest or rural background, who have been largely unable to learn French.

Since independence, the stated policy both of the government and opposition parties has been the prompt Moroccanization and Arabization of education and the civil service. By the late 1960s, however, it had become apparent that these goals were impossible of early attainment and in fact contradictory; the shortage of Arabic-trained teachers, bureaucrats, and technicians has required the continued use of French-educated Moroccans, as well as of French nationals, a substantial number of whom were training yet another French-speaking generation.

French therefore remains a language of prestige, essential for advancement in many fields and the medium of most higher education. Bilingualism and even trilingualism are common. Financial constraints have, however, prevented an expansion of educational and other facilities sufficient to offer equal access to French-language education to all children. For a number of years, therefore, the growing body of non-French-speaking Moroccans has demanded access to employment and prosperity, whether through Arabization or through equal access to French training. Language remains a crucial and highly volatile political issue (see ch. 8, The Governmental System and Political Dynamics).

THE PEOPLES OF MOROCCO

Except for the Jews and the Harratine, Berber-speaking Negro nomads, the ethnic communities in Morocco are distinguished by language. Arabic encroached gradually, spreading through the plains areas most accessible to migrants and conquerors. With minor exceptions, Berber remains the mother tongue in the mountains.

Because the present-day Berbers and substantial numbers of Arabs are descendants of largely the same indigenous stock, physical distinctions carry little or no social connotation and are, in any case, ordinarily impossible to make systemically. Identification with the Berber or Arab community is largely a matter of personal behavior rather than of membership in discrete and bounded social entities. Many adult Berbers also speak Arabic, and for centuries Berbers have entered the general society and melded, within a generation or two, into the Arab group. In some cases Arabic-speaking tribes adopted Berber.

Within his own territory the Berber is a tribesman deriving his primary social identity from membership in a specific tribal section. As long as he retains his connection with the tribe, whether physically present or not, he may be considered a Berber. It is unlikely, however, that an individual settled with his family away from the tribal home conveys to his children either a firm place in a specific tribal section or an adequate command of the Berber tongue. Berberhood may in this fashion be lost; the person considered a Berber either is or was formerly a member of a tribe.

This permeable boundary between the two major ethnic groups permits a good deal of movement and, along with other factors, prevents the development of rigid and exclusive ethnic blocs. It appears that whole tribal groups will in the future, as they have in the past, slip across the ethnic "boundary." In areas of linguistic contiguity, bilingualism is common, and in most cases Arabic eventually comes to predominate. This process has been noted in many places, such as in the foothills of the Rif.

Arabs

Arabs, or native speakers of Arabic, probably constituted approximately 60 percent of the 16.2 million people of Morocco in mid-1971; reliable statistics were not available. More than 2 million others speak it as a second language, although what level of mastery constitutes "speaking" is not known.

The earliest Arabs arrived in the mid-seventh century (see ch. 3, Historical Setting). Primarily soldiers, explorers, and Islamic proselytizers, they probably numbered no more than 150,000. Few women accompanied the invaders, so that many men married locally, hastening the introduction of Arabic culture and Islamic religion. The eleventh century brought a second wave of Arabs, this time nomadic beduins of the Beni Hilal and other tribes that had been displaced farther to the east. Their movement represented the migration of whole tribes spreading through the rural plains, diffusing their language, their religion and, to some extent, their nomadic way of life. Although some authorities estimate that the beduins could not have accounted for more than 2 percent of the population of North Africa, they exerted an important cultural influence on the peasants they encountered.

The fall of southern Spain to the Christians brought a third large-scale migration during the late fifteenth and sixteenth centuries. Significant numbers of Moriscos, Andalusian Muslims, mostly descended from Berber converts to Islam who had conquered parts of Spain in the eighth century, took refuge in Morocco. Largely urbanites, artisans, merchants, and intellectuals, they settled in Fes and other cities in large numbers. This migration heavily Arabized the coastal highlands near the Strait of Gibraltar, the route between Spain and the Moroccan plains. During the years between the three great migrations, Arabs also arrived as individuals or in small groups.

Authorities nevertheless estimate that the total number of Arabs who arrived in North Africa in the first two migrations could not have exceeded 700,000 persons. In the twelfth century population of 6 or 7 million they never constituted more than 10 percent. Therefore, despite considerable intermarriage, Berber descent heavily outweighs Arab in the Moroccan population. Moreover, Arabic cultural penetration was not complete. Although Islam was firmly and enthusiastically adopted in all parts of the country, a Berber cultural residue remains among the Arabized groups (see ch. 6, Social Structure). For example, marriage rites are pre-Islamic among both

Arabs and Berbers. Many farming terms used in colloquial Arabic, as well as proper names, come from Berber roots.

The varied Arabic dialects in Morocco reflect their several origins. Throughout the world Arabic exists in two styles: classical, including the language of the Quran as well as the form used in the modern press, and the local colloquials. In Morocco classical Arabic is used primarily by the traditional religious leaders and by modern bureaucrats in those organizations that have been Arabized. In addition, large numbers of men, including many Berbers, have learned Quranic quotations by rote but cannot be said to speak classical Arabic. Increasing interest in the language has developed among the educated young, particularly the nationalists. In the mid-1950s relatively few were able to read it; by the mid-1960s, however, their number had increased to an estimated 1 million. The low average age of these new readers indicates that classical Arabic will probably increase in importance.

Classical Arabic is written in an alphabet derived through Aramaic from Phoenician. As is usual in Semitic scripts, only the consonants are written and are arranged from right to left. Vowel signs and other diacritical marks are employed occasionally in printed texts only as aids to pronunciation. The modern form of written classical Arabic, often called literary Arabic or modern Arabic, is grammatically simplified and includes many words unknown in the Quran. It is used in the newspapers, on the radio, and for much public speaking; the classical form is still taught in schools and used for advanced Arabic scholarship.

The spoken Arabic dialects of Morocco belong to the Maghribi group, used throughout Libya, Tunisia, Algeria, and Morocco; the language of Malta is also a dialect of this group, as was the Arabic formerly spoken in Spain. These dialects are mutually intelligible, but they have diverged so far from eastern dialects that North Africans have some difficulty in conversing with a Syrian or an Iraqi. Dialectal Arabic, the local speech learned at home, is usually referred to as Moroccan Arabic. It is usually neither written nor used for literary purposes. The spoken language deviates so markedly from the classical that one observer reports that some Moroccan audiences can follow motion pictures made in Egypt with dialogue in classical Arabic only through the French subtitles. It has also been reported that 60 percent of a sample of radio listeners polled in 1957 did not understand the classical Arabic spoken but did understand Moroccan dialectal Arabic.

In most Arabic countries the dialect of the cities differs noticeably from that of the countryside, but in Morocco this divergence is exceptionally great because the dialects were introduced by different groups. Urban, spoken Arabic derives from the dialect of the first conquerors, as modified by that of the Spanish refugees. Rural speech is patterned on that introduced by the beduin immigrants. City dwellers ordinarily consider their speech pattern the more refined.

Berbers

Estimates of the number of Berber speakers vary but center on 40 percent. The Berber language, one of the Afro-Asiatic linguistic family, is related to other indigenous North African tongues, such as ancient Egyptian, the Cushite languages of the Horn of Africa, and the Chad language group. Berber speakers occupy the highlands that have been left relatively untouched by the advancing Arabic wave, primarily the mountainous regions of the Rif, the Middle Atlas, the High Atlas, and the Anti-Atlas. In some areas classification is difficult. Identification as a Berber is frequently relative rather than absolute and depends upon membership in a specific tribe. Although the foothills are becoming progressively Arabized, life in the mountain villages for the most part continues in the traditional manner. The territory in which Berber is spoken is contracting, but the number of Berber speakers continues to expand.

It is estimated that at least half of the Berber speakers also know another language, usually Arabic, as well as some French. Bilingual persons are ordinarily adult men or schoolchildren. One authority reports that in the early 1960s fewer than 1 percent of the women in the Rif knew Arabic or a European language. Arabic is often learned in school, and the numerous men who travel to the cities to work, often leaving their families behind, master the majority language, although they usually continue to speak Berber in their homes.

No generalized feeling of peoplehood embraces all Berbers; rather, each Berber is a member of a specific local group (see ch. 6, Social Structure). The language, which is found in various forms throughout North Africa, lacks the unifying vehicle of a written form and exists as a series of regional dialects that are mutually intelligible only with difficulty. The French attempted to emphasize the differences between Arabs and Berbers and to foster a Berber national spirit; but the fragmented nature of the Berber groups and the fact that they and the Arabs are distinguished largely by ecological, rather than by profound ethnic or cultural, differences prevented this (see ch. 3, Historical Setting).

Language, dress, and ecological adaptation vary from region to region. Methods of classification are also various. The numerous Berber dialects have been divided into three main groups: the Rifi of the Rif; the Tamazight of the Middle Atlas, the central High Atlas, and the Sahara; and the Tashilhit of the High Atlas and the Anti-Atlas. The numerous tribes have been grouped into two sedentary groups, the Rifians and the Shluh of the High Atlas and the Anti-Atlas; a third group comprises the seasonal migrant Beraber (whose name should not be confused with Berber) of the Middle Atlas and Sahara. The fourteenth-century historian Ibn Khaldun distinguished three main groups: the Sanhaja, the Masmuda, and the Zanata. Each of these groups is said to have given rise to one of the three great historic dynasties. Khaldun's divisions do not correlate with modern reality, although a number of theories exist tying them to various modern groups.

The largest psychologically significant unit is the local tribal section or confederation, although this may consist of nothing more than a number of related families farming adjacent land and sharing a historical tie to a now defunct tribal council. Each such group is known by a patronymic, preceded by the Arab or Berber prefix *Beni* or *Ait*, meaning "sons of" or "people." Reportedly, there are some 600 such groups.

The majority of those currently known as Berbers are sedentary farmers and part-time herders. The proportion of time spent in herding or farming and the techniques used vary with the ecological setting. The varied and rugged terrain has permitted and even compelled the development of differing local adaptations (see ch. 12, Agriculture and Industry). In addition, it hindered rapid diffusion and unity of culture.

A significant, but undetermined, number of countrypeople have settled in cities and retain a communal identity there. So many Shluh of the Sous region have established themselves in Casablanca as small retail grocers that in the slang of that city "going to the Soussi's" is synonymous with "going to the grocery store." They have also branched out into other businesses, including wholesaling; a majority of the small entrepreneurs in Casablanca are Berbers. In many cases families, rather than individuals, run a business, the male members rotating between the city and the family landholdings, usually leaving their wives and children in the country. A growing number of men, however, have brought their immediate families to town, weakening, and in some cases eventually breaking, their ties to family and village.

Jews

When the ancestors of many of modern Morocco's Jews arrived from Spain after its fall to Christendom in the late fifteenth century, they found a small and scattered community of their coreligionists who had already been settled in the country for centuries and who claimed ancient Palestinian origin. The original Jews, some of whom were Berber speakers apparently converted to Judaism, lived in various parts of the country—many in rural villages totally or predominantly Jewish in composition and others as single families or small groups in non-Jewish villages. In some areas small Jewish communities lived in a special quarter, or *mallah* (see Glossary). The Spanish, or Sephardic, Jews settled exclusively in cities, generally entering commerce and artisan trades.

Although significant in the economic life of the country, the Jewish community was never large. With the founding of the state of Israel in 1948 and with Moroccan independence in 1956, the number of Jews began to drop significantly through emigration to Israel, France, the United States, and elsewhere (see fig. 7). In addition to change in absolute numbers, this emigration caused an appreciable shift in the age structure of the Jewish community. In 1958 those over sixty years of age constituted only 8 percent of the community, but by late 1967 they accounted for 40 percent. Conversely, 58 percent of the community was between fifteen and sixty years of age in 1948, but in 1967 this productive age group accounted for only 25 percent. Furthermore, a significant internal migration emptied the rural Jewish communities into the cities until, by 1966, virtually no Jews remained in the countryside. In 1968 two-thirds lived in Casablanca, although in 1947 the city's share was only slightly over one-third.

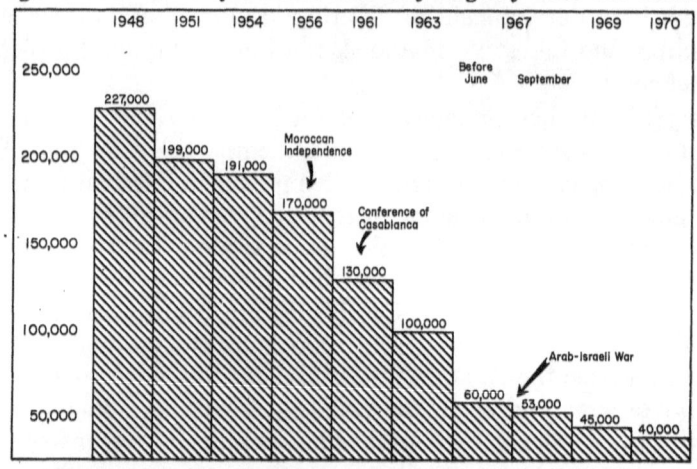

Source: Adapted from "Les Juifs d'Afrique du Nord," *Maghreb* [Paris], May 1968-June 1968, p. 32; and *African Research Bulletin* [London] (unpublished mimeo.), December 1970-January 1971, p. 1902.

Figure 7. *Jewish Population of Morocco, Selected Years, 1948-70.*

The departure of the Jewish community has been a particularly sharp loss because they constituted an important pool of scarce skilled technical, professional, and administrative manpower. Since the early days of French rule, the proportion of Jewish children receiving modern education has been much higher than that of any other indigenous group, and their departure aggravated the acute shortage of educated personnel, especially in managerial ranks. For example, of 141 lawyers admitted to Supreme Court practice in the Muslim year 1387 (1967/68), 34 were Jews. In addition, those leaving came disproportionately from the ranks of professionals and managerial Jews; their percentage of the Jewish community declined by two-thirds between 1947 and 1968, while that of businessmen and artisans increased by one-quarter. Those Jews who remain are also proportionately less active in economic life; in 1968 only 40 percent participated, as opposed to 46 percent in 1947.

The flight of the Jewish community arose from no policy of the government nor from any severe discrimination. Both before and after independence they have been recognized as a legitimate and valuable segment of society. Although they suffer some social discrimination, their local communities have official standing, including recognized leaders and schools, and Jews have held significant government positions. In 1968 three served on the city council of Casablanca, one on Rabat's, and two on Marrakech's. Nevertheless, Jews have always been excluded from certain social circles and did not get certain types of jobs. In 1968, for example, there was not a single Jewish career military man. On the other hand, warm personal relationships, often based on business friendships, have bound Jew and non-Jew for generations. During the June 1967 Arab-Israeli War, for instance, numerous Berber and Arab notables personally guaranteed the safety of Jewish associates at a time when an outbreak of anti-Jewish acts was feared.

The government has regarded the departure of the Jewish community as a serious loss to the country and at various times has taken steps to stem it. Between 1957 and 1961 agencies arranging Jewish emigration in Casablanca and Tangiers were closed by the police, and some arrests were made. A special section of the police was organized, and at certain times the borders were closed to Jewish emigrants. Jews obtained passports only with difficulty. Despite these provisions, however, 40,000 left during the period.

The June 1967 Arab-Israeli War created an atmosphere of high tension in the Jewish community. The government, throughout the period, acted forcefully to prevent any reprisals toward Moroccan Jews, and many Muslim private citizens acted with exemplary and unflagging friendship. The position of Jews in society did not alter. Nevertheless, some anti-Jewish sentiment was generated in radical nationalist quarters. Two Jewish youths celebrating the Israeli victory were murdered, and some politicians began an anti-Zionist boycott against Jewish business and professional men. The government quickly and firmly disavowed any anti-Jewish sentiment, although it declared itself opposed to Zionism. Nevertheless, the Jewish community panicked, and 7,000 quit the country between June and November of that year. Once again economic leaders bemoaned the loss of many of their most crucial employees, including a large number of accountants.

The departure of the Moroccan Jewish community came about largely because of the insecurity many felt in the face of the government's stated policy of Arabization and also because of the stagnant, and possibly worsening, economic conditions since independence (see ch. 11, Character and Structure of the Economy). More than any other segment of indigenous society, the Jews had adopted French culture; they also had gained full legal equality for the first time under the French. Before the protectorate, they had been a tolerated subject people (see ch. 5, Religious Life). They therefore regarded with nervous suspicion their prospects in an independent Morocco, fearing that nationalism might eventually exclude them.

Europeans

A substantial, but rapidly dwindling, European community remained, primarily in the cities. Accurate statistics were not available in mid-1971, but in 1970 there were an estimated 135,000, as compared to about 200,000 in 1965. The reported emigration rate of 1,000 per month probably increased in the aftermath of the Mehdi Ben Barka affair (see ch. 3, Historical Setting).

By 1971 the French numbered 90,000. Many of them worked under government contract; in 1971 nearly 9,000 teachers supplied by France taught in the schools. Together with their families they accounted for over 20,000 persons. In addition, several thousand technicians worked for the government and in public and private industry (see ch. 12, Agriculture and Industry).

Before the twentieth century no more than a few thousand Europeans resided in the country. During the colonial period this number increased to about 550,000 in 1955, with the Spanish dominating the northern zone and the French the southern, where they were responsible for the urban and industrial development of the region (see ch. 3, Historical Setting).

At independence 80 percent of the European population was urban, concentrated in the coastal cities. Europeans controlled over 80 percent of the industrial and commercial enterprises and virtually monopolized managerial positions, as well as controlling valuable farmland. The French, who constituted about 4 percent of the population in 1955, dominated the modern economic sector and administration. Of 130,000 economically active Frenchmen in the country, 25,000 were government functionaries; 50,000 were employed in industry as managers or workers; 10,000 were doctors or lawyers or were in other professions; 16,000 were merchants; and the remainder worked on the land. Europeans produced one-third of the tax revenue of the country and had a standard of living about seven times higher than that of the average Muslim Moroccan. These Europeans, about

65 percent of whom were not born in the country, usually maintained strong ties with their country of origin.

During colonial times the French presence was considerably more disruptive to the social equilibrium than the Spanish. Spaniards settled nearly exclusively in cities and did not come in large numbers. In 1955 they totaled under 100,000 persons. Many Frenchmen, on the other hand, came as farmers and displaced considerable numbers of local people. In 1955 Frenchmen owned 7 percent of the land in production and produced 40 percent of the country's agricultural income.

Between independence in 1956 and 1965 more than half the European population left the country. Between the census of 1952 and that of 1960, their number decreased by about one-quarter and thereafter by an average of 10 percent a year. Uneasiness about living as a minority in an independent Muslim state, as well as economic uncertainty, motivated their departure.

On the personal level, relations between Europeans and Moroccans are friendly, although their social circles do not often intersect. The Europeans, even those born in Morocco, identify firmly with the mother country and make no attempt to become Moroccan. Consequently, nationalistic, political, and economic policies threaten them directly. Whether the government's admission of the impossibility of rapid Arabization had improved the morale of the European community could not be determined in 1971. Nevertheless, the Europeans feared land reform, proposed in one form or another by all political parties, as well as the possibility of competition for jobs with the growing number of trained Moroccans, who by 1960 held 72 percent of all government administrative positions and over a half of the technical ones.

European farmers, who fear or have already experienced the loss of their lands; lawyers, faced with the gradual Arabization of the judicial system; and owners of small businesses are most likely to depart. Among those remaining are older technicians and professionals who do not wish to reestablish their careers elsewhere, teachers and public officials dedicated to the country and better remunerated than they would be in France, some skilled workers who do not fear replacement by Moroccans in the near future, and some retired and poor persons who cannot afford the expenses of a change.

LANGUAGE AND SOCIETY

Language is one of the central issues of Moroccan society. French colonial policy bequeathed a dual language system whose effects continue to reverberate through the social structure. Animated by their self-imposed civilizing mission of bringing the presumed blessings of French culture to the colonial peoples, French authorities attempted to assimilate the society, and particularly the elite stratum, into the French cultural community.

Throughout the colonial period and into the present, French has been the language of the modern sector of society. The French had little interest in teaching Arabic either to themselves or to the Moroccans except as a dead language of historical or antiquarian interest. Therefore, although Arabic remained the language of everyday discourse among the vast majority of the people, it failed to develop the flexibility and vocabulary needed for modern bureaucratic, industrial, financial, and intellectual affairs. In order to penetrate the modern sector with its desirable jobs, higher living standards, and generally alluring modernity, one had to learn French. As early as 1930 the urban commercial classes spoke French in both their business and personal lives. The transformation of the modern urban working class followed shortly.

Classical Arabic, meanwhile, remained the language of the traditional religious authorities, such as the *ulama* (see Glossary), who, separated from the dynamism of the developing modern sector by the ossifying traditional language, as well as by other factors, gradually lost influence. Because Arabic, the medium of the religious tradition and the historical glories of Moroccan society, became increasingly identified with an old-fashioned, out-of-date, and apparently inferior cultural milieu, problems of identity and self-image multiplied for the French-educated individual, or *evolué*. French, on the other hand, offered access to influence, professional security, and high social status but was nevertheless radically foreign and required an emotional and intellectual uprooting.

Because French was the language of modern education throughout the colonial period, it became the medium of literature and intellectual activity in the modern sector. Ironically, a good deal of nationalist writing, as well as the upbringing of the children of many nationalist leaders, took place in French. The radical estrangement of the modern sector, both from the mass of the people and from the traditional culture, is symbolized by the fact that, in 1964, only about 30 percent spoke French, however badly, and only about 6 percent could read it. Of literate persons, constituting perhaps 10 percent of the population, two-thirds knew French.

With independence, the mass of the people, formerly excluded by the formidable barrier of language, demanded action on their long-held desire for access to the modern sector. This meant both the replacement of French personnel by Moroccans and a widening of the primary route of access—the educational system. The policymakers therefore found themselves caught between the conflicting demands and requisites of Moroccanization and Arabization.

Most of those cut off from the modern sector were excluded by ignorance of the language of that sector. Access could be opened either by teaching French to the masses or by switching the modern sector to Arabic. Both alternatives proved unfeasible, and the education ministers, who have rapidly succeeded one another, have careened uneasily between these alternatives since independence (see ch. 8, The Governmental System and Political Dynamics). Arabizing the educational system and the bureaucracy proved impossible to achieve quickly because of insufficient Arabic-speaking staff. At the time of independence, for example, there was only one modern university-trained Arabic specialist in the country. Teachers trained in the traditional Islamic Arabic-language private schools, who had long been precluded from employment in the public schools, were hurriedly recruited but, because of their unfamiliarity with modern pedagogy, standards fell. The business and intellectual elite began withdrawing their children in favor of the cultural mission schools run by the French government, reinforcing once again the class distinctions that language differences had long symbolized.

The simultaneous and increasing demand for Moroccanization of government and business caused, if anything, a greater entrenchment of French because virtually all qualified Moroccans had been educated in that language. According to some authorities the masses, more interested in social mobility than in Arabic, would have accepted education in French rather than complete Arabization. This possibility has been foreclosed, however, by an absolute lack of personnel (despite large infusions of teachers from France) and by a skyrocketing birth rate which, in 1971, deprived half the children of any schooling at all (see ch. 7, Education, Communication, and the Arts and Sciences). In that same year illiteracy in the coming generation seemed to be increasing both absolutely and relatively; no progress could therefore be made on the language issue.

At the same time, interest in classical Arabic has been increasing among the intellectuals and elsewhere. Nationalist sentiment demands complete Arabization, despite the fact that in 1966 the minister of education and in 1970 the prime minister stated that it was impossible. A more devious goal has been attributed to well-to-do nationalists by French observers; they feel that, since French will probably continue as the language of influence and prestige for some time to come, encouraging the common people to accept education in Arabic while training the children of the elite in French will assure the preservation of existing privileges.

The nervously balanced and paradoxical situation finds expression in the behavior of the government. The king, for example, gives press conferences and consults with his advisers in French; he addresses the people on radio and in official pronouncements in classical Arabic. The government maintains the Bureau of Arabization in Rabat, which has produced wordlists on various subjects, such as 1,000 sports terms and 700 tourism terms; at the same time, much administration is conducted in French, and the Post Office has refused to accept cables in Arabic.

The problem is aggravated by the fact that French and Arabic (or Berber) represent differences far greater than those merely of language. In effect, they represent different world views and social contexts. An observer has noted, for example, that the French language permits social relationships between male and female acquaintances that are virtually impossible in Arabic (see ch. 6, Social Structure). Consequently, the confusion of identity suffered by the bilingual individual can be very great and is particularly painful to adolescents passing through an educational system that vacillates between two languages.

Authorities agree that, although French seems, for the time being, entrenched in the modern sector of society, the pressure for access for Arabic speakers is likely to increase. Data indicate that a stagnating economy cannot produce sufficient jobs for the unemployed graduates, particularly those of Arabic-language schools, whose number grows year by year (see ch. 11, Character and Structure of the Economy). Consequently, observers conclude that many of the social problems of Morocco are likely in the future, as they have in the past, to crystallize in the issue of language.

CHAPTER 5

RELIGIOUS LIFE

Islam, the faith of all Moroccans except a dwindling Jewish community and a small European colony, animates the nation's spiritual life and anchors the traditional social system. Both the rural and urban populations maintain a high level of loyalty to the faith, although practice in many regions is unorthodox and the exigencies of industrial and bureaucratic organization have made traditional devotion difficult for many employed in the modern sector.

The Constitution guarantees freedom of religion but not of proselytism to non-Muslim faiths; nevertheless, it describes the nation as Muslim and the king as the *amir al muaminin*, or commander of the faithful. The Ministry of Religious Foundations (Habus) and Islamic Affairs acts for the government to strengthen and support Islam. As recently as 1961 the *ulama*, the orthodox religious authorities and scholars, ratified the succession to the throne of King Hassan II in a manner long traditional in Morocco.

The sanction of religious authority and the king's position as the leading figure of the *shurfa*, the descendants of the Prophet Muhammad, have been significant in maintaining loyalty to the central government, which, as the embodiment of Islam, is probably the single institution commanding the loyalty of virtually all elements of society (see ch. 6, Social Structure; ch. 8, The Governmental System and Political Dynamics). Islam is a strong unifying force; veneration of the Quran, respect for the reputed descendants of the Prophet, and proud personal identification with the Muslim community cut across nearly all social, ecological, and linguistic distinctions and were significant in forging a dynamic sense of Moroccan nationhood in the late colonial period (see ch. 3, Historical Setting; ch. 4, Ethnic Groups and Languages). Although many practices and beliefs of the Berbers, as well as other rural and urban dwellers, deviate from, and are sometimes even antithetical to, the orthodox Islam of the Quran, personal devotion to the religion has rarely wavered.

Before central authority was firmly established throughout the country by the French Protectorate, religious personages and organizations, particularly *marabouts*, or local holy men, along with fraternal orders of their disciples, stood at the interstices of the highland social system, acting to maintain order among the various tribal groups (see ch. 3, Historical Setting; ch. 6, Social Structure). The establishment of central government authority in these areas has undermined this function, however, and during the last several decades membership in the religious brotherhoods has atrophied along with their usefulness as arbitrators. Nevertheless, the popular cults surrounding the graves and descendants of deceased local saints have remained vigorous in both country and town, as they have been for centuries. The unorthodoxy of these observances does not detract from their adherents' firm and personal identification with Islam.

ISLAM

Historical Background

In A.D. 610 Muhammad, a merchant of the Arabian town of Mecca and later known as the Prophet, began to preach the first of a series of revelations granted him by God through the Angel Gabriel. Muhammad denounced the polytheistic paganism of his fellow Meccans, his vigorous and continuing censure eventually earning him their bitter enmity. In 622 he and a group of his followers fled to Yathrib, which came to be known as Medina (the city) because it was the center of his activities. The flight, or *hijrah*, known in the West as the Hegira, marked the beginning of the Islamic era and of Islam as a force in history; the Muslim calendar begins in 622. In Medina he continued to preach, eventually defeated his detractors in battle, and consolidated both the temporal and spiritual leadership of all Arabia in his person before his death in 632.

After Muhammad's death his followers compiled those of his words regarded as coming directly from God into the Quran, the holy scripture of Islam; others of his sayings and teachings, as well as the precedents of his personal behavior, recalled by those who had known him during life, became the Hadith. Together they form a comprehensive guide to the spiritual, ethical, and social life of the Muslim.

Islam was rapidly transformed from a small religious community into a dynamic political and military force; during the seventh century Muslim conquerors reached as far as Morocco, and by the beginning of the eighth century the Berbers were substantially Islamized (see ch. 3, Historical Setting). The orthodox Sunni denomination, which is the larger of the two branches of Islam, was firmly established in Morocco by the Almohad dynasty during the twelfth century. The smaller branch, or Shia, which has little representation in Morocco, broke away during Islam's first century as a result of a bitter dispute over the succession to Muhammad's role of religious and secular leader.

Tenets of Islam

The *shahadah* (testimony) succinctly states the central belief of Islam: "There is no god but God (Allah), and Muhammad is His Prophet." This simple profession of faith is repeated on many ritual occasions, and recital in full and unquestioning sincerity designates one a Muslim. The God preached about by Muhammad was not one previously unknown to his countrymen, for *Allah* is the Arabic for "God" rather than a particular name. Instead of introducing a new deity, Muhammad denied the existence of the many minor gods and spirits worshiped before his ministry and declared the omnipotence of the unique creator, God. Islam means "submission to God," and he who submits is a Muslim. Muhammad is the "seal of the Prophets"; his revelation is said to complete for all time the series of biblical revelations received by the Jews and the Christians. God himself is believed to have remained one and the same throughout time, but men had strayed from his true teachings until they were corrected by Muhammad. Prophets and sages of the biblical tradition, such as Abraham, Moses, and Jesus (Isa), are recognized as inspired vehicles of God's will. Islam, however, reveres as sacred only the message, rejecting Christianity's deification of the messenger. It accepts the concepts of guardian angels, the Day of Judgment, general resurrection, heaven and hell, and the eternal life of the soul.

The duties of the Muslim form the "five pillars" of the faith. These are *shahada*, recitation of the creed; *salat*, daily prayer; *zakat*, almsgiving; *sawm*, fasting; and *hajj*, pilgrimage. The believer prays in a prescribed manner after purification through ritual ablutions at dawn, midday, midafternoon, sunset, and nightfall. Prescribed genuflections and prostrations accompany the prayers, which the worshiper recites while facing toward Mecca. Whenever possible men pray in congregation at the mosque under an *imam*, or prayer leader (see Glossary), and on Fridays are obliged to do so. Women may also attend public worship at the mosque, where they are segregated from the men, although most frequently they pray in seclusion at home. A special functionary, the *muaddhin*, intones a call to prayer to the entire community at the appropriate hours; those out of earshot determine the proper time from the sun.

In the early days of Islam the authorities imposed a tax on personal property proportionate to one's wealth; this was distributed to the mosques and to the needy. In addition, freewill gifts were made. Almsgiving, although still a duty of the believer, has become a more private matter.

The ninth month of the Muslim calendar is Ramadan, a period of obligatory fasting in commemoration of Muhammad's receipt of the Quran. During this month all but the sick, the weak, pregnant women, soldiers on duty, travelers on necessary journeys, and young children are enjoined from eating, drinking, smoking, or sexual intercourse during the daylight hours. The well-to-do usually do little or no work during this period, and many businesses close for all or part of the day. Since the months of the lunar calendar revolve through the solar year, Ramadan falls at various seasons in different years. A fast in summertime imposes considerable hardship on those who must do physical work. Each day's fast ends with a signal that light is insufficient to distinguish a black thread from a white one. Id al Fitr (also called Id al Saghir), a three-day feast and holiday, ends the month of Ramadan.

All Muslims at least once in their lifetime should, if possible, make the *hajj* (pilgrimage) to the holy city of Mecca to participate in special rites held at several spots there during the twelfth month of the lunar calendar. The pilgrim, dressed in the white seamless *ihram*, abstains from sexual relations, shaving, haircutting, and nail paring. Highlights of the *hajj* include kissing of the sacred black stone; circumambulation of the Kaaba, the sacred structure housing it; running seven times between the sacred mountains Safa and Marwa; and standing in prayer on Mount Arafat. The returning pilgrim is entitled to the honorific al Haj before his name.

The permanent struggle for the triumph of the word of God on earth, the *jihad*, represents an additional general duty of all Muslims. Although this has in the past been used to justify holy wars, modern Muslims see it in a broader context of civic and personal action. Abdul Karim, in his Rif rebellion of the 1920s, and later nationalist leaders invoked the concept of the preservation of Islam from the encroachment of Christian authority (see ch. 3, Historical Setting).

In addition to specific duties, Islam imposes a code of ethical conduct encouraging generosity, fairness, honesty, and respect and forbidding adultery, gambling, usury, and the consumption of carrion, blood, pork, and alcohol. A Muslim stands in a personal relationship to God; there is neither intermediary nor clergy in Islam. Those who lead prayers, preach sermons, and interpret the law do so by virtue of their superior knowledge and scholarship rather than any special powers or prerogatives endowed by ordination.

During his lifetime Muhammad was both spiritual and temporal leader of the Muslim community; he established the concept of Islam as a total and all-encompassing way of life for man and society. Muslims believe that Allah revealed to Muhammad the rules governing decent and proper behavior, and it is therefore incumbent on the individual to live in the manner prescribed by revealed law and on the community to perfect human society on earth according to the holy injunctions. Islam traditionally recognizes no distinction between church and state. Religious and secular life merge, as do religious and secular law.

In keeping with this conception of society, all Muslims have been traditionally subject to the *sharia*, or religious law, which covers most aspects of life, as interpreted by religious courts; in Morocco the Malikite school of Sunni law is followed. Consequently, when, by the Berber *dahir* (decree) of 1930, the French authorities symbolically and actually removed the Berber tribes from the jurisdiction of the *sharia* courts and from the unified Muslim community, Moroccan Muslims felt a sharp affront to the unity of Islam. What the French had intended as a divisive political tactic instead aroused the worst fears for the dignity and survival of Islam and, with them, a vigorous feeling of Islamic solidarity among all elements of the population (see ch. 3, Historical Setting).

During his lifetime the Prophet enjoined his followers to convert the infidel to the true faith. He specifically exempted, however, the "Peoples of the Book," Jews and Christians, whose religions he recognized as the historical basis of Islam. These peoples were to be permitted to continue their own communal and religious life as long as they recognized the temporal domain of Muslim authorities, paid their taxes, and did not proselytize or otherwise interfere with the practice of Islam. Consequently, the Jewish community of Morocco was, until the protectorate, a *dhimmi*, or protected subject people; in matters that did not concern Muslims their own religious law was valid. The Jews first gained legal equality under the French Protectorate and have since been recognized as fully equal Moroccan citizens.

The Christian community, however, arriving in substantial numbers only after French hegemony was established, was never a *dhimmi* group and, in fact, assumed control of the society. Although the Quran specifically discusses the position and treatment of subject Jews and Christians in Muslim society, it makes no mention of the reverse. A Muslim society permanently subject to non-Muslims has been called by one authority a situation inconceivable within the framework of Islam as God's final and authoritative revelation. Such a state of affairs is by its nature an affront to Islam and a reproach to the Muslims who permit it to persist; it must be ended as quickly as possible, and the true supremacy of Islam restored. For this reason, among others, Moroccan nationalism was, at base, largely a religious movement (see ch. 3, Historical Setting; ch. 8, The Governmental System and Political Dynamics).

Moroccan sensibilities notwithstanding, the French established their legal code as supreme except for marriage, divorce, and other aspects of personal life. The postindependence Moroccan legal code combines elements of secular law with the traditional law of the religious communities, which is still valid in matters of personal status (see ch. 8, The Governmental System and Political Dynamics).

FOLK BELIEFS AND FOLK RELIGION

Throughout the centuries since its introduction into North Africa, Islam has interacted with the indigenous, predominantly Berber culture to produce a style of religious belief and practice uniquely Moroccan. Both Arabs and Berbers are profoundly Islamized; religious terms, for example, are not translated into the Berber language. Paradoxically, however, the highly fragmented traditional social organization of the dissident tribesmen is antithetical to the unity envisioned by orthodox Islam. The religion in a sense therefore inheres in the individual rather than the group.

At various times in Moroccan history the Berbers' separatist aspirations and their reaction against Arab authority at the center have expressed themselves through the heretical and schismatic doctrines of particularly vivid Berber holy men. In addition, a residue of pre-Islamic belief and practice remains, coloring the worship of the uneducated. Popular Islam is thus an overlay of Quranic ritual and ethical principles on a background of belief in *djinns* (spirits), the evil eye, rites to assure good fortune, and the veneration of local saints. The educated of the cities and towns—merchants, artisans, professionals, and scholars—have been the primary bearers and guardians of the austere orthodox Islam.

Although orthodox Islam preaches the unique and inimitable majesty and sanctity of Allah and the equality of all believers before him, an important element of Moroccan Islam has for centuries been the belief in the coalescence of special spiritual powers in particular contemporaneous human beings. *Baraka* is a transferable quality of personal blessedness, holiness, and spiritual force that is said to congeal in certain individuals. Those whose claims to possession of *baraka* can be substantiated, either through performance of apparent miracles, exemplary spiritual insights, or genealogical connection with a recognized possessor, are viewed as saints. These persons are known in the West as *marabouts*, a French corruption of the Arabic *murabitin*, persons who have undergone *ribat*, a religious retreat. *Baraka* is said to be granted by God to certain persons and may be transferred by them to other persons and to inanimate objects. Beneficial effects accrue to those ordinary persons who come in contact with a possessor.

The human being to whom God granted the most *baraka* is said to be the Prophet Muhammad. Because it can be inherited in the male line, his *baraka* passed to his agnatic descendants among the *shurfa* (sing., *sharif*). *Baraka*, however, is not evenly distributed even among the *shurfa*; their descent gives them a hereditary tendency toward sainthood but does not guarantee it to any particular individual. Furthermore, *baraka* can be dormant for generations. At times, however, so great a quantity of it fuses in one person that he is undeniably accepted as a saint.

Saints

After death, a saint's *baraka* is thought to increase and to inhere in the persons and, particularly, the places associated with him, most especially his tomb, or *kubba*. After his death a saint often becomes the patron and protector of the locality or social group in which he lived. Persons seeking blessing, especially barren women and the sick, visit his tomb, usually a square whitewashed building with a horseshoe-shaped door and an octagonal roof, to perform rituals and absorb some of his blessedness through the osmosis of physical proximity.

The saint in his tomb is known in Moroccan dialect as the *mul bilad*, the owner of the land, and his connection with a given locality, quarter in a town, or craft group is strongly physical; the holiness inheres not only in his spirit but also very definitely in his body and the burial place. Thousands of saints' tombs, both large and small, dot the landscape, and nearly every settlement has a patron. One observer has noted that *sidi* and *mulay*, the honorifics given to saints, are as common on the map of Morocco as the term *saint* is on that of Europe and for a similar reason—the devotion of the common people of both regions to their local patron.

Migration to cities has, for this reason, strained the cults of saints among the newly urbanized. Countrypeople often continue in the city to venerate the saints of their home communities, but the cults, because of distance and the inaccessibility of the shrines, often gradually lose their viability. Sometimes such persons attempt to transfer their loyalty to the saints of their new home, although the change is frequently unsuccessful, either because the new devotee misses the strong force of tradition that tied him to his former patron or, as is often the case in Casablanca, the slum or quarter is so new that it lacks established traditions.

Sometimes an attempt is made to establish a new cult or embellish a weak one; in Casablanca, for example, the mushrooming shantytowns (*bidonvilles*) and suburbs have overtaken and absorbed old rural communities and, with them, their saints. The veneration of saints is widespread among the uneducated, particularly the rural and urban poor, and also among many urban middle-class women (see ch. 6, Social Structure). A long-term declining trend has been noted in the cities, however, probably caused by education, Western influence, the general secularization of life, and the greater tendency toward orthodoxy among reform-minded city dwellers. Among the leading saints are Mulay Idris, the patron of Fes, and Sidi Muhammad ben Isa, the patron of Meknès.

Moroccans generally also believe in the existence of a special group of spiritual beings called *djinns*, whose supernatural powers can be used either benevolently or malevolently. Many people fear them and protect themselves by magical incantations; petitions; offerings; animal sacrifices; and the use of *baraka*-impregnated objects, such as salt, iron, steel, and gunpowder.

Belief in the evil eye is widespread; the glance or look of certain individuals causes an evil or deadly spell, and danger is particularly great when accompanied by an "evil mouth," that is, by loose talk, praise, joking, or cursing. Protection is most commonly sought in incantations; incense; the use of magical colors, such as black, yellow, blue, and red; and symbolic forms of the number five or of the hand. Abstract forms of the number five or of the hand are frequently tattooed on the faces of women, particularly among the Berber tribes, and are a dominant motif in crafts and architectural decoration.

Unorthodox religious beliefs and practices of this type are probably more common among women than among men. Because they are excluded by the social segregation of the sexes from much of the formal religious life of the community, women attempt to meet their spiritual needs through informal and unorthodox religious beliefs and practices passed on from mother to daughter.

The government neither encourages nor discourages the cults of saints but is said to view them as a symptom of a vigorous folk culture. King Hassan II has ordered the construction of a traditional tomb for his widely revered father, the late King Mohammed V. The Alawite dynasty, as the leading sharifian family in the country, derives loyalty and a degree of legitimacy from their position as religious leaders, both ex officio and by descent. The special spiritual features of all sharifian families are held to occur most strongly in the royal line.

The descendants of an important saint, the *awlad siyyid* (saint's children), often form a saintly lineage, accepting the reverence of the laymen because of their illustrious ancestor. They frequently act as custodians of the tomb and shrine, living from the contributions received from pilgrims and devotees. The Muslim duty of pilgrimage has been widely reinterpreted in the popular mind to include pilgrimage to shrines of the saints. Some persons of the Rif are said to believe, for example, that seven pilgrimages to the shrines of Mulay Idris and Mulay Abd al Salam equal a pilgrimage to Mecca. The belief in pilgrimage also existed among many Jews, and persons of both faiths frequently visited the same shrines.

In addition to guarding the shrines, the saintly lineages, particularly in the highland areas, had served as mediators between tribal groups, adjudicating disputes, assigning rights, and granting asylum. Berber tribesmen in the past frequently came forward with claims of sainthood and sharifian descent. Although Berber culture was firmly established in Morocco long before the arrival of Islam and Arabic culture, many believe that those Berbers claiming to be *shurfa* are descended from originally Muslim families that later became Berberized. Consequently, a large proportion of the population claims, with varying degrees of success, sharifian descent, despite the logical contradiction implicit in history (see ch. 3, Historical Setting; ch. 4, Ethnic Groups and Languages).

Religious Brotherhoods

Groups of disciples have frequently clustered around particular saints, especially those who preached an original *tariqa*, a mystical or devotional "way." Brotherhoods of the followers of such mystical teachers appeared in North Africa at least as early as the eleventh century and during the instability of the fifteenth and sixteenth centuries became mass movements (see ch. 3, Historical Setting). The founder, an obvious possessor of great *baraka*, ruled an order of adepts who were ordinarily organized hierarchically. The authority of the leader, or *shaykh*, was often absolute; it was said that "He who has no *shaykh* has the devil for a *shaykh*." The brotherhood usually centered spatially on a combined lodge and shrine, called a *zawiya*. Although the *tariqa* was held to supplement and enrich the members' Islam, in practice it usually supplanted orthodox worship.

The cult of saints and the belief in sanctity and brotherhoods apparently antedate the arrival of Islam in Morocco, and the adaptation of these indigenous forms eased its acceptance by the Berber tribes. In fact, the brotherhoods were the most potent vehicles for the early spread of Islam in the highlands. The *zawiyiin* also served as hostels for travelers and sanctuaries from enemies, much as churches did in Europe during the Middle Ages. Because of their evident success and social utility, the orders were widely tolerated by the orthodox *ulama*, many of whom were said to be members in preprotectorate times. The orders came to exercise significant political influence.

The strengthened central government that developed under the protectorate has absorbed many of the traditional social functions of the brotherhoods, however, and an ideological shift within Islam has largely robbed them of their legitimacy. Although it was reported that in 1939 nearly 20 percent of Moroccan males belonged to one of the twenty-three largest brotherhoods, by the late 1960s the orders' vitality had waned. Observers stated that those *zawiyiin* still functioning consisted of older men and were not successfully recruiting among the younger generation. Evidence exists, however, that the *zawiya* as a social form is still vigorous, even among urban populations. A survey among Istiqlal (Independence) Party leaders in Fes, for example, indicated that a majority viewed their local party group as a *zawiya*, albeit one combining secular and religious overtones (see ch. 8, The Governmental System and Political Dynamics).

Religious Reform

The *zawiyiin* and *marabouts* for the most part coexisted easily with the French authorities. In the late nineteenth and early twentieth centuries there began to grow in the central Middle East a new drive for an Islam purified of unorthodox accretions (see ch. 3, Historical Setting). Founded by Jamal al Din al Afghani and Muhammad Abduh, this movement was known as Salafiya, from the Arabic *al salaf al salih* (the pious ancestors). A small group of men who had lived in the Middle East, including Abdullah Ben Driss Senoussi and Bouchaib al Doukkala, brought these ideas to Morocco after World War I. By the early 1920s study and discussion groups had been organized in Fes and Rabat. A student of Doukkala, Mulay al Arabi al Alawi, in turn instructed the future nationalist leader Allal al Fassi and his circle (see ch. 8, The Governmental System and Political Dynamics).

The members of the Salafiya taught that the salvation of society and of Islam, at that time both suffering disorganization and indignity at the hands of the French, lay in a return to the simple orthodoxy of the Quran. They rejected the profusion of popular beliefs and practices that had grown up around Islam and denounced the *marabouts* as frauds and as sycophants to the French authorities. Early nationalism in Morocco arose from this movement and therefore from the beginning carried heavy religious overtones (see ch. 3, Historical Setting; ch. 8, The Governmental System and Political Dynamics). The Islamic reformers were revolted by the deep inroads made by French culture, by the ignorance of the youth of their Arabic and Islamic heritage, and by the debasement of the Arabic language caused by the growing use of French by the educated. They began to organize private Arabic-language Quranic schools and nourished the interest in classical Arabic that has been growing in recent decades (see ch. 4, Ethnic Groups and Languages).

Because of the growing influence of Islamic reformism, the *marabouts* and brotherhoods quickly lost prestige. Throughout the struggle for independence, performance of certain public duties of Islam carried strong nationalistic overtones. Although the requirements of industrial and office work in many cases precluded daily prayer, the strict observance of Ramadan became a badge of solidarity with Islam and the Moroccan people.

In more recent years the public aspects of Ramadan have retained their symbolic importance, although the observance of other religious duties appears less widespread than the fast. During the month of fast, national wine consumption drops 30 percent. Violations of the rules of Ramadan occur mainly among the educated and Westernized and usually in secret. Observance is generally heartfelt; workers, even those doing hard labor, abstain from food and drink; smokers break their habit; many omit swimming for fear of swallowing water; and women give up garlic, which is said to have aphrodisiac properties. Each year hundreds of restaurant customers are arrested and fined under a provision of the penal code that forbids the public consumption of food or drink by Muslims during the fast period.

Because other religious duties are more private, observance is more difficult to measure. The number of pilgrims to Mecca continues to rise annually and includes a substantial number of women; in some years women constituted over 30 percent of the pilgrims originating in Casablanca. Particularly for city dwellers employed in industries or offices, halting work for the periods of daily prayer presents difficulties, and observers note that many, particularly the young and educated, omit this practice. Nevertheless, popular feeling toward Islam is said to remain very deep.

The government explicitly supports orthodox Islam through the Ministry of Religious Foundations (Habus) and Islamic Affairs, which administers the foundations established by charitable individuals for the advancement of the faith and of charity and also undertakes other projects. For example, during 1968 forty-one new mosques were constructed and thirty-seven, in the following year. Operation Quranic Schools, launched by the king, seeks to increase religious education among young children (see ch. 7, Education, Communication, and the Arts and Sciences). Lectures and sermons are broadcast on radio and television, and religious and cultural journals are published by the ministry.

The royal family participates conspicuously in religious activities, the king being frequently seen at prayer, usually dressed in traditional costume. In March 1971 the seven-year-old crown prince was circumcised at the palace, according to religious tradition, in the presence of the king and members of the *ulama*. To commemorate this event, the king absorbed the expenses of the circumcisions of 40,000 other boys of the same age in various parts of the country.

MINORITY RELIGIONS

Although the Constitution ensures the freedom to practice non-Muslim religions, proselytism among Muslims is not permitted. Consequently, conversions to Judaism and Christianity rarely, if ever, occur. A small number of non-Muslims accept Islam every year, primarily women marrying Muslims. Between 1959 and 1963, for example, some 144 such conversions were recorded in Casablanca.

Judaism

The Moroccan Jewish community, which in 1970 numbered approximately 40,000, relates to the larger Muslim society through official leaders in each locality and through officials representing the community as a whole (see ch. 4, Ethnic Groups and Languages). The religious courts and schools, which formerly functioned under the community committee, were in 1971 under the ministries of justice and education, respectively (see ch. 7, Education, Communication, and the Arts and Sciences; ch. 8, The Governmental System and Political Dynamics). The Institute of Jewish Studies, which accepts women students, in 1961 replaced an ancient seminary.

Judaism shares with Islam an uncompromising monotheism, as well as proscription on the consumption of pork. It emphasizes, however, the Sabbath as a day of rest and prayer and the unique mission of the Jewish people as bearers of God's law as embodied in the Torah, the scripture consisting of the Pentateuch. Other dietary restrictions, particularly on the mixing of milk and meat, are also observed. The level of religious observance is relatively high among Moroccan Jews; in 1968 an observer noted, for example, that 65 to 70 percent kept the Sabbath, which required closing businesses and absenting oneself from work.

The majority of the country's Jews are urban, descended from Sephardic Jews of Spain and Portugal or from Jewish migrants from the countryside (see ch. 4, Ethnic Groups and Languages). The Judaism of the Sephardim had certain distinctive features and profoundly influenced the groups already in Morocco when the Sephardim arrived from the Iberian Peninsula. Among these features was the use of cabala, an esoteric system of scriptural interpretation, which assigned an occult meaning to every word and letter of the scriptures, and the Zohar, a mystical commentary on the Torah that was sometimes invoked as a protection against the evil eye to exorcise the demons of sterility. These practices, as well as certain family regulations and rites of passage, continued among many Jews in 1971. Pilgrimages to local shrines have been customary among Moroccan Jews, and national officials have at times participated.

Among Jews who remain in Morocco certain aspects of the traditionalist religion are being discarded; the omission of family prayers and ceremonies is becoming a commonplace occurrence. Modernization of family life and the role of women affects them as much as Muslims (see ch. 6, Social Structure).

Christianity

Nearly all of the approximately 135,000 Christians in the country in 1970 were foreigners of European origin and members of the Roman

Catholic Church. A few Protestant foreigners resided in the country, and there was a limited number of Protestant missionary institutions.

The Roman Catholic Church was established in the country in the nineteenth century but has not been permitted to proselytize since the Algeciras Conference in 1906. It is, however, authorized, and even encouraged, to run private schools, hospitals, dispensaries, and other institutions. Until 1961 Sunday religious services were broadcast on the national radio network. Relations between the church and the government are cordial, although there is some anti-Christian sentiment among certain conservative Muslims.

The two Catholic archdioceses are centered at Tangier and Rabat. In Tangier the Catholic population is mostly Spanish with some French, Italians, and Portuguese. Religious orders of this archdiocese operate several schools, teaching mostly in Spanish with a few hours in Arabic each week, and run a few hospitals, three of which are under direct control of Spanish Catholic orders. In the Rabat archdiocese there are over 100 religious houses for contemplative and teaching orders, about 75 Catholic schools, about 90 hospitals and welfare institutions, and the internationally known Benedictine monastery at Tiouliline, where Muslims and Christians are brought together for study seminars. Whereas the foreign Christian population had been greatly reduced through emigration, the number of clergy had diminished only about 15 percent by 1965. At that time about 1,000 priests, monks, and nuns were still in the country. Organized congregations are found in Tangier, Rabat, Casablanca, and Fes, and other Christians are scattered in small groups throughout the country.

CHAPTER 6

SOCIAL STRUCTURE

In the early 1970s Moroccan social organization reflects the various periods of the nation's modern history, primarily in a profound social and cultural dislocation caused by the intervention of the French. Two substantially unintegrated sectors stand side by side, one dominating the life of the small but influential urban circles, the other receiving the loyalty of the vast majority of the rural people and the nonwealthy urbanites. A significant residue of the preprotectorate tribal-based traditional society remains, as modified by the direct and indirect results of French colonial policy, the most pregnant of which was the creation of a French-educated elite. Developments since independence have introduced additional elements and pressures, continuing the pattern of relatively rapid social change characteristic of Morocco during most of the twentieth century.

Although the nation's central symbol and religious authority, the monarchy, has existed for centuries, the nation lacks a single system of stratification and values binding all or even most traditional groups into a unified whole. The countervailing ancient tradition of *siba*, or tribal independence and dissidence, endures in many of the social practices and attitudes of the outlying tribes, despite the political centralization achieved by the French. Colonial policies, as well as subsequent developments, have nevertheless begun to dissolve the solidarity of the individual tribes and to modify their institutions (see ch. 3, Historical Setting).

The rapid, largely uncoordinated growth of commerce, industry, and the metropolitan centers began under the French; the effects of this uninterrupted development have restructured life both in cities and in the countryside. New urban elites, partially, but not entirely, based on the traditional ones, have assumed leadership. The sprawling slums and workers' suburbs that have mushroomed nearly out of control around most cities, particularly those on the coast, have transformed tens of thousands of largely illiterate former tribesmen into uneasy new urbanites, uncertain of their present environment and its values and alienated from the spiritual and social heritage of their tribes.

In addition, the mass media, increased ease of travel, contact with urbanized tribesmen, and other factors have brought city thinking and wants into the countryside, offering an outlet for the ambitious, an escape for the disaffected, and a galaxy of unsettling new possibilities and ideas for everyone. Although some tribes have retained a considerable solidarity in the face of urban influences, government policy has tended to speed the erosion of tribal organizations. During the early 1960s the government undertook the reorganization of rural groups into a number of communes, new local units founded on more rational and modern criteria than the traditional tribes (see ch. 8, The Governmental System and Political Dynamics). In some cases the boundaries of the new communes coincide with those of preexisting tribes, but more frequently they embody a new organization and at least a partial realignment of relationships.

Both in the city and the countryside the family remains the core of the social structure and the pivot of the value system. Arranged marriage and parental authority retain much of their traditional importance, although changing attitudes and conditions of life seem to have insinuated desires for greater freedom and individualism, especially among the modern educated and the urban young.

STRUCTURE OF SOCIETY

Traditional society consisted of relatively small groups, many of which recognized no sovereignty larger than their own. The traditional central government held sway over, raised armies in, and extracted taxes from only a central core of tribes loyal to the sultanate, which later became the monarchy (see ch. 3, Historical Setting; ch. 8, The Governmental System and Political Dynamics). Beyond the boundary of government territory, called the *bilad al makhzan*, stretched the much larger, though more sparsely settled, *bilad al siba*, or land of dissidence, the domain of the tribes effectively refusing fealty to the central authorities. The boundary between the two territories vacillated throughout history, and the tribes lived in a continuing relation to the *makhzan* (central government), even if it were only opposition.

As a result, the country does not yet constitute a single society. No integrating symbols exist for the country at large except for Islam and, to some extent, the monarchy. The government attempts to exploit in the interest of national unity what is probably the most potent symbol recognized by both rural and urban elements, the king as commander of the faithful, the representative and embodiment of Islam. Both through his sharifian descent and his position as the head of state, he personifies the leadership of the Muslim community and, as such, can appeal to the vast majority of his subjects in the name of the whole Moroccan people (see ch. 5, Religious Life; ch. 8, The Governmental System and Political Dynamics).

Another important, though less potent, symbol is Arabic language and culture. Up to 40 percent of the population, however, identify themselves primarily as Berbers rather than Arabs (see ch. 4, Ethnic Groups and Languages). The Berbers, in turn, identify with a multitude of tribal groups, rather than as one people. They are organized into numerous different structures and respond to different symbols.

A further significant split divides the townsman from the countryman; the former, including the recent urban migrant, is relatively individualistic, whereas the latter belongs to a tribe and thus is enmeshed in close and reciprocal relationships with a number of relatives. In Morocco, as in other Muslim countries, the division between town and country is relatively ancient, and the roles of townsman and tribesman have long been clearly distinguished. A cultural gap has for generations separated the two types of society, and differences of dress, custom, livelihood, and loyalty, as well as social barriers against close relationship and intermarriage, have symbolized and enhanced these distinctions.

Before the advent of the Europeans, both city and country were distinctive, but nevertheless complementary, parts of a single cultural tradition. During the colonial period, however, members of influential urban circles adopted elements of the radically foreign European culture, alienating themselves both from the tribesmen and their less affluent fellow townsmen. Urban social structure consequently shifted away from traditional forms, triggering further change elsewhere in society. Some authorities maintain, however, that the urban-rural gap, although still quite marked, has been slightly diminished by the tribesman's growing knowledge of, and familiarity with, city life.

Tribal Society

As a general rule, rural society, both Berber and Arab, is tribal society. A web of kinship relations binds the rural individual to his native place, to his immediate kinsmen, and to ramifying groups of his more distant kin. Authorities have noted, however, that these ties are often highly elastic, allowing personal desires and affections to outweigh the more formal requirements of structure in the formation of relationships. Many people perceive and explain their society in terms of the cultural ideal of segmentary organization, although that ideal does not always guide behavior. Because Moroccan tribes are independent and fractious, especially in the hills and among the Berbers, details of organization, terminology, and specific custom vary from region to region. In most places, however, the principles of organization are the same.

The traditional tribe was usually based on the principle of the segmentary lineage. That is to say, a group of kinsmen who trace descent through the male line to a common ancestor mass themselves into complementary but opposing groups of varying sizes to match the circumstances and the relevant degree of relationship. The founding ancestor, the presumed father of the entire tribe, also fathered a specific number of historical sons, who in their turn produced a known number of similarly prolific offspring, who continued the process until it resulted after several generations in the present members of the tribe, grouped in their small residential units or hamlets. Each of the various members can trace his ancestry through the preceding generations to the common founder, each more distant ancestor gathering under the umbrella of his "people" or "sons" an increasingly larger number of descendants until all are encompassed among the sons of the founder. Consequently, tribesmen visualize themselves as the son of D, the grandson of B, the great-grandson of A, joining at each level a progressively larger number of kinsmen recognizing the same descent at that level and above (see fig. 8).

The kinsmen who mass together as descendants of a common ancestor at each level view themselves as a unit in opposition to all other groups formed in that tribe at that same level. That is to say, the grandsons of brothers form two groups in opposition to each other, but they form one group in opposition to the descendants of the brother of their common great-grandfather.

Fellow tribesmen conceptualize their relationships to one another, often explicitly, by climbing up the generations to the nearest common ancestor. All other relationships, as well as all ramifying groups to which each belongs, are thus determined, and the exact degree of formal relationship is fixed. Especially among sedentary groups the segmentary scheme often closely parallels the spatial distribution of neighboring residential groups, building from the household, through the neighborhood, the hamlet, the village, and finally to an entire valley or region.

Disputes between fellow tribesmen are ordinarily settled at the appropriate level of complementary opposition. Because the constituent opposing groups are implicit in the relationships of all kinsmen but one's immediate household, disputes between kinsmen rapidly escalate to the highest relevant level of opposition, involving the members of the affected groups who may, depending on the circumstances, either attempt a reconciliation or resort to various means of conflict.

The structure of the tribe and relationships within it are consequently fluid and contingent. An opponent for some purposes is an ally for others. Individuals exploit the relatively wide leeway, emphasizing the most beneficial social ties and maneuvering among relationships. In addition, the complementary massing and opposition of the segments at various levels constitute an important form of social control within many tribes. Observers have referred to

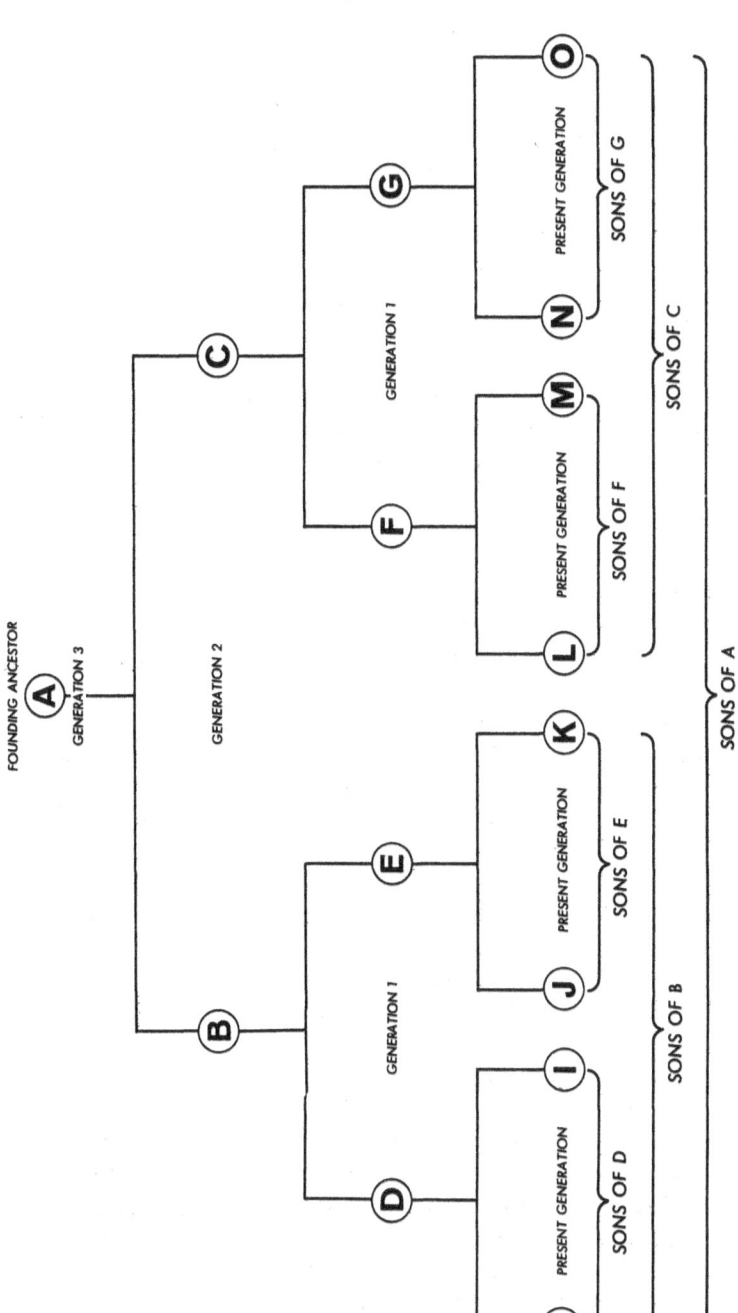

Figure 8. Schematic Representation of a Typical Segmentary System in Morocco.

organizations of this type as "tribes without government" because they lack a single uniform and organized system of authority and control but nevertheless function without undue turmoil or conflict.

Between the ultimate levels of neighboring tribes there were ordinarily no mediating genealogical connections. Consequently, *marabouts*, or local holy men, often functioned as mediators, deriving their authority from their reputations for exemplary holiness (see ch. 5, Religious Life). This function was of course modified after the establishment of central authority throughout the country.

The various self-conscious segments of a tribe call themselves by names reflecting their relationships. The distinctive title is ordinarily preceded by the Berber *ait* (people of) or the Arabic *beni* or *awlad* (sons or children of). Sedentary segments are usually distinguished by a geographic name; and seasonal migrant and nomad groups, most often by the name of the relevant ancestor. Each tribe consists, therefore, of a series of named segments nesting one inside the other, and each individual may recognize his group by any of a number of different names, depending on the context.

This relativity of membership vividly expresses itself in the system of personal names. Before the French no concept of a fixed multicontextual personal name nor any permanent transmittable surname existed. A small number of sophisticated persons required such a name for travel documents, but the average tribesman had no such need. (For that matter, neither do numerous tribesmen at the present day.) Within his group of personal acquaintances a man was known by his own given name and by that of his father, for example, Muhammad ben Hassan. If further clarification were needed the given name of the grandfather might be added, to make, for example, Muhammad ben Hassan ben Ali. Leaving his village or segment for a neighboring one, a man takes on the name of his home, for example, Muhammad ben Hassan al Hassuni (Muhammad of the people of Hassun). If he travels more widely he may take on the name of an intermediate segment of his tribe, or if he ventures out of the territories of his tribe or to the city, he is likely to assume the name of the tribe as a whole and become, for example, Muhammad al Srarhna.

Despite the fact that tribesmen believe that the genealogy by which they explain their tribal organization accurately represents their physical ancestry, authorities point out that such genealogies are not in most cases historically correct. Sometimes, new persons or groups are grafted to them. In many cases, modification and telescoping of generations occur over the years; only those ancestors defining socially significant contemporary segments remain in memory, the others falling away except in the case of lineages with pretenses to holiness. In that case each generation of saintly ancestors strengthens the group's claims to holiness (see ch. 5, Religious Life). Over a period of years the genealogy of nonholy lineages tends to remain approximately five generations deep.

The French, not fully understanding the fluid complexity of Moroccan tribal organization but nevertheless trying to preserve traditional forms while simultaneously establishing their authority among the tribes, instigated significant social change in the rural areas. Many of the tribes loyal to the *makhzan*, including the so-called *jaysh* (army) tribes who supplied levies of troops in lieu of taxes, had had a more stable and centralized organization than the tribes of the hinterland; in such cases protectorate officials integrated the tribal leaders into their colonial bureaucracy. They hoped to institutionalize some similar form of authority among the uncentralized groups in order to render them more manageable. They attempted to integrate any existing segment headmen, as well as the *marabouts*, whom they took for local leaders rather than mediators, into a formal structure of authority loyal to the protectorate. Many of the holy men cooperated, seeing their prestige and that of their religious followers enhanced. Nevertheless, their association with the unpopular French authorities ultimately undercut their popular appeal. As the independence movement developed, based heavily on orthodox religious doctrine, the *marabouts* came to be widely seen as procolonial collaborators and religious frauds (see ch. 3, Historical Setting; ch. 5, Religious Life).

A number of tribes traditionally had councils or assemblies of family heads or settlement representatives, often rather rudimentary in form and usually representing little more authority than consensus. Other tribes, however, had more developed systems of officials. Nevertheless, the French attempt to incorporate existing institutions into a colonial bureaucracy upset the equilibrium of tribal relations and, in many cases, gave certain favored individuals and groups an unaccustomed prestige and power. Despite these internal changes, the outlines of most tribal organizations and the sentiments of most tribesmen remained largely unchanged.

In some parts of the country, particularly the Sous region of the south, fairly rapid consolidation of authority was underway even before the French period. By the early twentieth century the *makhzan's* control had been slowly spreading into that region for some years. Powerful local authorities began to emerge, usually exploiting the wealth, power, and influence they enjoyed as favorites of the sultan. They became potent local leaders, sometimes posing as agents of the sultan, sometimes as defenders of the tribes. Several of these men, along with their families, quickly evolved into what the French called *grands seigneurs*, or a quasi-feudal nobility. Probably the most important of these new nobles was the house of Glaoui, whose leader ruled Marrakech and the tribes of its hinterland. The *grands seigneurs*, desiring stability, generally cooperated with the

French, whose support further entrenched them. This connection, however, proved damaging during the independence movement, when most of these families were discredited as collaborators and deprived of their power. The importance of the *grand seigneur* system and the tribal accommodations to it varied from region to region.

The most recent wave of change in tribal life resulted from the reorganization of rural groups in the early 1960s. The government, attempting to put rural life on a more efficient and manageable footing than the old tribal system, organized the countryside into units called communes, each composed of a number of hamlets and small settlements and grouped around a natural center of communication and social contact, such as a highway or *souk* (market) (see ch. 13, Trade and Transportation). Some of these new entities coincide with the boundaries of former tribes, but many combine elements of various traditional groups. As a consequence, relationships and power in many rural areas have been realigned, although some observers note that in many cases the longstanding habits of tribal life have so far remained largely undisturbed. With time, however, it is likely that the erosion of the affected tribal units will intensify.

Urban influence has been steadily increasing in the countryside. For decades a growing stream of migration to the cities has drained off much of the rural population's natural increase (see ch. 2, Geography and Population). Many city migrants, particularly Berbers, retain ties to their tribes, often keeping places in the tribal structure and rights to land. Many men leave their families in the country, and many of those who have moved definitively to the city visit their former homes regularly. As a result, communication flows continually between the city and the countryside.

The ability to earn money outside the tribal context has released many young men from the authority of their senior relatives, weakening family and tribal structures. In addition, city customs and practices are visible in some tribal groups. For example, the veiling of women, traditional among urban groups but not among Berber tribesmen, has become prevalent in some tribes of the Sous whose men work in Casablanca as grocers. In a neighboring tribe whose men work as miners, on the other hand, and thus do not come into contact with urbanites, veiling is not practiced.

Urban Society

The cities of Morocco have grown explosively during the twentieth century. At the beginning of that period there were only twenty-seven places of more than 1,500 inhabitants; by 1920 the number was forty; by 1936, fifty-six; and by 1962 it had reached 107. Although figures were not available in mid-1971, authorities assume that the number was greater still. During the 1930s only three cities had populations above 100,000; by 1968 they numbered eleven. Slightly over 30 percent of the population was urban in 1967, as opposed to a scant 8 to 9 percent in 1900. In only a few generations Casablanca had grown from a small coastal town to a giant, bustling metropolitan agglomeration, furiously building and industrializing and choked with more rural migrants than it could adequately house or employ. This growth is even more striking because it occurred during the exodus of the Jewish and European communities, both much more heavily urbanized than the Muslims (see ch. 4, Ethnic Groups and Languages).

From a social standpoint the frenetic pace of urban growth has produced metropolises populated largely by countrypeople or, at best, by persons very recently acclimated to city life. In 1952 only 6 percent of Casablanca's household heads were natives of that city, and only 8 percent were natives of any urban place. One observer has called Casablanca, the fastest growing center, an "urbanizing machine," because it annually absorbs thousands of former tribesmen and rural dwellers and transforms them and their children into city people, teaching them the unfamiliar values and habits of urban life. Because the migrants come from many tribes, regions, and social situations, they have little shared culture or consciousness. A perceptive scholar has called Casablanca "a city without a past," because of its lack of common tradition.

Although these trends stand out most markedly in Casablanca, they can be noticed in many other cities as well. The coastal cities have experienced the heaviest migration, but the sprawling squatter settlements, *bidonvilles* (tin-can towns), housing new arrivals now encircle most urban centers.

Because rapid urbanization coincided with the introduction and widespread adoption of many aspects of European culture, the growth of the cities represents more than new accretions of population. Rather, the various sections of many cities were built at different times, for different purposes, and for groups with widely differing values and ways of life. One observer has described the juxtaposition of the many modern European and traditional Muslim elements of architecture and city planning as "jarring agglomerations."

The traditional Moroccan city was, before the European arrival, organized around the *derb*, or quarter. Several of these composed a city, each consisting of a number of families that had lived in the same place for several generations and that were bound by a feeling of solidarity and common identification. Families of every economic standing lived in the same quarter, the wealthy and notable assuming leadership. Each quarter contained the services and institutions needed for daily life—a small *souk*, a fountain, a communal oven, a public bath, a mosque, and a Quranic elementary school; life went on in the context of the *derb*. Relationships were personal and intimate; reputation and family honor, the major means of social control. The Jewish population, if sizable, inhabited the *mallah*, or separate quarter. Each quarter had one or several leaders who represented it before the city at large. To a very great extent, the *derbs* formed small subsocieties functioning at an intimate level.

The economic backbone of city life was the large number of artisans, craftsmen, and small merchants, each plying a trade traditional in his family, often in association with sons, brothers, cousins, or other kinsmen. The *derbs*, with their narrow winding streets and closely placed houses, were often enclosed by walls or separated by gates and were well adapted to the needs both of small shopkeepers and traders running family businesses and of their pedestrian customers.

The arrival of the Europeans disturbed the equilibrium of urban life. Unaccustomed to the ways of life appropriate to traditional Moroccan housing, they built "new cities" along European lines, with wide streets, private lawns, and separate houses of European plan. As growing numbers of Moroccans began to emulate Europeans in dress, habits, and way of life, they increasingly used European mass-produced products, much to the detriment of local artisans, many of whom were driven out of business or into greatly reduced circumstances. The automobile, quickly adopted by many well-to-do Moroccans, proved singularly ill adapted to the streets of the old quarters. This, along with the general allure of fashionable modernity, attracted many of the affluent out of their homes in the *derbs* and into European-style housing in the new sections. As a result, the quarters lost much of their traditional leadership, and residential segregation by class and income became important for the first time.

The European-style houses were better adapted to the European style of life increasingly popular among prominent families. The *madina*, or old city, gradually became a neighborhood for the poor. In addition, the *mallahs* began to break up because the Jews, more than any other group of Moroccans, availed themselves of French education and succeeded in modern professional and economic pursuits.

A continuing housing shortage destroyed most of what remained of *derb* solidarity in the larger cities, especially Casablanca. With the exodus of Europeans at independence, large quantities of formerly European housing were opened to Moroccans, scattering persons from the various quarters throughout the city. Their places in the quarters were rapidly taken by the flood of rural migrants, usually relatively new to the city and unknown in their new quarters. In place of the old residential divisions, based primarily on ethnic background, the most thoroughgoing distinctions between residential neighborhoods were those of class in 1971.

The new governmental and economic systems, introduced whole, or in the words of one observer, "parachuted" by the French into Moroccan society, opened expansive new opportunities for the minority equipped with French education (see ch. 4, Ethnic Groups and Languages). Although Europeans staffed most modern institutions before independence, the demand for trained Moroccans became insatiable for a few years after 1956. Those able to assume important posts in the modern economic, governmental, and cultural structure immediately constituted a powerful new bourgeois elite. Recruited both from prominent families and from ambitious youths of modest social origin, the new middle class legitimates its recently attained social position by conspicuous consumption of expensive European-style consumer goods, such as swimming pools, lavish modern villas, fashionable clothing, and contemporary furniture.

The introduction of modern institutions drastically increased opportunities for social mobility through education and technical expertise; the relatively static traditional system had provided few possibilities for social movement. Nevertheless, by the 1970s the job market had become glutted with a far greater surplus of graduates, particularly in the liberal arts, than it could absorb into acceptable white-collar work. Although pure science also enjoyed great prestige, technical and engineering fields, especially those with manual overtones, attracted relatively few candidates because of the traditional disdain for working with one's hands. Consequently, although French and other European technicians held important technical posts for which trained Moroccans could not be found, the schools continued to produce applicants for white-collar positions that did not exist (see ch. 7, Education, Communication, and the Arts and Sciences). In mid-1971 many young people feared that the status for which their education was to prepare them would prove illusory, along with the opportunities for social mobility to which they believed independence entitled them. Much of this frustration found expression in agitation and criticism against the educational system and the language policy (see ch. 7, Education, Communication, and the Arts and Sciences; ch. 4, Ethnic Groups and Languages).

Because of these changes many of the older traditional elite find themselves stripped of the influence and, often, of the income they formerly enjoyed. A class of religious dignitaries and families claiming descent from the Prophet formerly occupied the social pinnacle, along with wealthy landowning and merchant families (see ch. 5, Religious Life). Although devotion to Islam remains strong, some traditional religious teachings and institutions have lost prestige with the advance of European culture and the spread of French education (see ch. 4, Ethnic Groups and Languages).

Traditional Islamic intellectuals adapted only reluctantly and uneasily to the challenge of European science, which has great prestige, particularly among the educated young (see ch. 7, Education, Communication, and the Arts and Sciences). Muslim learning had long assumed that the Quran, as God's complete and final revelation, contained all knowledge. Intellectual activity consisted primarily of the examination of the Quran by deductive means, in addition to theological and ethical studies. The inductive experimental method of Western science, assuming as it does the possibility of unknown and unforeseen results, was profoundly foreign to the traditional outlook.

Assured that the profane knowledge of infidels had little value compared to God's revelation, Islamic scholars nevertheless grudgingly had to recognize its undeniably impressive results. As a consequence, while science gained ground among the modern educated, the traditional Islamic authority, initially slow to react, lost ground. At first, however, the scientific method was little understood; when European education was introduced Moroccan students found classical literary authors and thinkers, such as Cicero and Jean Baptiste Racine, far more congenial than empiricists, such as René Descartes and Sir Isaac Newton. Among the sciences, mathematics, the least experimental, first gained wide acceptance. Nevertheless, the scientific method's widespread acceptance and prestige is symbolized by the king's statement in 1971 that Morocco aspired to participate in space exploration along with other nations. Many modernist intellectuals are attempting to integrate the teachings of Islam with modern science.

Although industrial technology provided enviable opportunities for some, it did not offer them to all. As mass production replaced handicrafts, many skilled artisans, who formerly occupied respectable positions in the community, were reduced to factory hands. Others managed to stay in business by changing their style or producing for the growing tourist trade. The government attempts to nourish the artisan tradition and find it markets abroad, but much of the work has become decorative rather than central to economic life (see ch. 11, Character and Structure of the Economy). Related changes occurred in the rural areas cultivated by the *colons* (French settlers in Morocco) where tribesmen became laborers for commercial farms.

Although some rural migrants have lost all roots in the traditional culture, others exploit their tribal connections to help in adjusting to city life. The serious shortage of jobs for both educated and uneducated persons prevents most new arrivals from finding work on their own (see ch. 2, Geography and Population). In most cases those who succeed in getting an industrial position do so through a network of fellow tribesmen or relatives already employed in industry. Often whole sections or departments of factories are staffed by men of the same tribe, village, or region, all of whom were either hired by a kinsman or friend working as a foreman or recommended by an established employee.

In some cases members of certain tribes specialize in certain types of city work. For example, Shluh groups of the Sous region own small grocery businesses in Casablanca on a family basis; various male members of the family spend time in the city working in the business and then return to the tribal home for a period. Members of the Zenaga tribes work in cleaning services in Casablanca and as waiters in Meknès. Tribesmen of the Tiznit plain become electricians and mechanics, and those of the region of Mogador constitute a high percentage of phosphate miners.

Many new arrivals who are unable to find any settled work swell the ranks of the underemployed, performing tasks of little or no economic value. Large numbers of makeshift peddlers crowd the sidewalks of every city selling snacks, trinkets, and other objects for very little profit. These individuals, although scarcely supporting themselves, nevertheless avoid the demeaning admission that they have no trade.

The disintegration of traditional social forms afflicts many new urbanites. Observers have noted that men who leave their wives and children in a tribal home, which they visit periodically, appear to enjoy better personal adjustment than those who move their families to town, although the former are less often transformed into permanent urbanites. Some succeed in maintaining a position in their tribe, marrying within it, and keeping up old relationships. Often members of the same family or tribe live together in the city slums, and family bonds endure for some years. Usually, however, these ties ultimately break down, as migrants, particularly those who came with their immediate families, integrate themselves into city life.

Nevertheless, the transition from the personal, intimate relationships of the countryside to the impersonal and bureaucratic ones of the city is traumatic and difficult for many. They miss the guidance and control of the small community and feel adrift in an individualistic value system they do not fully understand. Unaccustomed to being surrounded by strangers, many try to establish personal relationships by various means. The practice of *bakshish*, usually interpreted by Westerners as a bribe, often represents an attempt, through a gift, to place a formerly impersonal relationship on a personal footing. An interesting survival of the old personalism in the city is the many little shops with small, personally known clientele and prices determined through bargaining, which most people seem to prefer to the large, impersonal, fixed-price stores of European type.

The intense communal life of the old society expressed and nourished itself in community-wide festivals and holy days. Because they are socially diffuse and fragmented, Morocco's cities largely lack celebrations of this kind, along with the identity and solidarity they vividly affirm. Some individuals attempt, usually without success, to continue the traditional observances (see ch. 5, Religious Life). In place of the old participation rituals, large crowds gather for spectator sports, especially soccer, which, according to observers, substitute inadequately for the traditional fetes and represent the meager social and spiritual solidarity found in the cities.

THE INDIVIDUAL, THE FAMILY, AND THE SEXES

Social life in Morocco centers on the family. The household is composed of kinsmen, and among the tribes family ties ramify into tribal structure. The individual's loyalty to his family overrides most other obligations. Ascribed status often outweighs personal achievements in regulating social relationships. One's honor and dignity are tied to the good repute of his kin group and especially to that of its women.

Sexual segregation is basic to Moroccan social life, and sex is one of the most important determinants of social status. Men dominate women in most aspects of life. Although the systematic seclusion of women is rarely practiced, men and women constitute largely separate subsocieties, each with its own values, attitudes, and perceptions of the other. The character of separation varies; it is strictest among the traditional urban middle class and most flexible among tribesmen. Nevertheless, all groups observe it to some extent, and the lives of men and women often intersect only in the home.

Family and Household

Moroccans reckon kinship patrilineally, and the household is based on blood ties between men. Ideally, it consists of a man, his wife or wives, his single and married sons with their wives and children, his unmarried daughters, and possibly such other relatives as a widowed or divorced mother or sister. At the death of the father each son ideally establishes his own household to begin the cycle again. Because of the centrality of family life, it is assumed that all persons will marry when they reach the appropriate age; in addition, most divorced and many widowed persons remarry. In most areas adult status is bestowed only on married men and, often, only on fathers.

Traditionally, the individual was expected to subordinate his personal interests to those of his family and considered himself a member of a group whose importance outweighed his own. In mid-1971 it was still not common for persons to live apart from a family group. Grown children ordinarily lived with parents or relatives until marriage; for a girl of respectable family to do otherwise would be unthinkable. Despite the closeness of family ties, however, there still existed a reasonable leeway for individuals to maneuver within their status positions, exploiting relationships to their best advantage.

Marriage is a family, rather than a personal, affair. Because the sexes ordinarily do not mix socially, young men and women have few or no acquaintances among the opposite sex. Parents arrange marriages for their children, finding a mate through either their own social contacts or a professional matchmaker. In some regions—for example, the central High Atlas—unions between parallel cousins, or the children of brothers, are preferred. In such cases the young men of a girl's lineage have first claim on her hand and may effectively prevent her marriage to an outsider if one of them wishes her instead. In other areas, such as the Rif Massif, no particular preference or pattern exists, except that incest is prohibited and matches tend to occur between families of similar economic standing.

In Islam, marriage is a civil contract rather than a sacrament. Consequently, representatives of the bride negotiate a marriage agreement with those of the groom. Although the future husband and wife must, according to law, give their consent, they usually take no part in the arrangements. At times a young man might suggest to his parents the girl he would like to marry; girls usually have no such privileges. The contract establishes the terms of the union and, if they are broken, outlines appropriate recourse. Special provisions inserted into the standard contract become binding on both parties to the union.

Islam gives to the husband far greater discretion and leeway than to the wife. For example, he may take up to four wives at one time, provided he can treat them equally; a woman can have only one husband at a time. A man can divorce his wife by simply repeating "I divorce thee" three times before witnesses; a woman can initiate divorce only with difficulty. Any children of the union belong to the husband's family and stay with him in case of divorce. The husband, of course, exercises authority in the home. Men expect virginity of their brides, but no such expectation exists for bridegrooms. The Moroccan dialect distinguishes between virgins and women, the latter carrying a distinct connotation of sexual experience; it is assumed that a "woman" is married.

Nevertheless, despite the seeming stringency of Islamic marriage law, wives manage to exercise influence and protect themselves from mistreatment through a number of informal means. The code of personal status, for example, provides that a man may not take an additional wife if injustice to his existing spouse would result; it does not specify, however, who is to judge the likelihood of injustice. Moreover, the husband may not divorce his wife completely at once. The three repetitions of "I divorce thee" must come at different times, during which reconciliation is possible, and he must make a conciliatory gift of money to her at the time of divorce. Furthermore, during her marriage a wife has the right to housing apart from that of the husband's parents and in a neighborhood respectable enough to provide the witnesses to any mistreatment she might need in a divorce suit of her own.

In addition, stipulations and conditions of the marriage contract can work to strengthen the wife's position. At the time of marriage the bridegroom and his family make to the bride's family a considerable payment of money, usually collected from a wide circle of relatives and friends to whom obligations are thereby incurred. In many cases the bride's family insists that a portion of the bride-price be deferred, to be payable on demand or at divorce. In that case, divorce or displeasing the wife, for example, through marriage to an additional wife, entails for the husband the payment of a substantial cash sum in order to placate or rid himself of his present wife, as well as a similar substantial payment to remarry. During the 1960s brideprices rose appreciably, from the equivalent of a few hundred United States dollars at the beginning of the decade to US$1,000 or more by its end.

The bride comes to the marriage with a dowry from her father. This money is spent on the bride's trousseau and the furniture and equipment for the new household. Such household goods belong to the wife and leave the marriage with her. In most cases the bride's family does not permit the exact items composing the dowry to be enumerated, so that anything acquired after marriage may also be construed as belonging to her. Therefore, on divorce, the husband may stand to lose all his household goods except for his personal clothing and tools. Despite the weapons at her disposal, however, the wife ordinarily remains by far the weaker partner to the union and by far the more dependent.

Men and Women

The social milieu in which the family lives significantly affects the circumstances of the wife. In the countryside and among the urban poor, women fulfill important economic functions without which the family could not exist. Many women of poor urban families work in factories or elsewhere, and countrywomen help in all types of farmwork. As a result women occupy a position of relative importance and enjoy relative freedom, especially among the Berber tribes. Although casual social contact between the sexes of the type common in the West is not known, segregation of the sexes is much less pronounced than in the cities. Among the urban middle class, however, women fulfill fewer and less important economic functions. Artisan and merchant families earn their living from the skills of the men, and women make little contribution. Their responsibilities are most often limited to the household.

In such circumstances it is more likely that women are confined to the home and their social contacts and interests limited to an exclusively feminine sphere. The houses of financially comfortable urban families traditionally contained distinct men's and women's areas: the reception room where the men of the family entertained male guests, and the women's quarters, from which adult males other than relatives and servants were excluded. Unlike their rural counterparts, who moved freely in the fields and villages, urban women walked in the street discreetly in veiled pairs, avoiding cafés, *souks*, and other public gathering places, as well as any social contact with men. Some observers have noted that women of well-to-do bourgeois families, who have few material responsibilities and have little part in, or contact with, the outside world, tend to become "overfeminized," frivolous, and inattentive and to lack concentration and purpose. Among the rural and urban poor, however, girls assume responsibilities for housework and younger siblings at an early age.

Moroccans assume, often explicitly, that men and women are different types of creatures. Women are thought to be weaker than men in mind, body, and spirit; more sensual; less disciplined; and in need of protection, both from their own impulses and from the excesses of strange men. The honor of the men of a family, which is easily damaged and nearly irreparable, depends on the conduct of their women, particularly of sisters and daughters; consequently, women are expected to be circumspect, modest, and decorous and their virtue above reproach. The slightest implication of unavenged impropriety, especially if publicly acknowledged, could irreparably destroy the family's honor. Female virginity before marriage and sexual fidelity afterward are essential to its maintenance. In case they discover a transgression, the men are traditionally bound to punish the offending woman.

Arab societies generally value men more highly than women, and both sexes concur in this estimation. Their upbringing quickly impresses on girls that they are inferior to men and must cater to them and upon boys that they are entitled to demand the care and solicitude of women. The birth of a boy occasions great celebration, whereas that of a girl does not. Failure to produce sons can be grounds for divorcing a wife or taking a second. Barren women, therefore, are often desperately eager to bear sons and visit the shrines of saints and *marabouts* to seek fertility (see ch. 5, Religious Life).

Most women, except those of the more sophisticated urban families, marry in their middle teens men who, on the average, are ten years older than themselves. The young bride then goes to the household, village, or neighborhood of the bridegroom's family, where she may be a stranger and where she lives under the constant critical surveillance of her mother-in-law. A great deal of familial friction centers on the difficult relationship between mother-in-law and daughter-in-law.

A woman begins to gain status, security, and satisfaction in her husband's family only when she produces males. Therefore, mothers love and favor their sons, ordinarily nursing them longer than daughters. In later life the relationship between mother and son often remains very warm and intimate, whereas the father is a more distant figure. Observers suggest that women compensate for the emotional lack in their often rather impersonal marriages and submerged adult lives through their relationships with their sons, who often remain as adults in or near the parental household. The wife who enters such a home finds herself in a distinctly secondary position. Furthermore, her own parents are eager to have a girl married as soon as she reaches puberty to forestall any mishap to her virginity; she therefore is not encouraged to remain in her own family home.

Changing Values

Relations within the family and between the sexes, along with all other aspects of Moroccan society, have begun to show notable and accelerating change. The European settlers, admired and envied figures during much of their colonial tenure, embodied a set of familial and sexual values, attitudes, and customs much different from those traditional in the country. As education, the mass media, and European organizations began to percolate these ideas through the society, new perceptions and, to some extent, new practices began to appear, particularly among those Moroccans with the most European contact.

The traditional ideal of the polygynous extended family had never been widely practiced; reliable estimates place the number of polygynous workers and countrypeople at under 5 percent and among lower middle-class townsmen at approximately 10 percent. Nevertheless, the values permitting and encouraging this form of family were widespread. Contact with European notions of "modern" life have, however, begun to strip them of their appeal, substituting a desire for a more Western style of family life.

Increased opportunities for mobility, both social and physical, have undermined the old familial ties and the values that subordinated the individual to his kin group. Especially among the educated young, a growing individualism has appeared. Many young people prefer to set up their own households at marriage rather than live with parents, and the modern-educated view polygyny with scorn. At the same time, social security has lessened the dependence of the aged on their children and other relatives.

Among the most marked changes are those concerning women. The position and rights of women have become problematic under the influence of European models. Young women, especially in the cities, have begun to exercise greater freedom and equality than in the past, although the guidelines of traditional practice still broadly govern their lives. Western feminine fashion has appeared on city streets although not in its more extreme manifestations. Women have in recent decades begun to participate more in activities and interests outside the home.

During the political crises of the early 1950s that preceded independence, women for the first time took part in political action. Some authorities attribute this to the influence of radio, which brought political questions into the home and to women's attention. European movies have also been influential, especially among the young; the greater freedom they depict and their emphasis on romantic love as a basis for marriage have raised basic questions.

Despite masculine opposition, a number of women of respectable families have taken jobs in the modern sector. Many of these are poor women who work out of economic necessity, but a growing number come from financially secure families. Small numbers of women hold responsible posts in government, the courts, research, and other fields. Nevertheless, most end their careers at marriage; masculine resistance remains strong even in the new middle class.

Women enjoy increased opportunities for education, although facilities are limited in many country districts (see ch. 7, Education, Communication, and the Arts and Sciences). Observers have noted that educated women tend to convey fewer superstitious folk beliefs to their children and therefore can aid modernization even if they do not enter the work force. They point out, however, that because few countrywomen attend school, a substantial reservoir of these beliefs remain, especially among the poor, which are reinstilled in each generation.

City girls who attend school are not so closely chaperoned as formerly, although they rarely go out with friends in the evening. They also tend to marry later, often after working for several years. Some authorities also have noted a tendency to want fewer children than was common in the past, paralleling the desire for greater freedom for women.

Nevertheless, despite the liberalizing trends apparent in many areas, much of the tradition remains. The king symbolizes the national ambivalence on the woman issue. On the one hand, he encourages his sisters to lead the emancipation movement. Princess Lala Fatima heads the National Union of Moroccan Women, founded in 1969 to encourage social, cultural, and legal advancement of women. On the other hand, the king's wife lives in seclusion, taking no part in public life and receiving no mention in the press. Social, political, and intellectual trends point toward a further easing of restrictions on women but within the framework of the deeply ingrained Muslim tradition.

CHAPTER 7
EDUCATION, COMMUNICATION, AND THE ARTS AND SCIENCES

Since independence, Morocco has been striving to become a modern nation but at the same time assert its Arabic-Islamic cultural identity. Official statements have stressed the government's intention to extend the benefits of scientific and technological achievements to broad masses of the population. Simultaneously, policies related to creative activities and to the transmission of knowledge stressed the values of the Islamic-Arabic tradition. In 1957 the University of Rabat, the country's first modern institution of higher learning, was founded; legal provisions for universal, free education on the primary level were promulgated in 1962; and, during the 1970s, facilities for graduate technical and professional training were being expanded. King Hassan II had voiced the hope that his country might one day join other nations in the exploration of outer space.

While establishing institutions and adopting policies to implement modernization, the government was actively stimulating interest in the Arab-Islamic heritage through the rejuvenation of the traditional Quranic schools and through emphasis on cultural subjects in the school curricula. Numerous programs on religious and literary topics were conveyed to the population through the public radio and television network. The government newspaper reminded its readers daily of the value of the Arab linguistic tradition. Meanwhile, government agencies responsible for the implementation of cultural policies focused their attention on archaeology, ethnic crafts and folklore, and the restoration of historic sites. In the first two grades of public primary schools, Arabic was substituted for French as the language of instruction.

The government's efforts to establish a general, free public school system with uniform curricula and accessible to all have progressed since independence, although the expansion of facilities has been outpaced by the rapid population growth. Throughout the 1960s and early 1970s, education was the subject of intensive public interest and sometimes of acrimonious political debate. Students and parents alike voiced insistent demands for increased opportunities for education leading to future employment and economic security. Because of limited resources and its overwhelmingly academic and theoretical orientation, the school system could not fully respond to these demands nor to the pressing national needs for technically and professionally trained personnel. In most cases secondary schools and universities turned out graduates in classical, humanistic studies seeking jobs in already overcrowded fields of employment. At the same time there was a severe shortage of the technicians and scientists required to implement economic development plans. Other problems in secondary education stemmed from the introduction, in 1958, of Arabic as the teaching language in the early primary grades; without an early basis in French, many students subsequently found themselves unable to cope with more advanced courses given in French at the secondary level.

The government and leaders of public opinion have also been concerned with diminishing the residual French influence in education and intellectual expression dating from the colonial period. In 1970, however, French was still prominently used in the modern economic sector, making proficiency in that language a prerequisite for employment. French teachers conducted classes in many Moroccan-run secondary schools because of the shortage of trained Moroccan teachers, and the French University and Cultural Mission continued to operate a number of private schools attended by children of the urban elite. In the institutions of higher learning, foreign, primarily French, professors often outnumbered their Moroccan colleagues. Works of fiction, literary criticism, and articles on science and technology were mainly written in French. The government has, therefore, proceeded at a conservative pace in substituting Arabic for French as the language of instruction in public schools despite persistent pressure from both the left-wing opposition and traditional groups to hasten the change.

The government owned and operated both the radio and television facilities. Radio, the most influential of the communications media, was widely used to reach the masses of the population, including the often illiterate Berber-speaking tribesmen in the mountain areas who constituted about 40 percent of the population. Many of the programs dealt with various aspects of the country's artistic and intellectual heritage, including the Islamic tradition. They also constantly reminded the audience of the role of the king as an integrating symbol of cultural unity and religious authority.

Television facilities have been placed at government expense in many public areas, but in 1970 the network covered only limited parts of the country. Film production, also under government auspices, was limited mostly to documentaries on cultural topics. Films imported from Western countries have played a central role in presenting customs and values of technologically advanced societies to a growing segment of the population.

The privately owned press, comprising newspapers and periodicals in both French and Arabic, addressed itself to the politically aware, educated urban elite. Apart from a small group of French and Spanish owned and managed newspapers, they were primarily journals of opinion, concentrating on economic and political issues and often vehemently critical of government policies and officials. Government policy toward these newspapers during the late 1960s and early 1970s was increasingly restrictive. Bans and seizures were common, although there has been no prepublication censorship.

Three dailies were owned and published by French and Spanish enterprises. The two French dailies, providing effective news coverage and avoiding political commentary, offered keen competition to the Moroccan-owned newspapers but were permitted to publish despite vigorous protests by Moroccan newspapermen and by the political opposition against the continued existence of the foreign-owned press.

Fes, site of the ancient Karaouine University (founded in A.D. 859), is the center of traditional studies in Islamic theology and law pursued by a small group of scholars. Modern thought dealing with contemporary social and economic problems and with the role of Islam in a modernizing society is reflected in political essays in Arabic written by prominent journalists and other intellectuals.

EDUCATION

Background

Before the establishment of the protectorate in 1912, education was organized within the framework of traditional Islamic institutions. Young children attended Quranic schools at the local mosques where they were taught recitations of the Quran and in some cases the rudiments of reading and writing. Religious colleges (*madaaris*; sing., *madrasa*) in the cities taught Islamic theology, rhetoric, and Arabic grammar. Scholars from far and near flocked to the ancient Karaouine University at Fes to study Islamic law and letters.

The French established a modern school system primarily to serve the resident French population. Curricula, examinations, academic standards, and teacher certification closely resembled those in France. Admission of Moroccan children to these schools was not encouraged, although during the 1920s the French provided some schools for young Moroccans to help educate an elite for the protectorate administration. Moroccan nationalists in 1938 began a movement to establish private schools for Moroccan children, with instruction in Arabic. Yielding to the growing demand for public education, the French during the mid-1940s opened some Franco-Moroccan primary schools and began to admit Moroccans to some French secondary schools. The number of Moroccan children in these schools, however, was negligible. At independence only about 10 percent of all school age children were enrolled in school.

After independence in 1956 the government determined to consolidate the diverse types of schools into a single national public system and to make education accessible to a broad segment of the population. Official goals also called for the inclusion of social science subjects adapted to the Moroccan environment, the use of Arabic as the language of instruction, and the eventual replacement of French-speaking foreign teachers by Moroccans. The first step of the official program was to offer free primary education to as many children as practicable and to make Arabic the language of instruction in the first two grades. Secondary schooling was to provide personnel for the professions and for the civil service.

The extension of education to a rapidly growing number of children each year required an extensive school-building program and the temporary use of makeshift classroom facilities. Many severely underqualified, but Arabic-speaking, teachers were hired, and extensive use was made of so-called monitor teachers who had had only a primary education. Facilities were badly overcrowded, and the teachers were unable to provide the academic and linguistic grounding necessary for secondary schooling.

By the late 1950s academic standards had deteriorated markedly, evoking protest from middle and lower class parents who felt that poor schooling, especially in respect to French-language training, impaired the chances of their children for finding white-collar employment. Government officials and experts, many of whom had attended French schools, felt that the abandonment of the high academic standards of the French system was not in the national interest.

During the early 1960s two high-level commissions—the Royal Commission for Educational Reform and its successor, the Higher Board of Education—were established to deal with educational problems and requirements of the expanding population. Both indicated the need for unification of the school system and for continued expansion of educational opportunities but recommended a slowdown in the rate at which the language of instruction in the schools was being switched from French to Arabic.

Economic development plans during the 1960s called for an intensive construction program of primary school facilities, but the demand exceeded the rate of construction. Compulsory primary education, promulgated by law in 1962, has been only partially implemented—mostly in the urban areas—although enrollment figures have increased rapidly.

The low quality of academic achievement in the 1960s, however, caused the government to establish uniform standards for promotion, to institute entrance examinations for secondary schools, and to determine prerequisites for the award of diplomas and certificates. Curricula were revised to strengthen and expand Moroccan cultural subjects. At the same time there was a return to the use of French in teaching mathematics and science in the primary grades, and the number of hours of instruction in French was increased. Technical and science courses were developed for secondary school programs but, because of the lack of qualified teachers, few institutions could offer them.

Official measures to upgrade academic quality evoked widespread dissatisfaction among students, who feared their inability to meet the standards and therefore subsequently to obtain a civil service job. In March 1965 students staged massive protest demonstrations in Casablanca, which turned into widespread rioting against unemployment and high prices (see ch. 3, Historical Setting).

Throughout the 1960s the question of the use of Arabic in the school system was of crucial importance and the subject of strong and persistent public controversy. Students continued to have difficulty in making the transition from a primary education given partially in Arabic to French-language secondary schooling. Secondary school classrooms were crowded with repeaters, and an increasing number of secondary school students leaving before graduation were unable to find employment. At the same time, dissatisfaction among students was growing because of the inadequate number of scholarships, changes of prerequisites for technical secondary school certificates, and reorganization of teacher training.

Widespread student unrest in the early spring of 1970 disrupted teaching in many secondary schools and institutions of higher learning. In May of that year an assembly of students, parents, teachers, and government officials was called by King Hassan at the mountain resort of Ifrane to attempt a resolution of the major causes of public dissatisfaction. No specific measures were agreed upon, but the conference provided a forum for the restatement of official policies, including those governing the use of Arabic in the schools.

The School System

In 1970 some 53 percent of children seven to eleven years of age attended primary schools. Of the age group comprising twelve- to eighteen-year-old youths, about 17 percent were enrolled in the lower cycle; and some 4.7 percent, in the upper cycle of secondary schools. The school system included modern secular public institutions, traditional religious schools, and private schools. Traditional religious schools were part of the public school system; they served no more than 40,000 students on the primary and secondary levels in 1970, or about 2.8 percent of the total enrollment.

Although their enrollments were declining, private schools continued to attract some students, especially in the cities. In 1970 some 2.5 percent of primary school students and about 10 percent of secondary students attended private schools. Because of difficulties in providing sufficient public facilities and teachers, the government has permitted private schools to operate despite its commitment to a single public school system. Some such schools, notably those in Casablanca, have received financial aid from the municipal government in the form of grants and teacher salary supplements.

Some private schools were closely controlled by the government. French private schools, however, had a considerable degree of autonomy in accordance with provisions of cultural agreements between Morocco and France.

Administration

In early 1971 public education was under the jurisdiction of the Ministry of Primary Education and the Ministry of Higher, Secondary, and Technical Education. Each was responsible for school inspection, curricula, administration of examinations, teacher placement, and the issuance of official tests in the respective school levels under their jurisdiction.

The ministries shared a planning division in charge of research and statistical operations related to educational planning. The twelve field offices of the Planning Division studied local educational needs, furnished statistical data on the school age population of their respective regions, and estimated local needs for physical facilities.

The Higher Board of Education, a top-level consultative and planning body, was responsible for drafting policies on educational reform, including modernization of vocational and professional training. The board's permanent members included high-ranking government officials in education, economic planning, and public service; representatives from the ministries; deans of institutions of higher learning; and members of the Education Commission of the House of Representatives. Appointed members included teachers from primary and secondary private schools, university professors, and students.

Local authorities in each of the nineteen provinces and in the two urban prefectures had limited responsibility in the administration of education. There was, for example, some local participation in school construction, notably in Casablanca. Local initiative in matters affecting educational policies is rare although, during the 1960s, members of delegations representing local citizens have at times expressed themselves vigorously in matters of scholarships, curricula, and the assignment of children to various schools.

Finance

In 1970 the budget of the ministries of education totaled DH670 million (5.06 dirham equal US$1—see Glossary). Another DH38 million was earmarked for education and training programs in the budgets of the Ministry of Agriculture and National Development and the Ministry of Labor and Social Affairs.

Current expenditures of the ministries of education during the 1960s accounted for more than 20 percent of the government's recurrent budget. Taking into account educational expenditures of other ministries and official agencies, the proportion exceeded 23 percent in 1971. The Five Year Plan (1968-72) earmarked 39 percent of capital expenditures for education to primary schooling, 53 percent to secondary schooling, and 8 percent to institutions of higher learning.

A major portion—about 80 percent—of education funds was devoted to salaries; the rest, to scholarships, boarding expenditures, and teaching materials. Expenditures in 1971 reflected a 20-percent increase in teachers' salaries. High personnel costs on the secondary and upper school levels were related to the presence of many foreign teachers who received substantially higher pay than their Moroccan counterparts.

External sources complementing official budgets included funds from France, which contributed the equivalent of US$6 million in 1970. Between 1960 and 1970 the United Nations Development Program made available more than US$8 million for the establishment of secondary schools and institutions of higher learning. In 1971 a loan equivalent to US$8.5 million was extended by the International Development Association (IDA) for upgrading scientific and technical training in secondary education and the expansion of postsecondary-training institutions, teacher training, and educational research.

Preprimary and Primary Education

In October 1968 King Hassan launched a program to rejuvenate the system of Quranic schools, where young children are given religious and moral instruction, apparently in part to relieve some of the pressure on the standard primary system. Attendance was to be made compulsory for children between five and seven years of age; completion of the two-year program officially was recognized as the equivalent of the first primary grade. The king emphasized the importance of Quranic schools in instilling at an early age Islamic spiritual and moral values and fostering awareness in Arabic linguistic and cultural traditions. Urging all parents to enroll their children, the king stated that one of the important functions of the modern

Quranic school was to offer day care to the children of working parents.

The curriculum of the six-hour schoolday had been drafted by the Ministry of Primary Education, which also supplied the texts for instruction. The subjects included history and teachings of Islam, Islamic reading and writing, and civics, to which much importance was attached. The traditional custom of reciting the Quran by rote was continued. The schools were located in buildings and rooms used formerly by the traditional institutions operated in conjunction with the mosque and were equipped by the respective communities, which also appointed the teacher and paid him a nominal fee. Data on the number of Quranic schools and on their enrollment in 1971 were lacking.

Primary school enrollment during the late 1960s had been relatively stagnant and, between 1968 and 1969, there had been a slight decrease in the number of pupils attending primary schools. In 1969 seven out of a total of sixteen provinces reporting showed a decrease in the number of primary pupils; increases were noted in the remaining nine.

Enrollment in primary schools in 1970 totaled 1,142,810; girls accounted for about 33 percent of the total. Attrition rates were high, especially in the first grade; repeater rates tended to rise in the upper grades. In 1968, 121 out of every 1,000 students left school after the first grade, and 505 out of every 1,000 had to repeat the fifth grade.

Primary schooling was open to children seven years of age and was offered in a five-year course, although only 6 percent of the rural schools offered the full five-year program. The Certificate of Primary Studies, a prerequisite for entrance into secondary school, was earned at the end of the fifth grade.

In 1971, after extensive public controversy regarding the pace at which Arabic was being substituted for French as the language of instruction in primary grades, all subjects were being taught in Arabic in the first two grades. In the upper grades instruction was bilingual. Fifteen hours a week were taught in Arabic; and fifteen hours (in mathematics and science), in French. Among subjects taught were: religion and the history of Islam and the early caliphates, ethics, civics, Moroccan history and geography, mathematics, basic science, and Arabic and French. In the rural schools the program included elementary agricultural education.

Secondary Education

In mid-1971 the seven-year period of secondary education was divided into a first and second cycle of four and three years, respectively. Except for a few subjects offered in Arabic, the language of instruction was French. The first four-year cycle, taken by all secondary school students, led to the Certificate of Secondary Education. The first year of this cycle, called the observation class, was designed to facilitate the transition from primary to secondary studies. The four-year curriculum had general studies, including Arabic, French, another modern language (usually English), history, geography, civics, mathematics, handicraft, physical education, and music. In some institutions practical skill courses were added during the late 1960s.

Students who completed the first cycle could proceed to the second cycle where they followed a university-preparatory course leading to specialization in either commerce, industry, or agriculture. Students following the general academic course could major in literature, Arabic studies, economics, mathematics, or experimental science. Each of the major programs terminated in the *baccalaureat* (final examination), the successful passing of which represented academic achievement and qualified for university admission.

The three-year courses offering specialization in commercial and industrial subjects led to the Technician's Diploma. The commercial course offered specialization in commerce and bookkeeping, business administration, and secretarial work. The industrial course had majors in technical subjects or mathematics. The diploma earned upon completion of the industrial and commercial courses, however, was not recognized for university entrance qualifications and was not highly regarded in the respective occupational fields. The unsatisfactory status of these diplomas was the subject of much student concern during the late 1960s.

In 1970 official plans were in progress to upgrade industrial and commercial courses in order to enable the holders of the Technician's Diploma to enter institutions of higher learning. In the industrial program the diploma is to be replaced by a baccalaureate degree in mathematics or technology; prerequisite courses will offer a wider range of training in engineering techniques as well as a higher level of theoretical studies to qualify the holder of the industrial baccalaureate degree for university-level training in engineering and technology. In 1970 the new type of training was available only at the Mohammedia Engineering School and at the School of Mines, but government plans called for the introduction of these courses in ten other secondary schools by 1972. In the commercial courses persons majoring in commerce, bookkeeping, or business administration will earn a baccalaureate degree in economics, which qualifies for university admission. Students majoring in secretarial studies, however, continue to receive the Technician's Diploma.

Training in agriculture is also available. Under the auspices of the Ministry of Agriculture and National Development, four-year courses are offered in eight specialized secondary schools to train field assistants; the course for field agents is of two years' duration.

Training in hotel management and in the applied arts was added to the upper secondary cycle during the late 1960s, but data on this type of training were lacking in 1971.

Vocational training under the auspices of the Ministry of Labor and Social Affairs is available in training centers offering short-term courses in various technical and commercial occupations. Entrance requirements vary depending on the trade or craft in which training is offered. The courses, usually of one year's duration, offer about 80 percent practical and 20 percent theoretical instruction. Longer courses are available for selected advanced students, and special programs are offered for persons wishing to upgrade their skills. The centers train about 1,000 persons a year, mostly in basic level courses in mechanics, electricity, and automotive mechanics. The ministry plans to increase the annual number of graduates to 2,500 by 1972 and to open additional centers in Casablanca—for training in the building trade—and in Kenitra—for engineering trades.

Secondary schools were relatively less crowded than primary schools, but plans for the improvement and expansion of the facilities and curricula were made during the late 1960s in anticipation of the greater number of students who would be continuing after primary school. Enrollment has been increasing at a rate of 3.6 percent annually. In 1970 the total enrollment was 291,205, with 247,755 students in the first cycle and 43,450 in the second cycle. Officials of the Five Year Plan estimated that by the end of the plan period the number of secondary school students will exceed 390,000.

Only 26 percent of the 291,205 students in the two secondary cycles were girls; the comparative proportion in 1961 was 20 percent. A further analysis of the proportion of girls in secondary schools shows, however, that in the private schools they accounted for 40 percent of the student body, whereas in the public schools, the corresponding proportion decreased to 25 percent.

The general academic program, which included majors in literature or in experimental science, was the choice of the majority of students in the second cycle. The science program, however, suffered from the lack of qualified teachers and laboratory equipment and placed excessive emphasis on theoretical instruction. Only some 14.5 percent of the total of 43,450 students in the second cycle took technical and commercial courses. An analysis in 1970 of the enrollment in technical and commercial public secondary schools shows that of the 6,284 students enrolled, 3,429 majored in commerce, and 2,241, in technical fields; the rest took courses in hotel training, agriculture, or the applied arts.

Continuation of education after primary school has been encouraged by a program of government scholarships for secondary and higher education. Although the demand has been growing, many students were insufficiently prepared for academic work at the secondary level.

The French-language training available in primary schools was not sufficient to help the students master secondary level subjects offered in that language. Inadequately trained teachers, outmoded methods of instruction, and the lack of teaching equipment discouraged many from continuing their studies. The majority of students enrolled in the first year of secondary education fail to complete the two cycles; not more than about 8,000 students each year pass the *baccalaureat* examination.

During the late 1960s about 45 percent of first-cycle students proceeded to the three-year program of the secondary cycle. In the first cycle the attrition rate was 35 percent, increasing to about 40 percent in the second cycle. The incidence of failure was also high; completion of the first cycle took an average of 6.1 years; and completion of the second cycle, 4.4 years. Failures were especially common in the general academic course of the second cycle where the rates of failure doubled between 1965 and 1970.

Tuition and board in public secondary schools were free, but fees were charged to students for equipment, library services, and other items. A survey in 1969 of secondary schools in Casablanca showed that the average annual cost for a nonboarding secondary student was DH100 for boys and DH120 for girls. In general, the costs tended to rise in the upper grades.

In 1971 several plans were awaiting implementation to expand secondary school facilities and to resolve qualitative problems in secondary education. Construction of eighteen new secondary schools financed by a loan from the IDA was nearly finished in 1971. A substantial portion of another IDA loan has been earmarked for the construction and equipment of science laboratories in six existing secondary schools, for workshop and laboratory equipment in ten technical secondary schools, for modernization of thirteen commercial secondary schools, and for secondary teacher training.

Teachers

Primary school teachers were trained in seventeen regional colleges with an approximate enrollment of 1,600 in 1970. Completion of the first cycle of secondary education was an entrance requirement for the program, which consisted of one year of theoretical training followed by one year of practice teaching. Officials planned to raise entrance requirements and to add another year of theoretical training. Candidates for admission would be expected to complete four years of secondary schooling rather than three.

For teachers of the lower secondary cycle the training was of two years' duration, followed by one year of practice teaching. Fully qualified secondary school teachers must complete four years of higher education after earning the *baccalaureat* at the end of secondary schooling. The Higher Teacher Training School (Ecole Normal Supérieur) in Rabat offered a four-year program leading to a *licence* (certificate) in letters or science and a teaching certificate. The University of Rabat (sometimes called Mohammed V University) also offered training for teachers of the second cycle, with emphasis on subject specialization. Most secondary school teacher candidates during the late 1960s majored in the humanities. Of a total of 928 students enrolled in teacher training for the lower secondary cycle, only 152 majored in mathematics and sciences; the corresponding figure among trainees for the upper secondary cycle was 156 out of a total of 2,773.

Plans awaiting implementation in 1971 provided for teachers of the first secondary cycle to be trained in six regional teachers colleges in three-year courses. Completion of secondary education and possession of the *baccalaureat* would remain a usual entrance requirement, but some students would be admitted on the basis of entrance examinations. Teachers for the second cycle of secondary schools would be trained in the Higher Teacher Training School in a one-year course after they earned a university degree.

The training capacity of institutions for teacher education in 1970 was inadequate to meet national demands. During the late 1960s there was an annual need for 1,200 lower cycle secondary teachers, but existing facilities trained only some 500 a year. About 150 upper cycle secondary teachers were trained in various courses and institutions, although the need was for 300 annually.

Low remuneration of teachers was a primary reason for the lack of interest in teaching careers. In 1969 primary school teachers earned between DH380 and DH800 a month; and secondary teachers, between DH650 and DH1,500 a month, depending on the level of training. The much higher salaries of French teachers, ranging between DH1,700 and DH5,000 a month, were partly financed by French government funds.

The government paid tuition and board and an allowance to teacher trainees, who were required to pledge to serve in the public education system for eight years; otherwise, fees paid by the government became refundable. To stimulate interest in science teaching, supplementary allowances were announced for science teacher candidates in 1970.

By 1971 nearly all foreign teachers in primary school had been replaced, and the upgrading of the training of Moroccan teachers was progressing. In 1968, 30,248 of a total of 30,299 primary school teachers were Moroccans. Most of the teachers had at least partially completed normal school. The pupil-teacher ratio was approximately thirty-five to one. There were also 2,430 teachers in private primary schools; of these, 1,154 were Moroccans, and the rest were French, Spanish, or of other origin.

Moroccan statistics published in 1968 showed that more than half of a total of 12,365 secondary teachers were foreigners. The proportion of foreign teachers was most significant in the public secondary schools where they numbered 6,475 of a total of 11,206. A later survey prepared in 1970 revealed that almost 60 percent of the teachers of academic subjects in the first cycle of secondary schools were foreigners; in the second cycle the corresponding proportion was about 71 percent. In the private secondary schools the proportion of Moroccan teachers was highest in institutions offering the traditional religious curriculum, in schools of the Jewish Ittihad (Union), and in those operated by Muslim Moroccans.

A 1970 survey showed that only some 25 percent of teachers of academic subjects in the first secondary cycle were fully qualified. Of those not fully qualified, the majority had completed secondary schools; the rest had only partial secondary education. The proportion of fully qualified teachers in the second cycle was more favorable: 86.1 percent had completed higher education. Eight percent had partial higher education; the rest, complete or partial secondary education.

Private Education

Academically outstanding private schools were operated by the French University and Cultural Mission (Mission Universitaire Culturel Française—MUCF), established by a cultural convention signed between France and Morocco in 1957. Intended mainly for children of the foreign, especially of the French, community, the schools also admitted Moroccan children on a competitive basis and were favored by the Moroccan elite. Many leaders in public life had been trained in such prestigious schools as the Lycée Lyautey in Casablanca.

The MUCF had contributed part-time teachers, teaching supplies, and facilities to the public school system and, since the decline of the foreign community in the 1960s, had turned over many of its buildings and classrooms to it. In 1970 more than 11,000 children were enrolled in the MUCF schools, but the number of Moroccan children in this total was not known.

In addition to the MUCF schools, there were private secular Muslim schools, mainly in Rabat and Casablanca. They offered a modern academic program in Arabic and French based on the official curriculum. In 1970 these schools enrolled about 26,000 students on the primary and about 11,200 on the secondary level.

Other schools were operated by private individuals, mostly French, and by French and Spanish Catholic teaching orders. In 1970 enrollment in these schools on the primary and secondary levels totaled about 28,000 and 5,000, respectively.

Private education for Jewish children was available in the Ittihad schools of the Jewish community. Since the number of Moroccan Jews was rapidly decreasing, these schools operated on a diminished scale, enrolling about 2,000 students in secondary classes in 1970.

Higher Education

Higher education was offered at two universities, the renowned Karaouine University at Fes—an ancient center of Islamic studies with a famous library—and the University of Rabat. The former, the oldest university in North Africa, was founded in A.D. 859 as an appendage to the Karaouine mosque. Theology, Islamic law, and interpretation of the Quran constituted the mainstay of the curriculum. In 1963 Karaouine was reorganized and placed under the authority of the Ministry of Education. Some changes in the curriculum and teaching methods were made. Under the new organization a faculty of law continued to operate at Fes, and two other faculties, one for Arabic studies and one for theology, were opened at Marrakech and Tetouan, respectively. Three years of study at one of the faculties lead to a degree in the chosen field. In 1969 the university enrolled 898 students. Traditional Islamic fields were also taught at the Ben Youssef University in Marrakech with an enrollment of 1,100 in 1970.

The University of Rabat was opened in 1957. It had its roots in several earlier institutions founded by the French for advanced studies in law, science, and administration. In 1970 the university had four faculties and several specialized schools. Some of the latter had semiautonomous status and were located in Casablanca and Fes. A new campus for the main facility at Rabat was in the planning stage in 1971. The campus was earmarked to be the site of several planned institutions for professional and technical training.

The Faculty of Arts and Letters was based in Rabat and had a branch located in Fes. Courses in philosophy, literature, history, and geography were offered in French and Arabic; the faculty was also noted for its courses in Moroccan history and archaeology. The Faculty of Science had courses in mathematics and in the physical and natural sciences. In both faculties a year of preparatory study was followed by three years of specialized studies leading to the degree of *licence*. The Diploma of Higher Studies was awarded after two years of study to holders of the *licence*. The Faculty of Law, Economics, and Social Sciences, a major source of personnel for the civil service, had branches in Fes and Casablanca; it offered a five-year program for the Diploma of Higher Studies and a shorter course leading to a law diploma. The Faculty of Medicine had a six-year course preceded by a premedical year in the Faculty of Science. The attrition rate in the Faculty of Medicine was particularly high between the premedical course and the first year of study.

The Mohammedia Engineering School, in the port city of the same name near Casablanca, was affiliated with the University of Rabat. It offered a five-year course and had an enrollment of 260 students in 1970. University level training in agriculture was available at the

Hassan II Institute of Agronomy in Rabat. The course was open to candidates who had completed two years of preparatory studies at the Faculty of Science. In 1970 only two years of the planned four-year course were offered, with about thirty students enrolled. Plans in 1970 called for the expansion of the institute by the addition of a department of veterinary science; training in this department would be of four years' duration preceded by a preparatory year in the Faculty of Science.

Other institutions of higher learning affiliated with the University of Rabat included the Moroccan School of Administration, with a curriculum of bilingual courses in law, administration, and business management taught in French and Arabic. Associated with the Faculty of Law, Economics, and Social Sciences were the Center for Studies on Economic and Social Development and the Center for Preparation in Business Administration. The former offered a two-year program in economics and sociology in Rabat and Casablanca, mainly for high government officials; a *baccalaureat*, or special examination, was required for admission. The latter was for postgraduate students who had a university degree or could pass a special entrance examination.

According to data prepared by the Moroccan Statistical Office in 1969, there were 10,908 students of higher education, including 767 from foreign countries. Of the total, 9,400 attended universities, and the rest were in other institutions of higher learning. Some 14 percent of the 9,400 university students were women. The humanities and law were the major fields for 80 percent of university students; those in medicine and science accounted for the remaining 20 percent. In other institutions of higher learning, 70 percent of the students were enrolled in courses leading to administrative or teaching careers, and the rest were in technical courses. On the other hand, 90 percent of 2,700 Moroccan students enrolled abroad that year studied for science degrees.

Enrollment in higher education in 1970 was estimated at about 12,700; an additional 3,000 students were enrolled in institutions of higher learning abroad. The large majority of students in domestic institutions of higher learning followed courses leading to degrees in literature and in other liberal arts; only about 27 percent of the first-year students were enrolled in science and technical courses.

During the mid-1960s about 20 percent of university students received government scholarships. Those intended for students abroad were awarded mainly to candidates for degrees in scientific and technical fields. Scholarships for students in these fields were also awarded through the French technical assistance program. The proportion of scholarship recipients in 1971 was not known, but students voiced complaints that the lack of finances prevented many from attending institutions of higher learning.

According to education experts more than half of the students enrolled in domestic universities fail their examination, change their major field, or leave before completion of their course. The physical facilities for higher education were generally adequate and in many cases included modern laboratory facilities, but the latter were often underused because of insufficient enrollment. Throughout higher education, moreover, there was a severe shortage of teachers. In 1969 there was a total of 512 teachers in universities and institutions of higher learning; more than half of these were from foreign countries.

Literacy

Literacy in 1970 was estimated to be between 15 and 20 percent. The most recent analysis of literacy data available in 1971 derived from the 1960 census, which reported that 51 percent of those who could read and write could do so in Arabic; 41 percent, in French and Arabic; and the remainder, in French alone or a combination of French and Arabic or Spanish.

Immediately after independence in 1956, the Moroccan League for Fundamental Education and Literacy was organized under government sponsorship to introduce programs in reading, writing, simple arithmetic, domestic science, child care, and handicrafts at the local and national levels. The league also produced and distributed basic texts and newspapers for the newly literate. Many of the programs were offered in adult education and youth centers set up throughout the country. The number of persons reached, however, was limited, and enrollment tended to decrease after the first year of operation. Since the mid-1960s literacy training has been offered mostly in conjunction with on-the-job vocational instruction. The phosphate mining works, the Moroccan railroads, and the sugar enterprises were among the major public companies offering literacy training in 1968.

THE ARTS AND SCIENCES

Traditions

After the Arab invasions of the seventh century, decorative elements and architectural forms spread westward through North Africa to Morocco, where they were used mainly in the cities. In the countryside the local Berber forms of stone and mud architecture and geometric decorations continued, however, with relatively little change. Intellectual pursuits were almost exclusively the province of Arabic scholars and wealthy merchants or political leaders. Studies in Islamic theology, law, philosophy, and geography were concentrated at the Karaouine University.

Most of the renowned figures in intellectual life flourished during the medieval Berber dynasties (eleventh to fourteenth centuries). The Almoravids (1062-1147), who brought all of Morocco and much of Spain under their rule, introduced a mixture of Berber, Arab, and Spanish culture and inaugurated a period of four centuries of vigorous artistic and intellectual activity. Because both the Almoravids and their successors, the Almohads (1147-1212), gained power on waves of religious reform, their concern was directed largely to theology, philosophy, and Islamic law. Under the Marinid dynasty (1269-1465), less concerned with religious purism, Moroccan verbal and artistic expression became more intricate, and decorative motifs took on the luxuriance of detail that came to characterize later Moroccan work.

Ibn Bajja (also known as Avempace, d.1138) wrote treatises on music, mathematics, and astronomy, as well as the commentaries on Aristotle for which he is famous. Ibn Tufayl (d.1185) and Ibn Rushd (also known as Averroes, 1126-98), both of whom served as court physicians to the Almohad monarchs, represented the high point of philosophic thought in Morocco. The Aristotelian commentaries of Averroes had a marked influence on the development of European scholasticism. In other branches of knowledge the medieval period was equally rich. Scholars from Spain and all of North Africa came to the Karaouine University to study medicine, astronomy, astrology, technology, law, grammar, and rhetoric.

The works of Idrissi and Ibn Battuta took their place among the greatest geographical descriptions of medieval times. Ibn Battuta (1304-78) of Tangier reached Russia, India, Java, China, and Timbuktu and wrote a description of his travels for a Marinid prince.

Several types of writing were common in medieval Morocco: the *fahrasa*, a work describing the author's education and the professors he learned from; the *diwan*, or collection of poems; and biographies written in prose and verse. A biography of the Prophet, written in rhymed verse by the Cadi Jyaddh, has been a classic in the country since the twelfth century.

After the fall of the Marinid dynasty in 1465, political strife, foreign wars, and the growth of maraboutism wrought changes in intellectual life. Religious brotherhoods (*zawiyiin*; sing. *zawiya*—see Glossary) rather than the court became the centers of literary expression. Much of the writing from the sixteenth century on is tinged with mysticism. Biographies of saints and collections of the sayings and writings of leaders of religious brotherhoods became popular literary forms. Basic styles in the arts remained the same, and craftsmen limited themselves in large part to the imitation of the past. Intellectual and literary production and patronage were maintained, however, by a number of urban families, particularly those who had fled from Spain to settle in Fes and whose members wrote poetry, history, and legal treatises. In the sixteenth century Hassan Ibn Mohammed al Wazzi—

known in the West as Leo Africanus, who was converted to Christianity and became the protégé of Pope Leo X—wrote his famous *Description of Africa*.

Subsequent periods noted for architectural monuments and royal patronage of scholars and writers occurred under the Saads (1549-1660) and during the seventeenth- and eighteenth-century reigns of the two famous Alawite rulers, Mulay Ismail and Sultan Mohammed (see ch. 3, Historical Setting). Intellectual life was limited to a relatively small group of urban families who, by virtue of their alleged descent in the line of Muhammad, their status as government officials, or their wealth, were able to travel and study abroad. The completion of one's studies in Cordova, Baghdad, or Cairo was considered the final seal to education. As in all Muslim countries, religious education shaped intellectual life, and the most highly respected men in the country were religious scholars known as *ulama* (see Glossary), who had completed many years of religious studies and combined qualities of scholarship with religious insight. Some of them were advisers to the sultan, renowned members of the faculty of the Karaouine University, and judges in such matters as the succession to the sultanate (see ch. 3, Historical Setting; ch. 8, The Governmental System and Political Dynamics).

Literature continued to follow old forms and showed little originality, but at all times there seems to have been a few persons whose works were considered outstanding. Toward the end of the nineteenth century, there was some renewed interest in the work of Moroccan scholars of the past, and some of their works were lithographed in Fes and distributed. Much of Moroccan literature of the traditional period, however, has been lost over the centuries, and many manuscripts have remained in private libraries where they have received little attention.

The goal of education was the development of the cultivated man—intelligent, mannered, acquainted with the various divisions of knowledge considered important, fluent and clever in speech and in the writing of prose and verse, and appreciative of fine things. Less importance was attached to discovery or to originality, except expression, than to competence in discussing philosophy and theology, rhetoric, poetry, and law.

Artistic creativity in the cities was traditionally the province of a separate group, the master artisans, who after years of training gained recognition as experts and who designed and executed the intricate decorations of architecture and handicrafts. Similarly, professional musicians and dancers were trained in performance since childhood. These craftsmen and musicians lived by the sale of their skills or by obtaining the permanent patronage of a man of wealth or of the sultan himself.

Among the rural population music, dance, craftwork and design, and folklore have always been well established popular arts, both as vocations and avocations. Storytellers, musicians, and dancers still provide entertainment, as they have for hundreds of years, for market day crowds or tribal gatherings. Rural crafts are marked by considerable regional variation, and in some areas the Berber crafts seem to have been influenced little, if at all, by the more highly developed arts of the city.

French influence introduced under the protectorate was reflected in changing attitudes toward the traditional artistic and intellectual forms. The French schools in Morocco and visiting European musical or dramatic performers were patronized by increasing numbers of Moroccans providing contact with modern European secular and scientific thought and art forms.

Although the cultivated man, in the older sense, was still highly respected, persons of more utilitarian knowledge came to be recognized as better equipped to become leaders. The traditional view of higher education, however, remained strong, and most recipients of higher education continued to aim toward government jobs or the legal profession rather than medicine, engineering, or science.

Literature

The ability to express oneself in poetry is still considered a mark of the cultivated man, and, as elsewhere in Islam, poetry itself is valued as the highest use of language. Rhymed prose, second only to poetry in the admiration that it commands, has been used extensively in biography and even in scholarly treatises.

Modern Arabic literature, mainly in the form of political articles and essays, developed under the nationalist movement of the 1920s. The period also had its practitioners of traditional Arabic literary forms. Most prominent among these was Allal al Fassi, noted for his nationalistic poems rendered in classical Arabic verse form. After World War II the literature of political essays and editorials continued to flourish, providing important vehicles for social and political thought. Some essays, notably those by the journalist Muhammad Tazi, reached a high literary quality, providing a transitional form to fictional prose. Much of this literature written by leaders of political factions, journalists, and other intellectuals was published in political magazines. *Thawat al Haq*, of the Istiqlal (Independence) Party, represented conservative Arabic-Islamic values and conservative literary trends. *Aqlam*, an organ of the National Union of Popular Forces (Union Nationale des Forces Populaires—UNFP), published ideological essays, research articles, and free-form poetry.

French cultural influences had a strong impact on literary expression in modern Morocco. Difficulties in adapting both the classical and the dialectal Arabic to modern literary forms contributed to the lasting influence of French, especially in fiction writing, although a few novels have been published in Arabic since the 1950s. Whether writing in Arabic or French, however, Moroccan authors have a deep sense of mission to interpret the social and political changes of the postindependence period. Novels and short stories reflect concern with the role of Islam in the modern state, the status of women and, above all, the questions of cultural identity or alienation in relation to the Arabo-Islamic and French traditions of the country. The themes of cultural alienation and depersonalization in a developing country are often treated in subjective psychological contexts.

Driss Charibi is perhaps the best known contemporary author of fiction in French. Born in Casablanca, he studied chemistry in Paris where he has lived since the 1940s. His early works, among them *The Past Perfect*, written during the 1950s, express passionate protest against the cultural and social dicta of traditional Islam and of the West. His *Open Succession*, published in 1962, is autobiographical and deals with the problems of adjustment of an Arab expatriate in France. Charibi is also noted for his essays on the literature of the Maghrib, published in the French journal *Confluent*.

The other major author writing in French, Ahmed Sefrioui, won acclaim with his ethnographic novels, notably with the *Box of Miracles* portraying the life of humble craftsmen in the traditional sector of Fes, the author's native city. Sefrioui's short stories and tales, published in a volume entitled *Beads of Amber* are rendered in picturesque language, sometimes in the form of parables. Appointed to the post of director of fine arts in the Ministry of Culture during the late 1960s, Sefrioui has also written articles on tourism and traditional handicrafts.

Muhammad Khair Eddine is a representative of avant-garde literary forms, which he uses in both prose and verse. Living in Paris and a recipient of a French literary prize, he has explored the theme of identification of the present generation with its forebears.

Literary analyses and criticism by modern Moroccan and other Maghribian authors were written in French. These are published in *Soufflés*, a French-language literary review founded in Morocco in 1966.

Writing in Arabic, Abdulhamid Benjelloun has won acclaim with his novel *Memories of Childhood*, a volume of short stories entitled *The Valley of Tears*, and works of poetry. Benjelloun is a well-known public figure, having held the posts of ambassador to Pakistan, chief of mission to Africa and Asia in the Ministry of Foreign Affairs, and minister of education.

Another writer in Arabic, Muhammad al Sabbagh, is also a veteran of high government posts, including one in the Ministry of Islamic

Affairs. He is noted mainly for his poetic essays, including *The Tree of Fire*, published in 1955.

Bel Hachemy Abdelkader, a professor of Arabic, is a bilingual writer and playwright. He published tales in Arabic in a literary magazine and a work entitled *Thourya, or The Unfinished Novel*, published in Arabic and French in 1959.

Folklore

Storytelling remains one of the commonest forms of amusement among the people at home, in the café, or in the marketplace, and oral literature is far more widespread than written work. During the early 1970s professional storytellers were still found in the largest markets. Others travel from town to town for the weekly markets. The storyteller announces his presence by beating a drum, an instrument often used for punctuation and emphasis in the telling of the story. He collects from his listeners before he begins and often requires them to pay again to hear the ending. Tales are rendered dramatically and repeated again and again.

Much of the folklore concerns the characteristics of animals—why the bat has no feathers, why the owl is wise, the stork is sacred, or the donkey is ill behaved. Two of the recurrent human heroes of folk literature widely known in the Middle East and North Africa are Sidi Suleiman (King Solomon), revered for his wisdom, and Jeha, a picaresque hero and cunning clown of whom his neighbors try to take advantage but who outwits them in the end. Both good and evil spirits figure prominently in folk tales, as do the evil eye and methods of averting it.

The Visual Arts

Architecture and Decoration

Moroccan architectural style, designated Hispano-Moorish by Western art historians, originated in the eighth century in Umayyad Spain, evolved further in both Spain and North Africa, and reached its height in Morocco between the twelfth and fourteenth centuries.

As in other Muslim countries, architectural style found its highest expression in the mosques and Islamic school buildings adjacent to mosques and to a lesser extent in palaces, city walls, and gates. Most distinctive in Moroccan architecture is the repeated appearance of the horseshoe arch (both round and pointed) framing gateways, doorways, and windows or supported by slender columns in the colonnades that open into the courtyards of almost any sizable building. Decoration is so much a part of architecture that a building is as much the creation of the specialized craftsmen who adorned it with plaster, wood, mosaic, and tile as of the masons who outlined the basic structure.

Under the French Protectorate new European residential and business sections were constructed a mile or so from the existing old cities, leaving the *madina* (traditional Muslim quarters) untouched. In addition, some of the ancient mosques, Quranic colleges, and other buildings in the old cities were restored. Because of urban crowding, however, modern cities and the *madina* have grown together in many of the major urban centers.

A noted monument of the postindependence period is the Mohammed V memorial in Rabat, built by King Hassan in memory of his father and officially regarded as a national shrine. Consisting of the late king's tomb, a museum, and a mosque, it is executed in the traditional Hispano-Moorish style and is decorated with carved stucco and marble, chiseled bronze, and elaborate tile mosaics.

Handicrafts

In addition to the crafts used in architectural decoration, household articles made by the family for its own use or by highly specialized craftsmen are nearly all decorated in some way and are valued for attractiveness as well as utility. Leather, textiles, rugs, pottery, and articles of wood, copper, brass, and iron are the products of Morocco's most skilled artisans. Their tooled leather, brass trays, and wrought-iron grillwork have long been known outside the country.

The government operates cooperative centers for traditional artisans to encourage the production and marketing of handcrafted items. The centers also train the craftsmen in the operation of modern machinery for use in the production of traditional items. In 1967 a total of 8,000 craftsmen were trained in centers for weavers and leather, wood, and pottery workers. A "Month of Handicrafts" is celebrated each year under official auspices to stimulate interest in the traditional handcrafted works. National museums at Rabat and Tangier and regional museums at Fes, Marrakech, and Meknès preserve examples of the best Moroccan products.

In all Moroccan crafts regional variation is apparent both in the type of article made and in the designs and colors used. Designs in many crafts often incorporate motifs considered to bring luck or to be effective in warding off evil. Urban crafts, in the Arab and Andalusian traditions, are the more highly developed and specialized and are characterized by the use of floral motifs and arabesque designs.

Painting

Painting as a separate art rather than as a decorative element in architecture is a relatively new form. Exhibitions held in Casablanca and in other major cities during the 1960s and early 1970s attracted a small educated group of Moroccans and members of resident foreign communities.

A school of young painters, some of whom have been trained in France, gained national and international recognition, notably at the exposition of "2,000 Years of Moroccan Art" held in Paris in 1963. Farid Belkahia, director of the Casablanca School of Fine Arts, is the representative painter of this group, which also includes Ahmad al Yacoubi, Hassan Al Glaoui, Miloud ben Mokhtar, Radia Cherkaoui (Mokhtar's mother), Ahmed Laouidire, and Mohammed ben Allal.

Subjects are drawn generally from nature; some show street scenes and human figures, a departure from the Islamic proscription against representative painting. Others in the group, notably al Yacoubi and ben Allal, paint abstractions of the modern Western variety. The use of brilliant colors and pleasant harmonies are typical.

Music, Dance, and Drama

Moroccan music is of many types; it includes Arab, Berber, classical, and popular elements. Musicians perform in concerts, in cafés, at private homes, at circumcision ceremonies, marriages, funerals, and religious processions and in accompaniment to dancing and storytelling.

Classical music in the Moroccan sense is the Andalusian music of the tenth to fifteenth centuries. It is extremely complicated in musical structure, and its lyrics are characterized by the strict use of the Andalusian dialect or classical Arabic and by the construction of verse in the style of classical poetry. It is played by an orchestra composed of the *tar*, a form of tambourine; sometimes the *darbuqa*, a funnel-shaped drum made of clay; and three types of stringed instruments—the *rebab*, played by the leader and considered the most important; the *kemanjah*, now supplanted in most instances by the European violin; and the *oudh*, a lute. Students spend many years learning the theory and techniques of classical music at conservatories in Rabat and Marrakech.

Andalusian music is given regular performances by several orchestras, among them the National Broadcasting Orchestra and the concert orchestras of Fes, Marrakech, and Casablanca. Since independence the Association of Andalusian Music in Casablanca has attempted to preserve examples of this music, collecting and writing down the melodies and words, which have been transmitted largely by ear.

Moroccan Arab popular music, *griha*, is musically similar to, but simpler than, the classical music and uses the popular, rather than the classical, language. New songs are composed in this genre; they usually concern love, war, and adventure and often include topical satire, frequently directed toward another writer of verse. This type of music has also been adapted by some of the brotherhoods for religious chants.

Berber music, even more closely linked to poetry than Arab music, is usually associated with the dance and varies considerably according to region. Percussion instruments, drums, and tambourines provide the rhythm, while the melody is played on a flute or a single-stringed *rebab*.

Western classical music is little known outside the cities, although European orchestras visit Morocco on tour. Jazz and popular Egyptian music, however, have become popular and are heard regularly on the radio.

Dances are common, particularly in the countryside, at times of ceremonies, such as harvest festivals, marriage festivities, and religious celebrations. Traditional dances, Berber in origin, have survived in various local and regional forms in the various Arab- and Berber-speaking areas. Most public performances are accompanied by music and attended by most of the community or neighborhood.

Drama, not a traditional form of artistic expression in Islamic countries, was introduced in Morocco during the protectorate. The performances of French theatrical companies on tour in Morocco were patronized by members of the European community and European-educated Moroccans. During the 1950s amateur groups in the major cities, notably in Casablanca, performed plays in Arabic and some plays translated from French. The playwrights and actors included students, teachers, and low-level government functionaries whose efforts were limited by lack of experience and resources. Many of the plays dealt with the conflict between traditionalist parents and modern youth; others were replete with melodramatic plight. The audience included a wide range of social groups, from middle class to illiterate rural migrants, but because of problems of unintelligibility owing to language and overcomplicated plots, coupled with poor staging techniques, the presentations had limited success.

After independence in 1956 the Moroccan National Theater was established, and in 1959 a dramatic art school and the Moroccan Dramatic Research Center were opened in Rabat under government auspices. Young people interested in the theater are trained as actors, directors, and technicians at this school, as well as in Paris. They produce plays in French and Arabic—the former are usually examples of classical European drama, the latter are concerned with social mores and political themes of the day. Hammamet, a theatrical troupe under the direction of Ali Ben Ayed, has produced the plays of Shakespeare, Molière, and others in Arabic translation. Ahmed El Haj —a former carpenter turned playwright, actor, and singer—has gained popularity with urban audiences. Workers' theaters under the sponsorship of the Moroccan Labor Union (Union Marocain du Travail—UMT) have staged Western plays translated into Arabic, with a Moroccanized milieu and hero.

In general, however, theater performances attracted limited, French-educated audiences and have not gained wide popularity. Young directors and actors expressed concern over the continued reliance on the repertoire of Western plays and have urged the inclusion of more indigenous Arabic material.

Despite their lack of interest in the formal theater, Moroccans have a keen sense of the ridiculous, and the gift of mimicry is considered a social asset. Berber songs mocking the local *caid* (tribal chief—see Glossary) are widely enjoyed, and the mimicking of professors is a popular pastime among students. In the traditional quarters of the cities and on rural market days, wandering comedians attract crowds of people. Relying more on gestures and mime than on words, the comedians act out the escapades and tribulations of everyday man. These simple dramatic forms may well be the source of a new, indigenous type of comedy.

Scholarship and Research

Scholarly activities before independence were concerned mostly with Moroccan history, ethnology, and traditional crafts. Much of the knowledge in these fields rests on the investigations conducted by French scholars since the 1920s. Anthropologists and ethnologists have investigated Berber customs and have described ceremonies, folklore, and religious attitudes. Archaeological finds and ethnographic material are displayed in museums in Rabat and other cities.

French scholars also published works and bibliographies on early and modern Moroccan history, although most data on these works were based on European sources and translations of Arab historical studies. Morocco's libraries, archives, and institutions of traditional learning contain valuable historical sources in Arabic. Little of this material has been explored, although French scholars have described some of it in articles published in learned Moroccan journals. Moroccan scholars writing on the country's history and literary history include Muhammad ben Shenab, noted for his work on North African language and literature, and the historians Muhammed Hadj Sadok and Muhammad Umar al Hijwi.

Archaeologists have directed the excavation of Roman sites in the cities of Volubilis, northwest of Meknès, and Lixus, on the Atlantic coast south of Tangier. The foundations of buildings and forums from the Roman era have been discovered at these sites, and new explorations under government sponsorship were in progress during the late 1960s. Historical monuments were also being restored at the same time, including the necropolis of the Marinids in Rabat, the tombs of the Saad dynasty in Marrakech, and the gate and twelve palaces in Meknès built by the seventeenth-century Alawi ruler Mulay Ismail.

Institutions developed during the protectorate formed the nucleus of several facilities for scholarship. The Sharifian Scientific Institute for Research, founded in 1920, conducts investigations in geology, geography, and physics and other natural sciences. The institute has branches for seismological observations at Ifrane and Berrechid. The Pasteur Institute is concerned with epidemiological and bacteriological research. The National Institute for Research in Agronomy is engaged in soil and climatological studies.

Since independence the government has tended to favor the development of research branches within the various government agencies, many of which have their own libraries and archives. Chief among these agencies is the Secretariat of State for Planning, which carries out most of the statistical and conceptual research for the country's economic development plans. The National Center of Documentation, established in 1968 with the assistance of United Nations funds, operated under the Secretariat of State for Planning. The center is engaged in the preparation of an extensive, computer-based bibliography and microfilm collection on materials pertaining to Moroccan agriculture. The National Geological Survey, with an extensive library, was under the jurisdiction of the Ministry of Commerce in 1970.

The Center of Experimentation Research and Training in Casablanca, a study group under the Directorate of City Planning and Housing of the Ministry of Interior, was engaged in urban housing research in collaboration with the National Institute of Statistics and Applied Economics. The Hassan II Institute of Agronomy in Rabat coordinated data related to the Sebou River development project (see ch. 2, Geography and Population).

Social science research was also conducted by two institutes attached to the University of Rabat, but the scope of these activities was limited. The University Center for Scientific Research was noted chiefly for its scholarly publications, including *Hesperis-Tamuda*, the *Bulletin Economique et Social du Maroc*, and the *Revue de Geographie du Maroc*. The Institute of Sociology, also attached to the university, was being closed down according to information published in 1970.

The requirements of the government for personnel trained in science and technology have been so great that there has been a severe shortage of persons qualified to conduct theoretical and applied research. Most of the teaching and research personnel in the various institutions and in the science departments of universities have been supplied by foreign countries, mainly France.

The country's major libraries were repositories of research material. There are a total of eighteen public libraries in Casablanca and other major cities.

The Moroccan General Library and Archives (Bibliotheque Generale et Archives du Maroc) was the country's national library. Located on the campus of Mohammed V University in Rabat, it had holdings of more than 200,000 volumes in Arabic and in European languages and an extensive collection of Moroccan journals and newspapers. The archives were noted for their medieval books and manuscripts of interest to Muslim scholars and for their microfilm collection of historical documents. The Tetouan branch of the general library had extensive historical material, including manuscripts, administrative documents, and photographs. Its European section had some 45,000 volumes; the Arabic section, 15,000 volumes. The library of the Karaouine University in Fes was a repository of valuable ancient Islamic manuscripts. Materials of interest to traditional scholars could also be found at the Ben Youssef University in Marrakech.

COMMUNICATION

The Press

Historical

The press largely developed during the French and Spanish protectorates (1912-56), although a few periodicals were in existence before then. During the protectorate the dissemination of public information was controlled either by the French and the Spanish colonial governments or by publishers who represented their points of view (see ch. 8, The Governmental System and Political Dynamics).

Until 1936 the publication of Arabic-language journals by Moroccans was not permitted. During the early 1930s, however, a group of young Moroccans opposed to colonial policies published a French-language weekly, *L'Action du Peuple,* under a chief editor who was French. Some Arabic journals were printed in the regions of the Spanish Protectorate where the government appeared to be more conciliatory toward cultural self-expression.

In 1936 permission was granted by the French resident general for the publication of private Arabic-language journals in the region of the French Protectorate, provided that their tone was moderate; thereafter, several weeklies were published in Casablanca. The development of Moroccan newspapers or journalism, however, was not encouraged, and publications were strictly controlled by protectorate authorities. Despite these restrictions, a number of nationalist journals were published after the independence movement gained foothold during the late 1930s.

Although committed to the development of Arabic as a national language, each political group endeavored to publish a French-language organ as well, in order to reach a broader readership.

Because of their nationalist tone, however, these journals were tolerated for only brief periods of time by the protectorate authorities. Conflicts among nationalist groups and economic difficulties were added reasons for their brief lifespans.

Censorship restrictions introduced during World War II and applied rigorously against nationalist publications remained in force until independence in 1956. The Istiqlal Party was permitted to publish *Al Alam*; and the Democratic Independence Party (Parti Démocratique de l'Indépendance—PDI), *Al Ray al-Amm*. Both were heavily censored, however, and intermittently suspended. All nationalist journals were suppressed after the Casablanca riots of 1952 (see ch. 3, Historical Setting).

Throughout the protectorate period, a controlling position was held among newspaper publishers in the French zone by Pierre Mas and his son, Yves. In consistent editorial opposition to the Moroccan independence movement, they created an empire that, in 1956, included several of the largest and most influential newspapers in the country. The most important of these were the Casablanca dailies *Le Petit Marocain* and *La Vigie Marocaine*, the Fes daily *Le Courrier du Maroc*, and *Echo du Maroc*, published in Rabat. In addition, Mas and his son published several periodicals and controlled an important segment of the printing and advertising industries. The press in the Spanish zone, privately owned but reflecting official views, was less well developed. The Tangier daily *España*, however, was influential not only in northern Morocco but in southern Spain as well.

Development Since Independence

The removal of French controls after 1956 revitalized the domestic press. Politically sponsored newspapers proliferated after the Istiqlal Party split into factions in 1959. Like their predecessors before 1956, these newspapers aimed to convince rather than to inform. Their main goal of independence achieved, their polemic fervor turned on one another's political philosophies, as well as against government policies and high officials and on the social and economic shortcomings of the newly established order (see ch. 8, The Governmental System and Political Dynamics).

Several dailies and weeklies were published by the Istiqlal Party, the main opposition party, and by political groups that split from it and regrouped themselves as the National Union of Popular Forces (Union Nationale des Forces Populaires—UNFP). The conservative, loyalist Popular Movement (Mouvement Populaire—MP) and the Party of Independent Liberals (Parti des Liberaux Independants— PLI) were each represented by three journals. The Ministry of Information, in cooperation with the royalist Front for the Defense of Constitutional Institutions (Front pour la Défense des Institutions Constitutionnelles—FDIC), published two dailies and two weeklies.

The Moroccan Communist Party (Parti Communiste Marocain—PCM) published three newspapers until its proscription in 1959 (see ch. 8, The Governmental System and Political Dynamics).

Freedom of expression was proclaimed in King Mohammed V's Charter of Public Liberties of November 1958, which incorporated a basic press code. The latter contained provisions empowering the government to apply stringent measures to limit press freedom. Strengthened in 1960 and again in 1963, the code stipulated that the minister of interior might seize copies of any newspaper or periodical that appeared to threaten public order. Furthermore, he could suspend, or the prime minister could ban, any newspaper or periodical that in their judgment had attacked the political or religious foundations of the country. Official measures directed against the press for other offenses, however, had to be initiated through the courts.

Under pressure from the Istiqlal Party, provisions were also included in the press code that within six months of November 1958 all newspapers must be owned or controlled by Moroccan nationals. The government took no action, however, apparently because it believed the foreign press fulfilled a service the Moroccan press was not yet ready to assume. This attitude was strongly resented by opposition party leaders and Moroccan newspaper publishers.

In early 1964 the Istiqlal-dominated Moroccan Press Association brought suit against the French-owned Mas Publishing Company on the grounds that it had no legal right to publish according to provisions of the 1958 press code. The Rabat Appeals Court upheld the charge but, although it levied a small fine against the publishing company, it did not prohibit the firm from continuing to publish. The case put all foreign-owned newspapers on notice that their publications could be suspended at any time without cause, and since then they all have followed cautious editorial policies to avoid giving offense to the government. Shortly before the proclamation of the state of emergency in 1965, amendments to the code were passed under Istiqlal pressure to enforce the 1958 prohibition on newspapers owned by non-Moroccans, but Parliament was suspended before the amendment could be promulgated (see ch. 8, The Governmental System and Political Dynamics).

On October 6, 1971, the government announced that the prime minister had informed the owners of *La Vigie Marocaine*, *Le Petit Marocain*, and *España* that their temporary license to publish would be terminated as of November 1971. The prime minister stated that the decision had been made on instructions by the king.

The contest between the government and the opposition press gained momentum during the political crises of the mid-1960s. The suspension of the Istiqlal Party's popular daily, *La Nation Africaine*, in February 1965 for publishing an antimonarchical citation by a nineteenth-century Egyptian philosopher created a political crisis in Parliament. After the newspaper's director was sentenced in criminal court to ten months in prison and to the equivalent of about a US$1,000 fine, the Istiqlal hardened its opposition to the press code. When the code was put before the lower house of the then bicameral Parliament for revision in early June 1965, Istiqlal spokesmen led by the head of the party, Allal al Fassi, forced through amendments to the code that would eliminate the government's power to suspend or ban a newspaper. This signal defeat of the government was widely credited with having sparked King Hassan's decision to take personal control of the government in June 1965 (see ch. 8, The Governmental System and Political Dynamics).

Although the state of emergency was lifted in July 1970, the government acted with increasing stringency against opposition press criticism (see ch. 8, The Governmental System and Political Dynamics). The Istiqlal's Arabic newspaper, *Al Alam*, and French newspaper, *L'Opinion*, were the main targets of government restrictive measures in 1970 and 1971. In September 1970 Mohammad Berrada, editor of *L'Opinion* and member of the Party's Central Committee, was arrested for publishing an article on alleged maladministration in the armed services. Berrada was convicted on October 25 and sentenced to six months' imprisonment and a fine of DH1,000. The trial and the interpretation of the evidence by the prosecution aroused much public anger; Berrada was released in June 1971 by royal amnesty although, after an earlier appeal, his prison sentence had been increased to one year.

An attack by unknown persons on the printing press of *L'Opinion* and *Al Alam* in mid-February 1971 forced the newspapers to suspend publication for several weeks. They began republications in March but, because of subsequent seizures and bans by the government, the appearance of these dailies throughout the spring and early summer of that year was highly irregular. In April *L'Opinion* was seized on six separate occasions, and the May 1 issues of both *Al Alam* and *L'Opinion* were confiscated; official reasons for these measures were not given, however.

Le Monde, a French newspaper published in Paris, commented that official measures against the Moroccan opposition press evoked "anxiety in international opinion." Referring to *L'Opinion* in particular, *Le Monde* deplored official efforts to prevent the dissemination of opposition views in a newspaper that is often quoted in the international press.

Dailies and Periodicals

In 1970 the national press included six dailies differing in aims, political orientation, and language. The national newspapers, although diverse and politically vigorous, were weakened by frequent government seizures and powerful competition by the foreign-owned press. The leading Moroccan dailies have circulations of between 35,000 and 40,000, representing mostly street sales at the price of DHO.30.

Al Anba, the Arabic-language government daily, was published by the Ministry of Information. Its tone of serene optimism contrasted vividly with the passionate polemics of the opposition press. A mouthpiece for official views, *Al Anba* sought to interpret, disseminate, and seek public support for government policies. The activities of the royal court, royal speeches, and parliamentary debates were extensively covered. The government's identification with Islamic cultural and political traditions was expressed editorially and by elaborate photographic coverage of religious and court rituals.

The Istiqlal Party's Arabic-language daily, *Al Alam*, with a circulation of about 40,000 in 1970, was the most influential privately owned Moroccan newspaper. Its prestige and authority were derived from the prominent role in the independence struggle of its sponsoring party and of its founder, nationalist leader Allal al Fassi. Since its establishment in 1946, *Al Alam* had been the major opposition newspaper, regularly read by Mohammed V. Many of its essays and editorials were written by prominent intellectuals. A political and cultural newspaper of authority, *Al Alam* reported on the complexities and vicissitudes of national life in the light of Istiqlal's philosophy, endeavoring to popularize it among the general population. The newspaper abstained from sensational reporting and from publishing items of commercial appeal, such as cartoons, housewives' columns, and courtroom chronicles.

Istiqlal's French newspaper, *L'Opinion*, has the largest circulation among dailies—about 50,000. Founded in 1965 to replace the banned *La Nation Africaine*, it has many foreign readers and is frequently quoted in the international press. Shortly after it was first published, *L'Opinion* stated editorially that it intended to counter the influence of the foreign press by offering vigorous journalistic competition. It has supported the monarchy and institutions related to it but criticized in vigorous tones government policies, including information policies, and attacked groups and persons whom it held responsible for shortcomings in the implementation of social and economic programs.

Added to the domestic press in 1970 were three daily newspapers, all published under independent auspices. *Jaridatuk* was first published in Rabat in August 1970. Information is lacking on the other daily, *Al Kawalis*, but a satirical political weekly by the same name, sympathetic to the UNFP, was published during the early 1960s. *La Depêche* is published in French by Mehdi Bennouna, who is also director of the Maghreb Arab Press, the national news agency.

Most of the approximately forty periodicals appearing in 1970 were weekly publications of political parties or their affiliates. They covered a wide range of party journals, labor union and student magazines, and periodicals catering to special interests. The majority were published in Arabic, in tabloid format. Almost all had small circulations and were heavily dependent on subsidies and struggling to stay in business. Catering to a small, partisan readership, the opposition press expressed its antigovernment views with great verbal vehemence, and therefore its journals were frequent targets of government seizure and suspension.

Akbar al Dunya was an independent satirical weekly journal. Often seized because of its humorous allusions to the bureaucracy and public issues generally considered inviolable, *Akbar al Dunya* has been popular with educated readers and had a circulation of about 15,000 during the mid-1960s. *Maroc Informations*, a monthly, specialized in economic, commercial, and maritime news and was read mostly by French-speaking educated groups. During the mid-1960s the journal appeared under the titles *Maghrib Informations* and *Maghrib Maritime*.

Al Siyasa, a weekly, was founded in 1967; it succeeded *Al Dustur* formerly the newspaper of the Constitutional Democratic Party (Parti Démocratique Constitutionnel—PDC). *Al Saab* is a conservative weekly journal of commentaries reflecting the views of its founder and editor, Muhammad al Mekki al Naciri, a representative of early Moroccan nationalism advocating national rejuvenation through return to the simple orthodoxy of Islam. *Al Nidal* is an independent, liberal, literary-political weekly appealing to young readers.

The National News Agency

Since its creation in November 1959 Maghrib Arab Press (MAP), the national news agency, has been by far the country's most important news service. In 1971 it provided the domestic press with foreign news in Arabic and with domestic news in Arabic and French and transmitted and translated material from the foreign news services operating in Morocco. In addition, it supplied news to the radio and television services, to the royal court, ministries, foreign embassies, and some private enterprises.

Founded by Mehdi Bennouna as a private, independent joint stock company, MAP's news coverage and presentation reflected its agreement with government policies. The agency had permanent offices in Rabat, Casablanca, and Tangier; branches in Tunis, Algiers, and Paris; and correspondents in all major Moroccan cities.

MAP obtained world news from eighteen national news bureaus. With five of these—Agence France Press (AFP), United Press International (UPI), the British news bureau (Reuters), Algerie Presse

Service (APS), and Tunisie Afrique Press (TAP)—the agency maintained constant contact.

In early 1971 MAP had one radio teletype transmission daily, each in Arabic and French, and each of one and one-half hour's duration. The transmissions included political, economic, social, and international news; economic and sports reports; and items of interest to the diplomatic communities.

Radio

Radio broadcasting has been solely in the hands of the government since 1959, when, in accordance with a government decree promulgated early that year, all privately owned commercial radio stations were put off the air. The government purchased the facilities of the important Radio Tangier International and Radio Africa Maghrib, both based in Tangier, and Radio Dersa, based in Tetouan, and has since used these stations as part of its national network. Broadcasting in 1971 was handled by the Moroccan Radio and Television (Radiodiffusion Television Marocain—RTM), also known as Radio Maroc, an agency of the Ministry of Information, which controls its programming and editorial content. News was supplied for broadcast by MAP.

Rabat was the broadcasting center of the country. Most broadcasts of the national network originated in one of the main studios in Rabat, although studio facilities also existed in Casablanca, Tangier, Fes, Oujda, and other smaller cities.

Network A of the domestic service broadcast fifteen hours daily in Arabic. Most of the cultural programs were in classical Arabic, but news was broadcast in the colloquial dialect. Network B, known as the international network, had programs in French, Spanish, and English twelve hours daily on weekdays, fourteen hours on Saturdays, and seventeen hours on Sundays. The bulk of the broadcasting time was in French. Network C broadcast in three Berber dialects—Tashilhit, Tamazight, and Tarift—for nine hours a day. During the mid-1960s three hours were devoted to each of the dialects.

The former Radio Tangier operated as a separate network known as the Voice of Morocco, broadcasting a total of thirteen hours a day, of which eleven were in Arabic; the rest, in French and Spanish. Religious and educational programs were prominently featured in addition to music and variety, which constituted the bulk of the program. Readings and commentaries of Quranic texts were broadcast at least twice a day. The texts were related to social and political issues of the day, and the commentaries represented the official interpretations of these issues. Lectures by prominent Islamic scholars on timely social problems, notably on marriage and divorce, and on scientific and economic questions were broadcast weekly. Educational programs on the primary level were inaugurated during the mid-1960s, reaching more than 2,000 classrooms equipped with loudspeakers and radio sets. Moreover, there were broadcasts of interest to housewives, manual workers, and the youth; a program of medical information; on-the-spot interviews; quizzes; and sports broadcasts.

Radio Maroc broadcast special foreign service programs to Mauritania and other West African countries, the Middle East, Latin America, and Equatorial Africa, in Arabic, French, English, and Spanish. The Arabic program was broadcast for fifteen hours; the French, for 9-1/2 hours; the Spanish, for 2-1/2 hours; and the English, for one hour daily. Home service broadcasts were beamed abroad as well, by shortwave transmitters. The broadcasts to Africa included programs in classical and colloquial Arabic, Spanish, Poular, and Wolof (languages of Senegal), and English. The Arabic-language programs were aimed at explaining Moroccan policies and reflecting the country's ties with the Arab world.

Morocco had cooperated with other African countries in developing and coordinating cultural and educational programs for the audiovisual media. It was a member of the Union of African National Radio and Television Services, which met in Rabat in December 1970 to discuss program exchanges and to draft programs designed to develop African traditional music.

The government had worked steadily to improve the technical quality of its broadcasts, a difficult task since the mountainous terrain interfered with reception even of powerful local stations. In 1969 there were thirty-five transmitters, of which twenty-two were longwave and mediumwave; seven, shortwave; and six, ultra-shortwave. Domestic broadcasts were transmitted mainly on mediumwave; the shortwave transmitters were used to broadcast the home service programs to remote southern areas of the country, to other parts of Africa, and to the Near East. The most powerful facility was a 400-kilowatt longwave transmitter in Azilal used for external broadcasting.

There was a shortage of trained scriptwriters, producers, and communications technicians. Agreements have been signed between Radio Maroc and foreign countries, mainly France, for the training of such personnel.

In 1968 there were about 826,000 licensed radio receivers. According to unofficial sources the total number of receivers in 1970 was 934,689 (about 60 per 1,000 population), but it is not known whether this figure included unlicensed receivers. The domestic production of radio sets started during the mid-1960s. By 1968 some 150,000 sets were produced annually, according to Moroccan official sources; another approximately 60,000 were imported. Experts reported that all sets in operation could receive mediumwave broadcasts, and about half or more were equipped to receive shortwave broadcasts as well.

Broadcasting facilities in the country included shortwave transmitters of the Voice of America, located in Tangier, operating under a special agreement between Morocco and the United States. Under the terms of agreement, the Voice of America had granted permission to Radio Maroc to use the transmitters for a specified number of hours each week for broadcasts to West Africa and Mauritania.

Moroccans reportedly took great pride in owning a radio set and in displaying it. Almost every household was reported to own a radio of some sort. Sets were also set up in most cafés, village markets, and other gathering places, where they blare forth the entire day. The most popular hours for radio listening are between 7:30 and 8:30 A.M., between 1:00 and 1:30 P.M., and between 8:00 and 9:00 P.M.

In addition to Radio Maroc, a number of foreign radio stations could be heard throughout much of Morocco and apparently had large audiences. According to press reports during the mid-1960s, Radio Algiers was heard in the villages; Radio Paris, in the *madina*; the Voice of Arabs (Radio Cairo), in the cafés; BBC (British Broadcasting Corporation), in educated circles; and Nouakchott Radio (Mauritanian government radio), among the politicians. Radio Algiers and the Voice of the Arabs were particularly popular because they played Egyptian music.

Television

Television was introduced in 1954 by a private French company. Its facilities were taken over by the independent Moroccan government, and in 1962 the television service was incorporated with Radio Maroc. Since then telecasting has been an autonomous service within Radio Maroc and has shared with radio broadcasting the government administration and control mechanisms of the Ministry of Information.

In 1970 the area reached by television was limited, notably to the large cities and their environs in the northern portions of the country between Oujda and Fes and in the western coastal region. Plans were underway, however, to expand the network notably through a new station planned in Agadir. In 1970 there were television stations in eight locations telecasting through six channels for four hours daily. The system had been linked to Eurovision, the European television service, since 1965. The Arabic program was beamed for two hours and forty-five minutes; the rest of the time was devoted to French telecasts. Much of the programming was devoted to educational and cultural features. Programming material was supplied largely by foreign producers, notably in France and in the United States. Since early 1971 the country had also subscribed to Eurovision's daily television news service. Commercial telecasts first authorized in 1970 were beamed for six minutes each day.

The domestic production of television sets began during the early 1960s, but prices remained high. About 8,200 sets were produced in 1968, and another 2,000 were imported. Production was to be raised to some 11,000 sets annually under the Five Year Plan. The private ownership of sets was limited to the wealthy urban groups; other sets were owned by community organizations or by cafés where they were used for public viewing. The government had furnished television sets free of charge to various public places, such as youth hostels.

Films

Films were a favorite form of entertainment for urban Moroccans and for the small segment of the rural population to whom film showings were accessible. Films from Western countries had played an important role in exposing Moroccans to life and customs in technologically advanced Western societies and in many cases had altered traditional social attitudes, notably toward women. American westerns, French comedies, and mystery films provided good forms of temporary escape and were valued especially by urban low income groups. Egyptian films, because of linguistic and cultural identity, were especially popular. Many of the Egyptian films, however, presenting a Westernized social setting and values, complemented and even exceeded the influence of foreign films in modifying the views and ways of life of a growing segment of the population.

In 1969 there were 226 film theaters. Fifty of these were in Casablanca, accounting for about 40 percent of the box office receipts of all theaters. According to other data available in 1971, the country had 173 film theaters in 1969, equipped for showing thirty-five millimeter feature films and twenty-three theaters for showing sixteen-millimeter documentaries. The total seating capacity of the two types of theaters was 107,700, and the annual attendance was about 18.2 million. There were also eight mobile film units operated by the Ministry of Information, offering some 1,200 performances during the year.

Most of the feature films and short subjects were imported. Before being cleared for distribution by private enterprises, all imported films were officially censored for moral and political content. Films were also produced domestically by the government-directed Moroccan Cinematographic Center (Centre Cinematographique Marocain—CCM), established in 1961. The CCM had studios in Souisse and Ain-Chok (near Casablanca), both equipped for producing thirty-five-millimeter and sixteen-millimeter films, including television features. Full-length feature films had been officially encouraged but, because of budgetary limitations, CCM produced mainly newsreels and documentaries for various ministries. In 1969 CCM documentaries included *Folkloric Dances* and *Troubadour of Marrakech* (for the Ministry of Tourism) and *Andalousian Nights* (for the Ministry of Culture).

Despite limited scope of production CCM produced several full-length films in 1968. Two of the films, *Vaincre pour Mourir* (Win to Die) and *Le Soleil du Printemps* (The Sunshine of Spring), were presented at the government-sponsored Mediterranean Film Festival in Rabat in the fall of 1968. Several Moroccan film directors, including Muhammad Tazi Abdelaziz Ramdani and Larbi Bennani, have been acclaimed by Moroccan and foreign filmgoers.

SECTION II. POLITICAL

CHAPTER 8

THE GOVERNMENTAL SYSTEM AND POLITICAL DYNAMICS

On July 10, 1971, a military coup d'etat threatening to overturn the governmental system was directed against the king and a large assemblage of government and diplomatic notables gathered at the Skhirat Palace southwest of Rabat. By the evening of the same day the ill-conceived attempt had collapsed, leaving in its wake some 250 dead. King Hassan II, who survived unharmed, firmly resumed royal control, principally assisted by General Mohammed Oufkir. The armed forces remained loyal, and no substantial public uprising in support of the sudden eruption occurred.

The attempt, employing duped cadets of a noncommissioned officers training school, was organized by a small group of apolitical or conservative senior army officers apparently intent upon "purification" of the government and seizure of power, but under what form was not clear. The opposition parties—the Istiqlal (Independence) Party and the National Union of Popular Forces (Union Nationale des Forces Populaires—UNFP)—were not involved. No previously known political party or faction, domestic or foreign, was involved, and no specific political ideology was adduced. During the action, the antimonarchical Arab socialist government of Libya, apparently assuming that the revolt would succeed, broadcast support for the attempt in strong language which, in the succeeding days, resulted in the mutual withdrawal of the diplomatic missions of the two countries but not a formal break in diplomatic relations (see ch. 9, Foreign Relations).

The rapid and dramatic failure of the conspiracy attested to the basic stability of the governmental system and society as well as to the ineptitude of the plotters; it also illuminated a national characteristic of a political society in which balanced tensions required the role of the king as central arbiter. Of at least equal importance, the convulsion of July 10 was symbolic of interrelated dissatisfactions and stresses in the stagnated governmental-political and economic systems that had evolved in the wake of the French colonial period terminated by independence in 1956.

Sources and legitimation of national power are found both in the distinctive Moroccan-Islamic background and in a modern overlay embodied in the Constitution of 1970, a document endorsed by popular referendum in July of that year. In the country at large Moroccan society remained essentially traditionalist, Islamic, and authoritarian-deferential, as reflected in the constitutional identification of the king as commander of the faithful. Although the basic system of constitutional monarchy appeared virtually indispensable to the country, internal change and reform within that system appeared to be required. To this end Hassan II designated a new prime minister and government on August 6, 1971. In the aftermath of the bizarre and bloody but symptomatic outburst of July 10, the king charged this new government with prompt implementation of a four-point cleanup and reform program.

Political analysts observed in 1962 and 1963 that progress and stability depended upon cooperation between the throne on the one hand and the political parties and their associated interest groups on the other and questioned whether the country could afford both a multiparty system and the institution of a monarch who not only reigned but also ruled. Subsequent experience up to late 1971 showed that the country could live with this condition. Stability seemed to have prevailed but in a polity of balanced factional tension that tended to immobility rather than progress. Analysts described the dilemma as a balance of factors and conditions pointing strongly towards change but counterpoised by other factors, both traditional and modern, making change unlikely. In this equation the personality and leadership of the king, rather than the institution of his office, were described as most likely to provide the impulse for change or regression or, inertly, for continuation of the uneasy balance.

Underlying all sources of power and patronage, both in earlier and in modern times, is control of the armed forces; and this power also is in the hands of the king, confirmed in legal form in the Constitution. The loyalty of these forces is, in consequence, always a matter of the first interest. Among the rank and file, as shown by the failure of the coup attempt on July 10, 1971, military loyalty to the throne was not seriously in question. A subversive group, as shown by the same events, had formed among the senior leadership but was destroyed in the attempt and its aftermath.

CONSTITUTIONAL SYSTEM

Development of Constitutionalism

In December 1962, almost seven years after independence, Morocco received a written, Western-style constitution. There was no precedent in the country's history for a written charter limiting the power of the monarch. As early as 1908, however, a constitutional document was drafted but not implemented; and in the 1930s nationalists, in looking toward an independent Morocco, often referred to the form of their vision as a constitutional monarchy. Following a gradualist policy of balancing tradition with change, King Mohammed V acted to keep essential political controls in his own hands during the transition period after 1956. One of his first acts after independence was to create a cabinet, or Council of Government. The cabinet first headed by Embarek Bekkai, which functioned as an advisory and administrative body, was appointed by and responsible only to the sultan. Under the presidency of Mehdi Ben Barka, Morocco's first national consultative assembly was, like the cabinet, appointed by the sultan and had only consultative powers. From the opening debates in November 1956 until May 1959, when Mohammed V let its charter lapse, the assembly served as little more than a sounding board for the political parties and an initiation to the procedures of parliamentary government.

The next important move from the palace came on May 8, 1958, in the form of the Royal Charter, in which the king restated his contention that the best form of government for an independent state is democratic and that a true democracy, in which the people would participate increasingly in the affairs of government, could be evolved within the framework of a constitutional monarchy. In November 1958 the guarantees made in general terms in May were specified in the King's Charter of Public Liberties, and the basis of civil rights thus passed into law.

In May 1960 the palace announced that before the end of 1962 a constitution would be drawn up that would permit all Moroccans to participate in the government through the intermediary of elected representatives. In the same month the long-awaited elections for communal councils finally took place. Concerning the still-unanswered question of who would draft the constitution, the king chose a middle course between UNFP demands for a nationally elected constituent assembly and his own preference for a constitution drafted by a select group of experts. On November 3, 1960, he appointed the Constitutional Council, composed predominantly of Istiqlal leaders, to write a constitution, which would be approved by him and submitted to the people in a referendum. The absence of numerically small, but politically important, other elements ultimately undermined the council's authority, and it became defunct after King Mohammed's death on February 26, 1961.

On succeeding to the throne on March 3, 1961, Hassan II continued his father's work in the direction of the projected constitutional monarchy. His Fundamental Law, promulgated on June 2, 1961, reaffirmed the country's basic principles of adherence to the Islamic religion and the Arabic language and the preservation of monarchical government evolving toward "authentic democracy." In addition, he restated the basic rights and obligations of citizens that would later be found in the constitution, but the question of how and by whom the proposed constitution would be written remained unanswered. By late 1961 it was apparent that the king was planning to elaborate the constitution without a constituent assembly. The document that was finally presented to the people for ratification in December 1962 was the work of Hassan II and a small group of advisers, especially the minister of interior, Reda Guédira.

The Constitution of 1962

Despite many innovations, the new constitution embodied the essentials of Moroccan tradition and formalized the practices of government since independence. Importantly, it was open to legal revision, allowing for the evolution of the political system. For many politically sensitive Moroccans, however, the constitution fell short of expectations, both in content and especially in the manner in which it was drafted. The latter question continued thereafter to be a major issue for the political opposition in the country. Essentially, it reflected the larger contest between those favoring a single-party system and the royal determination that this should not occur.

On November 4, 1962, two weeks before the text of the constitution was made public, the procedures of the referendum were announced from the palace. All Moroccans over twenty-one could go to the polls on December 7 to vote yes or no to the question "Do you approve the draft constitution which has been proposed?" All authorized political parties, which excluded the Communists, were permitted to participate in the campaign. The Istiqlal supported the government for the last time, as it turned out, in a major action. Leading the opposition to ratification was the UNFP, joined by the Moroccan Labor Union (Union Marocain du Travail—UMT), which maintained that only a nationally elected assembly could draft the constitution. The outcome of the campaign and referendum was an overwhelming royal victory: 84 percent of the electorate voted, 95 percent in favor of ratification.

With the new constitution, effective on December 14, 1962, the kingdom of Morocco became a "constitutional monarchy," at least to the extent that it was endowed with a written statement of the legal bases of its authority. The constitution defined the kingdom of Morocco as a sovereign Muslim state, in form a social and democratic constitutional monarchy, with Arabic as the official language. The state was declared to be an African state and part of the "Greater Maghrib." Sovereignty was said to "belong to the nation," which exercised it directly through the referendum and indirectly through the intermediary of its representative institutions—a two-house national parliament and provincial and communal councils. The constitution supported political parties as a means to allow citizens to organize in their own interests; it specifically prohibited any single party from exercising a monopoly of political activity. All Moroccans were held equal before the law, as the highest expression of the will of the nation. Fundamental to the new constitution was the provision for representative government on the local level through the elected communal and provincial councils. Civil rights, based on the French Declaration of the Rights of Man, were spelled out, as were basic obligations of citizenship. Revision was provided for, to be initiated either by the prime minister or by a member of the Parliament.

Elections for the lower house of the national Parliament were held in May 1963 and for the upper house in the following October; by the end of the year all of Morocco's new institutions of representative government were in operation. King Hassan opened the first session of Parliament on November 18, 1963. Despite the separation of powers and cross-checking devices of the constitution, however, the decisive balance of power remained constitutionally and in fact with the throne.

The Constitution of 1970

On June 7, 1965, King Hassan II, in view of public disturbances earlier that year and the immobility of the Parliament, which had presented to him only two pieces of legislation since its opening, utilized the powers granted to him by Article 35 of the Constitution of 1962 to declare a national emergency, or "state of exception," under which he ruled directly, with his council of ministers, for the next five years. During this time he himself acted as prime minister until July 7, 1967. Parliament was suspended rather than dissolved, since its dissolution would have required new elections. Rather than conducting new elections, as advocated by the political opposition, the king and his government held that constitutional revision was first necessary to enable representative institutions to break out of their deadlock and provide legislation for national problems. King Hassan and a small staff of consultants prepared a new draft constitution, again without calling a constituent assembly for the purpose and again, as in 1962, incurring the opposition of the UNFP and now of the Istiqlal as well.

On July 24, 1970, the new Constitution was presented to the electorate through a referendum, was overwhelmingly endorsed by a 98.8-percent vote and became effective on July 31, 1970. Many provisions of the 1962 document were restated or modified only slightly. There were, however, significant changes—particularly in the manner of revision and in the shift from a bicameral to a unicameral legislature. The position of the throne was strengthened, both in the sections directly describing the monarchical functions and indirectly through interlocking provisions relating to other institutions.

The Constitution of 1970 consists of a preface stating the national identity and broad policies and twelve chapters totaling 101 articles. Chapter 1 sets forth basic principles and individual political, economic, and social rights; chapter 2 deals with the institution of the monarchy; chapter 3 describes the organization and powers of the House of Representatives; chapter 4 defines the executive agency of the government, comprising a prime minister and ministers; and chapter 5 covers relations between the various authorities. Chapters 6, 7, and 10 deal with the judiciary and courts; chapter 8, local government; chapter 9, the Higher Council for National Promotion and Planning; chapter 11, revision of the constitution; and chapter 12, transitional provisions empowering the king to conduct all affairs of state until the investiture of the new House of Representatives. (The House was elected in August 1970 and opened on October 9.)

The preface to the Constitution of 1970 declares that "Morocco is a sovereign Islamic state, with Arabic as its official language, and forms part of the Greater Maghrib." As an African nation, Morocco seeks the objective of African unity and, as a member of various international organizations, pledges support to their charters. Finally, the preface states a determination to continue working for world peace and security. Elsewhere in North Africa and the Middle East, constitutions propounded by Arab nationalist-socialist regimes frequently contain references to "Arab unity" and the "Arab nation." This particular language does not occur in either the 1970 or the 1962 constitution of Morocco; the country, however, belongs to the League of Arab States and has consistently aligned itself with the principal Arab causes (see ch. 9, Foreign Relations).

In the enumeration of basic principles and individual rights set forth in chapter one of the Constitution of 1970, Morocco is stated to be "a constitutional monarchy, democratic and social." Sovereignty resides in the nation and is exercised directly by referendum and indirectly through the constitutional institutions. Political parties, unions, communal councils, and professional chambers all participate in the organization and representation of the citizens. The last three of these elements were not cited in the parallel statement of the 1962 Constitution. Significantly, the 1962 constitutional prohibition of the single-party system is restated in the 1970 document. The rule of law and equality of all before the law are reaffirmed. Islam is again specifically given as the religion of the state, which guarantees to all the free exercise of religious worship. In the concluding sections of chapter one, the political, economic, and social rights and obligations of citizens are restated exactly as in 1962.

The Constitution of 1970, like its predecessor, contains provision for its own amendment, or revision, again specifying as exceptions that the monarchical form of the state and the provisions relating to Islam cannot be the object of such change. The manner of revision in 1970 is decisively altered from that of 1962 by placing the initiative for revision and the power of calling the required confirmatory referendum squarely in the hands of the king.

THE MONARCHY

Powers of the King

The Constitution of 1970, like that of 1962, confirmed the traditional role of the king as both secular and religious head of state and delineated the wide scope of his powers. The document of 1970, in fact, extended those powers. The king is commander of the faithful, supreme representative of the nation, symbol of its unity, and guarantor of its existence and continuity. He is the guardian of respect for Islam and the Constitution and protector of the rights and liberties of citizens, groups in the society, and organizations. He is the guarantor of the nation's independence and of the territorial integrity of the kingdom in its "authentic frontiers." His person is "sacred and inviolable."

The prime minister and ministers are appointed by the king, who presides over the cabinet, officially called the Council of Ministers. The king signs and promulgates laws and can put them to a referendum or send them back to the House of Representatives for a second reading. He can dissolve the House by decree (*dahir*) after consulting the president of the Constitutional Chamber of the Supreme Court and addressing the nation. In the event of dissolution, elections for a new House must be conducted not more than three months later; in the interim the king exercises both executive and legislative powers. The new House then formed cannot be dissolved less than a year after its election.

The king also has the right to address both the nation and the House by messages not subject to debate. He exercises the administrative power, and by decree, under Article 29, he may delegate defined administrative authority to the prime minister. In general, royal decrees are countersigned by the prime minister except in cases involving ministerial appointment or release, dissolution of the House, use of the referendum and revision of the constitution, and the declaration of national emergency.

The king is commander in chief of the armed forces and makes all civil and military appointments or delegates appointment power. He accredits Moroccan ambassadors, and foreign ambassadors are accredited to him. He signs and ratifies treaties, except that treaties involving financial expenditures must have the prior approval of the House, and any treaties having provisions contrary to the

Constitution cannot be ratified without prior constitutional revision. A declaration of war requires prior notification to the House.

Additionally, the king constitutionally presides over the Educational Higher Council, the Higher Council for National Promotion and Planning, and the Higher Council of the Magistracy. He appoints the judiciary upon recommendation from the Higher Council of the Magistracy and has the right of pardon by amnesty or commutation.

The capstone of royal authority, however, is the extraordinary power awarded by Article 35. When the national territory is in danger or the functioning of constitutional institutions is jeopardized, the king, after consulting with the president of the House and addressing a message to the nation, is empowered to declare by decree a national emergency and assume the full powers necessary to restore normalcy. The emergency period is terminated in the same way it is begun. It was under this power, stated also in the Constitution of 1962, that Hassan II ruled between June 1965 and August 1970.

Succession to the Throne

Under Articles 20 and 21 of the 1970 Constitution, as in that of 1962, succession to the throne is hereditary by male primogeniture in the line of King Hassan II, except when the king during his lifetime designates a successor other than his eldest son. If the king has no son, the succession passes to his nearest collateral male relative under the same conditions. Regularization of the succession was initiated on July 9, 1957, by Mohammed V when he officially named Mulay Hassan crown prince.

The king is not of age until the completion of his eighteenth year. During his minority the Regency Council exercises all powers of the crown except those pertaining to constitutional revision. (This means, in effect, that during a period of royal minority constitutional change is not legally possible.) The Regency Council is to be presided over by the nearest collateral male relative of the king who is himself more than twenty-one years old; the other members are the first president of the Supreme Court, the president of the House of Representatives, and seven others appointed by the old king during his lifetime. After the new king completes his eighteenth year, the Regency Council continues as a consultative body until the king completes his twenty-first year. The constitution specifies that the rules and procedures of council operations be fixed by an organic law; this requirement was fulfilled by the Regency Council Law of October 16, 1970.

Hassan II and the Royal Family

King Hassan II was born on July 9, 1929, in Rabat, the eldest son of Sultan Mohammed V, who had succeeded to the sultanate only in

1927. Mohammed had been elected by the *ulama* (see Glossary) in the traditional manner but only after approval by the ruling French colonial regime. His early life, despite his sharifian princely lineage, had been austere. His education was primarily in terms of Arabic classicism and the Quran rather than in the context of modern times. Later, by rigorous self-education, he repaired these omissions. Also, he ensured that his children should be educated in both modern and classical terms and that they should enjoy the comforts of life, which his station, even under the French, could provide.

Hassan II, from his earliest days, was prepared carefully by his father for his eventual ascent to the throne. He developed a wide range of interests, for which he became distinguished, ranging from athletics, automobiles, and aircraft to scientific technology, classical and modern literature, and a mastery of both the Arabic and the French languages. After graduating with honors from the Imperial College, he entered law studies at the Rabat Institute of Higher Studies, a department of the University of Bordeaux. He received the law degree from this university in 1951 and in 1952 the Diploma of Higher Studies corresponding to the Master of Arts degree. After independence he gradually became the king's principal representative and adviser. When Hassan II, at the age of thirty-two, succeeded as king on March 3, 1961, he had been well prepared. His legal, political, and military training, the combination of modern and classicial education he had received, and the experiences shared with his father and the nation enabled him to assume Mohammed V's role with a firm hand.

In 1960 Hassan II married Lala Latifa, a member of a leading Moroccan family. They have five children: Crown Prince Mulay Sidi Mohammed, born on August 21, 1963, three daughters, and a second son, Prince Mulay Rachid, born on June 20, 1970. The king's brother, Prince Mulay Abdullah, has actively assisted in various governmental affairs, including cabinet posts, and his sisters, Princess Lala Aisha and Princess Lala Fatima, have been active in public representation. In 1971 the latter was president of the National Union of Moroccan Women (Union Nationale des Femmes Marocaines—UNFM).

GOVERNMENT AND EXECUTIVE AGENCIES

The Prime Minister and Council of Ministers

The prime minister and the individual ministers together form the Council of Ministers, or cabinet. Collectively, they are constitutionally designated and referred to, in the European manner, as "the government." They are appointed and may be dismissed by the king and are responsible both to him and to the House of Representatives. The Constitution does not prescribe the number of ministries or any specific identifications except for the prime minister, and the composition of the cabinet is thus a royal prerogative. The king, at the time of appointment of a new government, habitually makes a policy address providing his guidance. The prime minister is then required to go before the House of Representatives and present the program he intends to carry out. The government is responsible for enforcement of the law and controls the administration.

The prime minister, as head of the government, coordinates the activities of the various ministries. He has the right, after discussion in the cabinet, to introduce draft bills into the House of Representatives. He countersigns laws, except those having to do with the basic royal powers, and may initiate and issue administrative directives under powers delegated him by Article 29 of the Constitution. In this case, the concurrence of the minister who will be charged with their execution is required. The prime minister may ask the House of Representatives for a vote of confidence. If the vote is negative he and all the ministers of his government are required to submit their resignations to the king. A House vote of censure has the same result. Ministers may simultaneously be members of the House and of the cabinet.

King Hassan has frequently changed one or more ministers without changing the prime minister and the government as a whole. The length of cabinet tenure has been generally less than two years. Changes have usually been made, especially since 1963, within a relatively small group of executives known for their loyalty and their experience in administration. The king has frequently consulted with ministers on an individual basis, using the council as a body of advisers somewhat like the council of *wazara* (executive officials of the sultan—plural of *wazir*) of the old *makhzan* (see Glossary). On August 17, 1971, however, Hassan II, under Article 29 of the Constitution, delegated extensive administrative power and responsibility to the government, a development likely to change the mode of cabinet functioning.

The Civil Service

The bureaucracy played a major role, exceeded only by the throne, in assuring national stability in the transition period of decolonization. Through the succession of cabinet crises, rural rebellions, border conflicts, political tensions, and strikes that disturbed the order of Moroccan society, the civil service continued to carry out the routine business of government, remaining loyal and relatively apolitical. Patterned after the French model established during the protectorate, the civil service replaced foreign personnel with Moroccans more rapidly than in other sectors of national life, except for the Ministry of Justice.

The bureaucracy established by the French to run the country under their colonial protectorate was a revolutionary innovation in Moroccan governmental experience, and by 1934 it had spread itself into every corner of the land. This bureaucracy provided a lucrative career field for the French, who occupied most positions of importance while in general relegating Moroccan employees to the lower grades and menial tasks. By the end of 1955 some 35,000 French were imbedded in the governmental system. In the four and a half decades of protectorate administration close links developed at all levels between the civil service and the private sector. Pork-barrel politics and the arrogance of office set a style for the bureaucracy that, in addition to modernized organizational forms, inevitably influenced administration after independence.

The public administration became the first major wage-earning group to benefit from independence; with the transformation of the administrative elite, position in the bureaucracy became a mark of prestige. Although exact and agreed figures were not available, informed estimates indicated that by 1970 the 35,000 French of 1955 had been reduced to less than 8,000; in the same period Moroccan civilians employed in the government service increased from about 12,000 to about 96,000.

By 1960 the Istiqlal Party, never able to displace Mohammed V as the symbol of national independence, had been split by the defection of the UNFP, and the king completed his consolidation and centralization of the power of appointment and patronage. In 1961 the UNFP and its ally the UMT attempted to generate a civil service strike, but the effort, securing partial support from employees of only two ministries, failed badly. When the three Istiqlal members resigned from the government in January 1963, the last party challenge to royal control of the government apparatus came to an end.

Since that time the emphasis has been on individual loyalty and apolitical routine management, producing a high degree of self-protection, security, routine competence, and continuity in the offices of chiefs of service (*chefs de service*) and below, with a recurring higher level rotation, or flux, of ministers and directors among a limited loyal elite. Basically, according to observers, this was simply the traditional system of the old preprotectorate sultanate, modernized in the style of the French example. Being essentially dependent, it was stable but also low in administrative vigor and vulnerable to collusion and corruption at all levels. The Istiqlal press complained in 1970 that, although the Constitution forbade the device of single-party rule, the administrative bureaucracy was actually the single party of the regime.

Civil service pay in all steps of the career grades has been frozen since 1960 and has never been high; this factor was at the base of much of the petty corruption in the service. That King Hassan was well aware of the problem as part of the national problem of wages and prices, as well as of government efficiency, was shown by his indication in early 1971 of an impending salary increase. The king's motive, accelerated by the events of July and August 1971, has been reform and rejuvenation within the system.

During the decade of 1960–70 five state-operated institutes were opened for government service training: the Mohammedia Engineering School, the Institute of Statistics and Applied Economics, the Kenitra School for Managers ("cadres"), the Hassan II Institute of Agronomy, and the Moroccan School of Administration. The programs at these institutions were designed to produce skillful, nonpolitical technicians for the career civil service. Their ultimate effect had not yet had time to be seen by late 1971.

The Higher Council for National Promotion and Planning

The urgent requirement for national development in a newly independent nation led to the formation in 1957 of a separate body, called the Higher Council for National Promotion and Planning, having quasi-executive and legislative attributes and free from many of the limitations of ordinary cabinet administration. This organization was constitutionally established in 1962 and again by Articles 89–92 of the Constitution of 1970. It is presided over by the king, and its composition is fixed by law to include certain ministers, technical advisers, and appointed union representatives. The draft plan drawn up by the staff is considered by the plan council and by the Council of Ministers.After approval by the Council of Ministers, it is presented to the House of Representatives for approval, where budgetary allocations are made (see ch. 11, Character and Structure of the Economy).

LEGAL SYSTEM, JUDICIARY, AND COURTS

At independence, the confusion resulting from the existence of several legal systems, each of which had its own court system, necessitated the creation of a unified legal structure and court system. The major portion of this reorganization had been carried out by 1958 without political complications.

Traditional Islamic law, Berber customary law, rabbinical law, and the French and Spanish legal codes of the protectorate were brought together into a hybrid system that maintains the distinction between modern law and court systems and the traditional secular and religious systems that are still a part of Moroccan culture. In the traditional sector of the society the *sharia* (Islamic law) continued to function, although gradually being integrated into the modern law system. In the modern sector statute law is used, combining elements of the French legal code system of the protectorate with some practices of Islamic law as established under the *makhzan*.

The implementation of this legal reorganization was begun by divesting the *caid* (local administrator—see Glossary) of all judicial functions. The Berber decree of 1930 that had institutionalized the Berber customary law courts was revoked in 1956, and Berber courts were replaced by *cadi* (Islamic law courts) (see ch. 3, Historical Setting). Hebrew law continued to apply to personal status questions in the Jewish community. The monumental task of rewriting a comprehensive legal code, which involved modernizing many traditional practices, was accomplished with relative speed. A new code of personal status, concerning the family, marriage, divorce, and inheritance, was compiled and promulgated in 1958. Despite pressure from progressive elements for a more rapid Westernization of law, many elements of the *sharia* were retained in the code, revealing the continuing influence of traditionalist thinking. A reformed penal code was published in February 1959, unifying criminal law and procedure and increasing the protection of the citizen against police errors and abuse. Under the code, the individual is presumed innocent until proved guilty, may not be held in police custody for more than forty-eight hours without indictment, and is guaranteed the right to legal counsel. Four classes of crimes are defined, with maximum penalties prescribed for each, and the jurisdiction of the various levels of courts is fixed.

Moroccanization, the replacement of foreign civil servants by Moroccan personnel, occurred somewhat more rapidly in the judiciary than in other sectors. This was due in part to the high number, compared with other professions, of Moroccan lawyers; law has been the favored subject for study by students from the Moroccan upper classes as preparation for entry into politics and public service. After independence it appeared that more than a third of university students were in this field.

In June 1964 Parliament voted to terminate all courts established under the protectorate. In the reorganized court system, Muslims appear before *cadi*, Jews before rabbinical courts, and foreigners before courts of first instance for matters of personal status. For penal, civil, and commercial questions, two parallel lines of jurisdiction exist: the traditional, functioning in the rural areas and old cities, incorporates the *sadad* (conciliation) courts, and the modern, operating in the Europeanized cities, such as Rabat and Casablanca, comprises courts of peace (*triunaux de paix*) and courts of first instance. Functioning in the modern line are labor courts, established in 1957 to arbitrate disputes arising in commerce, industry, agriculture, and the professions. Traditional, modern, and labor courts are under four courts of appeal, located in Rabat, Tangier, Fes, and Marrakech.

At the top of Morocco's court system, the Supreme Court—the highest court of appeals—is divided into five chambers: criminal, correctional (civil) appeals, abrogation and revision, administrative, and constitutional, numbered in that order. The administrative chamber deals with abuses of authority by administrative agencies. The constitutional chamber, provided for in the Constitution of 1962, determines the constitutionality of organic laws before their promulgation, decides disputes over location of powers, approves the internal rules of the House as to constitutionality, and oversees the regularity of elections and referenda. It consists of four members including its presiding officer, the first (senior) president of the Supreme Court.

Two other organs of Morocco's judicial structure are the Higher Council of the Magistracy and the High Court. The former regulates and disciplines the judiciary and ensures its guarantees. It is presided over by the king, with ten other members, four royally appointed and six elected within the judiciary. The High Court, sometimes called the High Court of Justice but not so named in the Constitution, decides on abuses of power and corruption in the government. Charges against a minister may be made by a secret ballot and a two-thirds majority in the House. The president of this court is royally appointed. The number of other members and their procedures are set by law; they are elected by the House of Representatives.

The basic judicial structure is stated in Articles 75-85 and 93-95 of the Constitution of 1970, specifying the independence of the judiciary, the rendering of judgments in the name of the king, the royal appointment of judges based on the recommendations of the Higher Council of the Magistracy, and the establishment of that council, the High Court, and the constitutional chamber. Detailed procedures for all bodies are promulgated by implementing decree; administration of the system is under the minister of justice, who is also vice president of the Higher Council of the Magistracy and head of the National Institute of Judiciary Studies, established by royal decree on January 29, 1970. The public prosecution is conducted under the king's attorney general in the Supreme Court and lower echelons.

LEGISLATIVE ARM AND THE ELECTORAL SYSTEM

The unicameral legislature is called the House of Representatives, also often given in English as the Chamber of Representatives. Within the structure of the House, multiple forms of representation were utilized: directly, by geographical electoral district; indirectly, from the councils of provincial and local government; and functionally, through professional chambers and unions.

Constitutional Organization and Powers of the House

The Constitution of 1970 provides for national election of the House of Representatives, specifying that the right to vote is personal and cannot be delegated. Freedom of expression and legal immunities of representatives during session and recess are delineated; critical challenge of the royalist system or Islam and disrespect for the king, however, are not permitted and, in general, legal immunity does not extend to any member caught in the act of a crime or misdemeanor.

The House of Representatives is required to hold two sessions annually: the first, commencing on the second Friday of October, is opened by the king; the second commences on the second Friday in April. Sessions lasting more than two months may be terminated by royal decree without dissolving the House. An extraordinary session for a special agenda may be called by decree or by an absolute majority of the members.

All government ministers may attend meetings of the House and of the committees by which its work is prepared. Meetings of the House are open to the public, and the record of discussion, like laws, is published in full in the *Official Bulletin*. Closed sessions may be held at the request of the prime minister or one-third of the representatives. The House makes its own rules of procedure by vote, subject to constitutional review by the Supreme Court.

Representatives are chosen for a term of six years, part by direct universal suffrage and part indirectly by electoral colleges of the communal councils and separate electoral colleges of the professional associations and wage earners. The Constitution does not specify the total number of representatives, the numbers in the representational categories, or the conditions of eligibility and method of election. These matters are required to be set forth in an organic law. The president and officers of the House are elected annually by the House, in proportion to participating groups, at the beginning of the October session. In September 1971 the president of the House chosen in the elections of August 21 and 28 continued to be the former foreign minister, Abdul Hadi Boutaleb. On October 11 Mahdi Ben Bouchta was elected president, replacing Boutaleb, who had announced his intended resignation at the beginning of the session.

The House of Representatives legislates by voting and, in some circumstances, can delegate authority to the prime minister and the government to issue decree laws. It has competence to legislate on individual and collective rights, principles of legal codes, the creation of courts, and basic matters pertaining to civil and military personnel of the government. It approves the budget and the development plan but cannot later change them. If the general budget is not approved by December 31, the government proceeds as if it were.

The king, the prime minister, and members of the House of Representatives all may introduce draft bills. The government is answerable to the House, and one meeting per week may be scheduled by the secretariat for the questioning of ministers. The failure of a vote of confidence motion to gain an absolute majority in the House or the passage of a no-confidence motion or vote of censure by an absolute majority causes the collective resignation of the prime minister and ministers. Only one censure vote may be passed in one year.

The Organic Law and Electoral System

The organic law pertaining to the membership and election of the House of Representatives, and implementing the Constitution, was promulgated as royal decree No. 1-70-206 of July 31, 1970, published in the *Official Bulletin* on August 1, 1970. This law, in addition to its own provisions, contains citations to numerous related decrees dealing with elections and constituent bodies. It provides that the House of Representatives shall consist of 240 members, of whom ninety shall be elected by direct universal suffrage, ninety shall be elected within the framework of the prefectures and provinces by assemblies or colleges of communal councilmen, and sixty shall be elected by colleges in the chambers of commerce and industry and in agriculture, crafts, and wage earners' unions. The professional and wage earners' unions seats were allocated as follows: agriculture, twenty-four; commerce and industry, sixteen; crafts, ten; wage earner representatives, ten. The ninety communal council seats were separately divided by proportion among the nineteen provinces and two prefectures.

Those eligible to vote in the direct election include Moroccans of both sexes over twenty-one years of age who are registered on the communal election lists; for the representatives in the other categories, additional factors of eligibility are determined by the bodies concerned. Candidates for the House must be citizens of at least twenty-five years of age at the date of election, registered voters, and members of the particular constituency from which they are seeking election. Certain categories of persons are not eligible to vote or run for office. Disqualification procedures are prescribed, as are definitions of the limits of incompatibility between status as a representative and other activities, and punishments for falsification or commercial exploitation of office are set forth. Detailed procedures required for the declaration of candidacy are also spelled out.

Articles 28 through 52 of the decree establish in extensive detail procedures regulating campaigning for and conduct and discipline of elections, maintaining electoral lists, opening and closing polls, counting votes at local and national levels, handling records, publishing results, and processing complaints and appeals. Single-member electoral districts for the direct vote segment are designated by separate decree. The machinery for election management and observation is highly organized and is administered under the minister of interior, provincial governors, and the representational chambers. The principle of voting is the secret written ballot, with color codes for the illiterate.

Reports from all polling stations and intermediate reviews must end up with the Constitutional Chamber of the Supreme Court in Rabat, where the national and final certification is made by a commission composed of the president of the constitutional chamber, a judge of the administrative chamber, and the minister of interior. Each party list may be represented by one delegate to the commission. Elections may be partially or fully nullified if one or more of the following conditions prevailed: if the election was not conducted in the manner prescribed by law, if voting was not free, if there was fraud, or if an elected person was found to be legally incapacitated.

LOCAL GOVERNMENT

Constitutional Provisions for Local Government

The Constitution of 1970 deals with local government under three short articles, with only minor changes in wording from the corresponding articles in the document of 1962. As in other categories of government description, delineation of details is left to be "created by law," meaning, in effect, by royal decree. Articles 86 and 87 state that the kingdom's local communities are the prefectures, provinces, and communes and additional communities as created by law. The communities elect councils, or assemblies, to manage their affairs democratically in accordance with conditions determined by law. Article 88 directs that in the prefectures and provinces the governors shall execute the decisions of the prefecture and provincial assemblies. Governors also coordinate administrative activity and watch over the application of the laws.

Evolution and Structure of Local Government

The principal characteristic of regional administration during the protectorate period was a highly centralized authority leading from the resident general down to the district officers in the military and civil zones. A double structure of European administrators and Moroccan officials appointed by the Europeans descended in parallel lines, but in every case ultimate power resided with the Europeans. At the lowest echelon the district officer reached the rural population through the Moroccan *caid*. After independence the double structure disappeared. Names of towns, titles of officials, and boundary lines changed, but the essential administrative system used under the protectorate remained as a hybrid system of European procedures adapted to Moroccan institutions, serving to bring the entire country under a single, central administration, after some initial rural turbulence from 1956 to 1959 (see ch. 3, Historical Setting; ch. 14, National Defense and Internal Security).

In the early years of independence the loose structure of rural administration imposed during the protectorate was modified to suit the requirements of a new nation. A major objective was the integration of Berber tribesmen into a national administrative system, attempted by rearranging rural administration on a basis of communal centers rather than tribes. In many rural areas this entailed bringing previously autonomous tribal leaders under the control of new administrators, who were often Istiqlal Party members from urban areas.

Under the administrative decrees of 1959 and 1960, implemented by the Ministry of Interior, the basic regional units are the constituency (*circonscription*), the circle, and the province. The constituency is based on the traditional unit of administration, the *caidat*. Constituencies are of two types, the rural and the urban, each of which exhibits hybrid characteristics of both traditional and French influence plus later accretions.

Administration in the rural constituency is headed by an official called the *caid*, whose functions are executive. (He does not have the judicial power of the old sultanic *caid*.) Subareas, or communes, under the rural *caid* are each administered by a *shaykh* (see Glossary); within each of these, the headman of a small village is called a *muqaddam*. There is no set geographical size for any of these divisions, their scope being determined by Ministry of Interior authority guided by custom and local conditions. Schematically, however, the structure is pyramidal and authoritarian. In the urban constituencies the senior official, parallel to the *caid*, is the *pasha* (governor, or mayor, of a city). Under him, administration of each municipal ward (*arrondissement*) is headed by a *khalif*.

The administrative level above the constituency is the circle, headed by a senior *caid*. It functions as an intermediate unit between the constituency and the province and has grouped under it two or more constituencies. Circles, in turn, are grouped under the nineteen provinces.

Although minor variations exist at the lowest level, the executive heads of the administrative chain from *muqaddam* to provincial governor are civil servants appointed usually by officials two levels higher upon recommendation from officials one level higher, but ultimately by royal authority. Each position, therefore, constitutes a key point of contact between the throne and all parts of the kingdom. The minister of interior, at the national level, is responsible for directing and administering the whole structure.

Partly because of the closeness of his contacts with the central government and partly because of his power, the governor of a province is one of the most highly regarded officials in government. He has a triple responsibility: to the king, whose direct representative he is; to the minister of interior, for the administration of the entire province; and to the representative provincial assembly, the decisions of which on social and economic questions he must consider for approval. The governor's functions include overseeing and executing the decisions of the provincial assemblies and coordinating provincial projects among various ministries. He receives local budgets from the *caids* and *pashas* and presents them, as well as the provincial budget, to the minister of interior for approval. He is usually consulted by the minister of interior before bills relevant to his province are taken up by the cabinet. Periodically, governors meet in conference with the king, thus assuring royal control and coordination.

Morocco's two largest cities, Rabat and Casablanca, are classed separately as prefectures, on the same administrative level as the provinces. Their *pashas*, at once governors and mayors, are appointed by, and therefore directly responsible to, the king. They are charged with overseeing and coordinating all administrative services as well as supervising the activities and executing the decisions of the prefectural assembly. A political and social service oversees the affairs of the wards into which the prefectures are organized for administrative purposes. A general secretariat for administrative and technical affairs coordinates urban planning and prepares the budget for the *pasha*, who submits it to the Ministry of Interior. The urban communes in municipalities elsewhere in the country are organized and function essentially like Rabat and Casablanca.

A far-reaching reform in Moroccan local government was achieved by the long-prepared and frequently postponed elections of May 29, 1960, which established urban and rural communal councils in the communes of the constituencies. Local elections again were held in 1963 and 1969. In practice, the power of the councils is restricted to the deliberation of social and economic affairs of the commune. Political questions are expressly excluded by law. Councillors prepare and vote on the communal budget, but all decisions are subject to approval by the *caid*, who may change or insert items on the budget, as he may on the agenda. The relationship between the local councils and the officers of the administration was not yet well clarified in 1971, but the essential powers lay with the latter group.

Councillors are elected for six-year terms by direct universal suffrage. According to the size of the commune, the council may have as many as fifty members. Its president, the highest elected official of the commune, is chosen from among them by secret ballot; he presents the budget, applies the decisions of the council, and represents the commune in court. Public sessions are held four times a year for two weeks each. As the representative of the central government, the *caid* or *pasha* attends all council sessions, and all decisions made by councillors are subject to his approval, as are all items on the agenda and in the budget.

Institutions of representative government on the provincial level, initiated by the assembly elections of October 1963, have little political weight, like the communal councils, but do exercise slightly wider legislative powers. Like the communal councils, the provincial assemblies vary in size according to the population of the province. In each province, assemblymen are chosen by communal councillors from among their own members. In addition to the elected assemblymen, one representative is chosen from each provincial chamber of agriculture, commerce, industry, and handicrafts.

Assembly sessions are held publicly, in the spring for two weeks and for three weeks in the fall, when the provincial budget is debated. The minister of interior, upon consultation with the governor, may dissolve the assembly. The agenda is established by the president, in cooperation with the assembly and the governor, although the minister of interior may include any items he sees fit. The budget is prepared by the governor and then submitted to the appropriate commission within the assembly where it is voted on; only after the approval of the minister of interior can it be enacted.

Municipal and communal elections were held nationwide on October 3, 1969, for the first time since 1963. Neutral or independent nonopposition candidates won 9,199 seats out of 11,166 contested. The opposition parties together won only seventy seats as compared to 850 in the 1963 elections and were thus swept aside at the local level.

Regions, Provinces, and Prefectures in 1971

A new development and further expansion of the consultative council device appeared in the designation in mid-1971 of seven administrative regions, each encompassing two to four provinces or prefectures. All the current nineteen provinces and both prefectures were included (see table 1). Announcement of the regions was made by decree No. 1-71-71 of June 16, 1971, published in the *Official Bulletin* on June 23. Under this decree, a regional consultative council is to be formed in each region to advise the government on all programs of social and economic development. The council is to be kept informed on the progress of development programs in its region and can request from pertinent authorities all necessary information on progress and problems. It can then make suggestions concerning implementation.

Table 1. Administrative Regions, Provinces, and Prefectures of Morocco, 1971

Region Number	Region	Components*
1	Southern	Agadir
		Tarfaya
		Ouarzazate
2	Tansilt	Marrakech
		Safi
3	Central	Al Jadida
		Settat
		Khouribga
		Beni Mellal
		Casablanca
4	Northwestern	Tangier
		Tetouan
		Kenitra
		Rabat-Salé
5	North-Central	Fes
		Taza
		Al Hoceima
6	Eastern	Nador
		Oujda
7	South-Central	Meknès
		Ksar al Souk

* Rabat-Salé and Casablanca are prefectures; all others are provinces.

Source: Adapted from Laws, Statutes, etc., of Morocco, U.S. Department of Commerce, Office of Technical Services, Joint Publications Research Service—JPRS (Washington), *Translations on North Africa*, "Decree No. 1-71-77, 16 June 1971, 'Creation of Administrative Regions'," *Bulletin Official*, Rabat, February 4, 1970, (JPRS:50,196, Series No. 882, March 31, 1970).

What executive arrangement would prevail in these regions was not clear. It was expected that one of the governors in each region would initially be designated as senior governor for regional purposes. Because of the coup attempt of July 10, 1971, the change of government on August 6, the military and security reorganizations underway, and the high priority of the reform program directed by King Hassan, it seemed unlikely to observers that rapid implementation of the new regional level of government would take place.

PARTIES, INTEREST GROUPS, AND ELECTIONS

Postindependence Party Development

On the eve of independence Mohammed V received delegations from all political elements in the country except the Communists. Of the four political parties that had cooperated in the struggle for independence three remained after independence: the Istiqlal, the Democratic Independence Party (Parti Démocratique de l'Indépendance—PDI), and the Party of Moroccan Unity (Parti de l'Unité Marocaine—PUM). The PDI reorganized in 1959, forming a new group, the Constitutional Democratic Party (Parti Démocratique Constitutionnel—PDC), and the PUM played no further significant role in politics after independence. The fourth group, the Islah (National Reform Party) of Abdel Torres in the Spanish zone, merged with the Istiqlal when Moroccan independence was achieved (see ch. 3, Historical Setting).

The Istiqlal's objective of forming a single-party government was obstructed not only by Mohammed V but also by the other parties and by newer forces, such as the labor movements, forming in the society. Consequently, the Istiqlal had to share portfolios in the first cabinet with the PDI and the Liberal Independents. The latter group, not formally a party, had coalesced in the late 1930s around Rashid Mouline and the "grey eminence," Guédira, a staunch supporter of both Mohammed V and, later, Hassan II, and a member of many cabinets.

The Istiqlal and, in general, the national political movement that had achieved independence were mainly Arab and urban. Many of the leaders came from the traditionalist inland cities, such as Fes, and from families of moderate wealth. It was to this group that most of the early fruits of independence went rather than to the large majority of rural Moroccans.

It was not surprising, therefore, that the first new political group to appear after independence in competition with the Istiqlal would seek to represent the interests of the countryside. The integration of the rural sector into the nation was begun at its own demand. There was apparently no direct connection between the new political party and the rural uprisings of 1957 and 1958, but its very existence gave a voice to the numerically important agricultural sector for the first time. Operating clandestinely in the mountains after 1957, the rural party survived both guilt by association with the rebellious Berber tribesmen and attacks by the Istiqlal in 1958 to register officially in February 1959 as a political party known as the Popular Movement (Mouvement Populaire—MP).

Friction within the Istiqlal, some aspects of which were publicly evident in 1958, became open in January 1959, when its younger, radical left wing became a party calling itself at first the "confederated" or "true" Istiqlal. This split was of central importance to the evolution of Moroccan politics for it marked the end of the widespread allegiance the Istiqlal had enjoyed since 1956 and of its hopes of becoming the single party in Morocco.

In September 1959 the confederated or "democratic" Istiqlal formally constituted itself the National Union of Popular Forces (Union Nationale des Forces Populaires—UNFP), which defined itself as neither a party in the traditional sense nor a front but a new organization whose structure and élan would no longer be based on personalities but on ideology—an essentially socialist ideology propounded by its leader, Ben Barka.

The dynamism and the radical program of the new UNFP attracted those who had been frustrated in the lower ranks of the Istiqlal, labor leaders, and many from other parties. They represented a faction of the Istiqlal that saw little in the program of social reform through traditionalist Islam, irredentist nationalism, and royalism that was relevant to the problems of national development in 1959. The UNFP leaders' talk of socialism at home and radical neutralism abroad appealed to those who, unlike many of the first generation of nationalists, felt that independence was not the ultimate goal but only the beginning of a new social order.

The popular approval of the Constitution of 1962 by referendum was a turning point in the political evolution of Morocco. The UNFP, however, complained that the king neglected party positions in drafting the document, that the new system formalized an excessive concentration of power in the hands of the executive, and that the referendum campaign was calculated to exclude from power those who differed with the king. The UNFP's ineffective attempt to boycott the referendum during the campaign was brushed aside by overwhelming popular support for the king. In addition to this disastrous defeat, the UNFP severely alienated its strongest allies, the labor unions, which refused to participate in the boycott.

The Istiqlal, which had backed the king during the referendum campaign, withdrew its support one month later in protest against the handling of the referendum. The three Istiqlal ministers in the government resigned, and the Istiqlal went into the opposition. This move prompted the formation of an electoral alliance among progovernment parties—the mass-based MP and Guédira's following among the Liberal Independents and the PDC—to secure a majority in the parliamentary elections of 1963. These groups joined in March 1963 to form a loose electoral alliance, the Front for the Defense of Constitutional Institutions (Front pour la Défense des Institutions Constitutionnelles—FDIC). Desirous of consolidating the government's advantage won in the referendum three months earlier and wary of an opposition now fortified by the Istiqlal and the prestige of its scholar-leader, Allal al Fassi, members of the FDIC readied themselves for the five elections, scheduled to take place between May and October 1963, that would create the institutions of representative government authorized by the Constitution.

In the first and most important election, conducted on May 17, 1963, for the House of Representatives, the FDIC obtained only a plurality, winning sixty-nine of the 144 seats; the UNFP won twenty-eight; and the Istiqlal, forty-one. Six seats were taken by unaffiliated members. The elections were immediately protested by both parties of the opposition—the UNFP and, since January, the Istiqlal—chiefly because the leader of the FDIC, Guédira, as minister of interior, controlled all electoral procedures. The UNFP was further alienated by the government's arrest of 130 of its leaders in July 1963 on charges of conspiring to assassinate the king and overthrow the regime. Newly elected UNFP members of Parliament were arrested and held in violation of immunity privileges, and the penal code was retroactively applied. These and other irregularities led the UNFP to withdraw its candidates and boycott the four remaining electoral contests. The absence of the major opposition party helped the FDIC in the subsequent elections, as did the proregime sentiment galvanized by the war on the Algerian frontier during the last elections, in October 1963. In March 1964 the government won its case in the UNFP trial. The party, publicly discredited, almost disappeared (see ch. 3, Historical Setting).

By October 1963 all the constitutionally authorized institutions were created and, just before the opening of Morocco's first elected Parliament in November, the king resigned from the position of prime minister, which he himself had occupied since 1961. He appointed Ahmad Bahnini, minister of justice in the preceding government, prime minister over a cabinet drawn exclusively from members of the FDIC and unaffiliated politicians. The two opposition parties, because of the need for national unity during the border war then current with Algeria, muffled their accusations of electoral illegalities and took their seats in Parliament.

After the elections of October 1963, which gave the FDIC 107 out of the 120 seats in the upper house of Parliament, or Chamber of Councillors, the FDIC began to break up. Guédira, who had formed the FDIC only a year before in order to defeat the opposition parties, now formed the Democratic Socialist Party (Parti Socialist Democrate—PSD) in April 1964. The party's name, however, was a misnomer for it was not, in fact, socialist.

By early 1965 the political parties experienced a decline in public confidence, and the failure of the government to alleviate the country's critical economic problems contributed to the spread of a general disillusionment with the regime as well. Morocco was in the throes of an economic and political crisis that had been in the making for more than a year. Economically, the crisis was characterized by increasing unemployment, rising living costs, declining production in the agricultural sector, and the continuing inability of the government to remedy any of these problems.

Related to and complicating the economic situation was a political stagnation that had persisted for eighteen months since the opening of the country's first Parliament. Finally, the situation erupted in the Casablanca riots of March 1965 (see ch. 3, Historical Setting). King Hassan, after a palliative general amnesty of political prisoners, endeavored to form a new national front government of all parties. This effort failing, he then invoked his emergency powers under Article 35 of the Constitution of 1962, and the 1965–70 period of direct rule began.

In Morocco's vigorous multiparty system, party leaders have participated actively in the affairs of the nation, and party newspapers, although subject to periodic suspension and seizure, enjoy some degree of freedom and diversity of opinion. Parties tend to be relatively nonideological, excluding the Communists and, perhaps, the UNFP, which inclines toward Marxian explanations and socialistic pronouncements. Political alignments are made on a pragmatic basis, and personalities are as important as issues. Hence, parties tend to revolve around a handful of leaders, whose followings cut across all sectors of the social spectrum. The political elite numbers no more than a thousand individuals, forming a close, if not closed, group of friends and enemies whose intimacy at once facilitates communication among allies and exacerbates rivalries. Parties in Morocco cannot be defined with precision in terms of left and right because of the diversity of their membership and the changing character of their policies. At the time of King Hassan's assumption of emergency powers in 1965, and so continuing in 1971, the political parties could best be classified into those opposing and those supporting the king.

In 1965 the opposition consisted of three main elements. The Istiqlal, founded in 1944 and headed by the esteemed Allal al Fassi, was the oldest and largest. Long featured by a high degree of cell and party organization, its leadership was essentially urban middle class. The UNFP, founded in 1959 and by 1970 headed by Abdullah Ibrahim and Abdul Rahim Bouabid, was Marxian socialist in character. The Moroccan Communist Party (Parti Communiste Marocain—PCM), headed by Ali Yata since its founding from French origins in 1944, was prohibited in independent Morocco, as it had been under the French, but enjoyed periods of comparative toleration. Definitely an opposition party, the PCM was occasionally able to make temporary expedient alliances with parts of the UNFP or Istiqlal or their affiliates in the labor and student movements. In mid-1965 it was small and almost extinguished. By 1970 its membership was estimated at only 400, with 2,000 to 3,000 other adherents.

Supporting the king was the loose FDIC alliance of four parties: the rural-based MP, founded in 1959 and headed by Mahjoub Ahardane and Haddan Abarkash; the PDC, formed in 1959 from the older PDI, headed by Mohammed Wazzani and Mohammed Sharkawi; the PSD, formed in 1964 and headed by Guédira, who was also ostensible leader of the FDIC; and the remnants of the old Liberal Independents of Mouline. Of these, the MP was by far numerically the strongest.

During the royal rule of the 1965-70 period political party activity continued at low key and under close government observation. Certain party changes and modifications occurred. The FDIC alliance broke up into its component parts. The influence of Guédira and, with him, the PSD declined. In July 1968 the PCM formed a front organization called the Party of Liberation and Socialism (Parti de Liberation et Socialisme—PLS) and registered it as a legal party. In September 1969, however, the government, recognizing the PLS simply as the PCM in disguise, banned it and its publications also and sent Yata to jail for several months. On the whole, when King Hassan announced in July 1970 that a new constitutional referendum and elections would be held, the basic alignments of opposition and royalists that had solidified in 1965 were still in effect, and these continued in 1971.

Labor and Youth Movements

Labor is the most powerful pressure group in Morocco. Organized in 1955 by Mahjub Ben Sadiq, the Moroccan Labor Union (Union Marocain du Travail—UMT) accounted for one-third the membership of the Istiqlal in 1956 and within the year increased its enrollment to an estimated 400,000. Like the parties, the labor federation soon developed its own affiliates such as the Moroccan Worker-Youth (Jeunesse Ouvriere Marocain—JOM) and the Progressive Union of Moroccan Women (Union Progressiste des Femmes Marocaines—UPFM). In 1961 it formed the Federation of Farmers' Unions (Union des Syndicats Agricoles—USA), unionizing for the first time thousands of farmworkers.

The UMT has at no time been a mere appendage of a political party but has always moved on the perimeters of politics and has been a frequent critic of both the government and the parties. Although it insists upon its independence from each, it has played an important role in both. The UMT has frequently been consulted by the king and has been represented in key government agencies. The power of labor is not confined to formal participation on the fringes of government. Its strike capacity can at any time paralyze Moroccan industry, but in 1971 the extent of urban unemployment appeared to have weakened this weapon.

The growth of Morocco's major labor movement followed that of the major political party, splitting into progressive and conservative wings in 1959 and 1960. The UMT found itself closer to the UNFP and withdrew its support of the Istiqlal. Hoping to recover its losses, the Istiqlal founded its own labor affiliate in 1960, the Union of Moroccan Workers (Union Generale des Travailleurs Marocains—UGTM) under its secretary general, Hachem Amine; this group has been moderately successful in certain regions and in various industries, but the UMT still commands the allegiance of the majority of workers. To counter losses to the UMT youth wing, the UGTM founded its own young workers' organization in 1962. As labor became increasingly political, disputes between the UGTM and the UMT sometimes broke into violence. After 1963, when the Istiqlal shared the opposition with the UNFP and the UMT declared its independence from that party, antagonism between the two labor wings diminished.

While the UGTM has remained loyal to the Istiqlal, the UMT has been more jealous of its autonomy, pulling away from the UNFP in late 1962 and formally declaring its dissociation from the party at its third national congress in January 1963. Although the move was based on the desire to keep free of any affiliation with a political party in order to maintain its own independence, Ben Sadiq insisted that the UMT had no intention of becoming uninterested in politics. Nevertheless, the UMT has continued to follow a policy that corresponds to that of the UNFP more than to that of any other political group.

Morocco's youth has been organized, with varying degrees of effectiveness, by the government, the parties, and labor groups. Each labor federation has its own youth wing, as do the two major opposition parties. By far the most active and politically significant element among Moroccan youth has been the university students, and student organizations, whether independent or affiliated with a party, constitute an active force in the political life of the nation. Enjoying more license than the opposition parties, they have sometimes been able to attack the government when parties or labor organizations could not.

The first significant student organization, the National Union of Moroccan Students (Union Nationale des Etudiants Marocains—UNEM), was founded in 1956 by Ben Barka, then in the Istiqlal. Paralleling its activity in the government, the Istiqlal secured near total control over the UNEM until its schism in 1959, when the student group remained uncommitted to either faction. Gradually, however, the progressive program of the new UNFP won over the UNEM, which remained closely associated with this party in 1965. Despite attempts by the government to restrict UNFP influence among youth, students from the secondary schools and in the universities both at home and abroad have remained generally sympathetic to its position. Alarmed by the students' drift toward the UNFP, the Istiqlal organized its own youth wing in 1962, the General

Union of Moroccan Students (Union Generale des Etudiants Marocains—UGEM).

Referendum and Elections of 1970

In the national referendum conducted on July 24, 1970, 4,536,407 voters participated, or 93.2 percent of the 4,869,168 voters registered, according to official figures. After discarding invalid ballots, the affirmative vote was found to be 4,443,561, or 98.8 percent approval, against only 55,101 negative votes. This overwhelming endorsement of the king's position made the elections to the House of Representatives, scheduled for the following month, virtually a foregone conclusion. Commenting upon the similar royal victory in the referendum of 1962, the North African analyst W.A. Beling wrote in 1964: "The referendum results revealed what subsequent elections confirmed, that Hassan II and the monarchy constitute the principal factors of Moroccan unity and stability." This conclusion was again decisively confirmed by the referendum of 1970.

Immediately after the referendum, what was probably the most significant political party development since 1965 took place. The Istiqlal and UNFP, both of whom had ineffectually campaigned for "no" votes on the referendum, announced on July 27, 1970, that they had formed the National Front (Al Kutla al Wataniya) to oppose the government. A central committee was to be the controlling device, and support from trade unions and students was claimed. Also, Yata of the banned PCM and PLS announced his endorsement of the opposition front and appeared to be endeavoring to align himself with it. By late 1971 the Istiqlal, still headed by Allal al Fassi, appeared to be leading the National Front, but it was by no means certain in Moroccan politics that this would continue. The Central Committee of the National Front was announced in this order as comprising Allal al Fassi; Ibrahim, president of UNFP; Boubakr Kadiri, Istiqlal; Mohammed Boucettar, Istiqlal; Bouabid, UNFP; Ben Sadiq, UMT-UNFP; Mohammed Labbabi, UNFP; and Mohammed Douiri, Istiqlal.

The parties of the National Front officially boycotted the communal-professional chamber electoral college elections on August 21, 1970, for 150 seats in the new House of Representatives and the direct general elections on August 28 for the balance of ninety seats. Nevertheless, some opposition party members, standing as individuals, were elected.

King Hassan and his supporters secured in these elections 221 of the 240 seats in the House as follows: neutral, or independent royalists, 159; the MP, sixty; and the PDC, two. The opposition parties secured nineteen seats, with eight to the Istiqlal, one to the UNFP, and ten to the Social Progress Party (Progres Social—PS), a new party from the trade unions. After these elections, the opposition parties called them illegal, alleging irregularities that the government denied. The new House of Representatives was convened on October 9, 1970.

POLITICAL STRESS AND CRISIS

Pressures for Change

By early 1970, before the referendum for the new Constitution and the elections of August, internal pressures for change were mounting, mostly through predictable channels, which had manifested themselves in the past among the opposition parties, labor, and students and which were becoming increasingly restless under the prolonged state of emergency. On Labor Day, May 1, 1970, the Istiqlal's Arabic newspaper *Al Alam* editorialized on the subjects requiring the attention of labor: increasing unemployment, burgeoning population growth, low wages and standard of living, inadequate educational facilities at all levels, slow development of agriculture and industry, oppression and inefficiency of the government bureaucracy, and political relegation of the working class and its organizations "on the sidelines as spectators." On the same day Allal al Fassi, speaking at UGTM headquarters, called for "termination of the state of emergency and building up of a true democracy." Also on May 1, 1970, the official UGTM statement of the day characterized Moroccan workers as living in a "gloomy and stormy atmosphere because of the lack of democratic institutions," called for an end to the emergency period, rejected the "theory of the elite," and, in different language, reiterated Allal al Fassi's stands calling for educational reform, adherence to Islam, Arabism, and the Arab language, and opposition to the "Zionist foe."

The Istiqlal editor of *L'Opinion*, Mohammed Berrada, was arrested on September 28, 1970, because of a news story pointing to maladministration in the army service forces. Despite a defense by fifty-three lawyers, he was convicted on October 25 and sentenced to six months in jail and a fine. He appealed the verdict and the sentence, which was then increased to twelve months. Before completing his sentence, he was released by royal amnesty. On November 16 Mohammed Yazghi, a leader of the UNFP, disappeared. Claims of other disappearances were advanced by the Istiqlal, amidst recollections of the Ben Barka affair (see ch. 3, Historical Setting). On November 28 six farmers were killed and others wounded near Kenitra in a melee with police and officials involving land sales. At the end of the year labor and student unrest again showed itself in the cities, although sustained strikes—the main political weapon of the opposition—were not feasible because of widespread urban unemployment.

Of further political significance in the security conscious, politically restive state in early 1971, and reminiscent of the plot and trials of the 1963–64 period, was the government's announcement on January 15 that 193 persons had been charged with plotting against the security of the state. Of the accused, 161 were under detention; thirty-two were to be tried in absentia. Among the latter were the UNFP leaders Mohammed Basri, reported by some sources to be in Iraq, and Yazghi, whose whereabouts were unknown. The plot, first detected in December 1969, allegedly involved contact with external radical Arab socialist movements such as the Baath (Resurrection) Party of the central Middle East. The trial, first scheduled to be held in a military court, opened on June 14, 1971, before the regional civil tribunal of Marrakech and ended on September 17. Although the prosecution had asked for forty-nine death sentences, only five were awarded. Of these, four were in absentia. Fifty-two of the accused were acquitted. The balance received sentences of imprisonment varying from six months to life.

Of all the sources of dissent and pressure for change, possibly the greatest, however, was the general complaint, not simply of stagnation, but of widespread corruption and malfeasance in government and government-related affairs. On November 19, 1970, in addressing the House of Representatives, Prime Minister Ahmed Laraki stated that bribery had become a "serious social disease" in Morocco and pledged a government attack on this condition. Earlier, on August 20, King Hassan observed with regret in a public address that integrity was becoming a "rare virtue" and that corruption existed on all sides—including "some in high places."

By mid-1971 measures directed at the principal economic, social, and administrative problems of the country had been undertaken, and all the legal and political forms of power, supported by tradition, were held by King Hassan and his supporters. The political opposition, however, remained alienated, insisting that progress was either too slow or nonexistent and maintaining their familiar demand for "democratic elections" and constitutional change as vociferously as the law and the watchful Ministry of Interior under General Oufkir would allow. To the public view, some minor changes of official position had again occurred among familiar figures in the recurring cycles of Moroccan elite politics. In what some analysts have called the Moroccan system of "balanced tensions," contending rival personalities seldom lost or won completely or permanently, and the throne was always the balance of power. The pressures for change had mounted, but so had the neutralizing pressures and power for stability. Some problems, such as education and Arabization, seemed virtually insoluble. Radical change had not occurred, and it was not clear how it could occur by constitutional and peaceful means.

The Attempted Coup d'Etat of July 10, 1971

Approximately 400 guests were assembled on July 10, 1971, at the royal seaside palace at Skhirat, fifteen miles southwest of Rabat, to celebrate King Hassan's birthday. The guests included Prime Minister Laraki and cabinet ministers, members of the diplomatic corps, and prominent Moroccans of official and private life. Among them were members of all political parties except the UNFP, including Allal al Fassi of Istiqlal and Abdulhadi Messouak, who had been associated with the PCM.

At about 2:00 P.M. the garden party came under sudden attack by troops employing small arms and grenades. King Hassan and General Oufkir withdrew to the private apartments of the palace. Outside, firing continued. The troops involved were all young and could be identified as noncommissioned officer trainees (widely reported as cadets) from the training center at Ahermoumou, about 135 miles east of Rabat.

Other rebel forces, meanwhile, under Colonel Mohammed Ababou, commandant of the Ahermoumou training center, seized the army headquarters in Rabat as well as the radio and television station. Rebel-controlled radio stations in both Rabat and Casablanca announced that a revolution was underway. The Rabat radio stated that King Hassan was dead and announced that "all responsibilities are deferred to the local military authorities," ending with the words "Long live the Republic." The Casablanca broadcast stated, "The army has just conducted a revolution for the people. The royal regime is abolished." None of these broadcasts, beyond proclaiming an army-sponsored republic for "the people," contained enough substantive content to show what sort of new regime was to be established.

About 2 ½ hours after the attack commenced, however, King Hassan reemerged from the royal apartments accompanied by a sergeant and several young soldiers. The troops present shouted "Long live Hassan the Second!" and the revolt began its precipitous collapse. As stated later by the king, he was informed by the sergeant that the troops had attacked the palace because they had been told the king was in danger. When they saw Hassan II, they put down their arms. Others, in confusion, mounted trucks and drove off to Rabat as ambulances began to arrive. King Hassan on the spot invested General Oufkir with full civil and military powers and commanded him to restore order. The diplomatic corps were freed to return to their embassies.

Moving immediately, General Oufkir found that communications were still responsive to him and that all regular troops and police, with the exception of the trainee attack unit from Ahermoumou and small elements in Casablanca, had remained loyal. The rebel group had called upon regular units, including the air force, to join the revolt but without avail. The counterattack was swift and became decisive by midnight. By noon on July 11 rebel elements had been mopped up. Soon afterwards General Oufkir announced that all those implicated were dead or in custody. Colonel Ababou of Ahermoumou was killed in the fighting.

Rabat quickly returned to usual surface patterns of life, but military forces remained on alert and took over the Casablanca port as part of the security operation. The reaction of the general public was passive on the whole because of the swiftness of events. Some public demonstrations had begun in various locations after the rebel broadcasts but quickly aborted because of the rapidity of the counteraction.

King Hassan addressed the nation by radio at 1:10 A.M. on July 11, thanking God and advising the population of his safety and the circumstances of the revolt. He identified General Mohammed Madbuh, killed on the afternoon of the attempted coup at the palace, as the coup leader of a group of officer conspirators not exceeding ten. He spoke of the dead and wounded, rich and poor, Moroccan and foreign, and then briefly described his deliverance upon being recognized by the deceived soldiers. This convinced him, he said, that the army was still sound. Citing the Libyan radio, which had broadcast support for the revolutionaries, he called upon the people to beware of troublemakers. The people, he said, would have been made orphans, but God had overcome the troublemakers.

Reaction to the Crisis

Messages of encouragement and congratulations on his survival quickly came in to Hassan II from the heads of state of most Arab and African nations, including Egypt but not Libya. On July 12 King Hassan, accompanied by King Husayn of Jordan, participated in the funeral of loyal officers and soldiers killed in the uprising. At 11:15 A.M. on July 13, after extensive interrogation, four generals, five colonels, and a major constituting the conspiracy leadership were executed by firing squad after decision by a ministerial war council headed by the king.

According to official figures, ninety-nine guests and staff personnel were killed and 133 wounded at Skhirat Palace; in Rabat and elsewhere 158 mutineers were killed, and about 900 were taken prisoner—all from the Ahermoumou training unit. Although the interrogations of the executed officers were not made public, government sources stated that the outburst was the work of "paranoid schizophrenics" who had grossly misled the noncommissioned officer trainees. The 900 prisoners were confined under continuing investigation but not treated in the same category as the executed officers.

General Oufkir, after returning from the executions on July 13, stated to the press that the plot had been in preparation for more than a year and that the principal leader was, in fact, Colonel Ababou rather than General Madbuh. He announced also that his special task was now finished, that his extraordinary powers were laid down, and that he was returning to his usual functions at the Ministry of Interior. The monarchy, he said, was the safeguard of unity, and only the king could head the country.

The executed generals, all of brigadier rank, were Khiati Bougrine, commanding the Fes-Taza Military Zone; Abdul Rahman Habibi, Marrakech Military Zone; Amazun Hammu, Rabat-Kenitra Military Zone; and Amirak Mustapha, commandant of the Royal Military Academy. Like General Madbuh, who had been the trusted chief of the Royal Military Household, all were regarded as right-wing conservative, austere, and honest disciplinarians. A common trait among them, according to international press commentators, was exasperation with the personality intrigues and influence traffic in all phases of public life generally included under the term *corruption*. Some were said to be impatient with any indications of liberalism or concession by the government to the political opposition, such as the king's effort to establish dialogue with students and the opposition in the conference at Ifrane in March 1970 (see ch. 7, Education, Communication, and the Arts and Sciences).

In the relatively small Moroccan military establishment, all senior officers had known each other long and well through many years of change and crisis since they were first in uniform. To what extent the coup attempt may have reflected intra-army power struggles and old personality conflicts was unknown. All the conspirators were of Berber origin, but so also were General Oukfir and a majority of the forces of all ranks. Particularly since independence, the ancient problem of Berber versus Arab, or *bilad al siba* (see Glossary) versus *bilad al makhzan* (see Glossary), has been better identifiable simply as rural versus urban politics, and, in any event, did not appear to be a major factor in the conspiracy.

The ultimate intentions of the conspirators, had they succeeded, as to the form of government or its foreign relations or the person of Hassan II were not definitely known. It was clear that the attempt was not a revolution of any radical ideology and that it developed from an internal source in the form of an essentially conservative, or puritanical, impulse to purify the government and national life. No evidence of actual foreign participation appeared, although the premature Libyan broadcasts of support after the attack was initiated resulted in the withdrawal of diplomatic missions by the two countries. More important, none of the well-identified opposition elements was involved—neither Istiqlal, nor the UNFP, nor the accused in the trial underway at Marrakech, nor labor, nor the student organizations. Among the neutralizing "balanced tensions" of Moroccan political, social, and economic life, the explosion of July 10, 1971, came from an unexpected direction and, as such, was symptomatic rather than determinant of the pressures for change.

King Hassan in public statements maintained that the intensity of opposition criticism had harmed national morale, and he cautioned opposition leaders that, if the coup attempt had succeeded, their situation, instead of being improved, would have been far worse. The noninvolvement of the organized political opposition, however, appeared to make possible a new effort for rapprochement. In an extensive interview with world press representatives on July 16, 1971, the king remarked: "I have come to realize that more seriousness, even strictness, by the state concerning the sphere of management and some fields of application of government policy will be necessary in the future. ... I again affirm that a change is going to take place. This will be in the means to be used, not in the democratic, social, and economic principles which Morocco, since its declaration of independence, has adopted."

Subsequently, Bouabid, a leader of the UNFP and chief defense counsel at the Marrakech trial, stated that a resumption of the dialogue between the monarchy and the opposition might now be possible, adding that the methods used by the government had thus far "resulted in stalemate." Allal al Fassi, who had been present at Skhirat on July 10 but was unhurt, observed that the abortive coup resembled old-time revolts against the sultans and emphasized that the rebel group had not made contact with either the Istiqlal or the UNFP. He said the attempted coup reflected the general malaise in the country and hoped that the lessons from it would lead to government reorientation in the direction of greater democracy.

NATIONAL GOALS

Hassan II's Assessment and Reform Program

On August 4, 1971, King Hassan, in a major address by radio, informed the nation that he had accepted the resignation of Prime Minister Laraki and his cabinet. Change was required, Hassan said, not in the fundamental principles of the nation but rather in means and emphasis. Article 29 of the Constitution specifically allows a wide delegation of royal powers to the prime minister and ministers. Although the heaviest and final responsibility still rested upon himself, the king announced that he would implement Article 29, abolish the post of director general of the royal, or personal, cabinet occupied by General Driss Slaoui, and hold ministers responsible for their performance. This statement was significant as indicating a limited withdrawal from the practice of direct royal rule. The new government, the king said, would have approximately eighteen months to draw up and implement a reform program centered in four related areas: education, distribution of the national wealth, administration, and justice. Speaking briefly on each of these, King Hassan decried the widened gap between rich and poor as intolerable, cited the need for improvement in land distribution and industrial organization, and was particularly emphatic on the "offense of corruption." The Quran, he said, is the true constitution, teaching equality and justice. He called also for reorganization of the judiciary so that "formal justice marked by great equity will be administered."

In the last section of his address the king recalled that in his speech on Youth Day, July 8, he had asked God for blessing and witness to the royal sincerity and love for the country's people. Then, he said: "Scarcely one day later, God supplied concrete proof of the sincerity of our speech. Thus did He spare us." Hassan called for harmonious national cooperation, with room for all "well-intentioned people ... without distinction between one faction or another."

In this important address, in addition to the announcements concerning the cabinet, several lines of analysis and a sense of urgency were apparent. Concentration of effort was to be on internal problems. Foreign policy, generally successful in the preceding five years, would not be changed, and no attempt was made to conceal internal difficulties by directing attention outward. King Hassan subjected himself to self-criticism and spoke in a strongly Islamic context virtually certain to be appealing to the mass of the Moroccan people. Because he was saved from the coup attempt, in remarkable circumstances and conceivably by the will of God, his link with the people as *imam* (spiritual leader) and commander of the faithful was reasserted and strengthened.

The Cabinet of August 6, 1971

The new government formed after the king's address of August 4 took the oath of allegiance on August 6, 1971, with Mohammed Karim Lamrani, the minister of finance in the previous government, as prime minister and minister of finance. The ministries and designees were: defense, and chief of staff of the armed forces, General Oufkir; justice, and secretary general of the cabinet, Bahnini; interior, Ahmad ben Boushta; foreign affairs, Abdul Latif Filali; higher, secondary, and technical education, Ahmad Laski; primary education, Haddou al Shigair; posts, telegraph, and telephone, General Driss Ben Omar Alami; agriculture and national development, Mati Jorio; religious endowments and Islamic affairs, Ahmad Bargash; public works and communications, Mohammed Burnousi; public health, Abdul Majid Ben Mahi; administrative affairs, Ahmad Majid Ben Jelloun; information, Abdul Qadir Sahrawi; and youth, sport, labor, and social affairs, Arsalan Jadidi. In addition, the posts of king's representative to the cabinet and director of the royal household, both of ministerial rank and occupied respectively by Ahmed Balafrej and Ahmad Osman, were retained. The office of director general of the royal cabinet was abolished, as were the four associated ministerial posts. In the government no nominations were made to the former ministries of maritime affairs, commerce, culture, and tourism; also, no ministers of state without portfolio were named.

As had been forecast by the king, the new cabinet was distinctly smaller than its predecessor, with seventeen ministers rather than twenty-eight. Reduced size indicated concentration for priority attention to the four-point program, as opposed to past diffusion. The personnel and functions of the disestablished ministries were presumably to be absorbed by the functionally related remaining ministries, but exactly how this would occur was not clear in early September 1971. Six members of the new cabinet held the same posts as in the previous one; five members of the preceding cabinet moved to different ministries in the new one. All members were familiar figures, well experienced in Moroccan politics, and royalist supporters.

Choice of the economist Lamrani as prime minister showed the emphasis to be placed in this area. The shift of General Oufkir from the Ministry of Interior, which he had headed since 1964, to the Ministry of Defense was of at least equal significance. Because the top military leadership had been decimated by the coup attempt and subsequent executions and in view of the critical importance of the armed forces' loyalty and effectiveness as the underlying source of power, General Oufkir's task was to scrutinize, reorganize, and retrain these forces. In speaking to the press, he postulated a new primary role for the armed forces as a socializing agency engaging in community action work.

The king had been ready to designate at least one minister from the Istiqlal and UNFP, and Bouabid of the UNFP remarked that there were in the king's address of August 4 "ideas which cannot be rejected." The Central Committee of the opposition National Front, however, declined to participate in the government and reiterated its familiar basic position calling for new elections and a "democratic constitution."

The delegation of powers promised by the king under Article 29 of the Constitution was formalized by decree on August 17, 1971, and announced at a meeting of the new Council of Ministers. King Hassan informed the new prime minister that eighteen months were allowed to implement the reform program. He described the delegation of powers as involving increased responsibility for ministers, individually and collectively, and stressed that "the administrative task has been entirely entrusted to the government." The cabinet showed early signs of response, among which was the announcement on August 29, 1971, by the minister of administrative affairs that a civil service reform law, replacing the old basic statute of 1950, had been approved by the cabinet and would be submitted to the House of Representatives in October.

Royal responsibilities and constitutional powers were not basically altered in the program of change. The king retained his constitutional rights to withdraw his delegation of powers, to appoint and dismiss the prime minister and ministers, to proclaim a state of emergency, to initiate popular consultation by referendum, to dissolve the House of Representatives, and to appoint the judiciary.

CHAPTER 9

FOREIGN RELATIONS

In late 1971 Morocco's foreign policy objectives continued to be concerned with the survival of the kingdom and its monarch, countering of foreign influence that might undermine the Alawite dynasty, procurement of significant amounts of economic and military aid and technical assistance for internal development and national security, adherence to the cause of the Arab states in the Arab-Israeli dispute, and technical nonalignment in cold war issues. Moroccan diplomats have sought to achieve these goals by active participation in the United Nations (UN) and its specialized agencies, the League of Arab States, the Organization of African Unity (OAU), and the Islamic Solidarity Bloc and by hosting numerous Arab, African, and Islamic conferences.

During the early years of independence, that is, from 1956 through the mid-1960s, key aspects of Morocco's foreign policy were based on its irredentist claims to parts of Algeria, Mauritania, the Spanish Sahara, and Mali. By 1971 these claims had been abandoned, except those concerning Spain's North African possessions, and a border dispute with Algeria apparently had been resolved (see ch. 2, Geography and Population). In addition, earlier disputes with France, which had been of a particularly bitter nature, had not so much been resolved as allowed to wither away, and French economic, technical, commercial, and military aid and assistance have been and remain of crucial importance to the country's development efforts (see ch. 3, Historical Setting; ch. 11, Character and Structure of the Economy; ch. 13, Trade and Transportation).

Moroccans on occasion have described the role of their country in foreign affairs as both a bridge for the transmission of European and American technological and philosophical ideas to North Africa and the Middle East and a mediator who offers his good offices to his feuding friends to resolve their differences. Thus, on the global level Morocco, by maintaining cordial relations with both the United States and the Soviet Union, has remained an important beneficiary of both super powers; on the regional level it has endeavored to remain neutral in the intra-Arab and intra-African rivalries and conflicts, yet it has played host to the numerous pan-Arab and pan-African conferences held to alleviate differences between the members; on the subregional level it acted as mediator between

Algeria and Tunisia in their brief border conflict. Its activities at all levels have redounded to the benefit of Morocco.

During the first year of independence, Morocco's interests abroad were represented by France and Spain, but the development of its own diplomatic corps soon made their assistance unnecessary. By 1971 Morocco had exchanged diplomatic representatives with over sixty countries. In 1971 King Hassan II continued to be the chief architect of foreign policy guidelines and on most important issues acted as the nation's chief spokesman and negotiator.

RELATIONS WITH THE STATES OF THE MAGHRIB

The Maghrib, the western Islamic world of North Africa, is held together by common threads of culture and historical experiences. As a geographical expression, the Maghrib is frequently used to encompass the modern states of Morocco, Algeria, Tunisia, and Libya; in political terms, however, many authors exclude Libya. Particularly since the coup in 1969, the government of Libya has manifested more interest in purely Arab, as opposed to Maghribian, affairs and in 1971 joined Syria and the United Arab Republic (UAR) in the formation of the Federation of Arab Republics. At the same time, Morocco has encouraged Mauritania to orient itself toward the Maghrib and has sought to include Mauritania in Maghribian affairs.

Morocco and its North African neighbors have long sought unity of purpose and goals in the formulation and implementation of domestic and foreign policies. The road to such a unity has, however, been arduous. Close collaboration between the states is, to some extent, inhibited by the differing natures of the regimes, yet psychological and economic imperatives have caused them to arbitrate their territorial differences and enter into a series of economic, cultural, technical, and political agreements (mainly bilateral) that might eventually pave the way toward a greater unity.

Although cultural and economic contacts between the peoples of North Africa had never ceased, even during the colonial period, a new kind of relationship—that of politically conscious students studying abroad—came into existence in the 1920s. Realizing the military and economic weaknesses of the individual states vis-a-vis the colonial powers, these students, most of whom were in France, talked about forming a federation as a potential force that would eliminate European hegemony from North Africa. These contacts were not very productive, however, because the colonial powers made it extremely difficult for the students to maintain ties with one another after their return from abroad. Thus, nationalist leaders had to await independence before concrete steps could be taken toward Maghribian unity.

Initial efforts to build North African unity were made in the fields of labor and education. Labor leaders and educators from Morocco, Tunisia, and Algeria met annually to consider the means by which the Algerian revolutionaries could be aided and discussed plans for a North African confederation. In March 1957 Morocco and Tunisia signed an agreement that provided that the two signatories would hold frequent consultations on a common foreign policy, have joint diplomatic representation in some states, take steps to abolish visas, and maintain a permanent commission to coordinate their economies and standardize their economic systems.

A year later, in April 1958, representatives of the Istiqlal (Independence) Party (Morocco), Neo-Destour (Tunisia), and the National Liberation Front (Algeria) met in Tangier and passed a number of resolutions on foreign and domestic issues that, among other things, expressed their common support for Algerian and Mauritanian independence. They also proposed a Maghribian consultative assembly, with powers to examine questions of mutual interest and to make recommendations to national executive organs. The conferees urged the governments to coordinate their defense and foreign policies and created a permanent secretariat of six members. Only a few of their recommendations were adopted by the governments.

Another significant step towards Maghrib unity was taken at the initiative of the United Nations Economic Commission for Africa, which in 1964 established the Maghrib Permanent Consultative Committee (MPCC) with headquarters in Tunis. Under the aegis of the UN, a committee of industrial studies was also set up for the Maghrib. The MPCC established a number of subcommittees on tourism, post and telecommunications, and transportation. In addition, the four Maghribian states have entered scores of agreements. These agreements cover numerous fields of cooperation, from a partial customs union to a judiciary arrangement that allows any lawyer in one country to take a case in another.

Algeria

Relations with independent Algeria have in the past been strained and often antagonistic, primarily because of their border dispute in the Colomb-Bechar and Tindouf-Djebilet areas. After eight years of discussions and abortive efforts at arbitration by a seven-member commission of the Organization of African Unity (OAU), interspersed with a series of border skirmishes and a bloody armed conflict in 1963, the disputants reached an amicable solution to the border dispute. Meeting in Tlemcen on May 20, 1970, King Hassan and President Houari Boumedienne signed an agreement that recognized the Algerian-Moroccan frontier established by France and gave Algeria undisputed sovereignty over the iron ore-rich region of Gara-Djebilet but awarded Morocco a share in a joint company to exploit the mines. The 1970 accord followed the procedure established in a March 1968 agreement between the two countries that had given Morocco the right to share in the exploitation of the zinc mines of Al Abid. In addition to settling the border dispute, the two leaders expressed the determination of the two governments to coordinate their efforts in respect to Spanish territories in North and Northwest Africa.

The Tlemcen meeting was preceded by President Boumedienne's first official visit to Morocco in January 1969, at which time Morocco and Algeria had signed a twenty-year treaty of solidarity and cooperation and set up mixed commissions of specialists to implement the provisions of the treaty. In an official communique published on January 17, the two parties expressed the wish to see the armament race ended, to abstain from the use of force for the solution of differences, and to mobilize the Muslim world for the support of the rights of the Palestinian Arabs. The two heads of state expressed their mutual desire to cooperate, especially in the economic field. The communique emphasized the need for pursuing a policy of nonalignment and of building a greater Maghrib.

Notwithstanding the Tlemcen agreement and the Treaty of Solidarity and Cooperation, the two neighbors remain suspicious of each other because of the dissimilarity of their political systems. After only a year of the Tlemcen agreement, for example, a regional Moroccan tribunal, which was trying 193 alleged conspirators charged with plotting to overthrow King Hassan, accused Algeria of providing military training to 17 of the accused (see ch. 8, The Governmental System and Political Dynamics).

Before Algeria's independence, Morocco maintained excellent relations with the leaders of the National Liberation Front (Front de Liberation Nationale—FLN). During the Algerian war Morocco provided the FLN with military, financial, and political aid and allowed Moroccan territory to be used as a sanctuary and training base. In 1958 Morocco was one of the first countries to extend diplomatic recognition to the provisional government of Algeria. Moroccan-Algerian collaboration not only caused serious friction between Morocco and France but also prompted the Moroccan government to develop cordial relations with the Soviet Union and the People's Republic of China (PRC), whose military help was believed to be essential for the FLN. Morocco was a conduit for arms shipments to the FLN from the Soviet and Chinese sources.

Before Algeria attained independence, Morocco signed with the Algerian Provisional Government a set of accords, including a secret agreement signed in 1960 that provided for a negotiated settlement of the Morocco-Algerian border dispute. The second agreement, signed in January 1962, dealt with a future Maghrib federation, but nothing came of this agreement because of the border conflict between the two soon after Algeria's independence.

Neither the secret agreement nor Morocco's material and moral support for the FLN, however, prevented the simmering territorial and ideological conflicts from resulting in armed border clashes within a week of Algeria's independence in July 1962. After a series of border skirmishes, the conflict was controlled for a little over a year, but it once again flared up into an armed conflict in October 1963. In the meantime, the ideological differences between the two countries manifested themselves in the form of charges by Morocco that Algeria was harboring and encouraging a group of antimonarchical elements, especially such individuals as Mehdi Ben Barka and Abdel Krim (see ch. 3, Historical Setting). Algeria countered by charging that Morocco had been supporting the antistate activities of former Algerian nationalist leader Belkacem Krim. Although Abdel Krim's death in 1962 alleviated King Hassan's apprehensions about Algeria's political designs in Morocco, Ben Barka's association with the Algerian head, Ahmad Ben Bella, remained a source of friction between the two countries, and this was further aggravated during the 1963 border conflict when Ben Barka publicly denounced the Moroccan government for its irredentist claims on Algeria.

When armed conflict began during the fall of 1963, Algeria quickly sought to internationalize the situation by eliciting support from its allies. It appealed to the League of Arab States, commonly known as the Arab League, which Morocco wanted to bypass because Syria and the UAR had sided with Algeria. Neither of the disputants could, however, take much satisfaction from the pronouncements of the league, which merely passed a resolution asking the belligerents to cease firing. After bilateral talks and mediation attempts by nearly a dozen heads of state, the Arab League, and the OAU had failed, President Modibo Keita of Mali and Emperor Haile Selassie of Ethopia finally brought together the Algerian and Moroccan heads of state at Bamako, Mali, on October 30, 1963. There the two belligerents and mediators signed an agreement to cease hostilities and formed a commission to establish a demilitarized neutral zone, the security and neutrality of which became the responsibility of Ethiopia and Mali.

Ten days later the foreign ministers of OAU member states met in Addis Ababa to name a commission to ascertain the facts of the Algerian-Moroccan quarrel and recommend a solution. Algeria and Morocco agreed to refrain from propaganda attacks on each other and from interference in each other's affairs and to settle all subsequent disputes by means of negotiations. After the cease-fire went into effect, there were no serious shooting incidents on the border, and the leaders of the two countries cautiously moved forward toward a rapprochement expressed in the form of a treaty of solidarity and a border agreement.

Although the conflict was eventually resolved amicably, it had created a disagreeable climate of opinion for Morocco's relations with a number of Afro-Arab states and put heavy strains on the country's economy because of the new military demands for arms. The border conflict adversely affected relations with the UAR, Syria, and Cuba, all of whom were reported to have given materiel and personnel aid to Algeria during the actual fighting. Morocco recalled its envoys from Cairo and Damascus and severed diplomatic relations with Cuba. Allegations that the United States and Spain had extended military assistance to Moroccan forces during this period further weakened Morocco's position among the countries of the Afro-Asian nonaligned bloc by casting doubts on its neutralist credentials.

Recognizing its economic and political limitations in an arms race with Algeria, in 1967 Morocco approached the OAU and the UN with a view to reaching an international arms inspection and control agreement for North Africa. In its proposal to the OAU, Morocco suggested strict control of armaments in North Africa and offered to hand over surplus arms to the UAR or any other country threatened by Israel. Both of these proposals were rejected by Algeria, which was reluctant to place restrictions on the expansion of its forces.

Tunisia

Morocco's relations with Tunisia have passed through stages of warmth and coolness. Compared with the intensity and duration of its difficulties with Algeria, however, Morocco's disputes with Tunisia have been minor. Soon after their independence Morocco and Tunisia entered into a series of agreements and treaties designed to move the two states toward Maghribian unity. A number of political irritants, however, prevented them from moving toward this goal. Friction was caused by a series of incidents and events, including the personal and political clash between Moroccan political leaders and Tunisian President Habib Bourguiba; the deposition of the bey of Tunis, an event that brought sharp criticism from Morocco; and Morocco's initial endeavors to establish close relations with the UAR and the Arab League, with both of whom Tunisia had strained relations.

These points of friction did not cause a break in Moroccan-Tunisian relations until 1960 when, despite Morocco's bitter opposition, Tunisia extended diplomatic recognition to Mauritania and sponsored its membership to the UN. Diplomatic relations between the two countries were suspended and were not restored until April 1964. This, however, did not prevent President Bourguiba from attending the funeral services of King Mohammed V in 1961. While in Rabat the Tunisian president conferred with King Hassan and expressed the hope that the two countries would soon normalize their diplomatic relations. By January 1963 Moroccan-Tunisian ties were sufficiently cordial for Tunisia to request King Hassan to use his good offices in bringing about a reconciliation between Algeria and Tunisia.

By this time a number of internal and external factors had prompted King Hassan to abandon the irredentist claims advanced by his late father and the Istiqlal Party and to make efforts to normalize Morocco's relations with its neighbors. During the January 1964 Arab Summit Conference in Cairo, meetings between Hassan and Bourguiba opened the way for an exchange of ambassadors, followed by visits by ranking officials of the two countries. In December 1964 Hassan paid his first official visit to Tunisia and, after discussing with Bourguiba a wide range of topics, notably projects for economic unity of the Maghrib, he witnessed the signing of several accords between the two states. Since then the two heads of state have exchanged several personal visits. The Hassan-Bourguiba talks have included such topics as the discussion of a Maghrib summit meeting, the progress of the OAU, and the possibility of creating a Maghribian common market. To increase social contacts and benefits, the two countries agreed to exchange information in scientific research, family planning, and the medical profession. In order to maintain high-level contacts, the two heads of state agreed to exchange visits every two years.

Mauritania

After refusing for ten years to recognize the separate existence of Mauritania, Morocco dropped its irredentist claims on its neighbor and, in 1970, full diplomatic relations between the countries were established. Initial steps for a reconciliation had been taken by Morocco during the preparatory work for the 1969 Islamic Summit Conference at Rabat, when Morocco invited Mauritania to the conference. It was a propitious time to extend the invitation because the Istiqlal Party, the major exponent of Moroccan irredentism, could scarcely criticize the government for inviting Mauritania to a conference that was being convened to express Muslim indignation against the burning of the al Aqsa mosque in the Israeli-occupied sector of Jerusalem.

Availing himself of the favorable circumstances created by the conference, King Hassan invited Mauritanian President Ould Daddah to a dinner-conference, during which the king reportedly assured the president that Morocco would forthwith drop its irredentist demands in the hope of creating better relations between the two countries. Soon after the Hassan-Daddah meeting, Hassan quietly eliminated the Ministry of Mauritanian Affairs from the Moroccan cabinet. This action and a series of exchanges of goodwill missions opened the way for the two countries to sign, in June 1970, a treaty of solidarity and good neighborliness. Under this treaty, the two signatories agreed to respect the other's territorial integrity; to refrain from any interference in the other's internal affairs; to strengthen their political, economic, social, and cultural relations; and to establish an interministerial joint commission to develop bilateral relations.

Morocco had claimed Mauritania on the ground that the territory had been under its suzerainty ever since Sultan Mulay Ismail (1672-1727) brought large portions of the area under Moroccan rule (see ch. 3, Historical Setting). Morocco asserted that Mauritania had been detached by France during its colonial ascendancy in North Africa. Morocco's claim to Mauritania was first verbalized in the 1950s by the Istiqlal Party's leading figure, Allal al Fassi, who, after obtaining King Mohammed's support, turned the irredentist demand into a top-priority national goal. Open support for the concept of a greater Morocco was expressed for the first time by King Mohammed on February 25 and by his cabinet on March 17, 1958. Two weeks later the monarch laid claim to Mauritania in more explicit terms by receiving four prominent Mauritanian public figures, who pledged him their allegiance.

On the international level the question of Mauritania was first discussed, at Morocco's request, by the foreign ministers of the Arab League in 1960. At that time, being in good standing with the Arab League, Morocco procured the ministers' support for its claim. In the hope of securing further international support for its irredentism, Morocco in the fall of 1960 took the case to the UN, where it failed in its efforts to muster sufficient favorable votes in the political committee of the General Assembly.

Morocco then turned to the Casablanca Bloc, in the formation of which the king had played a significant role, for legitimizing its claim to Mauritania. Meeting in Casablanca in January 1961, the heads of state of Ghana, Guinea, Mali, and the UAR and representatives of Libya and the Provisional Government of Algeria— the members of the short-lived Casablanca Bloc—passed a resolution stating that France had severed the southern portion of Morocco (Mauritania) in order to establish its hold in the Sahara on firmer grounds, to exploit wealth, and to assure itself of outlets on the Atlantic Ocean. The conference approved Morocco's efforts to recover Mauritania.

Although the political committee had failed to adopt any resolution on Mauritania, Morocco, with the help of the Soviet veto, was able to deny Mauritania's membership in the UN for two years. Thereafter, the Soviet Union withdrew its objection in an agreement with Western powers to admit Mauritania and Outer Mongolia to the UN simultaneously.

Libya

Before the 1969 Libyan coup, Morocco maintained warm and friendly relations with Libya, which was then also a monarchy. These, however, began to change, largely because of the new Libyan government's provocative attitude toward, and pronouncements against, the Moroccan monarchy. This attitude was openly expressed in the aftermath of the July 1971 coup attempt against King Hassan, who publicly accused Libya of encouraging the Moroccan dissidents. As a reaction to the Libyan broadcasts, which sought to incite the Moroccans against their government, Morocco expelled the Libyan ambassador and his staff in July 1971 and suspended, but did not formally break, diplomatic relations.

RELATIONS WITH OTHER AFRICAN STATES

Morocco's relations with African states have been generally satisfactory. Even before Morocco attained independence, its political leaders had established contacts with African intellectuals living in Paris and Cairo, and many of these contacts were renewed at the Bandung Conference in 1955. Morocco's active participation in African affairs, however, began in 1958, when the king sent delegations to pan-African conferences held in Cairo and Accra. Although little was achieved during these conferences, they provided the Moroccan leaders opportunities to exchange ideas with other African leaders.

The Congo crisis of 1960 provided the Moroccans another opportunity to take a keener and more constructive interest in the affairs of their continent. In answer to a UN call, Morocco contributed a 3,100-man military contingent to the UN Force in the Congo. Morocco was not satisfied with the UN operations in the Congo, however, and withdrew its forces in December 1960. Soon after the withdrawal, King Mohammed V took the lead, in January 1961, in forming the Casablanca Bloc, a political group of radical and neutralist African states that, like Morocco, had become disillusioned with the UN policies in the Congo. From this alliance the Moroccan government drew at least two significant benefits: it effectively immunized the king against the leftist attack on his conservative domestic policies and received the bloc's support for Morocco's irredentist claim on Mauritania.

Although the Casablanca Bloc soon disintegrated, Morocco continued to provide political and moral support to a number of revolutionary African groups fighting for the independence of Angola and Mozambique from Portugal. In August 1963 Morocco recognized the Angolan revolutionary government-in-exile led by Holden Roberto and soon thereafter broke off relations with Portugal.

RELATIONS WITH OTHER ARAB STATES

In 1971 Morocco's relations with most Arab states were friendly. It shared with them a mutual desire for a closer political, economic, cultural, and technical cooperation among the members of the Arab League. Taking into consideration its physical distance from the eastern Arab states, the meagerness of its resources, and its preoccupation with its own domestic and international problems, Morocco seems to have taken a keen interest in the affairs and well-being of its friends in the Arabian heartland. Within its capabilities, Morocco has sought to provide political, moral, and financial help to Arab states in the Arab-Israeli conflict, and Morocco has consistently supported the Palestinian Arabs.

Politically, Morocco has persisted in its efforts to elicit support of the major powers for the Arab cause and, financially, has given generously, relative to its capability, to both the Palestinian refugees and to the Palestinian Liberation Movement. Militarily, Morocco has twice offered military contingents to the eastern Arab states: in January 1964, to the Arab League if it called for a military action against the Israeli plan to divert the waters of the Jordan River; and in May and June 1967, when the king placed units of the Royal Armed Forces (Forces Armées Royales—FAR) at the disposal of the UAR. The 1964 offer was never put to test because the Arab League failed to adopt a military contingency plan for the Jordan River Project, and the 1967 expression of solidarity with the UAR and its allies did not make any material changes in the outcome of the war. Moroccan troops, which were en route to the Suez front, were in Libya when the call for a cease-fire was accepted by the UAR.

In the early independence period Morocco's relations with the UAR were warm and friendly; for some time Rabat considered Cairo its principal friend among the Arab states. This friendship was especially evident during their activities in the Casablanca Bloc. The activities of the Casablanca Bloc rapidly declined, however; as both Morocco and the UAR became preoccupied with their respective, though dissimilar, problems with Algeria and Yemen, the intimacy of former days changed into open hostility. The growing friendship between Algeria and the UAR and Radio Cairo's sharp criticism, in late 1962, of the monarchy in Rabat for its hesitation in recognizing the Egyptian-backed regime of Yemen caused serious damage to Moroccan-Egyptian relations, which continued to decline to the point of diplomatic rupture in the fall of 1963, when a group of Egyptian soldiers was captured at the Algerian-Moroccan front.

Formal diplomatic relations were normalized in February 1964, but Moroccan-Egyptian cooperation in the field of education and in technical and cultural activities was halted when Morocco declared *persona non grata* the Egyptian teachers, technicians, and cultural experts working in the country. By the end of 1964, however, Moroccan-Egyptian relations had improved and the vice president of the UAR attended Moroccan independence day celebrations. This trend toward a rapprochement was further strengthened, in March and September 1965, when King Hassan and President Gamal Abdul Nasser exchanged official visits. These exchanges were considered highly successful by the two rulers, who, in the joint communiques issued after each conference, expressed their complete agreement and support for African unity and the liberation of Palestine, Oman, and Aden. The countries also affirmed their solidarity with the peoples of Africa in their fight against colonialism.

Notwithstanding its diplomatic, moral, and military support to the UAR, Morocco has firmly opposed all efforts by the UAR for hegemony in the Arab world. At the 1969 Islamic Summit Conference of the Arab states in Rabat, Morocco opposed the UAR proposal for the establishment of a higher Arab command, to which each country would make firm financial, troop, and equipment commitments. Morocco, along with Tunisia, Algeria, and Saudi Arabia, made a counterproposal to increase contributions to the Palestinian Liberation Movement but not to the UAR military budget.

The Algerian-Moroccan border conflict in 1963 precipitated a Moroccan-Syrian crisis that culminated in a diplomatic rupture between the two countries. Accusing Syria of hostile action in the border dispute, Morocco withdrew its ambassador from Damascus. During the next two years relations improved somewhat, but diplomatic ties had hardly been restored when once again, in November 1965, Morocco felt obliged to suspend relations because of the alleged hostile attitude of the Syrian press in commenting on Moroccan domestic affairs. Relations between the two countries remained cool until a new Syrian government initiated negotiations for a restoration of relations, which were resumed in February 1970.

Morocco's relations with the rest of the Arab states have been cordial. It continued in late 1971 to maintain friendly ties with Iraq, Jordan, Saudi Arabia, Kuwait, and the sheikhdoms of the Persian Gulf.

RELATIONS WITH WEST EUROPEAN STATES

In late 1971 Morocco was on friendly terms with all the countries of Western Europe with the exception of Portugal. After five years of arduous and highly complex negotiations with the European Economic Community (EEC), Morocco signed an association agreement with it on March 31, 1969 (see ch. 13, Trade and

Transportation). The five-year accord provided for mutual trade preferences and included a stipulation that by the end of the third year talks would be resumed on advancing the association. As far as trade and aid relations were concerned, Morocco continued to rely most heavily on France but showed increasing interest in the opportunities for economic cooperation with its closest European neighbor, Spain. At the same time, it has obtained important industrial investment from Italy and the Federal Republic of Germany (West Germany). Morocco has continued to maintain excellent relations with West Germany, despite the pressure from the Algerian-UAR-Syrian front to break diplomatic ties with Bonn over its decision to recognize Israel in 1965. At that time, however, King Hassan expressed his displeasure at the German action by postponing his scheduled trip to Bonn.

France

Until December 1969 a number of political and economic issues complicated Morocco's relations with France, notably the Algerian war of independence, France's support for Mauritania, the French nuclear tests in the Sahara, the Moroccanization of French enterprises in the country, Morocco's membership in the now defunct Casablanca Bloc, and, particularly, the so-called Ben Barka affair. During the first ten years of Morocco's independence relations with France were suspended on three occasions: in 1956, in 1960, and in 1965. The breaks in diplomatic ties were accompanied by announcements of suspension of French economic and technical aid, which was usually restored, however, within a brief period.

The earlier episodes that had caused diplomatic breaks between France and Morocco—the French hijacking, in October 1956, of a Moroccan plane carrying FLN leader Ahmad Ben Bella and four of his close associates, and in early 1960 the French nuclear testing in a part of the Sahara that Morocco claimed as its own—had also touched off a spate of anti-French incidents in Morocco, but the issues were fairly easily resolved. The 1965 Ben Barka affair generated such unparalleled mutual resentment and an inflated sense of indignation and national self-righteousness that the scars made by this event did not fully heal until President Charles de Gaulle, who had made the incident a matter of personal and national honor, resigned and was replaced by Georges Pompidou, who did not share his predecessor's views on this issue (see ch. 3, Historical Setting).

As a result of the Ben Barka affair, France suspended its financial assistance to Morocco. After a break of approximately two years, French aid was gradually resumed until it reached a total of 323 million francs in 1970. As a prelude to a resumption of large-scale French aid, Morocco and France entered into high-level negotiations and an exchange of visits by senior officials. In May 1968 Moroccan Foreign Minister Ahmed Laraki made a hurried visit to Iran, where he was reported to have met with visiting French Prime Minister Pompidou. This meeting was followed by an exchange of visits between officials of French and Moroccan ministries of finance in July and August 1968. These officials discussed the Moroccan Five Year Plan (1968–72) and agreed to aid in the amount of 80 million francs for the development plan.

In February 1970 King Hassan, accompanied by his prime minister and minister of foreign affairs, paid a one-week private visit to France, where he and his party held a series of talks with ranking French officials, including President Pompidou. French-Moroccan relations were further improved when the French foreign minister, Maurice Schumann, paid an official visit to Morocco in December 1970. During his visit—the first by a French foreign minister since Morocco achieved independence—the two governments agreed to establish a permanent joint French-Moroccan commission to meet at least once a year to settle points at issue between the two contracting parties and to formulate bases for continued cooperation between them. The objectives of the new intergovernmental commission were expected to include discussions on increasing trade and other bilateral commercial exchanges, arms and military training, and the delicate question of compensation for the 90,000 French residents in Morocco whose commercial interests or property had been or were being Moroccanized.

In the joint communique issued at the conclusion of the Schumann visit on December 19, 1970, the two parties agreed that the Mediterranean should be a zone of peace and stability and stressed the similarity of their views on a settlement of the Middle East question. In the educational and technical fields, the two countries agreed to maintain the current level of French assistance, which provided nearly 9,000 teachers for Moroccan state schools (see ch. 7, Education, Communication, and the Arts and Sciences). The French foreign minister promised to extend the necessary credit to Morocco to buy modern military equipment.

Spain

Spanish-Moroccan relations have been close and cordial, despite the fact that the two countries have had territorial problems centering on the status of several parcels of land, some of which were still under Spanish rule in late 1971. Since independence Morocco has amicably resolved with Spain most of their territorial disputes, including the northern and southern zones of the Spanish Protectorate and the Atlantic coast enclave of Ifni (see ch. 3, Historical Setting).

The only territorial dispute still unresolved in 1971 centered on the North African coastal cities of Ceuta and Melilla and the island fortresses of Velez de la Gomera, Alhucemas, and the Shafarin Islands. With a view to resolving this dispute, the two countries have had intermittent negotiations, but Morocco has not gone beyond verbal demands for the return of the enclaves. In a speech in 1968 celebrating the seventh anniversary of his accession to the throne, King Hassan urged Spain to settle the territorial disputes over Ifni and the Spanish Sahara, but he made no mention of Ceuta and Melilla.

On the eve of the formal transfer of Ifni to Morocco on June 30, 1969, King Hassan, accompanied by his ministers of interior and foreign affairs, paid a five-day private visit to Spain, where he held meetings with Generalissimo Francisco Franco and other senior Spanish officials. Since that time a number of high-level visits have been exchanged between the two countries, in their continued effort toward evolving more meaningful ties. In addition to these visits, the ties have been further strengthened by showing special favors to each other's government. Such a favor was shown by Spain to Morocco in February 1970, when the Spanish government arrested two Moroccan opposition leaders and handed them over to the embassy of Morocco in Madrid. The two Moroccans had been tried in absentia and sentenced to death for their alleged role in a 1963 plot against the king. Although there was no extradition treaty between the two countries, the Spanish action was considered to be a manifestation of its desire to strengthen the Moroccan monarchy against revolutionary efforts to displace it.

In March 1971 Spain and Morocco took yet another step to improve their ties when they signed an agreement that established a joint commission for cultural, economic, scientific, and technical cooperation. The commission, which will be headed by the respective ambassadors of the two countries in Rabat and Madrid, was given the task of resolving the problems that exist or may arise between Morocco and Spain. These problems were not only concerned with various territorial claims, but also included matters relating to fishing rights and the United Nations' Law of the Sea in reference to the Strait of Gibraltar.

RELATIONS WITH THE UNITED STATES

Moroccan ties with the United States go back to the earliest history of the American republic, when the reigning monarch, Muhammed ben Abdullah, recognized the newly founded United States and, in 1787, signed a treaty of friendship with the union. Maintained in its essential provisions to the present day, it is the longest unbroken treaty relationship in American history. After establishing a consulate in Tangier in 1791, the United States during the nineteenth century obtained commercial and extraterritorial rights and privileges. These rights were also covered by the most-favored-nation and extraterritorial clauses of the Moroccan-United States treaties signed in 1836, 1880, and 1906, and these rights and privileges were confirmed by the Algeciras Conference of 1906 (see ch. 3, Historical Setting). After the establishment of the French Protectorate in 1912, the European powers renounced their extraterritorial rights in Morocco, but the United States continued to maintain its treaty rights until October 7, 1956, when, under intense pressure from Moroccan nationalists, it too renounced its extraterritorial rights.

Beginning in the early 1940s, American interest in Morocco began to change from primarily commercial to political-strategic affairs. In 1942 the United States took control of and expanded and modernized a naval base at Port Lyautey (later changed to Kenitra).

In January 1943, during his visit to Casablanca for a meeting of the Allied leaders, President Franklin D. Roosevelt met with Sultan Sidi Mohammed ben Youssef (later known as King Mohammed V) and was reported to have assured him of American support for Moroccan independence. This promise, if made, could not be kept, however, because the Moroccan struggle for independence was waged at a time when the United States did not consider it prudent to alienate France. Thus, during the UN debates and votes on Morocco in the early 1950s, the United States generally favored France. American-Moroccan relations were further complicated when, in December 1950, the United States and France entered into secret agreements that allowed the American government to build air and naval bases in Morocco. Although at the time of the negotiations for the bases the United States had requested France to inform Sultan Mohammed of the plans, the agreements were executed without his approval or knowledge.

Because the bases had been built during the period of French hegemony, and without reference to the sultan, Morocco, soon after independence, demanded the withdrawal of American forces from the country. The exigencies of Morocco's radical foreign policy in the late 1950s and the internal political pressures exerted by the leftist elements obliged the government to press for an early evacuation of the American bases. A visit by King Mohammed V to Washington in 1957 and a return visit by President Dwight D. Eisenhower to Rabat in 1959 finally produced an agreement that called for the evacuation of all bases by the end of 1963. The bases were returned to full Moroccan sovereignty in 1963, but Morocco has continued to permit the United States to use communications facilities at some of the bases.

Economic and technical assistance from the United States dates from 1956, when Morocco was looking for increased aid that would also counterbalance the preponderant influence of France. With the exception of a brief break in 1964, the American government has maintained constant aid commitments to Morocco. In February 1964 the United States suspended aid to Morocco because the 1964 Foreign Aid Act required that military and economic aid be withheld from countries that supplied strategic materials to the PRC whose flagships took part in trade with Cuba. In order for it to remain qualified for American aid, Morocco was told that it must stop deliveries of cobalt to the PRC and prevent its ships from calling on Cuban ports.

The Moroccan foreign minister criticized the action and said that those demands would put into jeopardy the policy of nonalignment that the country had pursued since independence. Furthermore, he maintained that it was essential for Morocco to sell cobalt to the PRC in order to obtain Chinese tea. Realizing that Morocco would face economic hardships if pressed to stop the cobalt deliveries and, perhaps, also appreciating the need to maintain telecommunication centers in the country, the United States government on April 15, 1964, granted a waiver in the case of Moroccan shipments of cobalt. At the same time Morocco was reported to have assured the United States that it had taken appropriate steps to discontinue carrying goods in Moroccan ships to Cuba.

RELATIONS WITH THE COMMUNIST STATES

In keeping with its avowed policy of friendship with all nations irrespective of their internal political systems, Morocco has maintained diplomatic, commercial, cultural, and military relations with most communist states. The monarchy does not perceive an imminent external communist threat to the country's integrity, though it bars communist activities within the state. Morocco has been generally nonideological in the formulation and implementation of foreign policy and expects the same from foreign powers. In this respect, the communist representatives in Morocco have, by and large, avoided taking sides in the country's political activities; they showed no hostile reaction, for example, to the ban imposed on the Communist Party (see ch. 8, The Governmental System and Political Dynamics).

Communist support to Morocco during the struggle for independence was limited to casting favorable votes in the UN and rhetorical denunciations of French policy in the country. Three months after Morocco's independence, the Soviet Union extended diplomatic recognition. This action was soon followed by the PRC and a number of other communist states, and diplomatic envoys were exchanged with Moscow and Peking in September 1958 and April 1959, respectively.

Before the exchange of envoys, however, Morocco had already entered into a series of commercial and cultural agreements with the Soviet Union and the PRC. Subsequently, similar ties were established with Poland, Romania, Yugoslavia, Hungary, Bulgaria, and Czechoslovakia. Under these arrangements a number of cultural groups as well as trade, labor, and student delegations were exchanged between Morocco and the communist states. A number of Moroccan national leaders also visited the Soviet Union and returned with high praise for Soviet achievements. In February 1961 Leonid I. Brezhnev, chairman of the Presidium of the Supreme Soviet, paid a two-day unofficial visit to Rabat, where he was cordially received by King Mohammed V. The Brezhnev visit coincided with the arrival of the first Soviet military consignment, which included a dozen MIG-17s and two Ilyshin bombers for the Royal Air Force. The military hardware was accompanied by a complement of two dozen Soviet technicians.

Morocco has received several additional consignments of military equipment from the Soviet Union and a number of other communist states. In 1967 alone the Soviet Union and Czechoslovakia sold to Morocco the equivalent of about US$20 million worth of arms. In an effort to acquire more Soviet military equipment, a Moroccan delegation led by the chief of staff, General Driss ben Omar al Alami, visited the Soviet Union in June 1969 and had talks with senior Soviet military and political figures. Results of the talks were not announced.

Although Morocco had played host to Brezhnev in 1961 and to Deputy Prime Minister Anastas I. Mikoyan in 1962, it was not until July 1966 that a Moroccan minister paid an official visit to the Soviet Union. The visit of the Moroccan foreign minister to Moscow was the beginning of a renewed effort to establish closer commercial and technical links with the Soviet Union. In August, as a sequel to the ministerial visit, a Soviet economic delegation arrived in Morocco to continue discussions concerning Moroccan-Soviet relations that the foreign minister had initiated in Moscow.

These visits laid the ground for King Hassan's five-day state visit to the Soviet Union in October 1966, which was the occasion for the signing of a Soviet-Moroccan economic and technical accord that provided for the extension of a number of projects already under study. In addition, the two countries agreed to increase substantially the volume of their trade. The trend toward closer ties was further strengthened when, in April 1969, Nikolai Podgorny, chairman of the Presidium of the Supreme Soviet, paid a six-day official visit to Morocco. In 1970 the two countries established a joint Soviet-Moroccan permanent committee for economic, technical, and scientific cooperation, which held its second meeting in Morocco in July 1971. As a result of this meeting, the two countries concluded a number of bilateral agreements to promote Soviet-Moroccan relations in the commercial, economic, and social fields.

Morocco's relations with the PRC have remained cordial, but there were no indications in 1971 that either country planned to expand ties beyond the scope of usual commercial, cultural, and economic agreements. Since Prime Minister Chou En-Lai's weeklong visit to Morocco in December 1963 and the participation of the king's brother in the fifteenth anniversary celebrations of the PRC in October 1964 no high-level visits have been exchanged between the two countries. Nevertheless, the volume of trade continues to grow, and a new trade protocol was signed on April 26, 1971.

THE UNITED NATIONS AND OTHER INTERNATIONAL ORGANIZATIONS

Morocco became a member of the UN on November 12, 1956. In general, the Moroccan delegation to the UN has voted with the Afro-Asian bloc; it consistently supports, for example, resolutions calling for an end to colonialism and color discrimination. Morocco is a member of all UN international agencies. In 1963 it was elected a member of the Security Council for two years.

Morocco became a member of the Arab League on October 1, 1958, and has attended all conferences and summits called by the league. Morocco is also an active member of the recently formed twenty-five-nation Islamic Solidarity Bloc, which seeks to foster closer relations among member states. Morocco continues to take a keen interest in the activities of the OAU, with which it has been associated since shortly after its inception in 1963.

MECHANICS OF FOREIGN POLICY

The making of Morocco's foreign policy is largely the responsibility of the king. According to the 1970 Constitution, the king receives foreign ambassadors and special representatives and appoints ambassadors to foreign countries and international organizations.

All major policy decisions are made by the king. His reliance on personal diplomacy, although not as extensive as that of some other heads of state, often takes him abroad several times a year to attend Arab, African, and Muslim leaders' conferences. Members of the royal family have also served as the country's representatives abroad. The minister of foreign affairs usually represents Morocco at other meetings.

CHAPTER 10
POLITICAL VALUES

The dominant system of political beliefs, opinions, and attitudes centers on the dual roles of the monarch as the spiritual leader and the secular ruler. In 1971 an overwhelming majority of the citizenry subscribed to the notion of the king as the commander of the faithful (*amir al muaminin*) and seemingly accepted the king's advocacy of his divine right to rule.

King Hassan II combines in his person the symbol of the legitimacy of the Alawite dynasty that has ruled, except for the brief interlude of French and Spanish occupation, since the seventeenth century. He was the appointed and unchallenged successor to the venerated King Mohammed V, who was the focal point of the struggle for independence (see ch. 3, Historical Setting). The king, and therefore his son and appointed successor, is recognized as a direct descendant of the Prophet Muhammad and, as such, is endowed with special grace and favor in religious and mundane matters (see ch. 5, Religious Life).

The widespread allegiance to the king and the infrequent and thus far ineffective resistance to his role as the arbitrator and manipulator of events have as their source a combination of historical-traditional and modern circumstances. Continuity with present times may be said to begin with the introduction of Islam in the seventh century A.D., which was followed by the establishment of the central authority of the sultanate, massive Arab immigrations, and, more gradually, the absorption of Arabic-Islamic cultural patterns from the eastern Mediterranean area. Previous conquerors and socioreligious systems had asserted themselves and declined, but Morocco attained its recognizable, independent identity with the coming of Islam and the sultanate (see ch. 3, Historical Setting).

Thereafter, regardless of the succession of dynasties, all were Islamic, and the people at large remained Muslims. In addition, regardless of how little or how much of the country particular dynasties or sultans firmly controlled, an indigenous central authority did exist. In the late medieval period, Morocco alone in the region of the Middle East and North Africa did not fall under the sovereignty of the Ottoman Turkish sultans but remained independent until succumbing to French colonial power in 1912. During the French period, native exercise of power was severely circumscribed, but the traditional Moroccan values, modes of thought, and social customs persisted.

The Islamic legal code called the *sharia* was the public law in Morocco, as in other Islamic states, until well into modern times, and its influence and, in some cases, direct application continued in 1971. This code, deriving from the scriptures of the Quran and associated traditions, is grounded in the concept that the purpose of government is to ensure obedience and worship of God by the community of faithful believers. Islam means "submission," and a Muslim is "one who has submitted."

As the relation between God and his creatures is one of absolute authority, so is the relation between the earthly ruler and the community essentially authoritarian. The Constitution of 1970, as had that of 1962, confirmed traditional practice by identifying the king as commander of the faithful. The mutually reinforcing influences of Islamic theocratic legalism and authoritarian social custom in 1971 continued to be the most basic and significant roots for the role and power of the historic monarchy.

Early nationalism, which began in the mid-1920s, was closely associated with Islamic reformism. The religious character of the nationalist movement was never entirely lost and accounts in part for the relative absence of secular European socialist or Marxist ideology in its subsequent development. Nationalist opposition to the protectorate spread to a broad segment of the population as the French hardened in their insistence that the sultan submit to protectorate government suzerainty. The exile of Sultan Mohammed V in 1953 for refusing to yield to French demands made him a symbol of national unity and Islamic solidarity against the infidel Europeans. Thus, popular devotion to the sultan in his sacred role was converted to a loyalty to the sultan as a secular leader and as the focus of national political unity. By 1955 the French realized that they could no longer maintain their status in Morocco peacefully and agreed to grant independence. Sultan Mohammed V was brought back from exile and enthusiastically accepted as the ruler of the new state.

The power of the throne was thus established, identifiable in its historic Moroccan outlines, and above party. Although not invulnerable to pressure from parties, unions, the press, or other interest factions, the king became the essential weight in any question of policy, preferment, or patronage.

Mohammed V, although inclined to act by gradual steps and only after careful study, nevertheless looked to the necessities of modernization and the future. He announced and moved toward the goal of a constitutional monarchy, actions that his son and successor, Hassan II, continued. Democratic institution building, however, often clashed with the forms and manners of the older monarchic way. Democratic innovations have been hampered by the two constants of the traditional political environment: the continuity of Islam as the state religion and the essential inviolability of the figure of the king as the commander of the faithful. Each reinforces the other, and both have been placed beyond constitutional change.

Although King Hassan has made occasional efforts to establish and work through democratic institutions, the attempts have been of short duration. In 1965 he terminated his brief experiment with a parliament and did not renew the attempt until 1970; according to most observers, the absence of a parliament was felt acutely by few other than the former legislators.

Hassan's rule, a mixture of traditional and modern forms, has been characterized as one of stalemate and tension management. With the exception of a few dissidents, such as the late Mehdi Ben Barka, the political scene has been, and in 1971 remained, devoid of ideology or ideologues. Hassan copes with and rules through a group of about 1,000 men in the military, political, civil service, business, landowning elite, men who, as one observer put it, have "known one another only too long and too well." The king manages and manipulates them, and they are dependent on him not just for advancement but also for continuance.

The bulk of the population, especially the large rural majority, continues to support this nonideological kingship. Tradition oriented, strongly religious, and preoccupied with local issues, they view the monarchy as the personification of Morocco. A relatively small middle class provides additional popular support for the monarchy. Deeply involved in economic affairs and generally conservative Muslims, members of the middle class may, privately, distinguish between the secular and sacred roles of the king, and they may, again privately, be critical of specific policies and arts, but they have remained a bulwark of royal support.

During the middle and late 1960s, however, there were increasingly vociferous and potentially powerful groups who viewed the concept of a virtually absolute monarchy as a political anachronism. By late 1971 King Hassan was one of only half a dozen monarchs who ruled rather than reigned, and to an unknown but apparently large number of urban proletarians, students, and professional-intellectuals, Hassan's role as secular ruler required revision and restriction.

The attitudes of Morocco's youth are difficult to ascertain. The most vocal groups among young people, and certainly the most politically aware, are the university student unions. The student unions do not necessarily represent the majority of Moroccan youth, and the radicalism of those for whom they speak may be exaggerated. Nevertheless, their opinions are often the only attitudes expressed by youth, and they have an important influence on political parties.

In general, students are likely to think about Morocco in terms of the development of an independent society; they are, for example, less likely than their elders to confuse irredentism and Islamic fundamentalism with nationalism. Idealistic, they are apt to seek solutions to Morocco's problems through some variety of socialism. The attitude of youth toward the king reveals an increasingly sharp awareness of the difference between his religious and his political functions and, on occasion, students have been hostile to the king.

In March 1965 peaceful antigovernment demonstrations by students in Casablanca provided the fuse to the serious riots, which were quelled only by harsh police and army measures (see ch. 7, Education, Communication, and the Arts and Sciences; ch. 8, The Governmental System and Political Dynamics). The riots were quickly joined by thousands of dissatisfied, unemployed, and poverty-stricken urban slum dwellers, who were unorganized but capable of producing the most serious threat to public order since independence. As a spontaneous, undirected outburst of population frustration, the 1965 riots—which spread from Casablanca to Fes and other cities—were significant as an expression of discontent not otherwise capable of being articulated in the political system. The shock of the labor unions and political parties and their inability to either deal with or take advantage of this discontent revealed their lack of communication with the urban proletariat.

A major complaint of the students is that there are not enough positions for them upon graduation, and this charge is echoed by a reportedly large group of unemployed intellectuals. In 1971 there was no information to indicate that this group had evolved a common ideology or general set of beliefs, but they were known to be increasingly disenchanted with arbitrary rule by the king. Journalists, subject to frequent seizures of their publications, are also critics, albeit discreet ones, of the monarchy.

None of the groups had, by late 1971, articulated publicly any direct attack on the sacred side of the king's role, no doubt reflecting their appreciation of the depth of commitment by most Moroccans to that kingly function. But, as many observers of Morocco have noted, Moroccans do not engage in long-range planning by choice, preferring instead to adjust to new situations as they develop. Politically, it is enough to cope with the problems of today and to seek protective alignments for the morrow.

SECTION III. ECONOMIC

CHAPTER 11

CHARACTER AND STRUCTURE OF THE ECONOMY

In late 1971 Morocco continued to have a centralized, capitalist, dualistic, underdeveloped economy, a terrain somewhat modestly endowed with natural resources, and a number of difficult economic problems that had been inherited along with independence in 1956. Its economic performance since independence had been commendable, considering the disadvantages it had had to cope with.

The country is a monarchy in which the economic decisionmaking power and other broad powers have been centralized in the person of the king. This had made for an unusual capacity for decisionmaking and for continuity and consistency in the evolution of the country's economic policy. From an economic viewpoint this centralization has probably been a source of progress since independence and, other things being equal, it may be expected to continue to be so, although it has posed some related political problems (see ch. 8, The Governmental System and Political Dynamics).

The economy is fundamentally based on private ownership of property, private enterprise, and a capitalist form of monetary apparatus. There is, however, a large measure of government participation in the economy. Ownership of the subsoil mineral rights is vested entirely in the government, which also enjoys large proprietary rights to the forest and nonagricultural surface areas of the country. The government has undertaken considerable participation in productive services, such as transport and communications, and to a less, and perhaps diminishing, extent in the economy's production process. The government, moreover, is dedicated to an as rapid as possible increase in the average per capita income and reduction in the spread between large and small incomes. On balance, however, the economy at the start of the 1970s was essentially private enterprise oriented.

Since the institution of the French and Spanish protectorates in 1912 the economy has leaned heavily on exports, especially to the large sheltered market created by the country's protectorate status. Largely as a function of this special market treatment, a modern economic sector grew up alongside the traditional sector. The modern sector was operated mainly by foreigners and for foreigners, both in Morocco and abroad. It tended to enjoy the use of the best of the country's resources—notably its agricultural resources—and to use up-to-date techniques and inputs imported from abroad. The traditional sector persisted in the old ways, which were not only inefficient but also actively wasteful of resources. Although the modern sector was appreciably more efficient than the traditional, its reliance on protected markets had tended to reduce its effectiveness below that of its potential competitors in other countries. This situation paved the way for difficulties after independence.

Since the early 1960s successive economic and social development programs have been undertaken by the government, with increasing measures of success, in a continuing effort to augment and redistribute the national income. At the beginning of the 1970s some 70 percent of the population was rural and dependent upon agriculture (including animal husbandry and forestry). The economy was therefore, by customary definition, still an underdeveloped one.

RESOURCES AND PROBLEMS

In the early 1970s the country's visible physical resources were largely limited to exceptional tourist attractions, reasonably abundant supplies of cropland and water, and large resources of phosphate rock. The ratio of cropland to population in 1968 was estimated at around three acres per capita. This ratio was about the same as in Algeria and somewhat lower than in Tunisia and Syria. Some 6 to 7 percent of the cropland was estimated to be irrigated, and this was considered to be about one-half of the area that was potentially irrigable (see ch. 12, Agriculture and Industry).

Apart from phosphate rock, most of the known mineral deposits had ceased, by the early 1970s, to be of positive economic significance. Either they had for practical purposes been exhausted or were of unimportant dimensions or they were being exploited at such high unit costs that export of their output was impracticable without subsidies or quotas. Their domestic utilization was based more on the desire to maintain employment or to limit imports than on considerations of comparative costs.

Energy sources included petroleum products, hydroelectricity, coal, wood, and dung. Petroleum products, practically all imported, represented some two-thirds of energy consumed. Hydroelectricity accounted for the bulk of domestic energy sources. The other domestic sources, including petroleum, were either not available in commercial quantities or were of inferior quality, making for high production costs.

As the economy entered the 1970s it faced a number of problems that promised to offer obstacles to its future progress. Foremost among them was the rate at which the population was increasing. Although this matter would continue to be somewhat obscured until the results of the 1971–72 census were available, it was generally accepted in 1971 that the population was growing at around 3.3 percent per year (see ch. 2, Geography and Population). For practical purposes, a rate of growth such as this meant that, unless the national output of goods and services could grow at a rate of around 3.5 percent per year (compounded), the per capita income would stand still.

A second major problem lay in the year-to-year instability of the rainfall pattern. This had its direct and its indirect effects. The direct effect resulted from the impact of inadequate rainfall on agricultural production, which caused foodstuff shortages, the need to consume stocks (even of seed grains), the need to turn to wheat imports to supplement domestic production, and the generalized economic debilitation induced by a decline of income in the agriculture sector.

The indirect effect lay in the difficulties that the foregoing situation created for an assured source of supply of the annually increasing amounts of petroleum products that are required under modern conditions by a developing economy. On the one hand, no adequate supply of petroleum had yet been discovered in Morocco. On the other hand, there had not as yet been developed an export category (including tourism) that could with certainty be depended on from one year to the next to provide the foreign currencies needed to purchase petroleum products abroad. The periodic droughts reduced the total value of export receipts, and the need for wheat imports, having first priority, resulted in further reducing the part of the already diminished export proceeds that would be available for the purchase of nonfood imports, including petroleum (see ch. 13, Trade and Transportation).

Over the long run, this problem should be alleviated by greater amounts of irrigation and flood control, new high-yield strains of wheat, the rapidly growing tourist trade, and greater efficiency both in industry and traditional agriculture. Offsetting these benefits, on present estimates, would be the continued rapid increase in population. For the time being, the problem depended for its solution upon foreign assistance.

Unemployment was also a major problem, although it was perhaps more a political than an economic one. In any case, it had economic repercussions in that it induced the introduction or continuation of certain costly production methods characterized by a high ratio of labor to capital investment that might not have been maintained or undertaken had it not been for the employment situation. Another problem was caused by the shortage of trained and experienced Moroccan management and administrative personnel.

GROSS DOMESTIC PRODUCT

In 1965, which could be called an ordinary year in terms of rainfall (and therefore in terms of agricultural yields), the gross domestic product (GDP) totaled an estimated DH10.79 billion (5.06 dirham equal US$1—see Glossary), measured in constant prices of 1960 (see table 2). In 1966, which was a poor year in terms of rainfall, the gross domestic product declined to DH10.61 billion (at constant prices). In 1968, the best agricultural year on record, the gross domestic product rose to DH12.74 billion (at constant prices), 21 percent above 1966. Provisional estimates for 1969 indicated an increase over 1968 of around 1 percent. In mid-1971 the latest available information suggested a further increase in 1970 of 4 to 5 percent to around DH13.35 billion to DH13.45 billion at 1960 prices, or about DH16.5 billion to DH16.6 billion at current prices. Assuming a population of around 15.7 million at mid-1970, this would have meant a per capita income in that year of around DH835, equivalent to about US$200.

The data available in 1971 suggested that over the 1956–65 period, at the time the economy was adapting itself to the country's new political status, the average annual rate of growth of the gross domestic product was around 2 percent (at constant prices), implying a probable decline over the period in per capita real income. On the other hand, a comparison of the gross domestic product for the year 1960 with that of the years 1967 through 1970 would give average rates of growth per year during those years varying from 3.3 percent over the 1960–67 period to 4.4 percent over the 1960–68 period and 4 percent for the 1960–69 period (compounded and adjusted for price changes). In mid-1971 it was not clear whether the improved gross domestic product growth rates in recent years reflected a movement of the economy to a higher plateau of productivity and output. In any case, they did represent achievement of the target average growth rate of 4.5 percent per year called for by the Five Year Plan (1968–72).

The breakdown of the gross domestic product by sectors indicated that agriculture has consistently been the most important sector of the economy, representing about 30 percent of the total, and that during the 1960s the breakdown remained stable. Although there appeared to have been a slight decline in the relative importance of agriculture, for the most part the year-to-year variations in the relative importance of the sectors were caused by the changes in the size of the agricultural output as a result of annual variations in rainfall. The sectors that appear to have improved their relative position over the period as the position of agriculture declined were

Table 2. *Gross Domestic Product of Morocco, by Industrial Origin at 1960 Market Prices, Selected Years, 1960-69* [1]

(in billions of dirham) [2]

Economic Sector	1960	1963	1965	1966	1967	1968	1969 [3]	Percentages			
								1960	1966	1968	1969 [3]
Agriculture, livestock, forestry, and fishing	2.65	3.06	3.15	2.78	3.07	3.98	3.63	29	26	31	28
Mining and quarrying	0.54	0.53	0.59	0.58	0.58	0.58	0.60	6	5	5	5
Manufacturing and craft industries	1.10	1.29	1.32	1.37	1.42	1.49	1.58	12	13	12	12
Construction	0.32	0.46	0.46	0.50	0.58	0.57	0.62	3	5	4	5
Energy	0.18	0.23	0.26	0.28	0.28	0.31	0.34	2	3	2	3
Commerce	1.91	2.18	2.13	2.14	2.28	2.44	2.56	21	20	19	20
Transport, storage, and other non-government services [4]	1.50	1.66	1.78	1.82	1.89	1.99	2.09	17	17	16	16
Government services	0.89	1.02	1.10	1.14	1.23	1.38	1.43	10	11	11	11
Gross domestic product	9.09	10.43	10.79	10.61	11.33	12.74	12.85	100	100	100	100
Index (1960 = 100)	100	115	118	117	125	140	142				

[1] The gross domestic product differs from the gross national product by not including the net factor payments (mainly interest, dividends, and profits) from abroad (whether positive or negative).
[2] After October 1959 the par value of the dirham equaled DH5.06 per US$1.
[3] Preliminary.
[4] Includes banking, insurance, communication, real estate, and ownership of dwellings.

Source: Adapted from *Yearbook of National Accounts Statistics, 1969*, New York, United Nations, 1970, pp. 486–487; U. S. Agency for International Development, *Gross National Product: Growth Rates and Trend Data*, Washington, 1971, pp. 12, 17; and *Statistical Yearbook, 1970*, New York, United Nations, 1971, p. 577.

construction, energy, and government wages and salaries. The relative contribution of nongovernmental services appears to have declined somewhat, but the item was so much of a catchall that it was impracticable to determine in what components of it the decline took place.

CONSUMPTION AND INVESTMENT

A breakdown of expenditure on the gross domestic product at the end of the 1960s indicated that about 75 percent of total expenditure was for private consumption; about 14 percent, for government consumption (wages and salaries); and the balance, for fixed investment and inventories. The total expenditures on consumption, in percentage terms, remained relatively stable except in 1968, when private consumption was reduced (in percentage but not in physical terms) to replenish the stocks that had been drawn down in 1966 and 1967 as a consequence of the drought in 1966. Public consumption may have increased somewhat over the period at the expense of private consumption, reflecting mainly increased employment by government.

Fixed capital formation apparently increased from around 10 percent of the gross domestic product at the start of the decade to close to 14 percent at the end of it, reflecting government investment for irrigation, transport, and communication facilities and both private and government investment for tourist facilities. The scanty data available in this connection suggested that at the end of the decade the government investment (including public sector enterprises) represented better than two-thirds of the total, despite persistent efforts by the government, through privileged tax treatment and other incentives, to stimulate an increase in private and especially foreign private investment.

The data on overall savings were also scanty. They suggested that the level of savings, both public and private, varied between 10 and 12 percent over the course of the decade—apparently representing around 12 percent at the end of it. An excess of imports over exports became characteristic of the economy in the years after 1965, as a consequence of the drought-induced grain imports in 1966 and 1967; the increasingly effective implementation of the government's Five Year Plan; and the private sector's increased participation in tourism, construction, and industry.

ROLE OF THE GOVERNMENT

Under the constitutions of 1962 and 1970 the right of private ownership of property was guaranteed, although provision was made that this right might be limited by law if the requirements of the economic and social development of the country should make that necessary. Expropriation was prohibited, except as expressly provided for and prescribed by law. Taxation applied to all citizens, according to their ability to pay. Laws might not be retroactive.

The role of the government in the economy at the start of the 1970s was widespread. The keystone of the governmental structure was the king, whose powers included those of initiating policy, promulgating legislation, appointing the ministers and, if need be, dissolving the legislature or abrogating the constitution. This concentration of control had made for continuity and freedom of action in evaluating and coping with the problems confronting the economy, including the enlistment of technical assistance from abroad when necessary.

Since early in the twentieth century the government had enjoyed a monopoly of all subsoil natural resources. By 1971 it had come to exert an increasing degree of direction over surface natural resources as well; this it had done through its investment in irrigation and by retaining control over a growing quantity of land that had been owned by Europeans under the protectorate and that since independence had been repossessed by the government but not redistributed to former owners or others. The government owned railroad, highway, power, and communication networks; the large-scale multipurpose irrigation installations; the phosphate, sugar, and tobacco-processing industries; and most of the airline and navigation services. It also held greater or lesser participating interests in most other major enterprises associated with mining and with the modern portion of the industrial sector. In the aggregate, these interests were estimated at around DH0.5 billion. In mid-1971 the government was proceeding with a policy of requiring that enterprises operating in the banking, insurance, and import-export sectors be incorporated and controlled in Morocco, though not necessarily nationalized.

In addition to its role as a direct participant in the productive activity of the economy, the government also exerted an appreciable indirect influence upon it. This it did through extension of low-cost credit to private sector agriculture, industry (including mining), and tourism; through tariff and other protection to agriculture and industry; through a statutory commission to screen projected new investments (domestic and foreign); through exchange and price controls; and through the use of customs duties and other taxes as inducements to investment in those parts of the private sector that the government desired to see expanded. Foreign trade was guided not only by exchange controls and physical quotas but also by the existence of government export-import agencies that monopolized most of the major exports and a number of important imports (see ch. 13, Trade and Transportation).

What was likely to be the net effect on the development of the economy of the attempted coup of July 1971 was not at once clear. The immediate reaction was a commitment by the king to eradicate corruption. Other actions suggested increased emphasis on agrarian reform and small-scale agriculture and on the social, at the expense of the strictly economic, aspects of the 1968-72 and 1973-77 five-year plans. This harbored possibilities of increased costs and decreased efficiency in agriculture and perhaps also in industry. Unless these were accompanied by increased assistance from abroad and compensating internal changes, the timetable of economic self-sufficiency might be delayed. The promised curtailment of corrupt practices, however, was itself important in securing economic assistance from abroad.

DEVELOPMENT PLANNING

Government programming for economic and social development began before independence. After independence interest in development planning was stressed and abetted by the United Nations and its specialized agencies, for example, the Food and Agriculture Organization (FAO), the International Bank for Reconstruction and Development (IBRD), commonly known as the World Bank, the International Monetary Fund (IMF), and the United Nations Development Program (UNDP). Since independence there have been four investment or development programs during the periods 1957-59, 1960-64, 1965-67, and 1968-72; in 1971 another was being readied for the five-year period 1973-77. The first three were overly ambitious and suffered from coincidence with bad crop years. The 1968-72 plan, although it was somewhat belated in getting started, benefited from the impetus of the better than average crops in 1968, 1969, and 1970 and the tourist-hotel and irrigation construction boom in 1969 and 1970. At the end of 1969 the plan was sufficiently on, or ahead of, schedule in its several sectors that the total projected outlay for the last three years of the plan (1970-72) was raised by nearly a quarter, most of the additional outlay going into agriculture, irrigation, and transport.

The constitutions of 1962 and 1970 assigned to the king the responsibility for presiding over the country's Higher Council for National Promotion and Planning, which includes all institutions dealing with the social and economic life of the country and makes the final recommendations to the king on matters having to do with social and economic development. Final decisions on development policy rest with the king. The Five Year Plan was given extra force by being issued in the form of a law.

The planning apparatus in 1971 was located in the office of the prime minister under the direction of a director general of planning and development. The office organization centered on the planning division, which was served by a statistical staff and which reported to the Inter-Ministerial Planning and Budget Coordination Committee. Its activities included planning, collection, and processing of statistical information; the coordination of technical assistance; and the supervision of a UNDP-sponsored statistical training office

The purpose of the 1968-72 plan, in aggregate terms, was to raise the level of gross investment over the plan period from about 14 percent of the gross domestic product to around 18 percent per year. This level of investment was expected to lift the average annual rate of growth of the gross domestic product (in constant prices) from 4.3 to 4.8 percent, depending on the performance of agriculture. Such a rate of growth would imply raising the average rate of increase of per capita income to the range of 1 to 1.5 percent per year.

The emphasis in the plan was upon the upgrading of agriculture, with special attention to the construction of multipurpose irrigation projects; upon the fostering of tourism; and upon the training of upper level government administrators and technicians. The indirect intention of this approach was to reduce the import of goods and services (including foreign technical services), to expand the export of goods and services (including tourist services), and to alleviate the pressure on the country's small availabilities of foreign exchange reserves. The necessary investments would be accompanied by those government reforms in the fields of public and private finance and exchange and tariff policy that were considered necessary to call forth the requisite savings and domestic and foreign investment.

Relatively little stress was placed on the social sectors. The latest information, however, indicated that substantially greater emphasis would be given to those sectors in the new plan (1973-77).

The 1968-72 plan consisted of a central government investment program and estimates of the investments by central government enterprises, local governments, and the private sector that would be needed to bring about the levels of growth decided upon by the plan (see table 3). Total outlays called for by the plan amounted to DH11.45 billion, of which DH7.68 billion represented outlays by the public sector and DH3.77 billion were expected to be forthcoming from the private sector.

Although the year-to-year framework of the plan was to be kept flexible and subject to change where desirable, the projected timing of the plan foresaw total annual outlays rising from DH2 billion in 1968 to DH2.75 billion in 1972. The central government's participation was projected at approximately DH1 billion annually.

Table 3. *Morocco's Five Year Development Plan, 1968-72, at Constant (1967) Prices, by Sectors and Investing Agencies*

(in millions of dirham)[1]

	Public Sector				Private Sector Total	Public and Private Total
	Central Government Capital Budget	Local Government Capital Budget[2]	Public Enterprises[3]	Total		
Agriculture	1,550	55	0	1,605	160	1,765
Dams	746	0	0	746	0	746
National Development	120	30	0	150	0	150
Tourism	171	10	230	411	349	760
Power	214	0	296	510	0	510
Mines	300	0	829	1,129	133	1,262
Industry	290	0	465	755	666	1,421
Crafts	22	0	0	22	0	22
Trade and public services	0	0	0	0	90	90
Education-training	276	0	0	276	0	276
Youth and sports	20	5	0	25	0	25
Public health	101	0	0	101	0	101
Transport	554	10	57	621	72	693
Telecommunications	170	0	21	191	0	191
Housing-water supply	181	83	15	279	1,000	1,279
Administrative facilities	196	2	0	198	0	198
Total new investment	4,911	195	1,913	7,019	2,470	9,489
Renewal[4]	0	205	317	522	1,300	1,822
Payments[5]	139	0	0	139	0	139
GRAND TOTAL	5,050	400	2,230	7,680	3,770	11,450

[1] After October 1959 the par value of the dirham equaled DH5.06 per US$1.

[2] Included nineteen provinces, two prefectures, seventy-four municipalities and autonomous centers, and some 730 rural communities.

[3] Excluding state contributions included in the central government budget. Public enterprises included (1969): phosphate monopoly; railways; tea and sugar monopoly; tobacco monopoly; sugar factories; export authority; electricity authority; National Agricultural Credit Bank; Industrial Office; Social Security Fund; and others.

[4] Renewal of equipment: materials, buildings, or public works.

[5] Settlement of treasury commitments for work carried out before 1968.

Source: Adapted from Morocco, Ministry of Economic Affairs, Planning and the Training of Senior Grades, *Five Year Plan, 1968-72*, I, Section II, Rabat, 1968, ch. 2, p.4.

The projected financing of the central government's outlays of DH5.05 billion foresaw the equivalent of DH1.94 billion (39 percent) from external sources and DH1.52 billion (30 percent) from new fiscal revenues and internal borrowings. This left DH1.59 billion (31 percent) still to be financed, either internally or externally, depending largely on future opportunities of obtaining favorable interest and repayment terms abroad. The authors of the plan expressed determination not to have recourse to inflationary financing. In point of fact, however, it did prove necessary to have recourse to the central bank for residual financing in each of the first three years of the plan. The manner in which the private sector investments were to be financed could not be defined in advance, inasmuch as it could not be known to what extent the private sector would react to official investment incentives and to what extent such reaction might involve direct foreign investment.

PUBLIC SECTOR FINANCES

The financial operations of the public sector occur at three levels—the central government, the various local government units, and the wholly or partly owned enterprises of the central government. Because the official data on the public sector's financial activities available in 1971 tended to be incomplete or inadequately identified, assessment of the full impact of the fiscal operations of the public sector on the economy was difficult.

The central government presents its annual estimates of budgetary receipts and outlays in a finance law that is divided into three parts: the general budget of the state, a group of separate agency budgets annexed to the general budget, and a series of special treasury accounts. In 1971 the estimated outlays under the general budget totaled some DH4.4 billion; the estimated outlays of the annexed budgets, about DH266 million; and the outlays under the special treasury accounts, DH823 million—for a total for the year of about DH5.5 billion. The overall budgetary resources of the government were estimated to exceed expenditures by some DH90 million.

The general budget of the state is presented in a threefold breakdown that comprises an operating budget resembling fairly closely the generally accepted prototype of a current budget; an investment budget consisting mainly of expenditures connected with the Five Year Plan; and expenditures on account of the public debt. The latter consist of interest and repayment of principle in respect to the amortizable debt and interest alone in regard to the so-called floating debt.

For practical purposes the expenditures for the public debt should be added to the current (operating) budget. In 1971 budgeted expenditures through the current budget (including DH354 million for the public debt) amounted to about DH3.1 billion, and budgeted outlays under the investment budget amounted to about DH1.3 billion.

The so-called annexed budgets relate to a number of government agencies—the Government Printing Office; the Casablanca Port Authority; the Other Ports Authority; the Ministry of Posts,

Telegraph, and Telephone; and the Moroccan Radio and Television Office. They are presented separately from the general budget of the state both for historical reasons and because they resemble commercial institutions in having some independent sources of operating revenue. They are linked to the general budget through the transfer of their current surpluses to the general budget resources and through the funding of their current deficits and investment outlays from the general budget expenditures.

The annexes may, therefore, be visualized as an extension of the general budget and may be added to it in considering the relationship of the government to the economy. Of the total anticipated expenditures of some DH266 million through the annexed budgets in 1971, about DH210 million was on account of current operating costs, and DH55 million was allocated to investment.

The treasury special accounts are accounts set up over the years in connection with special-purpose outlays and receipts. Their individual size, composition, and exact objectives are not readily available, but they apparently include accounts in connection with membership in international agencies; the counterpart funds created in connection with United States Food for Peace (PL 480) assistance; residual items connected with discontinued operating budget items; foreign grant and loan funds; and probably the accounts set up in connection with bilateral trading arrangements with communist countries. They are apparently financed in part with foreign loans and grants, specially earmarked current revenues, monies from the general budget, and treasury (medium- and short-term) bonds. Although determining their precise relationship to the general budget was not practicable, they also appeared on balance to represent an extension of the general budget.

Expenditures of the local government units (regional administrative offices, provinces, municipalities, and major urban centers) at the start of the 1970s were estimated to approximate 10 percent as much as the central government's expenditures under the general budget. An estimated 20 to 25 percent appeared to be financed with the units' own revenue collections; more than 60 percent, with central government transfers; and the balance, with other transfers and loans. About 60 percent of outlays seemed to be for current operating expenses, and 40 percent, for investment.

The major state enterprises included the transportation, power, phosphate, fertilizer, tobacco, and sugar monopolies, in addition to the posts, telegraph, telecommunication, and port authorities. To the extent that they were self-financing, they were not a burden on the government, but they did expand its operations. To the extent that they were not self-financing (this tended to result in plant obsolescence and inefficiency), they figured in the government's expenditures—especially in the form of investment outlays for rehabilitation and renewal of plant and equipment. Because this was being carried out in the framework of the Five Year Plan, it probably would not represent an addition to the plan outlays already incorporated in the central government's investment budget. Even where such renovations were not included in the investment budget, it was possible that they might be funded under one of the special treasury accounts and again, therefore, would not be added to outlays already accounted for.

Because of the definitional confusion surrounding the ideas of state enterprise and local governmental units, it was not practicable to aggregate the various components of public sector expenditure and reach an assured estimate of it and, therefore, of the ratio of public sector expenditures to the gross domestic product. Other factors contributing to this confusion were double-counting within the central government budget, the local unit budgets, and the annexed budgets and the large element of imprecision in regard to the content of the special treasury accounts. It seemed probable, however, that during the late 1960s perhaps close to one-third of the gross domestic product was directly or indirectly originating in the public sector.

The Budgetary Process

The public finance enabling legislation, under which the central government's annual finance law is drafted, voted, and implemented, was provided for in the constitutions of 1962 and 1970 and enacted in the Organic Finance Law of November 9, 1963. The finance law for each year consists of two parts, and it may be amended in the course of the year. The first part authorizes the collection of public revenues and the issuance of public loans. It also fixes global ceilings for expenditures and presents the measures necessary to implement the above provisions. The second part of the law sets forth, by ministry and in detail, the expenditures to be undertaken under the general budget. It authorizes the operations called for in the annexed budgets in some detail. It authorizes the special accounts of the treasury in global figures only.

A draft of the finance law is prepared annually by the Ministry of Finance in cooperation with the planning division of the Five Year Plan organization. The draft is presented not later than November 1 to the Council of Ministers for their consideration and approval and is then sent to the legislature to be discussed and voted into law. The provisions of the draft finance law may not be modified in Parliament if such modification would result either in reducing the projected receipts or in increasing the projected expenditures (see ch. 8, The Governmental System and Political Dynamics).

Expenditures

The central government's current expenditures, as set out in the general budget, have included the government's ordinary operating budget and the costs of carrying the public debt (see table 4). Over the 1966-70 period the projected ordinary operating budget increased about 35 percent, compared with an estimated increase in the gross domestic product (at current prices) over the same period of around 25 percent.

The current operating budget is presented by ministries, which are grouped in three categories: administrative, economic, and social service. In addition, relatively minor amounts are allocated for the expenditures of the crown and for a catchall miscellaneous item. The largest single allocation in 1971 was for national defense and police (34 percent), followed by allocations for education (25 percent), public health (8 percent), agriculture (7 percent), and finance (also 7 percent). Between 1966 and 1971 the administrative group increased its operating budget 70 percent; the social service group, 30 percent; and the economic group, 25 percent.

The central government's investment budget in 1971 contained projected allocations totaling DH1.3 billion, reflecting an increase of about 62 percent in the investment budget since 1966 (see table 5). The big jump from DH864 million in 1967 to DH1,130 million in 1968 resulted from the introduction of a "corrective budget" during the course of the year. The initial investment budget for 1968 apparently called for outlays of only some DH650 million, which was appreciably less than those for the year before, and also less than the DH1,010 million average annual share of the Five Year Plan.

The investment budget is presented in the same functional format as the operating budget, with the several ministries grouped as administrative, economic, and social service. By far the most important group in the investment budget in recent years has been the economic group, which in 1971 accounted for almost 80 percent of the budget, compared with 10 percent for the administrative group and 8 percent for the social service group.

Receipts

The means of financing the central government's budgetary expenditures are for practical purposes divided into current revenues and exceptional receipts (see table 6). The first consist of tax and other current receipts; they are intended to finance the government's current expenses, including the public debt charges. The exceptional receipts are for the most part made up of variable mixes of foreign and domestic borrowing. As presented, they are equal to the investment budget and are solely intended for that purpose. Before

Table 4. *Budget Estimates of Current Expenditures of the Central Government of Morocco, 1966-71*
(in millions of dirham)[1]

	1966	1967	1968[2]	1969	1970	1971	Percentage of 1971
Expenditures of the Crown	31	34	34	41	44	52	2
Administrative Ministries							41
Prime minister	16	17	22	22	24	24	
Youth and sports	--	--	19	20	21	22	
Information	4	14	5	5	5	5	
Justice	67	67	75	76	82	81	
Foreign affairs	44	44	48	51	52	55	
Defense and police	542	575	841	851	872	943	34
Chamber of representatives	--	--	--	--	--	15	
Total	673	717	1,010	1,025	1,056	1,145	
Economic Ministries							20
Tourism	7	7	11	17	14	17	
Finance	153	136	246	162	183	193	7
Commerce, industry, mining, and merchant marine	18	18	18	18	18	18	
Public works and communications	105	107	120	120	121	115	4
Agriculture and land reform	149	153	174	177	186	190	7
National Development and crafts	--	--	--	--	--	--	
Posts, telegraphs, and telephones	--	--	--	--	--	5	
Total	432	421	569	494	522	538	
Social Service Ministries							33
Education	507	497	553	594	625	690	25
Labor	11	11	13	14	15	15	
Health	190	200	204	213	216	217	8
Housing	--	--	--	--	3	3	
Total	708	708	770	821	859	925	
Reconstruction of Agadir	--	--	--	--	--	--	
Miscellaneous	75	72	88	117	123	111	4
TOTAL ORDINARY EXPENDITURES	1,919	1,952	2,471	2,498	2,604	2,770	100
Debt Service (interest and commissions)	215	242	264	274	324	354	
TOTAL CURRENT EXPENDITURES	2,134	2,194	2,735	2,772	2,928	3,124	

[1] At current prices. After October 1959 the par value of the dirham equaled DH5.06 per US$1.
[2] Revised estimates.
-- Less than 1.

Table 5. *Budget Estimates of the Investment Outlays of the Central Government of Morocco, 1966-71*

(in millions of dirham)[1]

	1966	1967	1968 [2]	1969	1970	1971	Percent of 1971
Expenditures of the Crown.	9	20	25	22	27	22	2
Administrative Ministries							10
Prime minister	n.a.	--	1	4	15	7	
Youth and sports	--	--	4	5	4	7	
Information	6	2	3	7	10	7	
Justice	1	1	2	2	3	2	
Foreign affairs	2	2	2	5	--	--	
Defense and police	20	24	57	n.a.	60	112	
Total	33	29	69	80	92	134	
Economic Ministries							80
Tourism	--	--	--	5	5	2	
Finance	188	204	222	184	126	195	
Commerce, industry, mining, and merchant marine	3	3	9	6	6	7	
Public works and communications	219	249	361	430	447	445	
Agriculture and land reform	290	296	344	347	332	295	
National development and crafts	8	--	--	n.a.	5	n.a.	
Posts, telegraphs, and telephones	--	13	--	1	22	3	
Total	708	765	936	973	943	1,040	
Social Service Ministries							8
Education	35	21	78	67	45	86	
Labor	2	1	1	2	2	3	
Health	13	8	13	14	21	14	
Housing	--	--	--	4	--	n.a.	
Total	50	30	92	87	68	104	
Reconstruction of Agadir	8	n.a.	6	2	2	--	
Miscellaneous	--	1	2	--	--	--	
TOTAL	808	864	1,130	1,164	1,132	1,300	100

n.a.—Not available.
--less than 1.
[1] At current prices. After October 1959 the par value of the dirham equaled DH5.06 per US$1.
[2] Revised estimates.

1969 the current budget was sometimes presented with an uncovered deficit; since then it has shown a nominal surplus.

Failure of the sources of financing for either the current or the investment budget to come up to expectations would probably mean that the central bank would be called upon to meet the shortfall, unless expenditures also had fallen sufficiently short of projections to offset the revenue deficiency. By the same token, an excess of receipts over outlays in the current budget would, other things being equal, have the effect of reducing the government's need to borrow from the central bank or from other internal sources. To the extent that foreign borrowing was being depended upon to finance the import of foreign goods and services for given investment projects, those projects would not be included in the budget in the absence of the corresponding financing from abroad unless the government's foreign exchange reserves had been sufficiently augmented in the meantime to sustain the extra load.

The current revenues for the most part comprise indirect taxes and customs receipts, direct taxes, stamp and registry taxes, and contributions of local units and public entities. Until 1968 the current revenues included a sizable item composed of receipts from government monopolies and enterprises; since 1969 these receipts have been treated as indirect taxes and included in that item. In the 1971 estimates of current revenues, indirect taxes, which included customs receipts, accounted for 65 percent of total current receipts; direct taxes, for 22 percent; and stamp taxes, for 6 percent. Between 1966 and 1971 projected total current receipts increased about 52 percent, compared with increases of about 35 percent in current expenditures and 25 percent in the gross domestic product over the same period. The growth in the current revenues resulted from increases in the tax base, increases in the tax rates, improvement in collection methods, incorporation into the budget of the profits of the phosphate monopoly, and retention of portions of the turnover tax that previously had been shared with the local unit governments.

The indirect taxes were of three types. The first consisted of excise taxes on commodities easily and profitably taxable at the source, such as petroleum products, tobacco products, sugar, alcoholic beverages, and certain luxury articles. The second was a turnover tax on most goods and services, at rates of around 12 to 15 percent and 6 percent, respectively. During the 1960s this tax was the most rapidly growing of the major revenue sources, and in 1970 it was expected to be the most productive.

The third kind of indirect taxes were the customs duties and surcharges; they formerly constituted the government's most important source of current revenues. Import duties affect most imported goods—at rates ranging from 3 to 150 percent—except low-income essentials and some capital goods and raw materials imported

Table 6. Budget Estimates for Financing of Current and Investment Outlays of Morocco, 1966-71

(in millions of dirham)[1]

Revenues	1966	1967	1968 [2]	1969	1970	1971	Percentage of 1971
Current Receipts							
Direct taxes	447	531	654	680	701	679	22
Agriculture	44	44	44	80	80	n.a.	--
Salaries	84	90	100	125	132	n.a.	--
Business profits	263	340	377	405	410	n.a.	--
Customs receipts	442	438	472	490	517	566	18
Import duties and taxes	340	383	410	420	455	n.a.	--
Indirect taxes	531	559	843	1,194	1,268	1,474	47
Turnover (tax on products and services)	195	215	440	590	n.a.	n.a.	--
Excise	336	344	403	604	n.a.	n.a.	--
Stamp and registration taxes	115	115	135	178	188	200	6
Receipts from government properties	79	54	53	53	57	--	--
Receipts from government monopolies and government enterprises	309	260	367	1	--	7	--
Contributions of local units, government agencies, and public entities	49	54	40	54	56	59	2
Other current fiscal income	101	95	134	124	146	140	5
TOTAL CURRENT REVENUES	2,073	2,106	2,698	2,774	2,933	3,125	100
Exceptional receipts, domestic and foreign borrowing, and use of counterpart funds	808	864	1,167	1,164	1,133	1,308	--
TOTAL BUDGETARY FINANCING	2,881	2,970	3,865	3,938	4,066	4,433	--

--not applicable.
n.a.—not available.
[1] At current prices. After October 1959 the par value of the dirham equaled DH5.06 per US$1.
[2] Revised estimates.

to be used in production by domestic enterprises. A flat-rate surcharge of 2 to 3 percent ad valorem is imposed on all imports. In 1970 export charges on minerals and other commodities amounted to about 12 percent of total customs receipts. In 1971 they were discontinued.

The direct taxes mainly included a tax on business profits, a tax on salaries, and an agricultural tax. The tax on business profits was assessed against both business enterprises and individuals, at fairly high rates (around 20 to 48 percent above DH24,000 for individuals and 40 to 48 percent above DH500,000 for enterprises in 1969); businesses were also subject to a business tax. The salaries (income) tax was assessed against upper level salaries and collected at the source at progressive rates; a compulsory government loan introduced in 1968 was tantamount to an increase in the salaries tax. The agricultural tax, representing less than 3 percent of current revenues in 1970, appeared meager in comparison with the importance of the agricultural sector in the economy. The stamp and registry taxes consisted largely of a property transfer tax and a unitary stamp tax.

The domestic debt portion of the exceptional receipts allocated to finance the investment budget apparently was composed of long-term (more than five years) government bonds plus the compulsory bonds introduced in 1968 to help finance the large in-year increase in the investment budget. Should such bonds prove insufficient for the local currency requirements of the investment budget, the deficit would presumably be absorbed by the treasury, if it had extra funds available, or by the central bank. The central bank statutorily, and within clearly defined limits, makes short-term (less than one year) advances to the government to smooth out the lags between its receipts and expenditures. It may also, by special written agreement, make additional advances to the government, which apparently have tended to accumulate rather than be repaid.

BANKING AND CURRENCY

Currency is widely used even in remote local markets, and the modern, urban sector of the economy has been served for many years by a highly developed banking system of public credit institutions and subsidiaries of foreign private banks. In 1971, however, the great majority of Moroccans made no use of banking institutions. Savings were invested in jewelry, livestock, and land. Borrowing—which was mostly for subsistence rather than investment purposes—was from a landlord, a merchant, or a moneylender.

When Morocco regained its independence in 1956, the country had three separate monetary systems. Since then the government's efforts in the monetary field have been directed mainly at integrating those systems into one and at creating new national monetary institutions, including a new central bank, named the Bank of Morocco, and a new currency—the Moroccan dirham. Although the government has indicated it would prefer not to nationalize the banking system, it has emphasized its purpose of reducing the extraterritorial ownership of the foreign units in the system.

Monetary Policy

Monetary policy in the years after independence was liberal, both with regard to credit to the private sector, the financing of rising budget deficits by the central bank, and the relative freedom from restraints on imports of goods and services and with regard to the repatriation of foreign (mainly French) investments. The result was excessive expansion of the money supply and deterioration of the foreign reserve position. This led to some stiffening of monetary and fiscal policy in 1961, which failed, however, to be adequate to the needs. In 1965, after a continued decline of the exchange reserves, the preliminary report of an indepth study of the economy by a World Bank survey mission, and the assumption of emergency powers by the king, the government instituted a restructuring of its monetary, fiscal, and foreign trade policies and machinery. Strict measures were taken to govern exchange movements (see ch. 13, Trade and Transportation). In 1967 basic legislation on money and credit was laid down to provide greater control over the money supply, and revised budgetary definitions and guidelines, based on the organic finance law of 1963, were introduced.

This strengthening of the government's fiscal and monetary posture was given additional impetus by the attempted coup in July 1971, though just how this would work itself out was still unclear in late 1971. Accumulated upward pressure on prices had, to date, been largely contained by rigorous governmental price and wage controls, but this was a continuing problem that would have to be dealt with if Moroccan exports were to be competitive in overseas markets.

The Money Market

The organized money market at the start of the 1970s consisted mainly of the central bank; some seventeen Moroccan commercial banks (including the Popular Credit Bank system); a dozen or so foreign commercial banks; deposit funds located in the post office and the treasury; a score or more important insurance and reinsurance companies; a stock exchange at Casablanca; and a number of government-owned or government-controlled special purpose banks and funds. The special purpose banks and funds included the Deposit and Investment Fund (Caisse de Dépôt et de Gestion—CDG), the

National Economic Development Bank, the National Agricultural Credit Bank, and the Construction and Hotel Credit Organization.

The government was engaged also in an effort to develop a network of credit cooperatives, but to 1971 that effort had not achieved a large measure of success. The appreciable amount of unorganized credit extended in the rural areas by landlords, local merchants, and moneylenders was not easy to quantify, but it probably represented a large part of the supply of credit available to small-scale agriculture, presumably at high rates of interest.

The total credit mobilized at the end of 1970 by the organized money market as defined and adjusted for double-counting was estimated to approach some DH7 billion, of which perhaps somewhat more than 50 percent represented claims on the government. Inclusion of the credit outstanding in the unorganized rural credit market would very likely have shifted the balance of indebtedness from the public to the private sector.

Of the organized credit to the private sector, apparently around 40 percent had been extended to industry (including fuel and power); perhaps 20 to 25 percent each to agriculture and commerce; 5 to 8 percent, to tourism; and lesser amounts, to transport, real estate, and other purposes. Between 75 and 80 percent of it was short-term credit.

The Banking Organization

The central bank (the Bank of Morocco) was created in 1959 as a public institution with all its capital subscribed by the state. The bank was designed to act as the sole issuer of currency, to hold and administer foreign exchange reserves, to act as financial adviser and agent for the government, to control the banking system and national credit policies (under guidance of the Ministry of Finance and the Committee of Money and Credit—Comité du Credit et du Marché Financier), and to have, in addition to the issue department, a commercial banking department. The bank had branches in the principal cities throughout the country. The law governing the Bank of Morocco requires that it maintain reserves in gold or convertible exchange equal to at least one-ninth the value of notes in circulation. As a means of controlling the economy, the bank may be required by the government to raise its reserves to one-third of the notes in circulation.

At the end of 1970 the commercial, or deposit money, banks (including the Popular Credit Bank system) operated under the provisions of the banking and credit law enacted in 1967. The central bank and the special purpose banks were controlled by the several statutes creating them.

The 1967 law established the minister of finance as the chief executive officer of the commercial banking system and money market, thereby affording more effective coordination of monetary and fiscal policy. It also provided for the advisory Committee of Money and Credit, of which the minister would be president and which would comprise, in addition to him, the governor and the vice governor of the Bank of Morocco, a number of government officials, and representatives of the special banks and of the banking profession. The Bank of Morocco was charged with carrying out the decisions of the committee relating to money and credit. In this the bank would be assisted by a banking association, also set up under the 1967 law and in which membership by the commercial banks was statutorily required. The association was instructed, in addition, to represent the banks in the study of matters of common interest to them and to the government.

After getting the opinion of the advisory committee, the minister of finance was authorized by law to establish or modify the relationship between any two or more components of the assets and liabilities of any commercial bank; to set the ratio of government securities to demand deposits; and to fix the ratio of reserves in the central bank to demand liabilities. The minister might also fix the maturity, as well as the amount and the interest rates, of the banks' various categories of credit. These additional discretionary powers were helpful in maintaining control over the money supply, inasmuch as the usefulness for that purpose of the discount rate had been largely nullified by the government's longtime desire to maintain it at the low level of 3.5 percent with the intent of stimulating the economy. At the end of 1970 the outstanding credit of the commercial banks to the private sector totaled about DH2.2 billion, most of it at short term. Around 45 percent was for industry; about 20 percent, for agriculture; a similar amount, for commerce; and appreciably smaller amounts for hotels, transport, and real estate.

The most important of the government's special purpose financing institutions seem to have been the National Agricultural Credit Bank system, the National Economic Development Bank, and the CDG.

In December 1961 all agricultural credit institutions were absorbed into the National Agricultural Credit Bank (Caisse Nationale de Crédit Agricole—CNCA). The CNCA makes loans only to credit organizations, public institutions, and cooperatives. Loans to individuals are made by regional or local agricultural credit banks or, if the borrower is in the low income group, by the agricultural credit and provident societies, which had a clientele of over 750,000 farmers. The whole pyramid of institutions is funded by CNCA, and their lending activities are directed by it. The societies perform a training and educational function as well as a financial one.

The National Economic Development Bank (Banque Nationale pour le Developpement Economique—BNDE) was also established in 1959, with the purpose of promoting the economic development of the country. Half of its DH20 million original capital was subscribed by the state; one-fourth, by private Moroccan interests; and one-fourth, by foreign banks in a number of countries. Three-fourths of a subsequent DH10 million stock issue was subscribed by the International Finance Corporation, an affiliate of the World Bank. Additional lending resources of the bank come from rediscounting loans at the central bank, from credits advanced by the government and borrowing on the open market, and from US$61 million in loans (up to mid-1971) from the World Bank.

The BNDE has been particularly active in financing two sectors, manufacturing and tourism, and is the main source of long-term finance for manufacturing. Although it may participate in ownership, it acts mainly through loans, which are limited to investment, not to working capital. Between 1962 and 1971 it had extended aggregate financing totaling more than DH500 million.

The CDG was established in 1959 as an autonomous public entity to receive and invest public sector deposits. Certain savings and retirement funds, including the national social security fund, are legally required to hold their deposits with the CDG, and other cooperative and mutual institutions may voluntarily do so. The CDG is responsible for the investment not only of the funds deposited with it but also of the national insurance and pension fund and the communal equipment fund, which is designed to extend loans or advances to local communal groups. The CDG may invest in government securities or private sector securities quoted on the stock exchange; it may lend to the BNDE and may purchase or construct real estate assets. In 1968 it invested about DH500 million in governmental obligations.

Interest rates charged by the various lending institutions at the start of the 1970s were low. They ranged from the central bank's discount rate of 3.5 percent, through heavily subsidized rates for agricultural credit and hotel construction mortgage loans, to rates on industrial loans of 6 to 7 percent. Rates on commercial bank credit varied from about 6 to 12 percent, depending on the purpose and term of the loan.

Currency, Money Supply, and Prices

The Moroccan dirham is a nonconvertible paper currency unit, consisting of 100 francs, issued by the Bank of Morocco. By agreement with the International Monetary Fund (IMF) on October 16, 1959, it was defined as equivalent to 175.61 milligrams of fine gold with a par value of DH5.06049 per US$1. The paper currency is issued in notes with denominations of five, ten, fifty, and 100 dirham; and the subsidiary currency, in coins denominated one, two, five, ten, twenty, and fifty francs and one and five dirham.

The money supply, as defined by the IMF in its monthly *International Financial Statistics*, is the sum of currency in the hands of the public and bank deposits subject to withdrawal on demand. Year-to-year changes in the money supply are attributable to the sum of changes in the country's net foreign exchange reserves, changes in credit extended by the banking system to the government (net of government deposits), and changes in credit extended by the banking system to the private sector, less changes in other balance sheet items (net). The Moroccan statistics, in defining the money supply, include certain other deposits in addition to the demand deposits. Because the *International Financial Statistics* definition is more satisfactory for purposes of intercountry comparison and its data are more current and convenient to update, its formula has been used here.

Between 1964 and the end of 1970 the money supply increased from DH3,593 million to DH5,543 million, or approximately 54 percent, which compares with an estimated increase in the gross domestic product of around 25 percent and suggests the possibility of some inflationary buildup (see table 7). During this period the proportion of currency in the money supply increased more rapidly than that of bank deposits, from 35 percent in 1964 to 41 percent in 1970, reflecting not only the improved crop conditions but also probably some increase in monetization in the rural parts of the country and possibly some increase in hoarding in the rural sector.

Analysis of the factors causing the increase in the money supply indicates that, taking the period as a whole, the major source of increase was bank credit, especially central bank credit, to the government. This credit accounted for more than 60 percent of the upward push on the money supply, compared with less than 30 percent attributable to bank credit to the private sector and about 10 percent attributable to improvement in the foreign exchange position.

After the drought in 1966 the foreign exchange position deteriorated rapidly. In 1969, however, the trend was reversed. It continued to improve in 1970 and buoyantly in the first four months of 1971.

Bank credit, including deposit money bank credit, to the government sector was restrained through 1966 but rose sharply in 1967, in step with increased food imports and the increase in development expenditures. It continued to rise until the end of 1970, though at a slower rate after 1969, reflecting the improvement in budget revenues and other sources, domestic and foreign, of budget financing. Bank credit, especially commercial bank credit, to the

Table 7. Changes in and Sources of Money Supply in Morocco, 1965–70 [1]

(in millions of dirham) [2]

Item	1965	1966	1967	1968	1969	1970	Total 1965–70	April 1971
Money Supply								
Currency	1,386	1,429	1,614	1,859	2,122	2,262	---	2,203
Demand deposits	2,425	2,370	2,527	2,829	3,076	3,281	---	3,418
Total	3,811	3,799	4,141	4,688	5,198	5,543	---	5,621
Year to year change in money supply	+218	−12	+342	+547	+510	+345	+1,950 [3]	+78 [3]
Sources of Change in Money Supply								
Gold and foreign exchange (net)	+231	−62	−94	−144	+105	+182	+218	+277
Bank credit to the government sector (net)								
Central bank (net)	+30	+21	+301	+270	+203	+164	+989	−187
Deposit money banks	+50	+12	+11	+67	+212	+37	+389	+47
Treasury and post office demand deposits	−79	−1	+33	−4	+108	−17	+40	+37
Total	+1	+32	+345	+333	+523	+184	+1,418	−103
Bank credit to the private sector								
Central bank	+27	+32	−26	+48	+62	−40	+103	+10
Deposit money banks	+22	+33	+133	+421	−119	+46	+536	+52
Total	+49	+65	+107	+469	−57	+6	+639	+62
Less								
Time and savings deposits	+42	−20	+42	+106	+71	−23	+218	+43
Other balance sheet items (net)	+19	+68	−26	+5	−10	+50	+106	+111
Total	+61	+48	+16	+111	+61	+27	+324	+154
Net total sources of change in money supply	+220	−13	+342	+547	+510	+345	+1,951 [3]	+82 [3]

[1] End of period.
[2] After October 1959 the par value of the dirham equaled DH5.06 per US$1.
[3] Totals differ presumably because of rounding.

Source: Adapted from International Monetary Fund, *International Financial Statistics*, XXIV, No. 8, August 1971, pp. 240–243.

private sector increased steadily from 1964 to 1968. In 1969 and 1970 it was restrained by the authorities in order to reduce the growing inflationary pressures on prices.

The available price indexes included a wholesale price index in Casablanca and a cost of living or consumer index. Both were limited in their coverage and heavily weighted with foodstuffs. The wholesale index had a 1939 base, and the consumer index, a 1959 base. Inasmuch as the prices of basic consumer foods, beverages, fuels, power, and transport were fixed by the government, the cost of living index had a built-in tendency toward stability. As a consequence, it is probable that changes in the index have tended to understate the actual decline in purchasing power of the currency unit. According to the consumer index, as presented by the IFS, prices increased about 1.6 percent from 1964 to 1967; from 1967 to 1970 the increase was about 4.8 percent, for an apparent, but probably underestimated, average of less than 1 percent per year between 1964 and 1970. From December 1970 to April 1971 there was an increase of about 2.3 percent, indicating a rapid rise in the tempo of inflationary pressures. This led in mid-1971 to a 16-percent wage increase for government workers, offset, in part at least, by reductions in some foodstuffs and increases in some taxes.

The Public Debt

Available estimates of the public debt differ appreciably, mainly as a result of differences in definition, coverage, and timing; when adjusted, they appear to agree fairly well on the general order of magnitude of the debt. A reasonably approximate estimate of the indebtedness of the central government (including the treasury) at the end of 1968 would seem to be in the range of DH6 billion to DH6.5 billion; a range is used to allow for the possibility of double-counting among the commercial banks, the insurance companies, and the CDG. This estimate includes the long- and medium-term direct and guaranteed debt of the government and the treasury (DH4.4 billion), as presented in the Finance Law of 1969 (adjusted for a number of statistical errors), of which some DH3 billion represented foreign debts; plus short-term treasury bonds held by the commercial banks, estimated at about DH0.6 billion; central bank advances to the central government of DH1.2 billion; and government and treasury bonds held by the CDG, estimated at up to DH0.2 billion. The estimate does not include supplier credits to state enterprises or the outstanding balance of payments agreements with communist and other countries, the total of which is not known; nor does it include the debt of the local government units, which in 1968 totaled around DH100 million, according to the Finance Law of 1969. The estimated indebtedness of the central government may be compared with the estimated gross domestic product in 1968 of DH15.25 billion at current prices. Service on the public debt in 1968 was estimated at DH264 million.

CHAPTER 12

AGRICULTURE AND INDUSTRY

Agriculture in 1971 continued to be the mainstay of the economy. About 70 percent of the active population was directly engaged in farming, livestock raising, fishing, and forestry, and some 75 to 80 percent of the total population was dependent on agriculture. It contributed over half of exports and roughly 30 percent of the gross domestic product (GDP—see Glossary), depending largely on the effect of weather on the harvests. Despite some sizable mineral deposits, increasing industrial output, and a rapidly growing tourist trade, the development of agricultural resources remained the key factor in the country's plans for economic expansion (see ch. 11, Character and Structure of the Economy).

The principal crops were cereals—barley, wheat, and corn. A large variety of vegetables, fruits and nuts was also grown, primarily for export. Although wide annual variations in rainfall threatened the agricultural economy with shortages, in years of normal harvest the country was largely self-sufficient in most foods except sugar and edible oils; in poor crop years, cereals had to be imported.

The industrial sector is defined to include energy, mining, and manufacturing (including handicrafts). At the end of the 1960s it accounted for about 20 percent of the gross domestic product; mining represented around 4 or 5 percent, power accounted for 3 or 4 percent, and manufacturing represented about 12 percent. By this definition, industry apparently employed at that time around 500,000 workers: 20,000 in the energy sector, some 40,000 in mining, 150,000 to 175,000 in large-scale modern manufacturing (more than 10 workers per workshop), and the balance (265,000 to 290,000) in handicraft and small-scale workshops. The sector, as defined, accounted for about 30 percent of exports.

In 1971 Morocco was one of the major producers of phosphate and the world's largest exporter. The phosphate rock reserves were estimated at some 40 billion metric tons, much of it of high quality. Other mineral deposits, however, such as coal, iron ore, and petroleum, either were of relatively low quality or were being, or had been, depleted. In 1971 extensive prospecting for liquid fuel deposits was continuing.

The country's work force continued in the early 1970s to grow more rapidly than the economy, thus exacerbating an already grave economic and political problem. Perhaps 50 percent of the agricultural workers were underemployed, and in 1968 an estimated 12.4 percent of a work force of approximately 5,575,000 were unemployed. The percentage of unemployed was projected to reach 14.2 by 1973, but in 1971 various observers estimated that urban unemployment was as high as 25 percent.

There continued to be a shortage of skilled laborers, technicians, and managerial and professional personnel. The official policy of replacing foreigners with Moroccans was being implemented cautiously at best, despite pressure from political opposition and labor union groups.

In 1971 less than 15 percent of the work force was unionized. The two leading union federations, the Moroccan Labor Union (Union Marocain du Travail—UMT) and the Union of Moroccan Workers (Union Générale des Travailleurs Marocains—UGTM), have a long history of political activities. The UMT in particular was an important element in opposition politics (see ch. 8, The Governmental System and Political Dynamics).

AGRICULTURE

Of the country's approximately 174,000 square miles (about 111 million acres), only some 18 percent was estimated to be arable in the mid-1960s; 17 percent was permanent pasture, 20 percent was forest land, and 45 percent was nonarable mountain, desert, or urban areas (see table 8). The agricultural area, comprising arable land and pasturelands, thus constituted approximately 35 percent of the total area. The plains and uplands of western Morocco between the Atlas ranges and the Atlantic Ocean, together with the intermontane valleys of the Middle Atlas range, constitute the main agricultural region. In crop year 1967/68 an estimated 13.5 million acres, or two-thirds of total croplands, were under cultivation, the remainder lying fallow. On the basis of farming methods, the agricultural area was divided into a traditional sector, accounting for about 85 to 90 percent of the total, and a modern sector, accounting for the remainder.

Roughly 1.25 million acres were under irrigation at the end of the 1960s. Nearly two-thirds were in the traditional sector and were irrigated by the use of springs and artesian and other wells, by the diversion of streams and, in the more arid areas, by horizontal tunnels connecting the irrigated land with water sources in the hills, in some cases many miles distant. Irrigation by these methods had been practiced for centuries, and the government, both before and after independence, continued to initiate small- and medium-sized flood control and irrigation water-control projects. It also embarked upon eight large multipurpose installations, called perimeters, designed to

Table 8. Estimated Land Utilization in Morocco, Mid-1960s [1]

Use	Area[2]	Percent of Total
Agricultural land		
Arable land	19.51	18
Permanent pasture	18.90	17
Total agricultural land	38.41	35
Forest land	22.23	20
Marshland	0.07	0
Nonarable land	50.29	45
TOTAL	111.00[3]	100

[1] There are a number of estimates of land utilization, in general resembling one another, but varying somewhat in date, definition, and coverage. Pending completion of a cadastral survey that was being designed in 1971 and the national census, including a farm census that was expected to be taken in 1972, the choice among them is probably not too significant.

[2] In millions of acres.

[3] Takes account of 1970-71 boundary settlements with Algeria.

Source: Adapted from U.S. Tennessee Valley Authority, *Morocco: Role of Fertilizer in Agricultural Development*, Muscle Shoals, 1967, table 1.

irrigate 1.6 million or more acres. At the end of 1970 these projects were in various stages of completion and probably were not providing more than half of their potential usefulness. In some instances the water had been brought to the edge of the fields to be irrigated, but the fields had not yet been leveled, and the internal ditching had not been finished.

Agriculture in Morocco is confronted with a number of difficulties. Predominant among these are the increasingly generalized lack of water as one moves from northwest to southeast and the year-to-year unpredictability of rainfall (see ch. 2, Geography and Population). This basic situation is compounded by historical factors in the traditional sector.

Primitive methods of cultivation, a lack of understanding of the use of fertilizers and insecticides, and the absence of means to acquire them contribute to low yields on the vast majority of farms. Continuous planting of one crop on the same land, despite a two-year plant-fallow cycle, has devitalized the soil and, as a result, annual yields are low and may be expected to become lower until something is done to remedy the situation. Fragmentation of land among heirs, resulting from the provisions of traditional Muslim inheritance laws, has created large numbers of minute, irregularly shaped, and often widely scattered plots that are inefficient to cultivate.

The physical situation makes difficult the use of modern equipment in the traditional sector and, together with extreme poverty, continues to tie the Moroccan peasant to the hoes, wooden plows, and pointed sticks used by his ancestors. Harvesting on these small holdings is done by hand, and threshing is done by animals. Expensive fertilizers are not used unless they are subsidized. Livestock fare poorly on the overgrazed pasture. Frequent droughts and insect plagues help to make the life of the subsistence farmer even more precarious. Attempts, both before and after independence, to consolidate these small holdings have met with little success. Under present conditions, an increase in the amount of land under cultivation could be achieved only by a reduction of the already insufficient grazing lands. Such lands, moreover, would be marginal and would not significantly increase yields.

In 1971 two categories of agricultural production were being carried on more or less side by side—the traditional subsistence agriculture of the bulk of the indigenous population and the modern agricultural production. The modern system had been introduced by Europeans, primarily *colons* (French settlers), in the first half of the twentieth century on land taken over by the protectorate government to be colonized or purchased from Moroccans by private owners. The modern sector included an estimated 2.5 million acres of agricultural land, most of which was under field or tree crops; this figure was down from the mid-1960s estimate of 3.7 million acres (see table 9). In 1971 perhaps 25 percent of this land was still owned by Europeans. The year 1971 was being referred to officially, however, as the "year of Moroccanization," and it was possible that most of the remaining foreign-owned agricultural land would soon be "recuperated." Lands that already had been "recuperated" by the government were apparently being retained within the modern sector in order to maintain their current yields rather than necessarily being returned to their former owners.

Although the modern sector comprised only about 10 or 15 percent of total agricultural land, it included some of the most fertile land in the country, and it contributed over 85 percent of commercialized agricultural production, including almost all of the citrus fruit, fresh vegetables, wine, soft wheat, and other export crops. Much of the agricultural land in the traditional sector was devoted to grazing, and the average yields per acre of cropped land were less than half of those in the modern sector. The traditional sector supported over 1 million families which, even in good years, consumed nearly all that they produced. Estimates at the end of the 1960s suggested that in the traditional sector farms had to be larger than ten acres in order to have the repayment capacity to support the use of fertilizers and that, where farms were larger than twenty-five acres in the rain-fed areas, they held promise of substantial development if adequately fertilized.

Table 9. *Estimated Distribution of Agricultural Land in Morocco, by Ownership, Mid-1960s*

Ownership	Area [1]	Percent of Total
Makhzan, jaysh, and habus land [2]	0.74	1.9
Traditional sector		
Collective land		
Permanent pasture	13.09	34.0
Arable land	2.47	6.4
Total collective land	15.56	40.4
Privately owned land (milk)		
Greater than 25-acre parcels	7.41	19.2
Less than 25-acre parcels	11.11	28.8
Total privately owned land	18.52	48.1[3]
Total traditional sector	34.08	88.5
Modern sector		
Owned by foreigners	1.11	2.9
Reacquired from foreigners [4]	0.62	1.6
Owned by Moroccans	1.98	5.1
Total modern sector [5]	3.71	9.6
GRAND TOTAL	38.53	100.0

[1] In millions of acres.
[2] Partly in the modern sector, partly in the traditional sector, without indication of the breakdown.
[3] Subtotals may not add to total because of rounding.
[4] Held by the government for distribution or rental.
[5] Includes an estimated 257,000 acres of irrigated land, without indication of their ownership.

Source: Adapted from U.S. Tennessee Valley Authority, *Morocco: Role of Fertilizer in Agricultural Development*, Muscle Shoals, 1967, table 1.

Ownership and Tenure

Traditional System

In the traditional sector the land tenure system was rooted in concepts and usages common to the Arab world. The system provided for five broad types of landholdings: *makhzan, jaysh, habus, milk*, and collective land.

Makhzan land was owned by the sultan or the central government (*makhzan*). In addition to a considerable amount of arable land, it included most forest land and all unused land and wasteland. The *makhzan* also owned the *jaysh* land, but the *jaysh* tribes had permanent usufruct of the land in exchange for the supply to the government of permanent military contingents (see ch. 3, Historical Setting). By 1971 all *makhzan* land was referred to as state land.

Habus land (land donated under Islamic law to a religious foundation) was in principle inalienable, but the protectorate government permitted holders to exchange or sell it in order to purchase other property.

Milk land was privately owned. In the mid-1960s *milk* land apparently totaled around 18.5 million acres of agricultural land, approximately 54 percent of the holdings in the traditional sector. *Milk* cropland consisted predominantly of parcels of less than 10 acres; more than 80 percent of it was rain-fed land, without irrigation. Under Muslim Arab usage, *milk* land had to be worked; if it were not worked, by definition it could not be treated as *milk* land—that is, privately owned.

Much of the *milk* land was worked under several forms of sharecropping. Under the most common system the sharecropper received about one-fifth of the crop in return for his labor, and the landowner, who supplied land, seed, tools, and sometimes clothing and food, received the remainder. In 1960, at the time of the last census, there were an estimated 120,000 sharecroppers.

Because of the importance of water, rights to it were traditionally dealt with separately from the land in customary law. An elaborate system of rules governed the transfer and exercise of water rights, and specialized customary officials saw to their proper application. Water rights could be acquired by inheritance, purchase, traditional right, or helping in the construction of the irrigation works. A well or other water source was rarely the property of a single individual, and the division of the available water among joint owners was either by alternating time periods of use or by a divider with various sized openings through which the water flowed from the source into the irrigation canals.

Modern System

Individual ownership with a clear, registered title was an outgrowth of colonization. Although some registration of titles existed under the traditional land tenure system, the procedure was not adequate for the needs of the European settlers. Therefore, in 1914 the French introduced a system under which registration became compulsory in cases where changes in ownership involved non-Moroccans.

Although large-scale colonization was discouraged in the early years of the protectorate, *colons* later began to arrive in large numbers, both with and without assistance from the French government. By independence in 1956 nearly 6,000 Europeans were in possession of more than 2.5 million acres of land, most of it in the fertile coastal areas and around Fes, Meknès, and Marrakech. Slightly more than a fourth of these lands was acquired under official colonization schemes and was provided by the government primarily from *makhzan* lands and *jaysh* lands and, when these proved insufficient, from supposedly unused communal and *milk* lands. The remainder of settler land was acquired by private purchase.

During the period of French rule some Moroccan landowners operating large-scale farms in the modern sector also had their land titles registered. Since independence the extent of Moroccan-owned land with clear, registered titles has been augmented both through the purchase by Moroccans of European-owned land and through the expropriation and redistribution to Moroccans of a part of the lands of official colonization. In this way the amount of land held outright by Europeans had apparently been reduced to less than 1 million acres by the end of the 1960s.

Under the protectorate, all water was declared to be public domain, but landowners were allowed the use of water on their land, and private water rights acquired earlier were recognized. Official authorization was required for any new diversion of waterways. The legislation was probably strictly applied only in the areas where governmental water-control projects were undertaken.

Agricultural Production

Crops

About 60 percent of agricultural income at the end of the 1960s was from crops. In the past the crops planted in the traditional sector were designed to minimize the risks of weather variability, even at the expense of forgoing large crops when the weather was exceptionally favorable. The principal crops were cereals, which were planted on over 80 percent of the arable land, including land held fallow. After cereals, the important crops were pulses, citrus fruits, grapes, vegetables, sugar beets, cotton, oil-producing plants, and nuts (see table 10). For the most part cereals were grown in the traditional dry-farming sector. The more than 1 million acres of irrigated land, as well as much of the best high-rainfall land in the northwest part of the country, were used to produce the modern sector's vegetables, citrus and other fruits, sugar beets, cotton, and rice.

The main cereal crops, which provide the staple diet of the country, are barley, hard wheat, and corn. These—with pulses—are the main crops grown by the subsistence farmers; they are also grown as cash crops, primarily by European settlers. Small quantities of sorghum, millet, and oats are also raised, and in recent years sufficient rice has been grown in irrigated areas to meet the small local demand. Cereals are affected more than other crops by the variable climate. In general, though by no means exclusively, wheat has been planted north of the Atlas ranges in the Fes, Meknès, and Chaouia regions and the Rharb and Tadla plains, where rainfall was greater than ten inches annually. The cultivation of barley predominated south of the Atlas from

Table 10. *Output of Principal Agricultural Commodities in Morocco, Average 1961-65, Annual 1966-70*

(in thousands of metric tons)

Commodity	Average 1961-65	1966	1967	1968	1969	1970*
Wheat	1,117	814	1,090	2,411	1,612	1,870
Barley	1,110	506	1,100	2,223	1,309	1,477
Sugar Beets	86	391	367	785	918	1,000
Oranges and tangerines	528	676	775	720	819	753
Milk	421	501	520	525	535	525
Grapes	396	448	450	470	400	420
Tomatoes	232	302	277	245	270	280
Corn	279	154	255	240	333	276
Meats	154	168	174	175	180	175
Potatoes	193	275	205	160	100	140
Dates	71	95	75	100	100	105
Chickpeas	42	33	67	70	57	94
Broad beans	77	50	52	113	75	93
Millet and sorghum	67	32	54	66	77	88
Figs (fresh)	76	59	65	65	60	60
Peas (dry)	34	30	32	47	41	60
Rice (paddy)	16	19	27	45	46	30
Olive oil	25	18	18	50	16	30
Canary seed	26	21	27	41	20	24
Oats	19	12	11	25	16	22
Lentils	15	9	15	18	20	20
Almonds (in shell)	18	20	24	20	20	20
Wool (greasy base)	15	14	14	12	14	14
Cottonseed	13	16	11	13	12	13
Sunflower seed	6	5	9	4	8	8
Cotton	6	8	5	6	6	7
Grapefruit	13	17	15	13	8	5
Flaxseed	6	3	3	5	4	4
Beans (dry)	4	3	5	7	4	3
Lemons	7	9	5	5	3	3
Tobacco	2	2	2	1	2	2

* Preliminary.

Source: Adapted from U.S. Department of Agriculture, *Indices of Agricultural Production in Africa and the Near East*, Washington, 1971, table 21.

Eastern Morocco to the Al Jadida, Marrakech, Safi, Essaouira, and Agadir regions.

The country in average years produced enough cereals to take care of internal consumption and allow for some export of hard wheat, barley, and oats. In low-yield years, such as 1957, 1961, and 1966, the country became a net importer of cereals. After 1966 it continued to be a net importer, even though the cereal crops from 1968 through 1970 were larger than in the past. Although the 1968 harvest was the largest on record, the accumulated shortages of 1966 and 1967 had apparently not been made up by 1971. Until 1968 there had been no significant change in the area or yields of land under cereals in three decades. Whether the continued large crops beginning in 1968 were fortuitous or represented a new trend of yields and production was still not clear in mid-1971.

Citrus fruits—primarily oranges and tangerines—have been locally cultivated for centuries, but after the 1920s they were grown commercially by Europeans, particularly in the area north of Rabat. Production has been developed rapidly, and it was hoped that exports would reach a level of 700,000 metric tons by 1970. Vineyards were cultivated primarily by *colons*, largely for producing wine for export to France. The economic importance of the wine industry has declined seriously in recent years, particularly since independent Morocco lost its preferential treatment in the French market, and it has been increasingly difficult to dispose of its surplus. The European Economic Community (EEC) and the Soviet bloc countries may be of help in disposing of its wine surplus, but there has been a tendency to shift out of raising wine grapes.

Other cultivated fruits and nuts included dates, figs, pomegranates, cherries, apricots, peaches, plums, apples, pears, almonds, walnuts, and pecans. Almonds in 1971 were the most important nut crop.

Olives were grown widely and were the principal source of vegetable oil. Oil was also produced from flaxseed, sunflower seed, cotton seed, and castor beans. The olive crop was subject to wide cyclical fluctuations.

Truck gardening near the large cities, particularly in the Casablanca area, was carried on by both Europeans and Moroccans. Potatoes, tomatoes, onions, green beans, eggplant, squash, sweet and red peppers, carrots, cabbage, and lettuce were the main truck crops. Some vegetables, especially tomatoes and potatoes, were raised as "early vegetables" for export to Europe, where they have a two- or three-week edge on the production of southern Spain, France, and Italy. France was a major, and protected, outlet for such vegetables during the protectorate period. The government has hoped that Morocco's association with the EEC and with the East European communist countries would expand this market. A major problem in this connection has involved the various aspects of marketing—timing, packaging, and delivery (see ch. 13, Trade and Transportation).

The cultivation of sugar beets has been actively encouraged by the government in order to reduce the import of sugar, one of the most costly import items in terms of hard currencies. From zero output in 1961 sugar beet production rose to around 1 million metric tons in 1970, enough to meet nearly one-half of the country's annual sugar needs.

Livestock

The livestock population exceeded the country's grazing and feeding capacity. Livestock raising, which has been estimated to contribute from 30 to 40 percent of agricultural income, was carried out on some 25 million to 35 million acres of pasture land and forest land, mainly by an estimated 100,000 seminomadic and nomadic families that customarily invested their savings in animals (see ch. 6, Social Structure). Because little feed was raised and stored, many animals starved during the dry season, and in years of very low rainfall the livestock population was subject to abrupt diminution. The large numbers of sheep and goats represented a threat to the natural pasture and state forests and to the delicately balanced equilibrium between crops and livestock. During the late 1960s some redress was attempted by reforestation and flood control, by the settlement of the nomad tribes, and by the gradual disappearance of the camel.

Sheep and goats were the principal animals raised and were the main source of meat and milk. In 1970 the livestock population included an estimated 15 million sheep, 6 million goats, and 3 million cattle. The cattle were raised more for their dairy produce than for their meat, but they were estimated to produce only about half as much milk as the sheep and goats. Estimated meat production totaled 150,000 to 175,000 metric tons, and milk production was estimated at 525,000 metric tons.

Wool production averaged approximately 15,000 metric tons a year and was used chiefly by local craftsmen in making rugs and other textiles. Hides and skins (dried) totaled around 22,000 metric tons, of which cattle hides represented about one-half.

Camels, mules, and donkeys were used as work animals, donkeys being the most common pack animals. In 1968 it was estimated that the country had 930,000 donkeys, 390,000 mules, 350,000 horses, and 216,000 camels. Pigs, estimated at 11,000, were raised primarily by and for Europeans.

Fish

The Atlantic coastal waters abound in sardine, tuna, mackerel, and anchovies. The fishing industry, one of the most important in Africa, has grown appreciably since 1922. In 1922 the catch (mostly sardines) amounted to 5,000 metric tons; in 1956 it had increased to 110,000 metric tons, and in 1963 the fish catch reached a peak of about 300,000 metric tons. In 1968 it declined to about 220,000 metric tons, but it was not certain in 1971 whether the decline was a result of obsolete equipment or a depletion of the fishing grounds.

Small amounts of fish are consumed locally. In the form of canned fish and fish products, fish has become an important export; some 40,000 to 45,000 metric tons of canned fish are exported annually. Fish canneries, largely French owned, are concentrated in Casablanca. A plant for the production of fish flour was constructed in the late 1960s in Agadir with the assistance of the Food and Agriculture Organization (FAO) of the United Nations. By the early 1970s both the fishing and processing aspects of this industry were suffering from obsolescence and high unit costs, making competition with other countries, especially Portugal, increasingly difficult. The Five Year Plan (1968–72) allocated public outlays of DH1.25 million (5.06 dirham equal US$1—see Glossary) to the modernization of the industry; this was expected to be supplemented by several times as much from private sources.

Forestry

Forests covered around 20 million acres in the mid-1960s, appreciably less than the 25 to 30 percent of the country's total area that is widely considered to be ecologically desirable in underdeveloped countries. The most valuable trees are cork and green oak, cedar, argan, eucalyptus, acacia, and pine. In addition, around 7 million acres are covered with esparto grass and scrub palm, the sources of esparto and vegetable horsehair. During the 1960s the forests provided work for about 40,000 families engaged in charcoal burning, cork gathering, and woodcutting.

The cork forests, all of which are state owned, cover about 775,000 acres and produce an annual 40,000 metric tons of cork, both for local industry and for export. The cedar forests, which cover around 375,000 acres and include trees several hundred years old, are among the finest in the world. Eucalyptus trees, introduced into the country to combat erosion and to supply cellulose for the textile industry, cover from 110,000 to 120,000 acres.

The argan, a tropical tree that grows in the southwest and is unknown outside that area, covers about 1.7 million acres of rather scattered forest in the Sous region. It is a spiny, evergreen tree of the ironwood family and produces a fruit about the size of a plum, which cattle and goats eat. An oil extracted from the fruit is used in place of olive oil by the southern Moroccans. The tree also supplies wood for domestic needs.

Esparto grass, or alfa, which covers large areas of Eastern Morocco and the Moulouya Valley, is baled and exported for the paper pulp industry. Vegetable horsehair, a fiber obtained from the leaves of the dwarf Mediterranean palm, has a wide foreign market as stuffing for mattresses and upholstery. Morocco is the world's leading producer of vegetable horsehair, which since World War II has become southern Morocco's most valuable forest product.

Depletion of the forests for purposes of land clearing, construction, fuel, and furniture making has been underway since the Arab invasions of the eleventh century. It was recognized as a national problem of serious proportions by the French colonial administration. The government could not effectively cope with the problem until the gradual expansion of the transportation network had opened up the country to efficient penetration by both law enforcement and technical agencies. It is estimated that more than 1 million acres of forest land were replanted during the period of French rule. Although much of this progress was lost during World War II, the introduction at that time of the eucalyptus tree provided a potent vehicle for renewed progress when conditions should permit. Since independence the government, with advice and assistance from international agencies, has continued to take steps to resolve the problem and, as a part of its successive development plans, has made appreciable headway. The Five Year Plan proposed to reforest around 175,000 acres at a cost of some DH70 million.

Role of the Government

Since independence the primary economic preoccupation of the government has been to increase the output of the agricultural sector, particularly cereals and sugar beets. This preoccupation has taken the form of attempts to increase the area and productivity of the traditional sector without sacrificing at the same time the greater efficiency and the specialized production and outlets that had been a byproduct of the colonial administration. To the extent that these objectives proved incompatible as they were pursued, the government support perhaps tended to favor the modern sector. If so, it was in large part because of the necessity to keep up production that could be converted into foreign exchange and thereby create an effective hedge against the food shortages resulting from the rising rate of population growth and the recurrence of droughts.

At the outset, the new government's approach to the problem took the form of a number of restricted programs, which met with only limited success. The first program was a series of land distribution by the king beginning a few months after independence in response to popular demands for the confiscation and redistribution to landless peasants of the lands belonging to Europeans and the Moroccan "traitors" who were considered to have collaborated with the French or to have profiteered under the protectorate. Because of a desire to maintain friendly relations with France and the resistance and political power of large Moroccan landowners only about 20,000 acres of the nearly 50,000 acres distributed were *colon* or "traitor" lands; the remainder were lands that had previously belonged to the state. About 2,000 peasant families benefited from these distributions, but only the first group of 270 received full title to the land. The others only received the right of usufruct, which enabled the government to impose controls on the kind of crops raised and the agricultural methods used.

The problem of the land held by the European settlers continued to be a critical one; the government was caught between mounting public demands for recovery of the land and its own reluctance to jeopardize French aid and the level of production on the foreign-owned farms, which were the most modern in the country and the source of most of the export crops. In September 1963, however, a *dahir* (government decree) was issued providing for the gradual takeover of all European-owned lands that had been received as grants under official colonization schemes during the protectorate. Since then, most of the colonization lands have been taken over by the government; a large part continue to be held by the government and operated under its aegis.

French financial aid, which had been blocked after the first takeovers, was resumed after an agreement was reached providing for indemnification to the Europeans for their livestock, machinery, and other property apart from the land. The land that had been purchased privately by Europeans was not affected by the government actions, but considerable amounts had been sold to Moroccans before such sales were subjected to regulation in 1959 and even afterwards despite the law.

A general land reform law was promulgated in 1966 that, it was foreseen, would affect not only erstwhile *colon* lands but also some state-owned lands, collectively held tribal lands, holdings of individual Moroccans in excess of specified limits, and a portion of the increment resulting from state-financed irrigation projects. Land was to be distributed in 10- to 25-acre parcels, on a twenty-year repayment basis, preferably to landless workers, who were to be provided with necessary credit for basic equipment and initial operating expenses. Of the approximately 600,000 acres originally included in the concession lands to be recovered, apparently less than one-half had been redistributed to landless farmers up to the end of 1970; simultaneously, some existing large landowners were able to increase their holdings.

In regard to its irrigation provisions, the 1966 law and supporting legislation provided for a virtual contract between the government and the farmer that presumably applied not only to *colon* lands and Moroccan privately owned lands served by already existing irrigation projects but also to all lands that should be benefited by future government-sponsored irrigation projects. Under this arrangement, the government would carry out the engineering works (external preparation) necessary to bring irrigation water to the farmer. The farmer for his part would carry out on his land the necessary internal preparations to enable the use of water. He would also acquiesce in governmental supervision and recommendations concerning the crops to be planted.

Contrary to expectations, events indicated that many farmers in the traditional sector, even some with large farms, were for a variety of reasons unwilling or unable to fulfill their part of the virtual contract. The government, moreover, observing the disparity in efficiency between large farms in the modern sector and the small farms of the traditional sector, appeared loath to forgo the advantages of large-scale production by extension of land redistribution to efficiently operating farms in the modern sector.

The relationship between the government and the agricultural sector was redefined in the Agricultural Investment Code of 1969. Under the code, the government would carry out both the external and the internal preparations needed for effective irrigation on the lands to be benefited. The farmer would make a monetary contribution to both, in lieu of the effort he would previously have contributed to the actual preparation process. He was furthermore constrained to regroup his land with other land, if necessary, in order to create viable-sized farms and not to subdivide his land for reasons of inheritance below the limits of viable size. He was expected also to accept the government's guidance in land use and crop rotation.

In case of persistent incapacity or resistance, farmers who had benefited from land redistribution could, in accordance with provisions of the code, be removed from their privileged status of usufructors, with the proviso that indemnification would be accorded them for capital improvements they had made to the properties. Although these arrangements were more easily and advantageously applicable to the large irrigation schemes, they were also available for application to the small-scale irrigation and rain-fed areas as the administrative and financial logistical resources of the government permitted.

The government's land policy was supported by a number of incentive programs. For the short run, perhaps the most important were fixed prices for bread, sugar, and edible oils; a fertilizer program that foresaw the expansion of effective fertilizer use from around 741,000 acres in 1968 to about 1.8 million acres by 1972; a mechanization program that included construction of local assembly lines for tractors that would produce a farm tractor count of more than 10,000 units by 1972; and a seed program involving more general distribution of selected domestic seed strains and experiments with imported high-yield strains.

For the medium term (five to ten years), the supporting program was the continuance of the policy of irrigation-flood control, which was expected to raise the effective irrigated area from around 1 million acres in 1968 to 1.2 million acres in 1972 and to around 2.5 million acres by the 1985–90 period. Another medium-term program was improved organization and effective supervision of markets for the small farmer's surplus production.

Long-run programs, in addition to the large-scale multipurpose irrigation projects, included the development of agricultural extension, agricultural credit, agricultural research, and rural education facilities. These facilities had largely depended on the colonial public administration and consequently had been decimated after independence and not yet replaced by 1971. A byproduct of these would be a network of cooperatives, which the government was actively fostering but which required greater amounts of management and training than were available in the early 1970s. In the meantime, as much advantage as possible was being taken of the assistance offered by various international and foreign national agencies.

Two special programs were the National Development Program (Promotion Nationale), acting under the direct responsibility of the king, and the Development of the Western Rif Program (Developpement Economique et Rural du Rif Occidental—DERRO). The first program was set up in 1961 to provide employment to the rural unemployed, reduce the drift of the poor to the cities, and carry out local flood and erosion control, minor irrigation, reforestation, and road construction projects that could be done by manual labor. During the late 1960s the project employed about 100,000 men (for 200 days a year) and was partly financed by the United States Food for Peace (PL 480) food grants. DERRO, set up in 1968 as a twenty-five-year project to carry out the same sort of activities as the National Development Program, was limited to an integrated rehabilitation program for the former Spanish Rif, one of the poorest and most undeveloped sections of the country.

Beginning in the early 1960s the government's agrarian policy and supporting programs were more and more implemented within the framework of the successive development plans (see ch. 11, Character and Structure of the Economy). Increasingly these tasks were performed by state agencies, as the French expertise in organizing and dealing with foreign markets was withdrawn, and as the inherited French markets themselves broke up and were replaced by the Soviet bloc countries and the EEC. The programs were progressively fortified by incentives afforded by subsidies, taxes, guaranteed prices, and exchange and trade controls (see ch. 11, Character and Structure of the Economy; ch. 13, Trade and Transportation).

INDUSTRY

Moroccan official statistics treat the industrial sector as comprising energy, mining, and manufacturing (see table 11). On that basis the sector represented about 19.4 percent of the estimated gross domestic product in 1969 (energy, 2.5 percent; mining, 4.8 percent; and manufacturing, 12.1 percent). From 1963 to 1969 energy output increased an estimated 40 percent, and mining rose 18 percent; manufacturing over the same period increased about 24 percent.

The Five Year Plan allocated some DH3.2 billion to the rehabilitation and development of the industrial sector: DH510 million to energy; DH1,260 million to mining; and DH1,440 million to manufacturing (including the handicraft industries). The actual allocation to energy is of course greater than indicated by these figures because a portion of the new power is to be hydroelectric and, as such, will be designed and developed as an integral part of the large irrigation projects (see ch. 2, Geography and Population).

Table 11. *Index of Industrial Production in Morocco, by Sector, Selected Years, 1963-69*

(base year 1958 = 100)[1]

	1963	1965	1967	1968	1969[2]
Energy	139	153	165	181	194
Mining	111	126	124	124	131
Manufacturing	128	128	142	150	158
Metal transformation	102	103	114	124	136
Ceramic and building materials	137	139	145	168	186
Chemicals	111	134	154	170	174
Fats and oils	145	125	136	140	121
Food products	121	127	144	145	141
Textiles	183	181	196	222	267
Leather	121	100	96	112	121
Paper and cardboard	134	133	147	157	178
Other	138	117	133	128	137
General Index	123	130	138	144	152

[1] Of weights totaling 1,000 in 1958, sector weights of 110, 375, and 515 were assigned to energy, mining, and manufacturing, respectively.
[2] Provisional.

Source: Adapted from Morocco, Ministère d'Etat Chargé du Plan et de la Formation des Cadres, Division du Plan et des Statistiques, *La Situation Economique du Maroc en 1968*, May 1969, ch. 4, pp. 2, 10; *Bulletin Mensuel* [Rabat], January 1971, p. 7; and Banque Marocaine du Commerce Exterieur, *Facts and Figures on Morocco* (4th and 5th eds.), Casablanca, 1969, 1970.

In general, the industrial sector since independence has been subject to overcapacity except the electricity subsector. Even in this subsector overcapacity has spasmodically occurred when the completion of large, multipurpose irrigation dams suddenly created more capacity than the demand or the distribution systems were temporarily capable of absorbing. In regard to mining and manufacturing, overcapacity was in part a function, directly or indirectly, of production having been geared initially to the French markets created by the country's special protectorate status and by the postindependence breakdown of those markets. In addition, unit costs became too high, through obsolescence or indifferent management, to permit efficient competition in other markets. Morocco's association with the EEC in 1969, as well as recent sizable increases in its virtually barter trade arrangements with communist countries, has improved but not basically cured the situation (see ch. 13, Trade and Transportation).

Energy

At the end of the 1960s Morocco consumed more energy than it produced. The domestic production of energy in 1968 from coal, lignite, petroleum products, natural gas, and electricity, as measured in coal energy units, totaled an estimated equivalent of 720,000 metric tons of coal, whereas the apparent consumption of energy totaled the equivalent of an estimated 2.64 million metric tons of coal, suggesting that almost three-quarters of the energy consumed in 1968 had to be imported.

Of the energy consumed in 1968, about 45 percent was estimated to be in the form of electricity; about 45 percent, in the form of direct use of petroleum products; and 10 percent, in the form of coal. (Small amounts of natural gas were available on the Atlantic coast.) The figures were adjusted for most of the double counting inherent in the use of coal and petroleum products in the generation of electricity. Approximately 50 percent of the consumption of electricity was in the cities, and almost 20 percent was in the rural areas. The remaining 25 to 30 percent was taken up by phosphate and other mines, the railroad system, municipal pumping systems, and other industries, most of which were in the public sector.

Since 1963 most of Morocco's electricity producing capacity has been concentrated in the National Electricity Authority. At the end of the 1960s the authority controlled from 90 to 95 percent of the total capacity of around 500,000 kilowatts. An additional 200,000 kilowatts of capacity was under construction, and a further capacity for 225,000 kilowatts was in varying stages of design. Production in 1970 was close to 2 billion kilowatt-hours.

Roughly 350,000 kilowatts (70 to 75 percent of the total) was produced largely as a byproduct of irrigation projects, and served large municipalities or industry in the modern sector areas. Another 145,000 kilowatts or so were produced either by large municipal thermal units, also in the modern sector, or to a less degree by smaller units used to provide peaking power in the large cities. In addition, there were around a dozen small units with a capacity of from 216 to 1,230 kilowatts, located in the small municipalities in the eastern and southern parts of the country.

The largest hydroelectric plant was the joint Bin al Ouidane-Afourer complex on the Al Abid River northeast of Marrakech, with a combined capacity of more than 200,000 kilowatts. The largest thermal unit was the three-stage plant at Jerada that was being constructed with financial and technical help from the Soviet Union. This plant was designed with the dual purpose of using Jerada coal, thereby keeping those mines open, and meeting the growing power demands of Oujda, Casablanca, and if necessary the northeast coast. When completed in 1972, its three stages are expected to have a total capacity of about 160,000 kilowatts. The high-tension power grid initiated by the French in the northwest has continued since independence to be extended, integrated, and upgraded. By 1971 it effectively included most of the industrially active sections of the country.

Although industrial demand for energy was growing, the spread between peak and regular loads was still high. This problem, together with the high cost of local fuels, the high cost of some of the large hydroelectric projects, and the necessity of maintaining extra thermal standby plants because of the unpredictability of the rainfall, has in the past made for higher energy costs than were desirable to make the domestic manufacturing industry internationally competitive. The unpredictability of the rainfall presents a specialized logistical problem: a certain ratio between hydroelectric and thermal production must, at least for the time being, be maintained as insurance against the danger of inadequate rainfall. The Five Year Plan provided for a reduction of power costs by reducing distribution costs, as well as production costs, especially for thermal power, and by revising the price schedule to benefit large industrial users of power, thereby increasing the use of publicly produced power in comparison with other power sources.

Mining

At the end of 1970 Morocco appeared to be only meagerly endowed with industrial mineral resources, with the exception of phosphate rock, which was abundant. After phosphates, the most important minerals were iron ore, anthracite coal, and pyrrhotite (see table 12). On balance, mineral production was either stagnant or declining, apparently as a consequence of obsolescence leading to noncompetitive unit costs or because of depletion of known deposits of liquid fuels. The estimated value of mineral output in 1968 was around DH850 million; most of it was exported in the form of ores or concentrates. Under the Five Year Plan it was proposed that around DH260 million should be invested in the mining industry during the plan period, approximately half of it for prospecting, especially for petroleum.

Mining legislation issued in 1914 provided that mineral deposits should revert to the state, unless they clearly belonged to the tribes or

Table 12. *Mineral Production in Morocco, Selected Years, 1964-70*

(in thousands of metric tons)

Production	1964	1966	1968	1969	1970 [1]
Phosphate rock	10,098	9,439	10,512	11,295	11,424 [2]
Iron ore	889	1,017	809	742	872 [3]
Anthracite coal	400	451	451	397	433 [4]
Pyrrhotite	0	282	418	390	392
Lead concentrates	104	119	121	117	130
Manganese	341	362	160	131	112
Crude petroleum	120	103	89	59	46
Zinc concentrates	81	94	68	71	32
Copper ore	7	9	10	9	n.a.
Cobalt [5]	1,850	2,198	1,840	1,700	1,600

n.a.—not available.
[1] Provisional.
[2] Of which 11,163,000 metric tons were exported.
[3] Of which 813,900 metric tons were exported.
[4] Consumption for the year totaled 550,700 metric tons, reflecting production of 450,000 tons (including 17,000 tons of agglomerates), exports of coal of 60,000 tons, imports of 68,000 tons, and (presumably) a draw down of stocks of 93,000 tons.
[5] In short tons of recoverable cobalt.

unless they could be mined by open-pit methods. Phosphate deposits were nationalized in 1920. In 1928 the Bureau of Mining Research and Participation (Bureau de Recherches et de Participations Minières—BRPM) was established by the government to prospect for coal and petroleum and to initiate production in partnership with private firms; other minerals (except phosphates) were added to coal and petroleum in 1938. In 1951 the earlier exemption from state ownership of open-pit mines was rescinded. By 1956 BRPM had acquired participatory interests in the production of all coal, petroleum, lead, and manganese.

Phosphates

Reserves of phosphate rock were estimated at some 40 billion metric tons at the end of the 1960s, and Morocco was, with the United States, the Soviet Union, and the Spanish Sahara, one of the world's major producers of phosphates and the largest exporter. Phosphate rock represented some 70 percent of the value of mining output. The major deposits at Khouribga are of high quality and command premium prices abroad. Other deposits, in the Youssoufia area and at Ben Guerir, are inferior in quality. In 1970 the Sharifian Office of Phosphates (Office Chérifien des Phosphates) produced about 11.4 million metric tons of phosphate rock, of which about 11.2 million metric tons were exported. Production was projected to increase over the period of the Five Year Plan to from 16 million to 18 million metric tons a year, under the stimulus of a DH720-million modernization program and projected stability of world prices.

The phosphate mines are the largest customer of the nation's railroad network and the second largest user of coal. Phosphates are exported through the modern ports of Safi and Casablanca. At Safi there is a modern chemical complex, which in 1968 converted about 350,000 metric tons of phosphate rock into triple superphosphate; this output could be expanded to 1 million metric tons a year should the local and (or) export demand for fertilizers increase.

Coal

As far as was known in 1970, the country had no coking coal. At Jerada there were deposits containing an estimated 100 million metric tons of anthracite coal that would continue to be difficult and costly to exploit unless the scale of production should be appreciably increased. Meanwhile, production was being heavily subsidized to maintain employment at the mines.

In 1968 the government engaged Soviet interests to construct a thermal powerplant at Jerada to use the local coal. Coal output would be about doubled, to some 800,000 metric tons per year; of the output, the new power plant would absorb about half, and other thermal plants and cement plants would use much of the remainder. Some part of the expanded output would be exported. It was hoped that expanded production would eliminate the need for subsidies.

Petroleum

Despite continuous exploration since 1950 (150 exploratory wells to the end of 1968), no sizable petroleum deposits had been found as of mid-1971. The largest output, in 1963, was about 150,000 metric tons; this compared with import requirements of 1.7 million metric tons in 1969, by which time domestic production had declined to about 60,000 metric tons. At the end of 1970 much of the Atlantic coastal area, which has been considered geologically the most potentially productive area, was held in short-term concession by foreign companies, in some cases under partnership arrangements with BRPM. These arrangements generally provided that the contracting company would meet the greater part of the costs and that, in the event oil was discovered in commercial quantities, a fifty-fifty or similar arrangement would be arrived at for exploiting the deposits.

In 1970 the country had two refineries: one, government-owned, at Sidi Kassem, with a capacity of 400,000 metric tons per year; and the other, privately owned, at Mohammedia, with a capacity of 1.3 million metric tons. The first was operated by the state oil production branch, the Sharifian Society of Petroleum (Societé Chérifienne des Petroles), and processed all domestic crude production, as well as part of the imports from Algeria and the Soviet Union. Both refineries were expected to double their output during the course of the Five Year Plan, and that at Mohammedia was expected to expand its range of output (thus making Morocco self-sufficient in all but highly specialized petroleum products), for a sizable saving in foreign exchange.

Iron Ore

Iron ore production in the 1960s was mainly concentrated near Nador in the northeast. The deposits had been mined by open pit methods, but it was expected that these would run out during 1971. An additional 25 million metric tons or so of not very high grade ore were available by going underground, but this would involve sizable capital outlays and an increase in wages. A pelletizing plant was set up in 1971; after the governmental decision to mine the underground deposits, it was further decided in 1971 to go forward with a small (240,000 metric tons per year) steel industry at Nador, based on local iron ores and coal from the coal mines at Jerada. Although this would be a high unit-cost operation, it was expected to have the desirable effect of reducing foreign exchange costs for iron and steel, and it would meet a significant proportion of the country's requirements in this basic part of the industrial sector.

Other Minerals

At the end of the 1960s the country was an internationally significant exporter of cobalt and manganese. It also produced, mainly for export, sizable quantities of lead, zinc, and pyrrhotite, and small quantities of copper, silver, barite, and gypsum.

Manufacturing

Manufacturing at the end of the 1960s contributed roughly 12.1 percent of the gross domestic product. In common with agriculture and, increasingly with mining, it was divided into modern and traditional sectors, comprising a few large-scale production units and many small-scale ones. In manufacturing the distinction between the two was perhaps less sharp than in agriculture, inasmuch as the major branches of manufacturing were probably even more a mixture of modern and traditional. To arrive at an estimate of the overall breakdown of the value of production in manufacturing between the modern and traditional sectors was impracticable with the statistical information available in mid-1971.

For the most part, the manufacturing sector produced light consumer goods, with emphasis on foodstuffs, textiles, matches, metal, and leather products. Heavy industry was largely limited to petroleum refining, chemical fertilizer production, automotive vehicle and tractor assembling, some foundry work, and cement manufacturing. The manufacturing sector also included production of electric motors, batteries, cables, and other light equipment; some light industrial metal and wire; and pulp, paper, and paperboard. Processing and assembly activities depended, in the main, on imported raw and intermediate materials.

A profile of the growth of the manufacturing sector emerges, albeit somewhat hazily, from a review of selected production data from 1965 to 1969 (see table 13). The value of the commodities produced was not available. The presentation of the data in volume terms has the advantage of showing the fluctuations in output, without adjustments necessary for price changes; however, the volume data do not provide any exact clue as to the relative (value) contribution of the individual industries or manufacturing groups. Although the available information on this matter was more than usually precarious, it seemed likely that at the end of the 1960s the foodstuffs, beverages, and tobacco group represented roughly 25 to 30 percent of the contribution of manufacturing to the gross domestic product. Textiles contributed perhaps somewhat less than that, followed more or less closely by metal transformation, and much more remotely by chemicals and fertilizers, leather goods, and building materials.

Although the ownership of manufacturing was mostly held in the private sector, the government participation in manufacturing was sizable and strategic. It included ownership of the phosphate-chemical fertilizer industry, and the bulk of the petroleum industry and a major participation, through partnership or financing, in much of the sugar milling capacity, the car and truck assembly facilities, and the manufacture of tires. Thus the government was a participant in most of the country's modern manufacturing sector, as well as the owner of the port, railroad, and power facilities (see ch. 13, Trade and Transportation).

LABOR

Although reliable data on the size and composition of the work force, the nature and extent of underemployment and unemployment, and related labor matters were not available in mid-1971, official Moroccan reports made clear that during the 1960s the rate of unemployment had increased rapidly and would continue to do so in the 1970s. In 1968 the work force totaled about 5,575,000 out of a population estimated at 14.5 million; the unemployment estimates ranged upwards from a minimum of about 690,000 (see table 14). This was about a 33-percent increase in unemployment since 1964 (from about 9.4 percent of the labor force in 1964 to approximately 12.4 percent in 1968). In 1971 it was conservatively estimated that unemployment would exceed 14 percent by 1973.

Table 13. *Manufacturing Production in Morocco, Selected Commodities, 1965-69*
(in thousands of metric tons)

Commodity	1965	1966	1967	1968	1969
Food and Beverages					
Flour milling (modern)	636	696	830	649	625
Sugar refining	334	358	340	384	409
Nonalcoholic drinks	259	284	291	352	407
Canned fish [1]	3	3	4	4	2
Textiles [2]					
Cotton textiles (modern)	7,156	7,237	9,302	9,711	13,037
Synthetic textiles (modern)	1,338	1,822	1,887	2,214	2,954
Woolen textiles (modern)	688	767	572	793	1,005
Chemical Products					
Superphosphates	160	249	247	253	282
Chemical fertilizers	77	65	120	111	78
Sulfuric acid	40	40	29	30	28
Paints	6	7	7	8	10
Metal Transformation					
Insulated wire cable	15	15	14	18	19
Foundry products	7	6	6	7	8
Construction Materials					
Cement	788	856	875	1,011	1,165
Red bricks	96	93	102	120	126
Miscellaneous					
Cars, assembled [3]	5,220	5,378	9,460	12,500	19,150
Paper and paperboard	38	44	43	44	55
Leather, tanned [4]	17	22	20	23	27

[1] Million cases.
[2] In metric tons.
[3] Units.
[4] Million square feet.

Source: Adapted from Banque Marocaine du Commerce Exterieur, *Facts and Figures on Morocco* (4th and 5th eds.), Casablanca, 1969, 1970; *Quarterly Economic Review, Morocco, Annual Supplement, 1971* [London], 1971, p. 9; and *Middle East Economic Digest, 1970 Annual Review*, XIV, No. 52, London, 1970, p. 1516.

In 1971 over two-thirds of the work force was engaged in agricultural pursuits, and the number of people in the rural area was steadily increasing. As a percentage of those employed, however, agricultural workers were decreasing, and it was estimated that perhaps half of the rural workers, many of whom were women, were underemployed.

Seasonal changes and migration affect practically all categories of the labor force. In agriculture the activity of both unpaid family

Table 14. Distribution of Work Force in Morocco, 1964, 1968, and 1973

Occupational Categories	Number (in thousands)			Percent of Employed		
	1964	1968	1973 [1]	1964	1968	1973 [1]
Agriculture [2]	3,250	3,400	3,675	72.4	69.6	67.5
Industry and handicrafts	420	436	458	9.3	8.9	8.4
Commerce [3]	250	287	332	5.6	5.9	6.1
Services [4]	148	225	282	3.3	4.6	5.2
Public sector [5]	200	215	258	4.5	4.4	4.6
Transportation and communication	87	110	146	1.9	2.2	2.7
Other [6]	134	212	290	3.0	4.3	5.3
Subtotal	4,489	4,885	5,441	100.0	99.9 [7]	99.8 [7]
Estimated Unemployment	467	690	900	9.4 [8]	12.4 [8]	14.2 [8]
TOTAL	4,956	5,575	6,341			

[1] Projected.
[2] An estimated 50 percent of the agricultural workers are described as underemployed; nearly half are female. Not included are children from six to fifteen years of age employed as herders or as helpers.
[3] Includes bazaar shopkeepers, street vendors, rural peddlers, and related occupations.
[4] Includes domestic workers, both in hotels and homes, and casual urban occupations, such as porters and shoeshine boys.
[5] Persons working for the central government, local governments, the social security service, and government-owned enterprises, which included the Moroccan railroads, the sugar and tobacco industries, and electric powerplants.
[6] Includes mining, construction and public works, energy and water, and special projects to alleviate unemployment by the National Development Program. Number under the program has increased from 19,000 in 1964 to 80,000 in 1968 and was projected to reach 150,000 by 1973.
[7] Does not total 100 because of rounding.
[8] Percentage of total work force.

workers and the small wage-earning sector decreases sharply after planting and harvesting. Between crops, many farmers take unskilled construction jobs, temporarily boosting the number of workers in that sector. There is a regular small-scale seasonal movement of farmers to handicraft shops in villages and towns. Some seasonal workers migrate from the cities to the plantations that offer high wages at harvesttime. Food processing, a major industry, extensively uses seasonal labor, since the scope of its operations depends on the quantity of harvest and of the fish catch.

The cityward migration of workers continues at a rate of approximately 100,000 a year, aggravating the problems of unemployment and spawning city slums (see ch. 2, Geography and Population). Despite the difficulties imposed by substandard housing and long periods of unemployment, most migrants eventually become permanently urbanized. The majority of seasonal and temporary workers are males, but permanent relocations to the cities usually involve entire families.

The Five Year Plan provides for the creation of about 710,000 new jobs during the plan period. Planning officials hope to place some 275,000 workers in the agricultural sector, 138,000 in transport, commerce, and services, and 43,000 in public administration; mining, utilities, industry, and public works, however, were expected to provide only some 29,000 new jobs during the period. Government-sponsored public works projects under the National Development Program were to employ another 70,000 persons. The optimum implementation of the plan would still leave unemployed more than 20 percent of jobseekers in 1972; reports published in 1970, however, indicated that the official goals of the plan may be exceeded because of increased activity in some economic sectors, notably in construction, commerce, and services (see ch. 11, Character and Structure of the Economy; ch. 13, Trade and Transportation).

The National Development Program offers temporary employment to jobless persons on various public works including roadbuilding, reforestation, and land restoration. The workers are paid DH2 per day, in addition to an equivalent amount in food rations, mainly wheat flour procured from the United States under the surplus agricultural commodities plan. The program benefits mainly the rural unemployed, although a growing number of urban jobseekers were employed during the late 1960s on slum clearance and construction projects. Employment under the program increased from an average of 13 million man-days per year before 1965 to between 15 million and 18 million man-days a year between 1965 and 1968. The Five Year Plan called for an increase to 25 million man-days per year by 1972.

A relatively small number of jobseekers find employment through one of the twenty-three government employment exchange offices under the Ministry of Youth, Sport, Labor, and Social Affairs (until August 6, 1971, called the Ministry of Labor and Social Affairs). Of 329,273 persons registered with these offices in 1969, employment was found for 26,340. A survey of these jobseekers showed that more than half of them were unskilled workers; unemployed were the next most numerous, followed by metalworkers and workers in the services sector.

Worker emigration to France, other West European countries, and Libya steadily increased during the 1960s. In mid-1971 agreements for the large-scale employment of Moroccans were in effect with France, the United Kingdom, West Germany, Belgium, the Netherlands, Switzerland, Spain, Algeria, and Libya. It was not clear what effect the rupture of diplomatic relations between Libya and Morocco in July would have on the status of Moroccans working in Libya. Morocco has appointed attachés to its embassies in six of these countries to aid immigrant workers and to facilitate their placement in jobs. With France and Belgium, moreover, social security agreements have been signed to provide for the transfer of family allowances to Morocco.

The volume of worker emigration under the auspices of the Ministry of Youth, Sport, Labor, and Social Affairs increased from an average of about 10,000 a year during the mid-1960s to more than 23,500 in 1969. In 1969 Moroccan workers abroad totaled an estimated 200,000; of these, there were about 130,000 in France, 14,000 in the Netherlands, and about 8,000 in Belgium and in Germany. In addition, an unknown number of workers emigrated through private rather than official channels.

The great majority of the work force is unskilled. In 1963 only about one-third of the industrial workers were classified as skilled or semiskilled; the situation was probably much the same in 1971.

To meet the need for skilled industrial labor and for trained industrial staff in general, training centers have been organized under the Ministry of Youth, Sport, Labor, and Social Affairs. Two centers, located in Fes and Casablanca, train skilled workers and technicians in milling, lathe-turning, mechanical and electrical engineering, welding, and automotive mechanics; other centers, also located in major cities, offer short-term courses in industrial skills and in such services as tailoring and office work. The centers are staffed by graduates of the National Institute for Technical Training in Casablanca. Vocational training programs were also offered by private technical schools, and various educational programs were administered by other government agencies (see ch. 7, Education, Communication, and the Arts and Sciences).

The Five Year Plan provides for the training of some 28,000 skilled workers and technicians, including 8,000 workers for the hotel industry, 3,500 skilled industrial workers, 2,000 public health workers, and 2,000 workers for projects of the Ministry of Interior. Although little detailed information was available in 1971, the military was believed to be actively engaged in training relatively large numbers of men in skills related to the expanding tourist trade (see ch. 14, National Defense and Internal Security).

Since independence the government has passed various decrees intended to reduce the number of non-Moroccans in the skilled and professional labor force. A decree of July 1959 provided that all salaried employees must be hired through public placement bureaus, and employers were instructed to give priority in hiring to Moroccans.

The replacement of skilled foreign personnel in the labor force by Moroccans continued at a modest pace during the late 1960s. According to French press reports in 1971, there were, in addition to the 7,000 to 9,000 foreign schoolteachers, about 12,000 foreign wage and salary earners in Morocco, mostly in high and intermediary positions. A Moroccan official during the same year stated that there were about 10,000 foreign technicians in the country, mostly from France and other West European countries.

Working Conditions

Extensive legislation, some of it dating back to the early protectorate period, regulates various aspects of working conditions. Both the old laws and those passed since independence are in many respects similar to the labor laws of France. Government practice has been to issue separate decrees as the need arises. In general, the laws cover workers in most occupations, except those employed in small agricultural enterprises and in handicraft shops. According to a statement made by the minister of labor and social affairs, a new labor code was in preparation in 1971; the minister said, moreover, that plans were underway to expand social security benefits and medical services for workers in industry and agriculture.

In late 1971 the enforcement of labor laws continued to be uneven, partly because of the lack of trained labor inspectors and partly because of the unfamiliarity of many workers with the rights and privileges provided by the laws. Compliance with labor legislation was most complete in the modern industrial enterprises of major cities. It tended to be slack in commercial establishments and small craft shops because these rarely employed more than ten persons and were therefore not subject to official inspections. In general, stricter compliance is required in foreign-owned enterprises than in Moroccan-owned enterprises.

The Ministry of Youth, Sport, Labor, and Social Affairs was charged with the administration and enforcement of labor laws. In 1970 its subdivisions included the offices of manpower, social security regulations, labor accidents, statistics and documents, social affairs, vocational training, and inspection of social laws in agriculture. The Manpower Council, a high-level consultative body under the ministry, was created by a royal decree promulgated in August 1967 to advise the government on all questions relating to employment.

Labor inspectors were responsible for the enforcement of labor laws through regular visits to industrial, craft, commercial, and professional establishments. They were entitled to make representations against employers who failed to comply with the laws. Special inspectors as well as regular labor inspectors ensured compliance with the regulations of the National Social Security Fund.

According to law, all workers must be hired through government labor exchanges, but this provision has not been enforced. Small-scale employers have generally preferred to hire relatives or friends rather than applicants referred to them by the official labor exchange. Even in large enterprises, the major portion of unskilled and casual workers were recruited through word of mouth and sometimes through advertising.

Reduction in force, incompetence, and several violations of discipline were legally recognized causes for dismissal, but workers must be given notice for periods that vary according to seniority, and they were entitled to compensatory pay proportionate to length of service. A royal decree regulated worker dismissal in enterprises that plan partial or complete closedown; dismissals in such instances must be authorized by local labor officials, and unauthorized dismissals were punishable by fines. The rates of compensation for legally dismissed workers were stipulated in two other royal decrees also promulgated in 1967.

A minimum wage was guaranteed by law for most occupations. For establishing minimum-wage levels, the country was divided into four zones with four different levels, according to the cost and standard of living in the respective regions. The highest minimum-wage zone was Casablanca. The rural areas comprised the lowest zone, with minimum wages about 14 percent below those in Casablanca. Minimum wages also varied according to sex and age. Young persons usually received 50 to 80 percent of the wages of adults, and women received about 80 to 85 percent of those of men. The level of pay was lower in the agricultural sector.

Since 1960 the legal minimum wage has been linked to the cost-of-living index. According to legal minimum wage provisions, wages and salaries were to be adjusted upward if the cost-of-living index rises by more than 5 percent. The index rose by 31 percent between 1959 and 1969, but as of mid-1971 no official wage increase had been granted since January 1962.

Wage levels varied considerably among industries. The metal and machinery industry, for example, paid the highest wages, largely because they employed many skilled workers and practically no women. The construction industry, however, employed large numbers of unskilled workers and paid low wages. Wages were still lower in the textile and clothing industries, which employed a high percentage of women as well as many unskilled and semiskilled workers.

In 1970 unskilled workers earned from DH1.10 to DH1.50 per hour; semiskilled workers, from DH1.25 to DH2.00; skilled workers, from DH2.00 to DH2.75; and highly qualified workers, from DH3.50 to DH4.00. The monthly wages of foremen varied from DH1,100 to DH1,500. According to information available in 1971, the minimum daily wage in agriculture in 1967 was DH3.89 for men and DH2.92 for women.

Various compulsory supplemental payments cost employers an additional amount equal to from 15 to 30 percent of the basic wage. Other supplemental payments varied according to industry. Miners, for example, were given housing and medical bonuses. Bonuses were given in the construction industry to foremen, nightworkers, and all workers involved in hazardous work. Employees and workers in the semipublic sector received various bonuses, including housing allowances and an end-of-year bonus not exceeding 10 percent of their gross annual pay. The latter type of bonus was quite common throughout the modern industrial sector.

Social security, effective since 1961, covered about 15 percent of the labor force; most of those covered work in modern industrial and commercial establishments (see ch. 2, Geography and Population). Compensation for accidents and occupational diseases was provided to the workers by law. Victims of industrial accidents or occupational diseases received one-half of their wages for the first twenty-eight days of disability and two-thirds of their wages beginning the twenty-ninth day of disability. A pension was payable to the workers in case of permanent disability.

Health, sanitation, and safety standards for a small category of workers were also prescribed by law. Establishments employing fifty persons or more were required to provide annual medical examinations and X-rays for all workers. Employers were also required to arrange for adequate drinking water and for food and shelter if the worksite is more than seven miles away from localities that provide these facilities. In addition, legislation provided standards for industrial safety and worker protection and for fire prevention. Sanitary and safety conditions were good in the modern sector, where many establishments also offered dispensaries, transportation facilities, lunchrooms, and vacation camps. Throughout most of the industrial sector, however, hygienic and safety facilities were marginal.

Organized Labor and Labor Relations

The right of workers to organize into unions and the right to strike were included in the Constitution of 1970. These general rights have been both limited and supported by governmental decrees and were the topics of pending legislation in mid-1971.

The largest union organization, the Moroccan Labor Union (Union Marocain du Travail—UMT), in 1970 claimed a total membership of about 700,000. The strongest unions within the UMT were the railroad, public works, mining, and transportation workers. The next largest labor grouping, the Union of Moroccan Workers (Union Générale des Travailleurs Marocains—UGTM), with a claimed membership in excess of 100,000, had as its main strength the teacher's and port worker's unions.

Union efforts aimed at the social and economic betterment of workers, such as demands made in 1970 for a 50-percent general wage and salary increase and a minimum income of DH300 a month for all workers. Union leaders also demanded an increase in social security family allowances, a minimum housing allowance of DH100 a month for workers in industry and commerce, improvement of vocational training programs, and a reduction of the price of medicine and sugar.

The unions have used strikes in attempts to achieve their goals. There were twenty-four strikes, mostly in low-wage food and textile factories, during the first six months of 1969. A major facet of union activity has been in the sphere of political opposition. The unions generally have been affiliated with, and sometimes are an important component of, a political party. The UMT, which has been affiliated with the National Union of Popular Forces (Union Nationale des Forces Populaires—UNFP), a leftist opposition party, and with the Moroccan Worker-Youth (Jeunesse Ouvrière Marocain—JOM), has long been viewed as a powerful political interest group (see ch. 8, The Governmental System and Political Dynamics).

Employer attitudes toward worker demands varied considerably, depending on the industrial sector and type of enterprise. Large, modern establishments generally maintained an attitude of progressive paternalism toward workers and readily negotiated with unions. Both union and nonunion members were hired and, although labor federations had not objected to this practice, they had been watchful to prevent discriminatory treatment on the basis of union membership.

A 1957 decree defined the form, coverage, and duration of collective bargaining contracts. These contracts may be negotiated for a period not to exceed three years. After they are written, they must be deposited with local authorities and with the Ministry of Youth, Sport, Labor, and Social Affairs and posted in the enterprises covered. If employers bound by the contract employ at least one-half of the workers in the occupation, industry, or geographic area named in the article defining the field of application, the ministry is empowered to extend coverage to all workers in those categories but only in the presence of "compelling economic reasons."

Collective bargaining is relatively new in the country and has been strongly favored by the UMT. Contracts usually have been negotiated on a plant-by-plant basis, although the UMT has favored more comprehensive agreements. Disparities in the level of economic development of the various regions have tended to limit the number of more comprehensive agreements. Most enterprises in the Casablanca-Rabat area practice collective bargaining, but the practice has spread slowly in the less developed areas.

Most collective disputes have been caused by dismissals and by worker complaints of inadequate wage and salary levels. In the absence of a government agency for arbitration or mediation in collective disputes, labor inspectors of the ministry have been assigned to act as go-betweens. Although their role has been technically minor, they have become increasingly important in settlement procedures. Because of the rather general nature of government legislation regarding disputes, collective contracts, negotiated on behalf of workers represented by powerful unions, spell out individual and collective dispute settlement procedures in some detail.

In 1962 a decree provided for the establishment of committees for the settlement of collective and individual disputes in enterprises employing more than 10 persons. In 1966, 310 enterprises representing some 4,530 workers resolved collective disputes through their committees on the enterprise level.

The legislation in effect in 1971 provided that grievances, if not settled on the enterprise level, could be taken to a labor court. Such courts functioned in Casablanca, Rabat, Meknès, Fes, Marrakech, Tangier, Tetouan, Nador, Oujda, Agadir, Beni Mellal, and Ksar al Souk. After a review of the facts involved, the conciliation committee attempted to resolve the case. If it failed to do so, the case was referred to the judicial committee, whose decision could be appealed if the court's competence was questioned. Both committees were headed by a senior legal or administrative official of the province in which the court was located.

CHAPTER 13

TRADE AND TRANSPORTATION

The share of trade, transportation, and other services in the country's gross domestic product (GDP—see Glossary) remained rather constant during the 1960s; it constituted some 36.4 percent in 1969 against 35.8 percent in 1963. At the launching of the Five Year Plan (1968–72) these sectors employed 387,000 persons out of an estimated number of 5,575,000 economically active Moroccans. The figures are expected to increase by the end of the plan period to 478,000 and 6,340,000, respectively.

In late 1971 domestic trade continued to be characterized by the existence of a modern sector juxtaposed to, but segregated from, the traditional system. The first existed primarily but not exclusively in the major urban centers (see ch. 6, Social Structure). It handled the distribution of imports and the selling of local products abroad.

The traditional sector, on the other hand, was prevalent in smaller towns, rural areas, and the older sections of the cities. Its basic features were the small retail shops, which carried wide varieties of merchandise, and the weekly *souks* (markets) where large numbers of farm producers, craftsmen, and other sellers gathered to sell their produce or merchandise.

Tourism and foreign trade were greatly helped by a well-developed transportation system that included the second best road network in Africa. Railroad and sea transport systems were well integrated with those of Europe and neighboring Algeria and Tunisia. European tourists reached Morocco either by air or by train or car via a regularly operated ferry service between Casablanca, Tangier, and Spain.

In the 1960s imports rose by an average rate of 3.4 percent and exports by only 2.7 percent annually, causing an increasing deficit in the balance of trade averaging DH150 million (5.06 dirham equal US$1—see Glossary) during the 1960–69 period. A decline in world phosphate prices and the liberalization of import regulations since 1967 contributed to the rising gap between imports and exports.

Major exports included phosphates, citrus fruits, vegetables, and canned fish; and leading imports were sugar, wheat, industrial goods, and petroleum. Because of the country's traditional French ties, a sizable portion of its foreign trade was conducted with France. Since independence, however, France's share in Morocco's imports and exports has been diminishing, while those of the United States, other Western European countries, and Eastern European countries have been growing.

The deficit in the balance of trade has been partially offset in the balance of payments by revenues from the expanding tourist industry, remittances from Moroccans working abroad, and multilateral and bilateral aid and loans. Tourism alone brought over DH700 million in revenue in 1970.

Because of the importance of tourism to the country's economic development, the government has provided a number of fiscal and credit benefits to private investors in tourist-related industries. Expansion in hotel capacity, however, has been concentrated in the first-class category despite an announced intention to increase the number of moderately priced hotels. Nevertheless, about 852,000 tourists visited Morocco in 1970, indicating that the target of over 1 million tourists by 1972 would be achieved.

DOMESTIC TRADE

In late 1971 commerce and business were composed of modern and traditional sectors. The modern sector emerged during the protectorate with the entry of European settlers and a subsequent expansion in domestic and foreign trade and finances. Because it had little to do with the traditional system and relied basically on the industrial and agricultural production of the Europeans and on foreign trade, the modern sector did not affect the economic life of the majority of the population. With more Moroccans becoming involved in this sector, however, by 1971 a greater degree of integration between the two sectors was gradually evolving.

Traditional Sector

The traditional market structure is characterized both by the small shops, opened regularly throughout the week, and the *souks*, where small local and farm producers and craftsmen gather once a week to sell their produce to town or city dwellers. In both the small rural and town shops and in the *souks*, a wide variety of domestic products is offered for sale. Price determination, except for the merchandise whose prices are fixed by the government, depends on supply and demand and the buyer's relative skill in bargaining.

Souks are held at three different levels: local, regional, and city. Local *souks* usually draw a small number of buyers and sellers from a radius of ten to twelve miles. Regional and city *souks* usually draw a larger number of buyers and sellers than local *souks* and hence result in a greater volume of sales. The exact locations where the regional and city *souks* are held are determined by both convenience and habit. Usually, regional *souks* are held at the convergence of transportation lines; and city *souks*, in the *madina* (ancient Muslim quarters in the urban areas).

Souks usually last for the whole day and are given the name of the day on which they are held. Thus, *souk al Arba* (Wednesday market) is held every Wednesday from early in the morning until sunset. If a seller does not sell his goods before the end of the day, he usually either carries them to another *souk* the following day or, if possible, returns to the same one the following week.

Because of economic development and gradual changes in taste the traditional system is slowly changing. Handicrafts have been particularly affected by the penetration of some modern manufactures sold at competitive prices in the small rural shops and the *souks*.

Modern Sector

The modern sector is found almost exclusively in the urban and industrial centers. It deals basically with the sale of manufactures, as well as with foreign trade and services. It is heavily concentrated in the Casablanca-Mohammedia area, which has replaced the principal older commercial cities of Fes, Meknès, and Marrakech, and is likely to remain as the country's main commercial and financial center for the foreseeable future.

Until independence practically all large business establishments were wholly owned by foreigners—mainly French. Since then many Europeans have left, and more Moroccans have become owners and managers. In some cases Moroccans have been accepted as minority partners in European-controlled establishments both as a gesture of goodwill and for security and public relations purposes.

Trade associations, such as the Moroccan General Economic Confederation and the Moroccan Union of Industrialists, Merchants, and Artisans, play an important role in establishing marketing channels and providing trade promotion. There are more than 100 associations covering most sectors of the economy, including industry and handicrafts.

Forms of Business Organization

In 1971 business activities were still governed by the Commercial Code of 1913 as amended. The code organized business establishments into five main types: sole proprietorship, general partnership, limited partnership, joint stock-limited liability company, and corporation.

The general partnership has a legal personality as an artificial being that can sue and be sued. The limited partnership has some partners with limited liability and some with unlimited liability; the former is neither responsible for management nor liable beyond their shares in the capital. Insurance companies, banks, and other financial institutions are prohibited from this type of organization.

In the limited liability company, shareholders are not liable beyond the value of the shares they hold. Such an organization could be formed by a minimum of two persons other than a husband and a wife, but its shares may not be issued to the public and may not be sold except with the consent of all concerned. Furthermore, it may not be changed into any other form of business except a corporation.

The capital of a corporation is divided into shares that may, after receiving an authorization, be sold to the public. This form of organization may be formed by a minimum of seven persons. It has to have a board of directors, whose members are selected by a general assembly vote for a maximum duration of six years. Board members are jointly responsible for the management of the corporation, and their shares are considered nontransferable, registered securities during the period of their service on the board.

Government Role in Distribution and Pricing

Government involvement in domestic trade aimed at maintaining relative stability in prices, raising revenues to finance certain projects, and raising productivity and volume of sale in some agricultural commodities. Government agencies in charge of these activities were: the Interprofessional Office for Cereals (Office Chérifien Interprofessionnel des Cereals—OCIC); the Office of Trade and Export (Office de Commercialisation et d'Exportation—OCE); the National Office of Tea and Sugar (Office National de Thé et du Sucre —ONTS); and the Moroccan Cooperative for Edible Oils (Cooperative Marocaine des Huileries Alimentaires—COMHA).

The main items subject to government price controls in 1971 were foodstuffs (bread, sugar, meat, milk, eggs, oils, wine, and some fruits), tobacco, fuels, water, charcoal, electricity, gas, and transport. The government also fixed wholesale prices or profit margins on flour, rice, salt, fresh and canned fish, butter, cheese, some fruits and vegetables, cotton textiles, soap, tea, coffee, school supplies, and farm machinery and supplies.

Government price and profit controls on these commodities along with a virtual freeze on salaries succeeded in stabilizing prices during the 1960s. The cost-of-living price index, used by the government, reached only 129 by mid-1970 (1958 = 100). This index, however, did not include imported consumer goods, the cost of which rose steadily during the late 1960s.

In announcing a 15-percent increase in grain prices in mid-1971, the government noted that such an increase was the first since 1965 and announced that its aim was to motivate farmers to grow more wheat and hence reduce the country's growing dependence on imports. The government was also encouraging farmers to use cooperatives in the marketing of grains.

TRANSPORTATION AND TELECOMMUNICATION

Road Transport

Morocco has a well developed road network. Until 1910 the country had only few roads, mainly in the sections leading toward the major cities. The present roads are relatively new and have been well planned.

Of the total of about 31,000 miles of principal and secondary roads in 1971, some 14,820 miles were well paved, and 12,600 miles were earth roads of good quality. The distinction between principal and secondary roads was based on their economic and tourist value. The latter were, however, mainly constructed to connect principal or trunk roads.

Major principal and secondary roads include those connecting Tangier and Oujda, the coastal or subcoastal towns and cities from Tangier to Goulimine, Marrakech to the Algerian border, Fes to Marrakech, Fes and Meknès to Ksar al Souk and Rissani, Marrakech to Ouarzazate, and Agadir to Figuig (see fig. 9). Each of these highways passes through a number of cities and towns, and the number of lanes varies in accordance with the expected volume of traffic at the time of construction.

A number of secondary roads were being constructed under the Five Year Plan to link various population centers to irrigation and development projects, either recently completed or still under construction, as well as to sites of tourist interest. In 1971 work was in progress on a road between Ifni and Tarfaya and another between Tangier and Fridek. The International Bank for Reconstruction and Development (IBRD), commonly known as the World Bank, was also providing some assistance to a number of road maintenance and construction projects and feasibility studies.

All land transport of goods and passengers was under the jurisdiction of an autonomous public agency, the National Transport Office (Office National de Transport—ONT). In practice, this agency has restricted its activities largely to the field of intercity, common-carrier road freight. It set freight rates, maintained an extensive system of freight depots, and allocated freight among all trucks with a carrying capacity over two metric tons that were for public hire.

Motor vehicle registrations reached 278,000 in 1969; of these, 191,000 were passenger cars and the remainder were trucks, buses, and other transport vehicles. This was more than double the total number of cars registered in 1957. In terms of geographic distribution,

Source: Adapted from *Investment in Morocco* (2d ed.), Rabat, July 1969.

Figure 9. Railroads, Principal Highways, Ports, and Airports of Morocco, 1970.

about 50 percent of the cars on the roads in 1969 were registered in Casablanca; 20 percent, in Rabat; 6 percent, in Meknès; and 6 percent, in Marrakech.

Many of the cars used in Morocco were assembled locally. The largest plant, Somaca, produced 21,000 vehicles in 1970, compared with 19,000 the previous year. Some of the needed parts and components, such as radiators, safety glass, tires, and mufflers, were also being produced locally.

Rail Transport

In 1971 the railroad system was owned and operated by the Moroccan National Office for Railroads (Office National des Chemins de Fer Maroc—ONCF). Previously it had been under the control of three separate private firms, whose concessions were terminated in 1963.

The rail network covered a distance of 1,062 miles, of which 440 miles were electrified and the remainder diesel operated. Principal lines extend from Casablanca eastward to Oujda and the Algerian frontier and southward to Marrakech.

The Casablanca-Sidi Kassem-Tangier section of the Moroccan railroads links Tangier with the European system via ferry service across the Strait of Gibraltar. A train ride from Paris to Casablanca takes fifty-two hours; and from Geneva to Casablanca, about three days, with a change in Madrid.

To encourage more Moroccans, tourists, and industries to use the railroads, ONCF started a program to improve freight and passenger services and establish new lines over the decade of the 1970s. The program provides for the acquisition of thirty-three high-powered electric and sixteen diesel electric locomotives and 1,000 new thirty-metric-ton freight cars and for the modification of existing railroad cars. In addition, some of the tracks that were not strong enough to carry heavy mineral and freight traffic at high speeds were to be relaid; these included the tracks between Youssoufia and Safi, Youssoufia and Marrakech, Casablanca and Rabat, and south of Casablanca to Sidi al Aidi. ONCF also had a number of long-term plans of expansion in the present network.

During the late 1960s the annual passenger traffic in the rail system averaged about 270 million passenger-miles; and freight traffic, about 17.6 million tons and 1,482 million ton-miles. This compares with 6.2 million metric tons of freight carried by road transport in 1969. About 85 percent of the railroads' revenues come from freight, and minerals, particularly phosphates, accounted for the major part of it. All the railroad operations were operating at a loss except for phosphates.

To arrive at a greater coordination in the Maghrib transport system, Morocco along with Algeria and Tunisia established the Maghrib Rail Transport Committee, composed of representatives from the three states. In a meeting held in Tunis in May 1971, the committee agreed on a number of measures, including the Arabization of rail documents, exchange of personnel, and the operation of the permanent secretariat of the Rail Transport Committee.

Sea Transport

The country has four major ports (Casablanca, Tangier, Safi, and Mohammedia), three regional ports (Kenitra, Agadir, and Al Hoceima), and ten minor ports. Casablanca is by far the largest, accounting in 1969 for over 75 percent of the 16.8 million metric tons of goods loaded and unloaded in Moroccan ports. Some of the export items shipped through this port are phosphate, citrus fruits, cereals, and vegetables. Casablanca also handles part of the country's passenger traffic and oil imports.

Tangier is the major passenger and tourist port and the only one in the country with a free trade area. It is also the point of entry for a number of important import items, such as cereals and sugar. Safi is primarily a sardine export port; however, it also handles a portion of phosphate exports. Along with Casablanca, Kenitra and Agadir are important for shipping citrus fruits.

Most of the oil imports come through Mohammedia. In 1970 improvements in port facilities and work on pipeline installations were completed, allowing 100,000-ton tankers to supply the refinery at Mohammedia. The refinery itself was linked to the port with a two-mile pipeline.

Warehouses at Casablanca are under the control of the Casablanca Port Authority (Regie d'Aconage du Port de Casablanca—RAPC). Most imported consumer goods may be stored free of charge for ten days at the port's facilities. Inflammable and other dangerous goods, however, are limited to four days of free storage. Goods declared for transshipment or in transit are allowed twenty days free of charge in the port's warehouse. At the end of these various periods continued storage becomes subject to charges calculated on the basis of gross weight. These charges increase at an accelerated rate.

The largest shipping company is the Moroccan Shipping Company (Compagnie Marocaine de Navigation—COMANAV). It is 96 percent government owned and has a fleet composed of eight vessels with a combined capacity of over 39,000 metric tons, about 60 percent of the merchant fleet. Its regular lines include services to the major ports in the other Maghrib countries, France, Poland, the Soviet Union, and the Scandinavian countries.

Recently the company opened a travel agency and began operating an auto-ferry service connecting Casablanca with Rouen, Southampton, and Lisbon. The purpose is to make it possible for European tourists to reach Morocco in their own cars, thus providing an added incentive to potential visitors.

Air Transport

Morocco has some fifty civil airports administered by the Directorate of Aviation, an agency of the Ministry of Public Works and Communications. In terms of their capacity, installations, and traffic, these airports were classified roughly into three main categories: principal, secondary, and tourist.

The principal airports—Casablanca-Nouasseur, Rabat-Salé, Casablanca-Anfa, Tangier-Boukhalf, Agadir, Marrakech, Oujda, Al Hoceima, and Fes—have a volume of traffic and the type of terminal installations and equipment of international airports. Until 1969 the Casablanca-Anfa airport was the most important in the country, but in 1969 the Casablanca-Nouasseur airport was opened for civil aircraft and replaced the operational structure of Casablanca-Anfa. Originally built as a military base for the United States Air Force, Nouasseur was turned over to the Moroccan authorities in 1963. Work on its reconversion and adaptation to make it suitable to receive large-size aircraft and meet the requirements of international civil aviation was started in 1967 with an initial loan granted by the United States Agency for International Development (AID).

The Tangier-Boukhalf airport is the oldest in Morocco and one of the oldest in Africa. In 1971 it was being enlarged to accommodate more and larger aircraft. When work on this airport is completed, it is expected to be the best equipped in the country. The Rabat-Salé airport was also being enlarged and modernized in accordance with the Five Year Plan.

The airport at Fes-Sais, opened for international traffic only in 1969, would be able to receive such aircraft as the Boeing 727 by 1972. In terms of volume of traffic, it is expected to become the fifth most important airport in the country.

Most important cities have an airport in the tourist category, serving the needs of light planes and sport aviation. The most heavily used of these airports is Til Mellil, which is thirteen miles from Casablanca. Most of the aircraft using this airport and the other tourist airports are private, belonging to either tourists or businesses.

Morocco has subscribed to the Chicago Convention of Air Transport, the International Civil Aviation Organization, and the World Meteorological Organization. It has also signed bilateral air agreements with twenty-four countries. Some of these bilateral agreements provide for absolute equality between the national airline of one party and an airline designated by the other and for the elimination of identical routes. Examples of these are the agreements signed with France and Spain. Some of the other agreements are less rigid, providing for equality of opportunity and allowing a certain degree of permeability. Examples of the latter are the agreements signed with the Federal Republic of Germany (West Germany) and the United Kingdom.

Morocco has two national airlines: Royal Air Maroc (RAM) and Royal Air Inter (RAI). RAM, founded in 1957, operates regular flights to Europe, Africa, and the United States. It is 63.6 percent state owned, and the remainder of its capital is distributed between Air France (about 17 percent) and various other air transport companies and individuals. RAI was created in 1970; it is 80 percent owned by RAM. It operates domestic flights between major Moroccan cities.

In addition to RAM and RAI, sixteen foreign airlines serve the principal airports in Morocco—ten European, five African, and one American. To attract more foreign airlines to extend their services to Morocco, the Ministry of Public Works and Communications and the Directorate of Aviation allow the establishment of regular services with Morocco even in the absence of an air agreement between Morocco and the country where the airline company is registered.

Most of the foreign airlines serving Moroccan airports have representatives in Casablanca, Rabat, or Tangier and are subject to the Moroccan Commercial Code, as is any other business enterprise. Because only the national airlines have the right to intervene directly with the Directorate of Aviation, foreign airlines do not have direct access to responsible government agencies; instead they assign a spokesman to deal with RAM. Representatives of these airlines have also formed a professional organization, the Board of Airline Representatives (BAR), to formulate common policy and deal with their problems in a collective fashion.

In 1971 the three Maghrib countries—Morocco, Algeria, and Tunisia—announced their intention to merge their national airlines by 1972. Should this plan materialize, the air transport system in the three countries would undergo some change, and previously established agreements and regulations would be revised.

Postal Service and Telecommunication

Postal service and telecommunication are operated by the Ministry of Posts, Telegraph, and Telephone. The private concessions for telecommunication in the former Spanish Protectorate in the north and in Tangier were ended in 1964 and 1967, respectively.

Direct cable connections with France, Algeria, West Africa, and Italy and a newly established satellite communications ground station provide an adequate link between Morocco and the rest of the world. All major cities are connected by telegraph and an automatic telephone network. In 1969 there were over 160,000 telephone subscribers, mostly concentrated in Casablanca and other major cities. Increases in demand for telephone subscriptions have been at the rate of about 4 percent per annum.

Postal service was adequately provided, although it still did not reach some of the more remote villages and towns. In 1966 there were 128 post offices and 500 agencies serving the country.

TOURISM

Tourism has become a major industry. The number of tourists visiting the country in 1970 reached an estimated 852,220, up from 255,520 in 1962 and 482,000 in 1965. In 1970 visitors came mainly from France (23.2 percent), the United States (15.8 percent), Great Britain (11.3 percent), and Algeria (8 percent), and most of the remainder came from Belgium, the Netherlands, Italy, and the Scandinavian countries.

The expansion of tourism may be attributed both to natural factors and to conscious efforts by the government and the private sector to increase and expand the needed services and facilities. Aside from the country's location, which makes it accessible from Europe by air, sea, and land, Morocco is endowed with such natural assets as a favorable climate, historic sites, 1,700 miles of white beaches along the Atlantic and the Mediterranean Sea, and scenic mountains and countryside (see ch. 2, Geography and Population).

The diversity in weather conditions in the different parts of the country, coupled with the moderate year-round climate in the lowlands, makes seasonal variations in tourist traffic less pronounced than in many other Mediterranean countries. About 40 percent of all visitors arrive between July and September, most of the remainder being dispersed throughout the rest of the year.

Importance to the Economy

Tourism is Morocco's fastest growing industry. It brought in an estimated DH700 million in gross revenues in 1970, against only DH332 million in 1965. This is an increase of 20 percent a year, which is above the world average of about 11 percent a year during the same period.

Aside from bringing in substantial quantities of foreign exchange, the tourist industry interacts with other sectors of the economy to bring about an expansion in employment and in the construction, food, amusements, transportation, and handicrafts industries. Its impact on the construction industry is reflected in the expansion in hotel capacity needed to meet the growth in the number of tourists. Investments in hotel construction and expansion during the 1965-67 period amounted to DH295 million, and the Five Year Plan allocated DH671 million for hotel development.

The target of the Five Year Plan was to increase hotel capacity and other tourist accommodations to provide about 50,000 beds for tourists at any one time, compared with 20,000 when the plan was launched. This would create new employment opportunities for about 2,400 Moroccans.

The pattern of tourist expenditures indicates the relative income received by the various sectors of the economy from this industry. In 1968, for example, 30 percent of tourist payments were for shelter; 25 percent, for food and drinks; 25 percent, for purchases (handicrafts); 5 percent, for amusements; 5 percent, for domestic transport; and the remaining 10 percent, for other purchases and services. Hotel income from tourism in that year amounted to about DH290 million, of which DH158 million, or 55 percent, was for food and drinks provided to customers. Domestic transport received another DH22.5 million and the handicrafts industry about DH113 million.

Government Role in Tourism and Planned Expansion

In 1971 the main branch in the government in charge of tourism was the National Tourist Office; it was the executive organ of the

Ministry of Tourism until that ministry was eliminated in August 1971. Its functions include the formulation of the state's policy on tourism, disseminating the information abroad, attracting potential investors, and regulating the businesses involved in the industry.

Because of the great importance of tourist revenues to the country's well-being, the government has encouraged investment in tourist-related projects by both the public and the private sectors. As an incentive, investors have been exempted from a number of taxes, and government-backed organizations were established to provide assistance and loans for hotel expansion.

The Investment Code of 1960 exempts investors from a number of taxes and offers foreign investors in hotel and other projects a number of guarantees concerning repatriation of capital and profits. A royal decree of July 17, 1965, further exempts hotel, motel, and holiday resorts and tourist complexes from the tax on services and provides that the state may extend a guarantee on the repayment of loans for the construction, expansion, or improvement of hotels.

Investments necessary for tourist development have been estimated at nearly DH1.3 billion for the 1960–72 period. Investment allocations for tourism by the public sector alone in the Five Year Plan amount to over DH171 million, of which DH92.5 million was directed to hotel construction. In addition, investments by semipublic organizations and local cooperatives have been estimated at another DH437.9 million. The private sector, both domestic and foreign, is expected to invest an additional DH151 million during the same period. Aside from these direct investments in tourist-related projects, expenditures on beautification and the development of public utilities are of a special tourist value but included under different accounts.

Promoting Investment

Three organizations participate in the development and financing of the tourist sector through loans or financial and technical aid: the Construction and Hotel Credit Organization (Crédit Immobilier et Hotelier—CIH), Morocco-Tourism (Maroc-Tourist), and the Moroccan Company for the Development of Tourism (Societé Marocaine pour le Développement du Tourisme—SOMADET). CIH was founded in 1928 to extend loans to investors in tourism and has since contributed to many projects. Loans made between 1959 and 1968 amounted to about DH121.6 million.

Under a law of December 1968, CIH was permitted to grant loans as high as 80 percent of the costs of hotel building construction or renovation and 70 percent of the value of needed furnishings and materials. Reimbursement of the loans may include a five-year grace period, and interests are set at 4-1/2 percent for twenty years on new construction and for ten years on equipment.

The other two organizations also contribute to the development of tourism, but their approach is different. Morocco-Tourism operates large tourist complexes and has investments in a number of hotel companies, whereas SOMADET conducts studies and establishes new joint projects with interested foreign partners to increase tourist traffic and revenues. The latter is particularly concerned with carrying out studies for large-scale tourist projects and joining with foreign interests in implementing them.

Prospects for Expansion

A target of the Five Year Plan was to increase tourist traffic to over 1 million a year by 1972. With a growth record of 20 percent between 1965 and 1970, this volume seems to be realizable. The most important impediment was the high cost of hotel accommodations and other expenditures as compared to other Mediterranean countries, such as Italy and Spain.

According to one estimate in 1970, the cost of one week in a four- or a five-star hotel with complete board averaged the equivalent of DH230 in Spain, DH320 in Tunisia, and DH520 in Morocco. Although the Five Year Plan provided for the construction of more moderately priced hotels to attract more tourists, in 1971 construction of first-class hotels was still the major part of new hotel construction.

BALANCE OF PAYMENTS

The balance-of-payments position improved in the late 1960s despite a widening deficit in the merchandise trade balance. It reached a critical deterioration in the 1961–64 period because of a succession of sizable deficits, resulting in large part from the outflow of capital and an unfavorable trade balance. This situation prompted the establishment of strict exchange and trade regulations in 1964.

The balance of payments and the volume of foreign exchange reserves improved significantly in 1969 and 1970, showing surpluses amounting to about DH131 million in 1969 and DH170 million in 1970. Although figures for the merchandise balance showed that imports exceeded exports by DH288 million in 1969 and DH600 million in 1970, these deficits were more than offset by transfer payments from abroad and foreign aid and loans. As a result, foreign exchange reserves at the end of 1970 increased to DH600 million, an increase of about 43 percent over 1969.

Balance of Trade

The volume of foreign trade and its importance to the economy rose sharply during the protectorate period because of the increase in the number of European settlers, whose needs for consumer and capital goods were not available domestically and had to be imported, as well as a sharp increase in the export of minerals and agricultural products, mainly to France and Spain. Thus, although the volume of foreign trade was only about DH10 million a year at the beginning of the twentieth century, it reached about DH35.5 million in 1913 and about DH576 million by 1930, of which about DH435 million represented imports of consumer and other goods. The volume of imports consistently exceeded that of exports during the protectorate period.

The deficit in the balance of trade was offset by French economic aid until 1956. After independence, however, French aid was periodically interrupted because of political difficulties, while the deficit in the balance of trade continued to grow (see ch. 9, Foreign Relations). Exchange restrictions were imposed in 1964, with a total ban on imports during the month of October.

Improvements in the balance of payments in 1965 led to a gradual liberalization of trade policy, particularly after 1967, which in turn led to a widening deficit in the balance of trade. The only noticeable improvement in the trade balance was in 1969, when a significant increase in olive oil exports and a drop in wheat imports reduced the gap between imports and exports. In 1970, however, imports were up again because of a resumption of wheat imports. Preliminary figures indicated that imports increased by 17 percent over the 1969 level; but exports increased by only 3 percent, causing an estimated balance-of-trade deficit twice that of 1969.

Tourism, Transport, and Insurance

The 1969 balance-of-payments figures indicate that gross receipts from tourism amounted to DH614 million (see table 15). Net receipts reached DH346.7 million, the difference representing expenditures by Moroccan travelers abroad. During the same year, receipts from maritime transport and insurance amounted to DH88.3 million, against total payments of DH239 million; of these, foreign exchange receipts by RAM came to DH11.5 million against payments of DH56.4 million made to foreign airlines.

Income from Investment and Cash Receipts

The income from the investments account included the repatriation of profits and interests by the private sector and interests payments and receipts by the public sector. Receipts in this account increased slightly in 1969 because of a rise in interests collected by the public sector, but expenditures remained relatively stable. Transfers by the

Table 15. *Balance of Payments of Morocco, 1969*

(in millions of dirham)[1]

Item	Receipts	Expenditures	Balance
Goods and Services			
Goods f.o.b.[2]	2,450.1	2,634.3	−184.2
Gold for industry	0	6.6	− 6.6
Transport charges and insurance on international shipments	88.3	239.0	−150.7
Other transport	25.6	73.9	− 48.3
Travel	614.0	267.3	+346.7
Income from investments	58.7	264.7	−206.0
Governmental transactions	151.1	265.3	−114.2
Other services	47.2	100.6	− 53.4
Total goods and services	3,435.0	3,851.7	−416.7
Cash Transfers			
Private	532.1	260.1	+272.0
Public	153.5	73.9	+ 79.6
Total cash transfers	685.6	334.0	+351.6
Nonmonetary Capital			
Private			
Balance of commercial credits	77.2	0	+ 77.2
Loans and investments	77.3	44.1	+ 33.2
Other	50.6	208.8	−158.2
Total private	205.1	252.9	− 47.8
Public			
Commercial credits	193.3	75.4	+117.9
Loans in foreign exchange	155.4	87.7	+ 67.7
Loans in dirham	70.9	16.3	+ 54.6
Other	3.5	0	+ 3.5
Total public	423.1	179.4	+243.7
Total nonmonetary capital	628.2	432.3	+195.9
GRAND TOTAL	4,748.8	4,618.0	+130.8

[1] 5.06 dirham equal US$1—see Glossary.
[2] Free on board.

Source: Adapted from *Monthly Bulletin of Information* [Rabat], March 1970, p. 20.

private sector represented 44.2 percent of the total in 1969, down from 52 percent the previous year.

In 1969 cash receipts from salaries, pensions, and gifts amounted to DH532.1 million, of which DH302.3 million represented remittances by Moroccans working abroad. Cash expenditures, on the other hand, reached DH260.1 million, of which DH231.3 million was in salaries repatriated by foreign citizens working in Morocco.

The surplus in government cash transfers fell to DH79.6 million in 1969, against DH96.2 million in 1968 and DH117.4 million in 1967. This resulted from a drop both in receipts from France for payment of the salaries of French citizens working in Morocco under the technical assistance program and in American grants usually obtained from private sources.

The Capital Account

The deficit in Morocco's private capital account has persisted since the mid-1950s. In 1968 it reached DH81.1 million, dropping to DH47.8 million in 1969. Public capital transfers, however, had a surplus of DH243.7 million in 1969, resulting in an overall surplus in the capital account amounting to DH195.9 million. Total public grants, gifts, and loans registered DH423.1 million in that year, whereas repayments of public debts reached only DH179.4 million.

Exchange Controls

Exchange control regulations are set and administered by the Exchange Control Office (Office des Changes), an agency of the Ministry of Finance. Authorized banks act in some cases on behalf of the Exchange Control Office in the execution of some exchange control measures (see ch. 11, Character and Structure of the Economy).

According to regulations in force in 1971, foreign exchange brought into Morocco must be declared and exchanged for dirham at authorized banks. The par value of exchange of Moroccan dirham was set at 0.175610 gram of fine gold, or DH5.06049 equal US$1, and the rate per French franc at DH1.09755.

Importation of Moroccan banknotes is prohibited, and foreign banknotes brought in must be declared upon entry. For resident travelers, foreign exchange must be surrendered within fifteen days of entry.

Morocco does not have a foreign exchange market. Sale and purchase of foreign currency are centralized in the Bank of Morocco; authorized banks that are permitted to handle foreign exchange transactions on behalf of their customers are required to purchase from or sell to the Bank of Morocco the balances of their daily foreign exchange transactions.

The Exchange Control Office classifies countries for prescription of currency purposes into three groups: the French franc area countries, the payments agreement countries, and the area of convertibility countries. Transactions with the franc area are made in francs or in dirham through the French Franc Area Accounts (in which Moroccan dirham are held by franc area residents for use in any settlement except imports).

Transactions with the payments agreement countries are debited or credited in the payments agreement accounts. Countries with which Morocco has entered into such agreements are Bulgaria, the People's Republic of China (PRC), Cuba, Czechoslovakia, the German Democratic Republic (East Germany), Guinea, Hungary, Mali, Poland, Spain, the Arab Republic of Egypt, and the Soviet Union.

Although a distinction is made between the franc area and the area of convertibility, exchange controls apply equally to countries in the two areas. Unlike the franc area, however, transactions with the convertibility area are settled in convertible currencies negotiated by the Bank of Morocco. Some of the countries included in this category are Austria, Belgium, Canada, Denmark, West Germany, Italy, the Netherlands, Norway, Portugal, the United Kingdom, Switzerland, and the United States.

FOREIGN TRADE

Since independence, and particularly during the late 1960s, the role of foreign trade in the economy of Morocco has been declining steadily despite the increase in import-export volume. Exports, which constituted about 19.5 percent of the national income in 1964, made up only 17.3 percent of it in 1969; and imports, which were 20.7 percent of the national income in 1964, dropped to 20 percent in 1969.

Exports

Exports in 1969 totaled DH2,455 million, compared with DH1,942 million in 1963, DH2,168 million in 1966, and DH2,278 million in 1968 (see table 16). Most of this increase is attributed to growth in the export of foodstuffs, raw materials, and processed goods.

Exports of food and beverages reached DH1,185 million in 1969, or about 48 percent of the total. Morocco is the world's second largest exporter of citrus fruits. Some 551,000 metric tons of these fruits were exported in 1969—mostly to France, the Soviet Union, West Germany, the Netherlands, and Belgium—bringing a revenue of DH388.5 million. Fresh tomatoes, of which 133,142 metric tons were exported in 1969, brought an additional revenue of DH145.6 million. Canned fish is third in importance, with a total metric tonnage of 46,908 valued at DH133 million. France and West Germany were the two leading customers for Moroccan tomatoes and canned fish.

Agricultural raw materials constituted about 9.7 percent of total exports in 1969, bringing DH238 million in revenue. Olive oil, cotton,

Table 16. *Foreign Trade of Morocco, 1966–69*
(in millions of dirham)*

	1966	1967	1968	1969
Imports				
Food, drink, and tobacco	659.6	722.7	618.7	452.2
Fuels and lubricants	117.1	126.9	165.7	164.6
Products in bulk of animal and vegetable origin	294.4	268.9	327.2	291.8
Minerals	23.5	22.4	36.1	50.6
Semiprocessed goods	516.3	550.1	616.0	731.1
Manufactured goods				
Manufactured for industry	385.1	528.9	588.4	663.3
Manufactured for consumption	415.8	396.8	433.3	483.6
Gold for industry	6.1	3.5	4.7	7.2
TOTAL	2,417.9	2,620.2	2,790.1	2,844.4
Exports				
Food, drink, and tobacco	1,051.7	1,061.9	1,168.5	1,184.9
Fuels and lubricants	6.5	10.7	16.3	7.8
Products in bulk of animal and vegetable origin	137.7	140.9	134.2	238.2
Minerals	777.5	753.7	737.7	768.2
Semiprocessed goods	110.1	122.3	155.0	.1445
Manufactured goods				
Manufactured for industry	4.8	2.1	8.3	2.9
Manufactured for consumption	43.7	54.6	57.1	108.9
TOTAL	2,132.0	2,146.2	2,278.1	2,465.4

*5.06 dirham equal US$1—see Glossary.

Source: Adapted from Banque Marocaine du Commerce Exterieur, *Bulletin Mensuel d'Information* [Casablanca], No. 105, May 1970.

and cork were the major items in this group. Olive oil exports showed a significant increase in 1969; about 32,765 metric tons valued at DH91.4 million were exported in that year, compared with 2,430 metric tons valued at DH7.2 million in 1968. This increase, however, does not necessarily reflect a trend because Morocco's olive oil production is subject to a triennial cycle.

Minerals contributed about DH776 million, or 31 percent of total exports, in 1969. Morocco is the world's leading exporter of phosphate, the country's leading export item. Revenues from phosphate exports in 1969 amounted to DH551 million, or 22 percent of total export value. Major customers, in order of importance, were France, the United Kingdom, the Belgium-Luxembourg Economic Union, Spain, Poland, the Netherlands, PRC, Japan, and Italy. Other minerals exported are lead, iron, manganese, zinc, cobalt, and coal.

Imports

Total imports reached DH2,844 million in 1969, compared with DH2,790 million in 1968, DH2,418 million in 1966, and DH2,310 million in 1963. Food, beverages, and tobacco constituted 15.9 percent of total imports in 1969; fuel and raw materials (including food oil), 17.8 percent; and consumer goods, about 17 percent.

Morocco imports large quantities of sugar, but the amount imported has been declining in recent years because of the government's encouragement of sugar beet production and an expansion of sugar-refining capacity (see ch. 12, Agriculture and Industry). Thus, although sugar imports were valued at DH327 million in 1964, they dropped to DH262 million in 1965, DH191 million in 1966, DH149 million in 1967, DH119 million in 1968, and DH109 million in 1969. Long-range plans aim at self-sufficiency in sugar production by 1985.

The two other leading food imports were tea and wheat. Tea was second to sugar in value in 1969, reaching DH103 million. This was more than double the 1963 value of only DH51 million and a sharp rise over 1968, which registered DH82 million.

Morocco became a net importer of cereals early in the 1960s. Between 1966 and 1970 yearly imports averaged 63,420 metric tons. According to an estimate by the Ministry of Agriculture and National Development, improved methods of cultivation could increase the country's wheat production to almost 3 million metric tons a year by 1977. If this level were achieved, import needs from this commodity would drop by 80 percent of the 1970 level. The alternative would be a rise in imports to a level of 1.3 million metric tons by 1977.

Fuels and raw materials imported include crude oil, lumber, lubricants, gasoline and diesel fuel, peanut oil, and other food oils. Imports of these items rose from DH377 million in 1963 to DH435 million in 1966 and DH507 million in 1969. Morocco depends on imported petroleum for most of its oil needs; crude oil imports rose from DH65 million in 1963 to DH79 million in 1966 and DH102 million in 1969. The Soviet Union and Algeria were the major suppliers.

Semifinished products imported consist of metal products, cotton and synthetic textile yarn, intermediate paper products, fertilizers, and other chemicals and industrial goods. In 1969 the value of these imports amounted to DH731 million, constituting some 25.7 percent of total imports against 20 percent in 1963 and 21.4 percent in 1966.

Imports of agricultural and industrial equipment were valued at DH663 million in 1969, a sharp increase over 1963 and 1966 figures of DH370 million and DH385 million, respectively. Most of this increase was in the industrial equipment and machinery category (as opposed to agricultural equipment), which accounted for DH415 million in 1969 against only DH154 million in 1963.

Consumer goods imported in 1969 amounted to DH484 million. Automobiles and auto parts, hardware and appliances, and pharmaceuticals were the major items in this category. Because of the expansion in domestic textile production, the value of textile imports dropped significantly in the 1960s—from DH165 million in 1963 to DH97 million in 1966, DH71 million in 1967, and DH25 million in 1969.

Trade Pattern

France, West Germany, and Italy are Morocco's leading partners (see table 17). These three states and the other three members of the European Economic Community (EEC) received 58.8 percent of Morocco's exports in 1969 and supplied it with 52.3 percent of its imports.

Table 17. Principal Suppliers and Customers of Morocco, 1969

Suppliers	Value*	Percent	Customers	Value*	Percent
France	866,206	30.5	France	862,838	35.1
West Germany	279,313	9.8	West Germany	209,493	8.5
United States	213,869	7.5	Italy	200,328	8.2
Soviet Union	159,439	5.6	Great Britain	143,492	5.8
Italy	152,193	5.3	Netherlands	102,924	4.2
Great Britain	147,821	5.2	Spain	99,982	4.1
Other	1,025,580	36.1	Other	836,397	34.1
TOTAL	2,844,421	100.0	TOTAL	2,455,454	100.0

* In thousands of dirham; 5.06 dirham equal US$1—see Glossary.

Source: Adapted from *Monthly Bulletin of Information* [Rabat], June 1970.

Although France's relative share in Morocco's trade declined during the 1950s and 1960s, in 1971 it remained the principal supplier of Morocco's imports and the major market for its exports. In 1969 France supplied 30.5 percent of Morocco's total imports and received 35.1 percent of its exports. Morocco was also one of France's leading suppliers and customers, ranking twelfth among both its sources and its customers.

After a long period of negotiation, an association agreement between Morocco and the EEC came into effect in 1969. In accordance with this agreement, about 75 percent of Morocco's exports to the EEC get preferential treatment on tariffs and quotas for industrial products and tariffs for farm products. Moroccan citrus exports get an 80-percent reduction in the common external tariff, and canned fruits and vegetables get a 50-percent tariff cut. Special consideration is also given to fish products and olive oil.

In return for these concessions Morocco agreed to reduce tariffs on imports from the EEC by an average of 12.5 percent and establish some quotas guaranteeing the maintenance of the same level of imports on certain items traditionally obtained from member countries. The establishment of these quotas, however, did not imply any new purchasing obligations, since they were based upon the share of the EEC members in Morocco's imports before the association agreement was signed.

This agreement did not show any immediate favorable results with regard to an increase in volume or a change in direction of trade. Provisional figures for 1970 even indicate a small drop in the volume of goods traded. Moroccan citrus fruit exports to the community dropped slightly in that year because of competition from Spain and Israel, and total Moroccan exports to the six member countries dropped from DH1,443 million in 1969 to DH1,087 million in 1970, while its imports from the community fell from DH1,448 million to DH1,296 million.

The United States is Morocco's major trading partner in the Western Hemisphere. The United States had for many years maintained second place among Morocco's suppliers. A good wheat crop in 1969, however, resulted in a reduction of Morocco's imports of this commodity, which in turn reduced that year's volume of American exports to Morocco and caused it to rank third among Morocco's sources of supply. In addition to wheat, Morocco imports vegetable oils, cotton, tobacco, and tallow from the United States.

Although total American exports to Morocco in 1969 amounted to DH213 million, or about 7.5 percent of the total, its imports from Morocco registered only DH47 million, or about 1.9 percent of the total. The reason for the low level of American imports from Morocco is that the United States is a major producer of most of Morocco's traditional exports. It is, for example, the world's major producer of phosphate, which is Morocco's main export item. The United States, however, still imports a number of items from Morocco, including chemical manganese ore; zinc ore; dried vegetables and spices; canned vegetables, fish, and olives; agar; barium; and hides and skins.

The Soviet Union has been Morocco's major trading partner among the communist states. In the early 1970s it was Morocco's second major crude oil supplier and the second largest buyer of its oranges. The total volume of Soviet-Moroccan trade, however, was still small, as was the total value of trade with all the communist states, whose total share amounted to only 12 percent of Morocco's foreign trade in 1969.

A permanent Soviet-Moroccan commission for economic, scientific, and technical cooperation was established in 1970 to enhance trade and other relations between the two states. They also signed a new three-year trade agreement covering the 1970–73 period, according to which the Soviet Union would sell Morocco hydroelectric power and refrigeration equipment, tractors, and agricultural machinery worth about DH222 million. Payments for these imports would be made in citrus fruits, cotton, cork, and canned sardines.

Morocco's trade with Africa has risen steadily since the mid-1960s. In 1969 alone it rose by 30 percent, total imports amounting to DH130.8 million and exports to about DH137.1 million. Over 65 percent of this trade is composed of commodity exchanges with the other three North African countries: Algeria, Tunisia, and Libya.

Most of Morocco's trade with Asia is conducted with Japan and the PRC. Imports from Japan amounted to DH55.5 million in 1969, up 83.7 percent from the previous year; exports were DH37.6 million, up by 41 percent.

Imports from the PRC were greater in volume in 1969 than those from Japan, reaching DH66.6 million, of which DH55.2 million represented payments for green tea. Morocco's exports to China in the same year were composed of phosphate and cobalt ore and amounted in value to DH34.5 million. In mid-1971 negotiations were underway for the sale of Moroccan-assembled buses to China.

Government Role

Until 1963 the government's direct involvement in export trade was restricted to the phosphate industry. The production and export of this mineral have always been handled as a government monopoly. The Sharifian Office of Phosphates (Office Chérifien des Phosphates —OCP) was founded in 1920 and has since been responsible for the production and exportation of phosphates.

In 1965, because of disappointment over the slow growth of the country's export earnings and suspicion that some exporters were resorting to underinvoicing to repatriate capital, the government established the Office of Trade and Export (Office de Commercialisation et d'Exportation—OCE), giving it a monopoly over the export of citrus fruits, fresh and canned vegetables and fruits, fresh and canned fish, and fruit juices. In 1966 wine and cotton were added to the list of controlled items.

Direct government involvement in the import trade is limited to tobacco, sugar, and tea. Tobacco and tobacco products have for many years been handled exclusively by the Tobacco Authority (Regie de Tabacs), but control over sugar and tea imports was started only in 1963. The National Office of Tea and Sugar has since been given a monopoly over the importation and wholesaling of these commodities.

Foreign Trade Regulations

During the protectorate, Morocco's foreign trade was theoretically regulated by the Act of Algeciras of 1906, which provided, among other things, for equal treatment of all states in Morocco's foreign economic policies and trade regulations and established a maximum tariff rate of 12.5 percent on all goods imported. France and Spain, however, established quotas and currency restrictions as a result of which each secured a major share of trade in the zone under its control. Thus, French products were imported freely into the French Protectorate, but goods imported from other areas were subject to import quotas.

Accordingly, by the 1930s Morocco was importing 34 percent of its needs from France and the French franc zone, and by 1950 this share had reached about 68 percent. In the meantime, most importers, exporters, and retailers, as well as a significant portion of the potential consumers, were French.

After independence, Morocco's foreign trade policy was governed by its balance-of-payments situation. The strict measures taken in 1964 were prompted by the deterioration of the balance-of-payments position and the drop in foreign exchange reserves. As soon as circumstances allowed, however, import regulations and controls were gradually eased.

In 1967 new simplified import regulations divided imports into three categories or lists (A,B, and C). Goods in category A do not require import licenses, goods in category B are subject to import licenses, and those in category C are forbidden entry to the country because they are either injurious or unnecessary.

It is indicative of the increasing liberalization of trade that items in category A, originally described as essential goods and materials needed for domestic industry, increased steadily. In the 1971 General

Import Program, about three-fourths of all imports were included in this category, and very few items were left in the C category.

Import licenses for items in the B category, described as either already produced locally or restricted because of the state of the country's foreign finances, are secured from the Exchange Control Office. A deposit of 25 percent of the f.o.b. (free on board) value of the shipment is to be made by the importer, upon applying for a license, at a bank designated by him to handle the transaction.

In common with most trading nations, Morocco has adopted the Brussels Tariff Nomenclature and has a two-column tariff system, in which one column indicates how high the rate could go without a prior announcement and the other the current rate. Duties are assessed on an ad valorem basis, and value is decided in terms of wholesale price at the country of origin and costs of transportation.

In an effort to increase exports, minimum export controls have been used in Morocco, and export taxes were completely abolished in mid-1971. Items that are neither under a government export monopoly nor of a critical nature, such as gold, jewelry, petroleum, and cereals, are exported freely. Items that are considered of a critical nature or of special importance are subject to export declarations, which remain good for a period of six months, as do import licenses.

FOREIGN INVESTMENT

Sizable amounts of French capital were invested in Moroccan industry, agriculture, housing, and trade during the protectorate. A 1952 study made by the Bank of Morocco indicated that about 68.7 percent of the private capital invested in Morocco in that year, estimated at the equivalent of about US$1.9 billion, came from France and that most of the remainder belonged to French *colons* (settlers in Morocco). This put the French in strong control of most of the modern industrial and business sectors in Morocco, accounting in 1955 for about 80 percent of investments in commerce, industry, and mines and 40 percent of investments in the construction industry.

As the prospects of Morocco's independence became clear, many French merchants and property owners decided to return to France, carrying with them the proceeds from the sale of their businesses and properties. It was estimated that capital flight amounted to the equivalent of US$60 million in 1955, increasing to US$285 million in 1956, the year of independence. Big property owners, industrialists, and financiers remained, however.

Unlike many newly independent countries Morocco did not resort to large-scale nationalization of foreign-owned businesses. As a result, there were still about 3,000 French firms in Morocco in the mid-1960s, of which 450 accounted for more than half of the country's industrial production.

The closest that the government came to nationalization was the 1963 takeover of some 556,000 acres of land from French owners. These properties, however, had originally been taken over by the protectorate government and distributed among French *colons*. French-owned *milk* (see Glossary) land, which at the time amounted to 800,000 acres, was not affected by these measures, although many of the *milk* landowners later preferred to sell their lots to Moroccans (see ch. 12, Agriculture and Industry).

Other instances sometimes cited as government takeovers were the ending of the concessions of the private electric power and railroad companies before their expiration dates and participation by the government in a French metal-box manufacturing company. In the latter case the public sector put up DH10 million in fresh capital, thus doubling the company's capital and establishing a fifty-fifty participation in the management of the firm. One reason given for this partial nationalization was that the higher prices paid by Moroccan processing and canning industries for cans produced by this firm caused Moroccan canned fish, vegetables, and fruits to be less competitive internationally.

Although foreign investment in Morocco continued in 1971 to be primarily French, other European and American investments have increased significantly since independence and particularly since the mid-1960s. In 1969 alone, out of a total inflow of foreign investment of DH68.8 million, some 40.3 percent was from the United States; 34.1 percent, from France (compared to 64 percent in 1968); 13.2 percent, from Switzerland; and 5.5 percent, from West Germany.

The number of American ventures and branch offices in Morocco rose from forty-six in 1967 to sixty-four in 1969. They were basically involved in tourism, banking, agricultural projects, petroleum distribution and exploration, and tire manufacturing. Recent estimates of the total value of these ventures were the equivalent of about US$40 million.

Policy and Incentives

In 1971 foreign firms could operate in Morocco either through a branch office or a subsidiary company. The first was treated under law as a sole proprietorship, without regard to its legal status in its mother country, and was treated for tax purposes on that basis. On the other hand, subsidiaries of foreign firms were registered as Moroccan firms and were subject in their formal structure to Moroccan legal requirements.

In 1958 the government promulgated an investment code to assure private and foreign investors of the safety of their properties and provide some incentives to attract new foreign capital. In the same year an investment commission was established to administer the application of the incentives offered in the code.

In 1960 a new investment code became operative that applied to productive enterprises, both foreign and domestic, which had received approval from the investment commission. Basic incentives provided under this code include: increasing the rate of depreciation to a limit up to twice its permitted level; allowing the maintenance of a tax-free reserve for the acquisition of new equipment up to a level of 40 percent of the total value of approved investment and 50 percent of net annual profits; providing a guarantee for the total or partial repatriation of capital in the currency originally brought into Morocco to start or expand the venture; allowing an equipment premium or a direct government subsidy of up to 20 percent of investments made in Tangier and 15 percent in the other parts of the country (except the Casablanca-Mohammedia area); providing total or partial exemption from customs duties on imported tools, machinery, equipment, and other capital goods (provided that they are new and are not produced locally at competitive prices and are needed to increase productivity); reducing company registration and license taxes on new construction and equipment; and granting a ten-year stabilization guarantee on profit, license, urban, and local taxes.

Repatriation of profits and transfer of salaries and wages earned by foreign employees and workers were provided for under the foreign exchange regulations that were set and administered by the Exchange Control Office. These regulations provided that profits after taxes, dividends on shares in Moroccan firms held by nonresidents, and undistributed profits were transferable to the investor's country of residence after receiving the proper authorization from the Exchange Control Office. Salaries and wages earned by foreign employees and workers qualify for transfer up to the limit of 50 percent if the employee's or the worker's family does not reside in Morocco and 30 percent if he is single or his family lives in Morocco.

In 1967 an investment promotion center was established by a royal decree to provide information on available opportunities and incentives, assist with feasibility studies, act as a basic point of contact between local and potential foreign investors, and serve as a reception and documentation center for investors. This center, therefore, supplements the work of the investment commission.

As an additional incentive to foreign investors, Morocco has signed investment guarantee agreements with the United States, West Germany, Belgium, and Luxembourg. The agreement with the United States covers expropriation; convertibility; risk of war, revolution, and insurrection; and extended risks. Furthermore, it has ratified the convention drawn by the World Bank for the settlement of investment disputes.

Moroccan Control over Trade and Services

Increasing the share of Moroccan nationals in business activities and employment without resort to stiff nationalization measures has been an area of concern in Morocco. In 1970 the government finally announced its intention to Moroccanize the trade and services sector (tertiary sector). Firms in this sector are to have a minimum of 51 percent Moroccan capital, and two-thirds of the members of their boards of directors are to be Moroccans. In cases in which private Moroccan capital cannot be obtained, the government-controlled National Investment Company (Societé Nationale d'Investissements) would make available the necessary capital.

Government spokesmen, however, were quick to explain that unlike nationalization, which is usually undertaken through specific legislation, what is referred to by Moroccans as Moroccanization of the tertiary sector is a form of joint venture or partnership between national and foreign private capital and is to be arrived at through negotiations and mutual agreement. Furthermore, no specific deadline was announced, although some Moroccan officials referred to 1971 as the year of Moroccanization.

Specifically, the companies expected to Moroccanize were: import companies representing specific brands (exclusive agencies); enterprises subject to authorization, such as freight forwarders, transportation companies, pharmacies, and the press; and wholesale and retail businesses. With regard to banks and insurance companies, joint committees, composed of government officials and representatives of foreign chambers of commerce and other concerned trade associations in Morocco, have been formulated to study the possible approaches to the Moroccanization of these financial establishments.

FOREIGN AID

France has traditionally been the major supplier of aid to Morocco. After independence it was joined by the United States and, since the mid-1960s, by the World Bank, the Soviet Union, West Germany, and a number of other countries. Figures released for 1970 indicate that Morocco received a total of DH756.5 million in foreign loans and grants in that year. Of these, about 40.4 percent came from the United States; 18.9 percent, from France; 11.2 percent, from West Germany; 10 percent, from the World Bank group; and 8.5 percent, from the Soviet Union. It was estimated that about 40 percent of investments included under the Five Year Plan would be financed through foreign aid and loans.

French Aid

Following independence, negotiations were held for a new French aid program, but the French kidnapping of five Algerian leaders and the subsequent anti-French riots in Morocco caused a deterioration in French-Moroccan relations and a breakdown in the negotiations. As a result, the flow of French aid remained below the expected level, and in 1959 it was completely suspended for about three years. During the 1960s another break in the supply of French aid resulted from the 1965–66 Ben Barka affair (see ch. 3, Historical Setting; ch. 9, Foreign Relations).

After 1968 French aid to Morocco became totally tied, much to the satisfaction of French businesses and French-owned establishments in Morocco. French firms were contracted to carry out projects financed by French aid, and needed purchases also had to be obtained from French businesses. Some of the projects completed under this aid program were the Sidi Bennour Sugar Works and the expansion of the petroleum refineries.

In mid-1971 France and Morocco signed three protocols on new French aid amounting to 530 million francs, of which 380 million was directed to financing a number of projects, including laying an underwater cable between the two countries, the construction of an assembly plant for French cars and a cement works, the expansion of a cellulose factory, and the installment of a thermal center in Roches-Noires. The remainder of the aid would be used for the purchase of telecommunication equipment and conducting a number of feasibility studies on public works and other projects.

United States Aid

United States aid to Morocco began in 1957 at the level of US$20 million. It was later increased to an average of US$40 million between 1959 and 1964.

In the early years of the United States aid program, assistance was mainly in the form of loans to the government of Morocco, but starting in 1962 greater emphasis was given to technical assistance and the financing of some major projects. A substantial program was also started during the 1960s to supply Morocco with surplus grain and other agricultural commodities under United States Food for Peace (PL 480).

By the end of 1970 total United States aid to Morocco amounted to some US$700 million, approximately 60 percent of which was in the form of long-term loans and about 40 percent in gifts and grants. Substantial amounts of Morocco's wheat imports were still being obtained under PL 480 titles I and II, the Commodity Credit

Corporation (CCC) credits, and a small part of them under AID agriculture sector loans.

The Export-Import Bank has also participated in extending aid to Morocco with its financing of two Boeing 727s received by RAM. In 1971 it was also involved in financing the iron ore pelletization plant at Nador and an earth satellite station.

Aid from the World Bank and the United Nations Development Program

The World Bank has extended to the government of Morocco a number of loans for projects in agriculture, tourism, and transportation. In 1969 it agreed to provide US$46 million to finance irrigation works in the first phase of the Rharb-Sebou project. Part of this loan was allocated to the construction of a dam at Arabat on the Inoauene River.

The United Nations Development Program (UNDP) has provided some assistance in a number of projects, including a manpower and technical requirements study and a project to improve methods and quality of economic statistics. In addition, it has helped both financially and technically in mining studies in the Anti-Atlas and in studies aimed at improving the protein concentration of fishmeals.

Other Sources of Aid

The Soviet Union, Italy, Canada, and Kuwait have extended varying amounts and forms of aid to Morocco. In 1966 the Soviet Union provided the equivalent of US$42 million for project financing, basically in agriculture, and long-term trade credits. This was followed by another long-term loan for the construction of a hydroelectric power station at Ait Adel near Marrakech, totaling $19.2 million. In 1970 new loans from the Soviet Union amounted to DH64 million.

Italian aid to Morocco was about DH50.6 million in 1971, directed basically to projects under the Five Year Plan. On the other hand, the bulk of Canada's aid until mid-1971 was devoted to financing and supplying technicians and equipment to the Development of the Western Rif Program (Développement Economique et Rural du Rif Occidental—DERRO). Morocco has also received a number of loans from the Kuwait Fund for Arab Economic Development (KFAED), including a US$16.9 million loan in 1965 and a US$28 million one in 1966.

SECTION IV. NATIONAL SECURITY

CHAPTER 14

NATIONAL DEFENSE AND INTERNAL SECURITY

In late 1971 the loyalty to the monarchy of the Royal Armed Forces (Forces Armées Royales—FAR) and therefore its future role in politics and government were for the first time since independence the subjects of extensive speculation by observers and of apparent concern to the king. An attempted coup d'etat on July 10, 1971, not only resulted in the death of nine of the thirteen generals then on active military duty but also revealed that five of the nine had been engaged in a plot either to kill the king or to make him a prisoner and thus force him to comply with their demands. As of late 1971 the exact nature of the conspirators' demands had not been made clear by the government, but a reported goal of the coup leaders, who were depicted by various spokesmen as of a conservative, puritanical, reactionary bent, was to eliminate corruption and the corrupters as an initial step in a vague program that would purify and preserve the kingdom (see ch. 8, The Governmental System and Political Dynamics).

King Hassan II had been, as crown prince, a member of the royal commission appointed by his father in 1956 to establish a military force, which in 1971 continued to be a part of the royal household rather than an integral part of the apparatus of government. As the first and only chief of the general staff and as the supreme commander since his succession to the throne in 1961, Hassan has given unremitting attention to the selection and promotion of military personnel. For several years before the coup attempt, Hassan had relied heavily upon several score mid- and senior-level military officers to discharge administrative duties at all levels of government, and in 1971 most of the nineteen provincial governors were army officers.

Not surprisingly, Hassan at first belittled the coup attempt as a clumsy effort by a few dissident officers to seize power, and he reiterated his faith in the loyalty of the FAR. On August 6, however, he appointed a new government in which General Mohammed Oufkir, since 1964 the minister of interior and widely regarded as second only to the king in power, was designated as the new minister of defense and FAR chief of staff (see ch. 8, The Governmental System and Political Dynamics). Because of Oufkir's reputation for ruthless efficiency and unalloyed allegiance to the king, it was generally assumed that Oufkir had been assigned the task of ensuring that the king could continue to rely upon the FAR as the main bulwark of his regime (see ch. 3, Historical Setting; ch. 9, Foreign Relations).

In 1971 the main component of the FAR was the army, with nearly 50,000 officers and men. The air force, with about 4,000 men, was lightly armed and served largely as a support element of the army, as did the navy, a small force with slightly over 1,000 men. The Royal Guard, a small force of a few hundred men attached directly to the royal family, also is technically a part of the FAR.

In addition to the FAR, the kingdom's security forces included the Auxiliary Forces, a paramilitary command of about 20,000 men; the Royal Gendarmerie, a rural police force of about 7,000 men; and the Sûreté Nationale, the national police force with about 16,000 men (see fig. 10). The commanders of these units were personally appointed by the king, and the director general of the police was responsible directly to the monarch. The Auxiliary Forces were attached to the Ministry of Interior, and the Royal Gendarmerie received operational control from the Royal Moroccan Army.

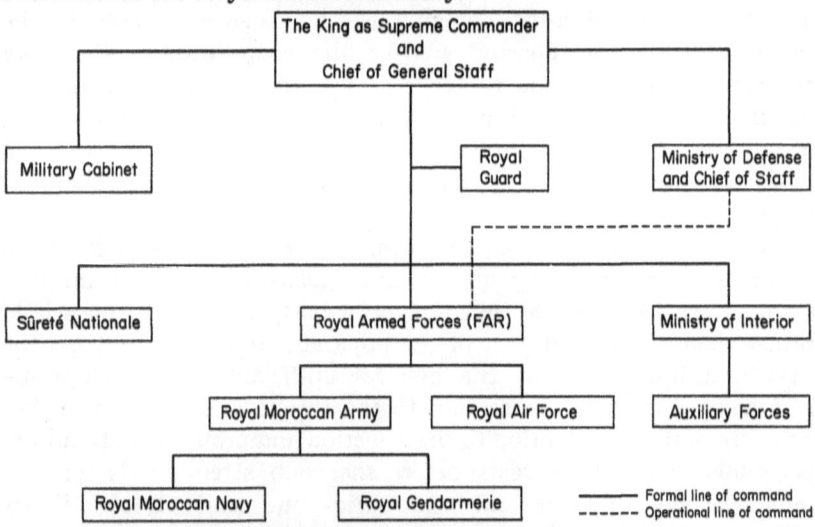

Figure 10. *Defense and Security Forces of Morocco, 1971.*

The only foreign military threat to the nation's security came during the brief border war with Algeria in 1963, during which the FAR fought skillfully and, on the whole, successfully (see ch. 3, Historical Setting; ch. 9, Foreign Relations). Serious internal threats to security have been infrequent, but on those few occasions the government has reacted vigorously. In response to four days of rioting by students and workers in 1965, for example, the king declared a state of emergency that was not lifted until 1970. Individuals have frequently been sentenced to death or life imprisonment on charges of conspiracy, and in late 1971, five of the 193 persons on trial on conspiracy charges were sentenced to death, and a number of others were sentenced to life imprisonment.

Despite a serious lack of modern equipment, the national police force has been successful in coping with normal law and order problems. The rate of serious crime has been relatively low. Morocco, however, has experienced some difficulty in coping with law violations by a fairly large transient and tourist population. The government has sought the help of, and cooperates as fully as its resources allow with, international agencies in the control of illegal drug and narcotics traffic.

THE ARMED FORCES

Throughout the period of the French Protectorate (1912–56) the armed forces in Morocco consisted of French and Spanish forces stationed in their respective zones to maintain order and enforce the laws (see ch. 3, Historical Setting). Moroccans were accepted for service in both armies in enlisted and commissioned grades along with French and Spanish nationals.

After independence a military commission was appointed by Sultan Mohammed V to decide on the details of establishing the armed forces. The commission included the sultan, Crown Prince Mulay Hassan, ranking cabinet ministers, and French and Moroccan army officers. On March 22, 1956, the sultan announced the creation of a ministry of defense and a general staff. Reda Guédira, a close associate of the sultan, was named minister of national defense, and Hassan was appointed chief of the general staff.

In subsequent negotiations with the French and Spanish, it was decided to establish a 20,000-man force to be known as the Royal Moroccan Armed Forces and to permit the French and Spanish forces to remain in the country for an indeterminate transitional period. For the first several years the government concentrated on creating an army. A small air force was established in late 1956, but a navy was not created until 1960; both were subordinated to the army.

The army was formed initially by the transfer of Moroccan units, mainly from the French occupation army. By May 1956 the army comprised 14,000 men; during the following year the army was expanded by the integration into it of about 10,000 Moroccans who had served in the Spanish occupation forces.

The new army lacked trained Moroccan officers and noncommissioned officers. The French supplied nearly 1,000 officers and a like number of noncommissioned officers on one-year contracts in order to fill the immediate need. A longer range solution was sought by agreements under which the French and Spanish governments opened their national military academies at St. Cyr and Toledo to Moroccan officer candidates for one-year accelerated training programs. About 200 officer candidates entered each school in the summer of 1956. The French also undertook to staff and conduct officer training at the Royal Military Academy at Dar al Bayda, a suburb of Meknès, where, since its founding, the Moroccan officers corps in the French army had been trained. The course at the academy was compressed to ten months and included academic studies as well as military science and tactics. About 100 candidates were accepted for the course beginning in the summer of 1956. After the pressing need for Moroccan officers had been satisfied, the course at the Royal Military Academy was lengthened to two years and in 1965 was extended to three years, where it has remained.

One of the problems that faced the new army was the necessity to bring the guerrilla forces of the Army of National Liberation (Armée de Liberation Nationale—ALN) under governmental control. The ALN, which had been formed in October 1955 around a core of Berber tribesmen who had been trained in the French army and had fought in World War II and in Indochina, considered itself the only authentic Moroccan army. It had maintained a loose relationship with the nationalist movement headed by the Istiqlal (Independence) Party and had fought to achieve independence not only for Morocco but also for all of North Africa. By March 1956 the ALN had seized from the French control over the Rif and much of the Middle Atlas (see ch. 3, Historical Setting).

Between March and July 1956 Prince Hassan negotiated with the leaders of the various ALN sectors the details of their integration into the army. By the time final agreement was reached in July, the ALN had grown to 10,000 men. Integration proceeded slowly; about half the ALN joined the army by the end of 1956, increasing the size of the army to about 30,000 officers and men. Those that were acceptable were sent to a six-month training course for instruction in military and civic duties. Many had to be taught to read and write. From the graduating class of May 1957 only twenty-nine officers were accepted for integration into the army. Those ALN forces that declined to be integrated continued to harass the French and Spanish troops and civilian population and proved an embarrassment to the Moroccan government.

With a new general staff that had never before functioned, an untried and inadequate logistics system, a shortage of officers, and troops that had never operated together, the army was soon called upon to prove its ability to protect internal security. In October 1956, infuriated by the French kidnapping of five leaders of the Algerian National Liberation Front who were flying in a Moroccan plane from Rabat to Tunisia, Moroccans in Meknès rioted and attacked French settlers and their property. European casualties totaled about fifty killed. Moroccan army troops did not arrive until the next day. An army officer was given supreme military and civilian authority, with two battalions of troops at his disposal. Within a week order was restored in the Meknès area, over 1,500 arrests were made, and those responsible for the disorders were tried by military courts. Although the army's role in the Meknès affair was more an occupation than an aggressive operation, it disclosed many weaknesses in staff operations that called for correction.

In January 1957 the governor of Tafilalt Province refused to accept the appointment of local administrators, police, and judges made by the ministries of interior and justice. Sympathizers in the adjoining province of Fes joined the revolt and established roadblocks on the single road from the north. The premier issued an order to the governor to give up the post office, reopen communications, remove roadblocks, and report immediately to Rabat. Hassan ordered two battalions south from Fes to open the roads. Opposition continued, and Hassan replaced the rebellious governor with an army major. The army battalions entered Midelt on January 22 without resistance, and the governor surrendered three days later and was placed under house arrest in Rabat. The prompt and decisive action displayed in this affair resulted in a bloodless military operation that accomplished its purpose.

During the fall and winter of 1958 and 1959 the Moroccan army was called upon to suppress a widespread rebellion in the Rif. The police arrested and jailed some of the leaders, but the tribes around Al Hoceima and north and south of Taza in the Middle Atlas took to the hills in armed revolt. A battalion of army troops with mountain artillery was sent in with orders to encircle the rebels, avoid open combat, and await a surrender. By the end of December the area was under control, but the remainder of the rebellious tribesmen in the Rif continued to revolt.

In January Prince Hassan took personal command of operations. He established his headquarters in Tetouan and prepared to mount an offensive against the rebels in the vicinity of Al Hoceima. Leaflets were dropped, and a radio appeal was made promising pardon and a review of their grievances for all who returned to their homes by January 7. Order was restored in most of the country, but several thousand rebels around Al Hoceima and Taza continued the fight. About 20,000 army troops, formed in three columns, moved from the east, the south, and the southwest toward the troubled areas. Al Hoceima was relieved on January 12, 1959, but the rebels had retreated to the mountains. Hassan moved his headquarters to Fes on January 23 and proceeded with mopping-up operations around Taza. On February 13, 1959, the army was commended for its accomplishment.

During the first two years of independence Morocco was unable to pay much attention to the defense of its eastern frontier. It had neither a plan nor the strength for its adequate defense, and as a consequence the border with Algeria was largely unguarded from the Mediterranean almost to the Atlantic, although the ALN had more or less assumed the responsibility for border control. The first 350 miles of the border south from the sea to Figuig was fairly well marked, but beyond that the demarcation line was undefined and open to dispute. It was mid-1958 before even token forces of the army were stationed in Oujda Province. Minor border incidents were frequent.

Immediately after Algeria gained its independence in 1962, border difficulties multiplied. In July 1962 Moroccan troops moved into Zegdou and Saf-Saf in the area where the border was undefined. They were driven out of Saf-Saf by stronger Algerian forces that then laid siege to Zegdou. Morocco claimed this area and also the area around Tindouf where there are large iron ore deposits. Fighting occurred in the Tindouf area in September and October 1962.

By the summer of 1963 the border disputes with Algeria had reached an impasse. In September Moroccan troops occupied strategic points on the route from Colomb-Bechar to Tindouf. On October 8 Algerian troops reoccupied the area, killing ten Moroccans. Moroccan troops in considerable strength were moved on October 14; fighting continued until the end of October. A cease-fire was arranged at a meeting between King Hassan and President Ahmad Ben Bella presided over by Emperor Haile Selassie in Bamako, Mali. By February 20, 1964, it had been announced that by agreement a demilitarized zone would be established by each country pulling back its forces 4.3 miles from positions occupied on October 1, 1963. An exchange of prisoners followed.

Since the end of 1963 there have been occasional border clashes on the Algerian border and around Ifni, but none has been on a scale to precipitate a shooting war. Concern over the mounting stockpile of Algerian weapons has made Morocco anxious to negotiate differences as they arise or refer them to the Organization of African Unity for settlement (see ch. 9, Foreign Relations).

THE PLACE OF THE MILITARY IN NATIONAL LIFE

As institutions, the elements of the FAR have the dual missions of protecting the nation from an external military threat and of providing assistance to the police forces for internal security. Military personnel, however, have been called upon to perform a wide range of governmental functions. Numerous generals have held cabinet and other senior positions. In 1971 there were two generals in the Council of Ministers, most of the nineteen provincial governors were army officers, and many of the ministries that were particularly concerned with social welfare and development programs were heavily staffed by mid-level army officers. In the rural regions many, if not most, of the local administrative officers were on detached duty from their military units.

On assuming his new post as defense minister and chief of staff on August 6, 1971, General Oufkir stated that in his view a major role for the army would be to act as a "staff school" to train large numbers of citizens in various administrative and technical skills. Oufkir's statement suggests a probable intensification of a program launched in the late 1960s whereby several hundred recruits were trained in office procedures, hotel work, mechanics, and other skills.

In addition, the army had been active in relief and rescue work in times of natural disaster and in various aspects of public works. Information available in 1971 indicated that roadbuilding, bridge construction, assistance on irrigation projects, and similar activities by the army would be increased during the 1970s.

With a population of about 16.2 million in 1971 and an armed forces strength of about 55,000, Morocco had a relatively low ratio of military personnel to total population. Less than 0.34 percent of its population was in the military. With the addition of the estimated 20,000 men in the paramilitary Auxiliary Forces, the ratio is increased to only 0.46 percent of the population. The size of the armed forces did not constitute a drain on the labor force because there was widespread unemployment, and any significant reduction in the size of the armed forces would in fact increase the rate of unemployment (see ch. 12, Agriculture and Industry).

The funds allotted to the FAR fall under two headings, the operating budget and the equipment budget. Personnel expenses and the continuing day-to-day operations of the military establishment are charged to the operating budget, and the purchase of new armament, vehicles, and equipment is made from the equipment budget. The operating budget has shown a large, steady increase since independence, reflecting both increases in the size of the military establishment and upward revisions of the pay scale. The equipment budget, in proportion, has risen less rapidly but does not represent the actual costs of new armament and equipment, which have been and are furnished from time to time by foreign countries under foreign aid programs.

In 1969 defense and police expenditures totaled DH851 million (5.06 dirham equal US$1—see Glossary), somewhat over 34 percent of the total budget. The defense portion was probably about two-thirds of the defense and police expenditures, which were slightly above earlier figures; there was probably little change for the 1970 and 1971 budgets.

During the protectorate period Moroccans, particularly Berbers, were used in the French and Spanish armies. During both world wars Moroccan units fought with the French army; in World War II about 300,000 Moroccan troops fought in North Africa, Italy, and France. After the end of the war Moroccans served with the French forces in Indochina. At the time of independence over 50,000 Moroccans were still in the French and Spanish armies.

Berbers made up the bulk of the Moroccans in the French and Spanish armies. In 1971 they were still estimated to constitute about 80 percent of the troops in the FAR and over half of the officers commissioned before independence. Rural Berbers have proved their worth as combat soldiers and with proper training make excellent troops. They have long been conditioned to hardship in a harsh physical environment where the land is not productive and violence is prevalent. They make fierce and tenacious fighters, capable of great endurance, and have a strong sense of loyalty to the king and to their officers.

Service in the armed forces is open to all Moroccan male citizens who are able to meet the qualifications for enlistment. The army is a professional army in which the rate of reenlistment is high; soldiers prefer to remain in the service until forced out by age. Since independence there have been three large inductions or increases of army personnel—some 2,000 original five-year enlistments in June 1956; the integration between 1956 and 1960 of the ALN; and the recall of some 25,000 ex-servicemen in October 1963, at the time of the Algerian border conflict.

The more sophisticated urbanites have tended to view a military career with suspicion and disdain, partly because of the repressive role of the army during the colonial period and partly because of the use of the army to suppress the occasional student and worker riots. The rural population, however, has been attracted to the military, which is viewed as an honorable vocation and which offers economic security, and volunteers have always exceeded the annual enlistment quotas. In 1967, however, the king issued a decree that provided for an eighteen-month compulsory service.

In 1971 it was unclear as to the percentage of physically eligible youths conscripted annually. Various Moroccan government publications, however, suggested that perhaps 4,000 conscripts a year were given basic military training followed by training in skills that would be of immediate use in the economy, particularly in the tourist trade, and then were returned to civilian life (see ch. 13, Trade and Transportation).

The source of officers for the FAR is usually the Royal Military Academy at Dar al Bayda or a foreign military academy approved by the government. There are, however, certain exceptions. Noncommissioned officers of the grade of chief or junior-grade warrant officer, with a minimum of twelve years' service (of which two years have been in one of the warrant officer grades), may become officers. Individuals holding a university degree in certain fields, such as engineering, may become officers, as may individuals holding a doctor's degree in medicine, chemistry, veterinary medicine, or dentistry. Officers commissioned from civilian life are required to undergo six months of military training at the Royal Military Academy as officer cadets and must agree to serve not less than five years in the armed forces.

Within the officer corps there are several distinguishable groups, according to experience and background. Fewer than 100 officers who had served in the French and Spanish armies before independence form the older, higher ranking group. Nearly all were educated at the Dar al Bayda military school near Meknès under French tutelage. A second group of officers was integrated from the ALN in 1956 and 1957. They were given a six months' course of training that included, for some, reading and writing. Tension existed at first between this group and the regular officers who had fought against them in the Rif, but these former Maquis officers seem to have satisfactorily integrated. Another distinguishable group is made up of those who joined the army after independence and have attended French and Spanish military schools or the Royal Military Academy. This group is younger, with an urban background, and is more interested in politics. A fourth, small, and quite different group is made up of former noncommissioned officers who have earned commissions.

Maximum age-in-grade limits, ranging from fifty-one for lieutenants to sixty-one for generals, have been fixed by law. Statutory age limits for noncommissioned officers and enlisted men range from forty-five for privates to fifty for warrant officers. Highly qualified noncommissioned officers or enlisted men who perform special duties may be authorized to serve beyond their statutory age limit, however.

WEAPONS AND EQUIPMENT

Since 1956 the armed forces has had to depend on foreign sources of supply to fill its needs for weapons and military equipment. The initial requirements of the FAR were supplied by the transfer of weapons, transport, and equipment from the French and Spanish armies in Morocco. The French contribution was valued at the equivalent of US$40 million; the value of the Spanish contribution is not known, but it was considerably less.

Morocco has accepted military aid and made purchases from both East and West in keeping with its policy of nonalignment. In 1960, when its leaders felt that French and United States military assistance was inadequate and was coming too slowly, they turned to the Soviet Union for help. The first large shipments of Soviet arms and equipment reached Morocco in late 1960 and early 1961. In March 1962 a second sizable purchase of Soviet arms was made, including twelve MIG-17 jet fighter-interceptors and two MIG-15 jet trainers. Soviet technicians accompanied these shipments.

As a result of this dependence on a number of different foreign sources, the FAR is saddled with a wide range of types of arms and equipment, making standardization next to impossible. The air force, for example, had a mix of American, French, and Soviet jet interceptors and trainers, although most of the Soviet aircraft had been retired by 1970. In 1970 the army had 120 Soviet medium tanks and an equal number of French light tanks. The armored cars and personnel carriers were mostly of World War II vintage and were of Soviet, French, Czech, and American origin, as was the artillery.

Ranks and Pay

The rank structure of the army and the air force corresponds to those of the French and United States armies, except that there are only seven enlisted grades. The rank structure of the navy section corresponds to that of the French navy. Until March 1965 the navy was commanded by a *capitaine de frigate* (commander) on loan from the French navy. The navy was then turned to Moroccan control.

Members of the Moroccan armed forces are paid a basic monthly salary augmented by certain allowances. Within each rank there are several base pay steps based upon length of time in grade or total years of service or a combination of both. At the time of commissioning and throughout their military careers, officers holding a baccalaureate degree, indicating completion of secondary school, receive two years of service seniority as regards pay. Married officers receive slightly higher housing allowances than bachelors; other allowances are based on the number of children in the family.

Officers' pay schedules set in 1956 were lower than the schedules for similar duties in other government departments. This discrepancy, plus the fact that military pay scales were not increased for the first seven years after independence and that promotions in the military service were slower than in the other governmental services, created growing dissatisfaction among the officers, particularly among the junior grades. Some junior officers resigned their commissions and sought higher paying positions in the civilian branches of the government.

Prompted by the drop in officer morale, the king approved a new pay scale in July 1963, retroactive to March 1, 1963. In early 1971 a new pay scale was approved, but by late 1971 not all personnel had received the increase that was to have placed them on a par with the civil service.

In April 1965 official announcement was made of an air service allowance and a maritime allowance. The air service allowance is granted to military personnel belonging to airborne units of the armed forces. A 50-percent increase in base pay is granted to military personnel holding a parachute badge, a pilot certificate, an observer certificate for artillery observation air units, or an air force flying certificate. A 25-percent increase is granted personnel authorized for air service training with a view to obtaining any of those badges or certificates. The maritime allowance grants a 50-percent increase of base pay to naval personnel during their assignment to a ship of the Royal Moroccan Navy. A 25-percent increase of base pay is granted maritime personnel during their assignment to an instructing unit of the navy as an instructor or as a trainee. If the recipient has been absent without leave or has been disciplined, the allowances are suspended for the duration of the absence or the disciplinary sanction. In the case of air force personnel a yearly test for proficiency is required for a continuation of the allowance.

A pension program for all military personnel is based on longevity and rank at retirement. In addition, disability pensions are provided for all who have become incapacitated through injury or disease incurred while on active duty. Rates of disability pay depend on rank and degree of disability. Widows, orphans, and parents of military personnel who die or are killed while on duty are entitled to compensation.

Uniforms and Insignia

Four types of uniforms are worn by the army: field, service, semidress and service, and full dress. Army uniforms closely resemble those of the French army with the exception of the officers' semidress and service uniforms, which more closely resemble those worn by officers in the United States Army. The field uniform for all ranks is of olive-drab cotton and consists of a jacket over which a web belt is worn. The trousers are straight, with deep side patch pockets, and are generally tucked into short canvas leggings. A steel helmet or a green beret is worn by all personnel in field uniform. The service uniform for all ranks is of olive-drab wool or gabardine and consists of an Eisenhower-type jacket with two breast pockets, belted at the bottom. The trousers are full length and straight. With the winter service uniforms enlisted men may wear canvas leggings. The semidress and service uniform is of olive-drab gabardine or cotton cloth. The semidress blouse with notched lapels is similar to that of the United States Army. A shirt of the same material may be worn with black tie in the summer in lieu of the blouse. With this uniform officers wear a garrison-type service cap with black headband and visor; enlisted men wear the green beret as headpiece. When the blouse is worn with the semidress uniform, officers wear a white shirt with a black tie.

When the air force was made a separate and autonomous service in February 1964, it adopted a distinctive uniform made from United States Air Force blue uniform material supplied through the United States Military Assistance Program (MAP). The cloth supplied was winter-weight serge and summer-weight and overcoat material sufficient to equip 5,000 men. Officers wear a blue service cap or beret; enlisted men wear only the blue beret for headgear. The style and pattern of the air force uniform is similar to that of the army.

Officers' insignia of rank is displayed on red shoulder boards, or epaulets. Warrant officers wear a silver star insignia on the shoulder loops of the coat or shirt. Enlisted insignia of grade is indicated by green diamond-shaped patches overlaid with a gold crown and various combinations of red and (or) yellow chevrons, worn on the left sleeve of the winter uniform midway between the elbow and the shoulder. With the summer uniform the same enlisted insignia of grade is worn suspended from the left breast pocket of the shirt. Insignia for all officer ranks and enlisted grades includes a gold crown. The cap insignia consists of a gold palm wreath with the Moroccan star in the center, a smaller size for enlisted and warrant officer grades and a larger size for officers. The warrant officers' cap insignia is a silver wreath, and the field grade officers' is a combination of an outer gold wreath and an inner silver one. A dark leather pocket medallion bearing the army crest is generally worn suspended from the right breast pocket. Within the army, the branch of service is designated by shoulder boards of various color and fabric.

Air force officers wear gray shoulder boards instead of red and a distinctive pocket medallion. Grey shoulder boards denote officer status, the rank indicated by sleeve stripes of gold braid. The air force cap insignia consists of various sizes of gold wreaths and silver wings and crown to denote senior officers, junior officers, senior and junior noncommissioned officers, and basic airmen. In 1962 the air arm adopted flight badges (wings) to denote different categories of flying personnel, pilots, navigators, radio-navigators, and flight engineers, to be worn by both officers and enlisted men.

Military Justice

A code of military justice applicable to all members of the armed forces was promulgated by a decree of November 10, 1956; it has since been amended by several decrees. The code provides that penal justice for members of the armed forces is rendered in peacetime by the Tribunal of the Royal Forces (Tribunal Des Forces Royales) or, in time of war, by the Armed Forces Military Tribunals (Tribunaux Militaires aux Armées) and by the Supreme Court.

The code established a single permanent military court, which usually sits at Rabat but can be moved to another site upon order of the minister of national defense. It specifies that the president of the military court shall be a civil magistrate of the regional tribunal or a magistrate of the court of appeal from the same jurisdiction as the accused. For the trial of misdemeanors and minor offenses the president of the court is assisted by two military officers as assistant judges; and for the trial of criminal offenses, by four military assistant judges. The military assistant judges must be of a higher seniority than the accused on trial. When the accused is a general officer, the court is composed of a president of a chamber of an appeals court as president and two officers senior to the accused.

The competence of the military courts covers three categories of offenses: military offenses, including disobedience, desertion, surrender, abandoning post, disrespect toward the flag, rebellion, striking a superior, abuse of authority, or offenses involving military property, such as embezzlement, receiving stolen goods, and selling military property; miscellaneous offenses not specified by the code of military justice but covered by the ordinary penal code, which become triable offenses when committed by military personnel; and offenses against the external security of the state or aiding and abetting the enemy. For the trial of offenses of the third category two magistrates from an appeals court are added to the panel of the court for criminal offenses.

According to the code, sessions of the court during trial are open to the public. The accused is authorized counsel of his own choosing. If the accused refuses to appear after legal summons, he may be tried in absentia. The decision of the judges is rendered by secret written ballot, a majority vote deciding guilt or innocence. In criminal matters it takes four votes to one for a conviction, and in crimes against the external security of the state a vote of five to two is required. The death penalty may be imposed for crimes against state security. Sentences pronounced by the military court may be appealed before the penal chamber of the Supreme Court. The condemned has eight days in which to avail himself of the right of appeal.

The prompt execution of the conspirators in the coup attempt of July 10, 1971, indicated that there are exceptions to the provisions of the code. On July 11 the king announced that the conspirators would be executed as soon as they had provided the details of their crime; the king surmised that this would be within twenty-four hours. The conspirators were not executed until July 13, but there was no suggestion that any sort of trial or hearing in a legal sense had been held. The International Commission of Jurists, in response to the king's July 11 statement, had sent him a message urging that the accused be tried in a court of law, and the commission also sent a message of protest after the execution had been announced. Neither the king nor his government took official notice of either message.

ORGANIZATION OF THE ARMED FORCES

The army is by far the most important and well developed branch of the FAR; a small air force became independent of army control only in 1964, and a weak navy section remained, in 1971, under the control of the army. The gendarmerie is operationally subordinate to the army but administratively within the jurisdiction of the Ministry of Interior.

Territorial organization of the army has been gradually strengthened and simplified since 1956. Originally based on strongpoints and scattered troop camps inherited from the French, army control of the country was placed on a regional basis in 1959. The sixteen military zones were only approximately contiguous with administrative provinces. No provision was made for commands specifically responsible for frontier protection. The shortage of trained senior officers prevented the creation of a strong general staff or of large military units. Rather, battalions were scattered around the country under the command of junior officers.

By 1965 the army had enough senior officers to attempt a more centralized territorial organization. The country was divided into three military zones and one independent sector. By 1971 this had been changed to six military zones, each commanded by a general with the title of military governor.

In the aftermath of the attempted coup in July 1971, the military zone system was abolished, possibly reflecting the fact that three of the five generals who took part in the coup attempt were governors of military zones but also reflecting the decimation of the high command of the FAR. As of August 6 the senior officers included an octagenarian marshal who did not hold a responsible military post; Oufkir as defense minister and chief of staff; a general serving as minister of posts, telegraph, and telephone; a general serving without title as an adviser to the king; and three other generals.

The army in 1971 was broken down into one armored brigade, two motorized infantry brigades, one light security brigade, one paratroop brigade, twelve independent infantry battalions, and two camel corps battalions. There were in addition three desert cavalry detachments and four artillery groups, plus various support elements.

Traditionally the Ministry of Defense was concerned basically with logistics, supply, payrolls, pensions, and related matters. A separate chief of staff stood between the various commanders and governors of military zones and the king as chief of general staff and supreme commander. Although the information was at best fragmentary in late 1971, it appeared that the various brigade and battalion commanders reported directly to Oufkir, as did the air force and navy commanders.

INTERNAL SECURITY FORCES

Sûreté Nationale

The Sûreté Nationale (national police force) has primary responsibility for internal security and political intelligence and shares responsibility for the maintenance of law and order in the major urban areas. In 1971 the force was commanded by a director general, who was appointed by, and responsible solely to, the king. The director general, in common with some other senior police officers, was an army officer.

The government, which means the king, appears to have a policy of avoiding a clear delineation of authority and responsibility among the various agencies of government. Because there are nineteen provinces, two prefectures, ten police regions, seven development regions and, until August 1971, six military regions, coordination among the various regional chiefs is difficult, perhaps intentionally so. In addition, the police and the Royal Gendarmerie share responsibility and authority in some police duties, a situation that makes it impossible to determine ultimate responsibility in some gray areas.

There are four broad police sections: the internal security service, the Mobile Intervention Companies (Compagnies Mobiles pour l'Intervention—CMI), the Judiciary Police, and the Urban Corps. The country is broken down into ten operational regions (called *sûretés*, such as the Rabat Sûreté), each under the command of a commissioner. For administrative purposes, however, the police force has five subdirectorates (see fig. 11).

Over two-thirds of the Sûreté Nationale are in the Urban Corps, a uniformed detachment whose members are stationed in all cities and major towns. Their basic assignment is the all-encompassing one of the maintenance of public order. They perform foot, bicycle, motorcycle, and automobile patrols; man traffic control stations; respond to emergency requests for protection; and discharge related control and protection functions.

The Judiciary Police, on the other hand, is a specialized criminal investigation corps of about 3,000 officers and men. The individual policemen are assigned or attached to courts of law and conduct their

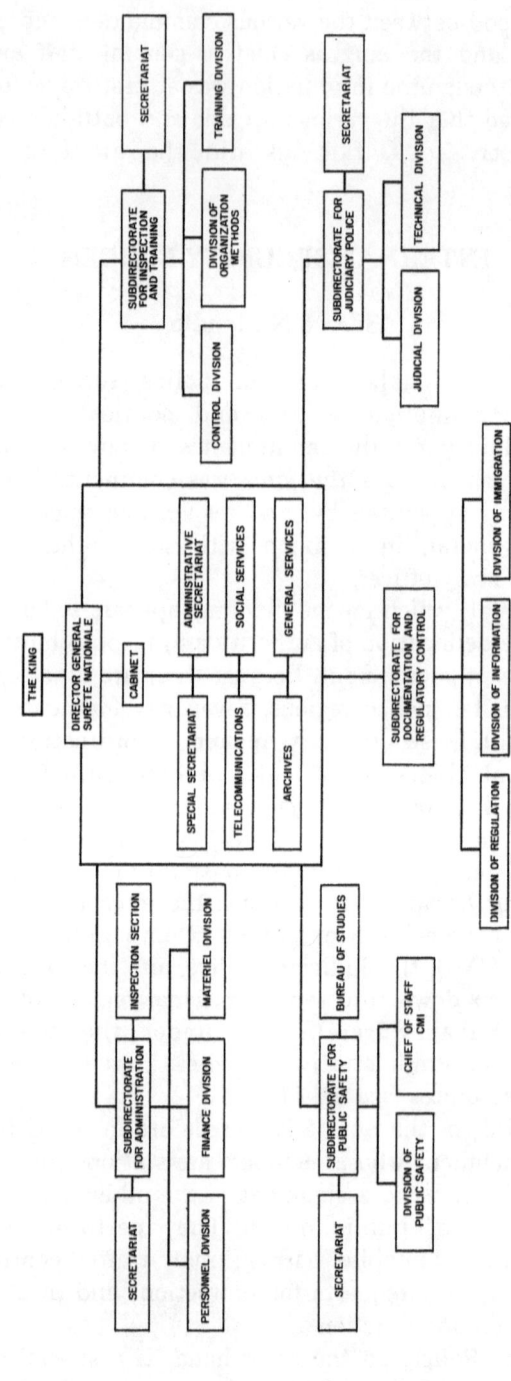

Source: Adapted from Thomas M. Finn, et al., *Morocco: Police Survey Report*, Washington, 1966, pp. 28-29.

Figure 11. Organization of the Moroccan Sûreté Nationale.

investigations at the instruction, and under the supervision, of an officer of the court (see ch. 8, The Governmental System and Political Dynamics). It would appear that members of the Judiciary Police feel a stronger sense of attachment to the court system than to the police force, and the working relationship with the court officials reportedly is a close and cordial one.

The responsibilities of the internal security police are roughly analogous to a combination of the United States Federal Bureau of Investigation and the special branches of the departments of treasury and justice that are charged with narcotics control, counterfeiting, immigration control, and related topics. The section operates clandestinely as the kingdom's counterespionage and counter-subversion arm, and little is known as to its size and organization. It reports directly to the director general and, although it is known as the Sixth Subdirectorate, it does not appear on the Sûreté Nationale organization chart.

The CMI is an active reserve police force of about 3,000 officers and men. In addition to its mobile support role, for which each company of some 250 men is equipped with transportation and radio communication, the companies are called upon to police public functions at which important dignitaries are present. It frequently forms the honor guard and provides personal protection for the king, senior officials, and foreign heads of state or diplomats. The companies of the CMI are located near or in the major metropolitan areas, and the CMI staff forms the second level of command in the Subdirectorate for Public Safety.

Within a region, the various parts of the Sûreté Nationale, with the exception of the internal security section, are placed under the administrative and operational control of a commissioner (see fig. 12). The relationship of the *sûreté* commissioner to elements of the Royal Gendarmerie serving in the region was not clarified, however, by the information available in late 1971.

Royal Gendarmerie

Although it is an integral part of the FAR, the Royal Gendarmerie is basically a police unit. The commander and many, if not most, of the officers are army officers, but the remainder of the corps is made up of volunteers for five-year tours of duty.

The gendarmerie, which has its headquarters in Rabat, is organized by companies that are located throughout the country. The companies are in turn subdivided into sections and brigades, the size of the units varying widely in response to functions and assignments.

The basic unit of the gendarmerie is the brigade. There are four types of brigades—motorcycle brigades, jeep brigades, criminal investigation brigades, and village police brigades. The special Mobile

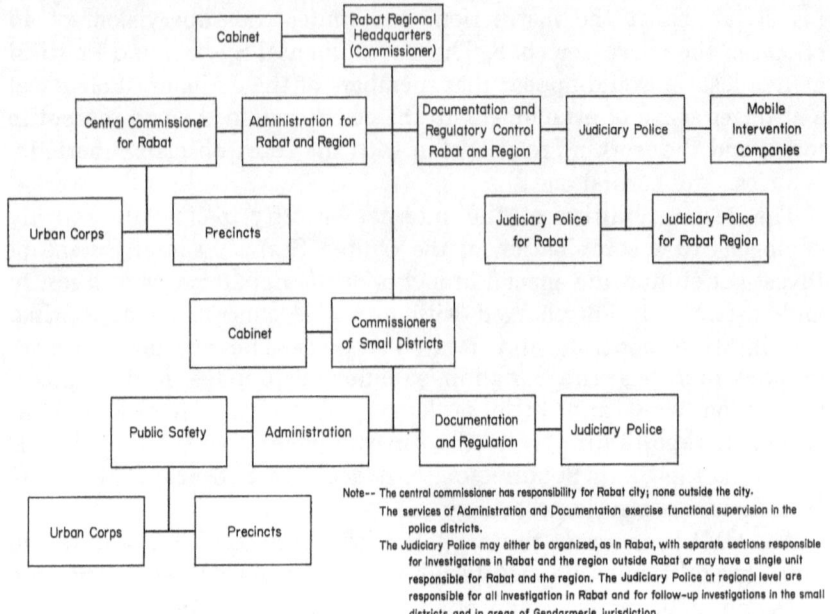

Source: Adapted from Thomas M. Finn, et al., *Morocco: Police Survey Report*, Washington, 1966, pp. 41-42.

Figure 12. Organization of a Police Region in Morocco.

Group is maintained for rapid response deployment to assist in riot control or other special projects. In addition to these mainly, but not exclusively, rural police functions, the gendarmerie serves as a military police unit for the FAR, collects unpaid and delinquent taxes, and checks the registration of automobile radios.

Auxiliary Forces

The Auxiliary Forces are made up of the Administrative Maghzani and the Mobile Maghzani. In 1971 the total number of officers and men was reportedly about 20,000, but from 50 to 75 percent of these were in the Administrative Maghzani. The Administrative Maghzani is a nonuniformed force whose members guard buildings, bridges, wells, and other "sensitive" areas; act as messengers and minor clerks for local officials; patrol markets; serve as arbitrators of grazing and water disputes; and perform related supplemental and support duties for the uniformed police. Many members are military or police pensioners and are paid a small stipend in addition to their pension.

The Auxiliary Forces are commanded by an inspector general who is responsible to the minister of interior. The inspector general and most of the officers are serving on detached duty from the army.

To the extent that the Administrative Maghzani is armed, it is equipped with sidearms or rifles of World War II or earlier origin. In the general course of their duties, the members are controlled by the civil servant to whose office they are assigned. On certain occasions the guards are called upon to support either the FAR or the Sûreté Nationale, in which instance the military or police unit to which they are assigned is supposed to provide arms, equipment, and transportation.

The Mobile Maghzani, however, is a relatively well equipped paramilitary force. In 1971 it had between 4,000 and 6,000 men, perhaps more, organized into units or companies of about 150 officers and men. The units were motorized, and the men were specifically trained to control riots and civil disorders.

The companies are stationed individually or as groups near the major population centers. The Casablanca Intervention Group, for example, in 1965 was composed of eight companies of Mobile Maghzani; the group was available either for use in the Casablanca Prefecture or for rapid deployment anyplace in the country. The units of Mobile Maghzani are also trained to provide assistance to the FAR in the event of a border disturbance.

PRISONS

During the colonial period prisons were under the control of the police, but at independence the Ministry of Justice assumed full responsibility. In 1971 the ministry's Penitentiary Administrative Division (Direction de l'Administration Penitentiare) operated some thirty-five prisons and correctional institutions. There were three maximum security prisons and one juvenile reform center; the remainder were medium security prisons. The information available in 1971 suggested that prison conditions were grim. Sanitary facilities ranged from minimal to inadequate, and the food ration was low in quantity and quality.

Small detention facilities are attached to all large and most small police stations. The penal code stipulates that those arrested must be formally charged or released within twenty-four hours of arrest. Political prisoners and foreigners apparently are an exception to the code, but information on this subject was not readily available in late 1971.

BIBLIOGRAPHY FOR THE NOVEMBER 1965 EDITION

Section I. Social

RECOMMENDED SOURCES

American Friends of the Middle East, Inc. *Education in Morocco: A Survey Prepared April, 1963.* Washington: AFME, 1963.
Ashford, Douglas E. *Political Change in Morocco.* Princeton: Princeton University Press, 1961.
Ayache, Albert. *LeMaroc: bilan d'une colonisation.* Paris: Editions Sociales, 1956.
Barbour, Nevill. "Two Problems in Modern Morocco," *Civilisations,* XI, No. 3, 1961, 265-274.
Bernard, Augustin. *Le Maroc.* Paris: Librairie Félix Alcan, 1931.
Berque, Jacques. *Les Arabes d'hier à demain.* Paris: Editions du Seuil, 1960.
――――. *Le Maghreb entre deux guerres.* Paris: Le Seuil, 1962.
Buttin, Paul. "La Relève au Maroc des cadres français par les cadres marocains," *Civilisations,* XI, No. 1, 1961, 52-60.
Centre d'Etudes Nord-Africaines. *Annuaire de l'Afrique du Nord, 1962,* I. Aix-en-Provence: Centre National de la Recherche Scientifique, 1964.
Centre de Recherches sur l'Afrique Méditerranéenne. *Annuaire de l'Afrique du Nord, 1963,* II. Aix-en-Provence: Centre National de la Recherche Scientifique, 1965.
Gallagher, Charles F. "Morocco Goes Back to School." (AUFS, Morocco, CFG-10-'58.) New York: American Universities Field Staff, 1958.
――――. "New Laws for Old: The Moroccan Code of Personal Status," (AUFS Reports Service, North Africa Series, V, No. 1.) New York: American Universities Field Staff, 1959.
――――. "North African Problems and Prospects, Pt. III: Language and Identity." (AUFS Reports Service, North Africa Series, X, No. 5.) New York: American Universities Field Staff, 1964.
Great Britain. Naval Staff. Naval Intelligence Division. *Morocco.* 2 vols. (Geographical Handbook Series.) London: HMSO, 1941.
Julien, Charles-André. *Histoire de l'Afrique du Nord.* 3 vols. Paris: Payot, 1951-52.

Lacouture, Jean and Simonne. *Le Maroc à l'éprueve.* Paris: Editions du Seuil, 1958.

Lahlou, Abbès. "La Bourgeoisie, symbole et reflect direct de l'occidentalisation de la société marocaine," *Civilisations*, XIV, Nos. 1-2, 1964, 62-80.

Landau, Rom. *Moroccan Drama, 1900-1955.* San Francisco: American Academy of Asian Studies, 1956.

Le Tourneau, Roger. *Evolution politique de l'Afrique du Nord musulmane, 1920-1961.* Paris: Librairie Armand Colin, 1962.

Marais, Octave. "La Classe dirigeante au Maroc," *Revue Francaise de Science Politique*, XIV, August 1964, 709-737.

Mikesell, Marvin W. *Northern Morocco: A Cultural Geography.* (University of California Publications in Geography, XIV.) Berkeley: University of California Press, 1961.

Morocco. Ministry of Education. *The Educational Movement in Morocco during the School-Year 1963-1964.* (Report made to the 27th International Conference on Public Education.) Rabat: 1964.

Noin, Daniel. "La Population du Maroc," *L'Information Géographique*, XXVI, No. 1, 1962, 1-12.

U.S. Department of State. Bureau of Intelligence and Research. External Research Staff. *Second and Third Generation Elites in the Maghreb*, by Douglas E. Ashford. Washington: 1963.

OTHER SOURCES USED

Abu-Lughod, Ibrahim. "The Islamic Factor in African Politics," *Orbis*, VIII, Summer 1964, 425-444.

Adam, André. *La Maison et le village dans quelques tribus de l'Anti-Atlas.* Paris: Larose, 1951.

_____. "La Population musulmane dans l'ancienne medina de Casablanca," *Bulletin Economique et Social du Maroc*, XIV, No. 48, 1950, 14-26.

American Friends of the Middle East, Inc. *Basic Facts on Morocco.* (Comp., Richard J. Blake.) Washington: AFME, 1964.

_____. *Education in Morocco: Supplement, 1964.* Washington: AFME, 1964.

Arab News and Views, XI, February 15, 1965.

Awad, Hassan. "Morocco's Expanding Towns," *The Geographic Journal*, CXXX, Pt. 1, March 1964, 49-64.

Barbour, Nevill (ed.). *A Survey of North West Africa.* London: Oxford University Press, 1959.

Basset, André. *La Langue berbère.* London: Oxford University Press, 1952.

Bastide, Henri de la. "L'Islam dans le Maghreb contemporain," *Documents Nord-Africans* (Etudes Sociales Nord-Africaines), No. 591, January 16, 1965.

Benabud, Ahmed. "Aspects psychopathologiques du cannabisme au Maroc," *Bulletin des Stupéfiants*, IX, October-December 1957, 1-17.

Bernard, Augustin, and Despois, Jean-Jacques. "Physical Features of Morocco," *Encyclopaedia Britannica* (1958 ed.), XV, 808, 809.

Berque, Jacques. *Structures sociales du Haut-Atlas*. Paris: Presses Universitaires de France, 1955.

Berry, James R. "Moroccan Dilemma," *America*, March 8, 1958, 668-670.

Bousquet, Marie. "Les Rapports de la bourgeoisie et de la monarchie au Maroc," *Temps Modernes*, XVII, April 1962, 1483-1491.

Bovill, E. W. *The Golden Trade of the Moors*. London: Oxford University Press, 1958.

Brenier, Henri. "History of Morocco," *Encyclopaedia Britannica* (1958 ed.), XV, 809-812.

Catroux, Général. *Lyautey le marocain*. Paris: Librairie Hachette, 1952.

Charconnet, André. "La Radio et l'education des masses," *Confluent*, No. 16, November-December 1961, 658-661.

Crowe, Sibyl E. "The French Protectorate in Morocco," *Encyclopaedia Britannica* (1958 ed.), XV, 812-815.

Daoud, Zakya. "Ceux qui restent," *Jeune Afrique*, No. 228, April 18, 1965, 19-22.

──────. "Le Temps de la sueur et des larmes," *Jeune Afrique*, No. 227, April 11, 1965, 14, 15.

Delisle, Stephane. "Le Proletariat marocain de Port-Lyautey." In *L'Evolution sociale du Maroc*, I (Cahiers de l'Afrique et l'Asie). Paris: Peyronnet, 1950, 109-228.

Demographic Yearbook 1963. New York: United Nations, 1964.

Desanti, Dominique. "Les Ecrivains maghrébins d'expression française ne sont pas des touristes de la langue," *Jeune Afrique*, No. 212, December 27, 1964, 28, 29.

──────. "La Marocaine entre deux mondes," *Jeune Afrique*, No. 188, June 15, 1964, 31.

d'Esme, Jean. *Le Maroc que nous avons fait*. Paris: Librairie Hachette, 1955.

d'Etienne, Jean. "Une Famille marocaine." In *L'Evolution sociale du Maroc*, I (Cahiers de l'Afrique et l'Asie). Paris: Peyronnet, 1950, 1-51.

El Fassi, M. Nacer. "Les Perspectives de l'education nationale au Maroc dans le cadre du plan quinquennal," *Confluent*, No. 12, March-April 1961. 176-184.

Etudes Sociales Nord-Africaines. *Documents Nord-Africains*, No. 582, November 9, 1964.

──────. "Les Travailleurs migrants en Europe occidentale," *Documents Nord-Africains*, No. 591, January 16, 1965.

Faits et Idées. "La Famille marocaine." *Les Cahiers de Faits et Idées*, I, 1955.

———. "Le Role de la communauté européenne au Maroc," *Cahiers* (Cahiers de Faits et Idées), III, 1957.

Foreign Education Digest, "Education in Morocco," XXVII, January-March 1963, 191–195.

Forget, Nelly. "Attitudes Towards Work by Women in Morocco," *International Social Science Journal*, XIV, No. 1, 1962, 90–124.

Gellner, Ernest. "Patterns of Rural Rebellion in Morocco: Tribes as Minorities," *Archives Européennes de Sociologie*, III, No. 2, 1962, 297–311.

Hagopian, Elaine C. "The Status and Role of the Marabout in Pre-Protectorate Morocco," *Ethnology*, III, No. 1, 1964, 42–52.

Halstead, John P. "The Changing Character of Moroccan Reformism, 1921–1934," *Journal of African History*, V, No. 3, 1964, 435–447.

Hance, William A. *The Geography of Modern Africa*. New York: Columbia University Press, 1964.

Hitti, Philip K. *History of the Arabs*. (6th ed.) London: Macmillan, 1956.

Hoffman, Eleanor. *Realm of the Evening Star*. Philadelphia: Chilton Books, 1965.

Human Relations Area Files. *Morocco*. (HRAF Subcontractor's Monograph, HRAF-62, Johns Hopkins.) New Haven: HRAF Press, 1956.

International Yearbook of Education 1962. Geneva: United Nations Educational, Scientific and Cultural Organization, 1963.

Joly, Fernand; Ayache, Albert; Fardel, Jean; and Suech, Léon. *Géographie du Maroc*. Paris: Delagrave, 1949.

Lewis, William H. "Feuding and Social Change in Morocco," *Journal of Conflict Resolution*, V, March 1961, 43–54.

Middle East Journal, "Chronology," Winter 1965, 80.

Le Monde (Paris), January 19, 1965.

Monteil, Vincent. *Maroc*. Paris: Collections Microcosme, 1963.

———. *Morocco*. (Trans., Veronica Hull.) New York: Viking Press, 1964.

Morocco. Embassy in Washington. *News of Morocco*, II, January and April 1959; III, October 1960.

———. Press and Information Department. "Education in Morocco," *Statements and Documents*, II, March 1959.

———. "The Housing Problem of Morocco," *Statements and Documents*, IV, April 1963.

Morocco. Laws, Statutes, etc.

The Constitution of the Kingdom of Morocco (*As Approved at the Election of December 7, 1962*). Washington: Embassy of Morocco, 1963.

Morocco. Ministère de l'Economie Nationale. *Population legale du Maroc*. Rabat: Service Central de Statistiques, 1961.

――――. *Population rurale du Maroc*. Rabat: Service Central de Statistiques, 1962.

――――. *Résultats du sondage au 1/50e du recensement de 1960*. Rabat: Service Central de Statistiques, January 1963.

――――. Division de la Coordination Economique et du Plan. *La Consommation et les dépenses des ménages marocains musulmans (résultats de l'enquête 1959-60)*. Rabat: Service Central des Statistiques, 1961.

Morocco. Ministère de l'Education Nationale. "La Rentrée scolaire, 1964-1965." (Press Conference by Youssef Ben Abbès, Minister of National Education, September 24, 1964.) Rabat: 1964 (mimeo.).

――――. Direction des Affaires Culturelles. *L'Education Nationale*. (Numéro spécial relatif à la Conférence Internationale des Organismes Familiaux.) Rabat: July 22-28, 1962.

――――. *L'Education Nationale*, 2d quarter, No. 4, 1963; 3d quarter, No. 5, 1963; 4th quarter, No. 6, 1963.

――――. *Notes et Documents*, No. 10, January 1959.

――――. *Notes et Informations*, No. 6, October 1962; Numéro Spécial, July-August 1963.

Morocco. Ministère de l'Education Nationale. Service de la Planification et de la Carte Scolaire. Bureau des Statistiques. *Statistiques de l'enseignement, année, scolaire 1962-1963*. Rabat: 1963.

Morocco. Ministère de l'Information, des Beaux Arts et du Tourisme. *Le Maroc*. Rabat: August 1961.

Morocco. Ministère des Travaux Publics. *Industries et Travaux*. Rabat: 1960.

Morocco. Ministry of Foreign Affairs. *Morocco*, No. 1, May 1957; No. 4, June-July 1957.

Nouacer, Khadidja. "The Changing Status of Women and the Employment of Women in Morocco," *International Social Science Journal*, XIV, No. 1, 1962, 124-129.

Ogrizek, Doré. *North Africa*. New York: McGraw-Hill, 1955.

Rickards, Donald R. "Northern Africa: Doors Closed and Closing," *Christianity Today*, VIII, July 31, 1964, 7.

Robert, Jacques. *La Monarchie marocaine*. Paris: Pichon et Durand-Auzias, 1962.

Selosse, Jacques. "Perception du changement social par une population citadine marocaine," *Revue Française de Sociologie*, IV, April-June 1963, 144-158.

Shuster, James R. "Bureaucratic Transition in Morocco," *Human Organization*, XXIV, Spring 1965, 53-58.

Sterling, Claire. "Morocco's Troubled Young King," *The Reporter*, June 17, 1965, 21-24.

Strasser, Daniel. *Réalités et promesses sahariennes*. Paris: Encyclopédie d'Outre-Mer, 1956.
Terrasse, Henri. *History of Morocco*. (Trans., Hilary Tee.) Casablanca: Editions Atlantides, 1952.
Terres d'Afrique. *Communautés en terres d'Afrique*. Meknès: Terres d'Afrique, 1947.
——. *Problèmes humaines en terres d'Afrique*. Meknès: Terres d'Afrique, 1948.
Theis, Jean. "Les Institutions publiques du Maroc indépendant." *Revue du Droit Public*, 1961, 543–555.
United Nations. Economic and Social Council. Economic Commission for Africa. *Industrial Growth in Africa*. New York: UN, 1963.
——. *Report of the ECA Industrial Co-Ordination Mission to Algeria, Libya, Morocco and Tunisia*. Addis Ababa: ECA, 1964.
United Nations Educational, Scientific and Cultural Organization. *The Development of Higher Education in Africa*. (Report of the Conference on the Development of Higher Education in Africa, September 3–12, 1962.) N.pl.: UNESCO, 1963.
——. *World Survey of Education*, III, Pt. 2. New York: International Documents Service, 1961.
United Nations Statistical Yearbook 1962. New York: UN, 1963.
U.S. Army Medical Service. Medical Information and Intelligence Agency. *Health and Sanitary Data for Morocco*. (Project No. PO 2311.) Washington: 1960.
U.S. Department of Health, Education and Welfare. Public Health Service. Division of International Health. *Morocco—A Geomedical Brief*, by Rose Belmont. Washington: HEW, 1960.
Westermarck, Edward A. *Wit and Wisdom in Morocco, A Study of Native Proverbs*. New York: Liveright, 1931.
World Health Organization. *Second Report on the World Health Situation 1957–1960*. Geneva: WHO, 1963.
——. Regional Office for Europe, Copenhagen. *Report of the Regional Director, July 1963–June 1964*. Geneva: WHO, 1964.
Zartman, I. William. *Morocco: Problems of New Power*. New York: Atherton Press, 1964.

(Various issues of the following periodicals were also used in the preparation of this section: *Christian Science Monitor*, January through June 1965; *Jeune Afrique* [Tunis], from November 1964 through June 1965; *Maghreb* [Paris], from May 1964 through June 1965; *Maghreb Digest* [Los Angeles], from April 1964 through June 1965; *Maroc Informations* [Casablanca], from June 1963 through June 1965; *La Nation Africaine* [Rabat], from September 1964 through June 1965; *Revue de Presse* [Algiers], from July 1962 through June 1965; and *La Vie Economique* [Casablanca], from February 1964 through June 1965.)

RECOMMENDED FURTHER READING

Beneitez Cantero, Valentin. *Sociologia Marroqui.* (1st ed.) ("Publicaciones del Instituto General Franco de Estudias y Investigacion Hispaña-Arabe.") Tetuán: 1952.

Bourilly, Joseph. *Eléments de l'Ethnographie Marocaine.* (Bibliothèque de Culture et de Vulgarisation Nord-Africaines.) Paris: Librairie Coloniale et Orientaliste, 1932.

Brunot, Louis. *Au Seuil de la Vie Marocaine. Ce Qu'il Faut Savoir des Coutumes et des Relations Sociales chez les Marocains.* Casablanca: Librairie Farrairre, 1950.

Cambon, Henri. *Histoire du Moroc.* Paris: Librairie Hachette, 1952.

Coon, Carleton. *Caravan, the Story of the Middle East.* New York: Holt, 1951.

1957 Editor and Publisher International Yearbook, XC, No. 9, February 28, 1957.

Gárcia Figueras, Tomás, and Roda y Jimenez, Rafael de. *Economia Social de Marruecos.* 3 vols. (Consejo Superior de Investigaciones Cientificas.) Madrid: Institute de Estudios Africanos, 1950–1955.

Gellner, Ernest. "Independence in the Central High Atlas," *The Middle East Journal,* II, No. 3 (Summer 1957), 237–252.

Grandidier, Guillaume. *Atlas des Colonies Françaises. Protectorats et Territoires sous Mandat de la France.* Paris: Société d'Editions Géographiques, Maritimes et Coloniales, 1934.

The Istiqlal (Independence) Party of Morocco. *Morocco under the Protectorate: Forty Years of French Administration.* New York: Moroccan Office of Information and Documentation, 1953.

Johansen, O. Lund. *World Radio Handbook: Broadcasting-Television, 1957.* (11th ed.) Copenhagen: Det Berlingske Bogtrykker, 1957.

Joly, Fernand, et al. *Geographie du Maroc.* Paris: Librairie de Grave, 1949.

Landau, Rom. *Moroccan Drama, 1900–1955.* San Francisco: The American Academy of Asian Studies, 1956.

———. *An Outline of Moroccan Culture.* Rabat: Morocco Publishers, 1957.

Lewis, William, H. "The New Nomadism in North Africa," *Middle East Journal,* 11, No. 3 (Summer 1957), 269–281.

Montagne, Robert. *La Naissance du Prolétariat Marocain. Enquête Collective, 1948–1950.* (Cahiers de l'Afrique et de l'Asie, Vol. III.) Paris: Peyronnet, 1951.

"Morocco '54," Encyclopédie Mensuelle d'Outre-Mer (Special Issue). Paris: 1954.

"Morocco: History," *Encyclopedia of Islam,* III, 583–589.

Patai, Raphael. "The Middle East as a Culture Area," *The Middle East Journal,* VI, No. 1 (Winter 1952), 1–21.

Sjoberg, Gideon. "The Preindustrial City," *The American Journal of Sociology*, LX, No. 5 (March 1955), 438–445.

Terrasse, Henri. *Histoire du Maroc, des Origines à l'Establissement du Protectorat Français*, 2 vols. Casablanca: Editions Atlantides, 1949.

——. *Histoire du Maroc, des Origines à l'Establissement du Protectorat Français*. (Edition abrégée.) Casablanca: Editions Atlantides, 1952.

Le Tourneau, Roger. "Social Change in the Muslim Cities of North Africa," *The American Journal of Sociology*, LX, No. 6 (May 1955), 527–535.

Westermarck, Edward A. *Pagan Survivals in Mohammedan Civilization*. London: Macmillan, 1933.

——. *Ritual and Belief in Morocco*. London: Macmillan, 1926.

OTHER SOURCES USED

Adam, André. "La 'Bidonville' de Ben Msik à Casablanca: Contribution à l'Etude du Prolétariat Musulman au Maroc," *Annales d'Institut d'Etudes Orientales*, VIII (1949–1950), 61–199.

——. *La Maison et le Village dans Quelques Tribus d'Anti-Atlas*. (Institut des Hautes-Etudes Marocaines, Collection Hesperis, No. 13.) Paris: Larose, 1952.

——. "La Prolétarisation de l'Habitat dans l'Ancienne Medina de Casablanca." *Bulletin Economique et Social du Maroc*, XLV–XLVI (1950).

American Jewish Committee. *American Jewish Year Book, 1957*. (Vol. 58.) Philadelphia: Jewish Publication Society of America, 1957.

Ayache, Albert. *Le Maroc, Bilan d'une Colonisation*. Paris: Editions Sociales, 1956.

Basset, André. *La Langue Berbère*. London: Oxford University Press, 1952.

Basset, Henri. *Essai sur la Litterature des Berbères*. Algiers: Carbonel, 1920.

Bencheneb, Saadeddine. "La Littérature Contemporaire en Afrique du Nord," *l'Islam and l'Occident*. Paris: Cahiers du Sud, 1947.

Benet, Francisco. "Explosive Markets: the Berber Highlands." Pages 188–217 in Karl Polanyi, et al. (eds.), *Trade and Markets in the Early Empires: Economies in History and Theory*, Glencoe, Illinois: The Free Press, 1957.

Biarnay, E. *Etude sur les Dialectes Berbères du Rif*. Paris: Leroux, 1917.

Boothe, Louise Worthington. "The Evolution of Moorish Art," *Gazette des Beaux Arts*, XXVIII (1945), 113–122.

Brockelman, Carl. *History of the Islamic Peoples*. London: Routledge and Kegan Paul, 1952.

Brunot, Louis. *Introduction à l'Arabe Marocain*. Paris: Maisonneuve, 1950.

———. *Textes Arabes de Rabat*. 2 vols. Paris: Geuthner, 1931.

———. *Textes Arabes de Rabat*. 2 vols. Paris: Geuthner, 1952.

Capot-Rey, Robert. "Le Nomadisme Pastoral dans le Sahara Francais," *Travaux de l'Institut de Recherches Sahariennes*, I (1942), 63-86.

Cauneille, J. "Les Nomades Regueibat," *Travaux de l'Institut de Recherches Sahariennes*, VI (1950), 83-100.

Célérier, Jean. "La Modernisation du Paysant Marocain," *Revue de Géographic Marocaine*, XXXI, No. 1 (1947), 3-29.

Chouraqui, André. *Les Juifs de l'Afrique du Nord; Marche vers l'Occident*. Paris: Presses Universitaires de France, 1952.

Cid, Kaoui S. *Dictionnaire Français Tachelhit et Tamazir't*. Paris. Leroux, 1907.

Coon, Carleton S. *Tribes of the Rif*. Harvard African Studies, IX.) Cambridge, Massachusetts: Peabody Museum of Harvard University, 1931.

Corval, Pierre. *Le Maroc en Révolution*. Paris: Bibliothèque de l'Homme d'Action, 1956.

Delawarde, J. B. "Inesgane: un Exemple d'Organisation de la Vie Indigène au Maroc," *La Géographie*, LXXI, No. 4 (April 1939), 193-204.

Destaing, E. *Etudes sur le Dialecte Berbère des Air Seghrouchen*. Paris: Leroux, 1920.

———. *Textes Arabes en Parlers Chliuhs du Sous (Maroc)*. Paris: Geuthner, 1937.

Doutte, M. Edmon. "Organization Sociale et Domestique des Haha," *Comité de l'Afrique Francaise*, V, No. 1 (January 1905), 1-16.

Duquaire, Henri. *Anthologie de la Littérature Marocaine, Arabe, and Berbère*. Paris: Plon, 1947.

Ellis, Walter Crosby. *Communism in Education in Asia, Africa, and the Far Pacific*. Washington, D.C.: American Council on Education, 1954.

Fisher, Sir Godfrey. *Barbary Legend*. Oxford: Clarendon Press, 1957.

Fischer, Roger. "Essai sur le Paysage Agraire du Plateau de Meknès," *Revue de Géographie Marocaine*, XXXII, No. 4 (1948), 121-146.

Fogg, Walter. "Villages, Tribal Markets and Towns: Some Considerations Concerning Urban Development in the Spanish and International Zones of Morocco," *The Sociological Review*, XXXII, Nos. 1-2 (January-April 1940), 85-107.

Food and Agriculture Organization. *Per Caput Fiber Consumption Levels*. (Commodity Series, No. 21.) Rome: December 1951.

———. *Sugar.* (Commodity Series, No. 22.) Rome: September 1952.
Foucald, Charles Eugène de. *Reconnaissance au Maroc, 1883–1884, Ouvrage Illustré.* Paris: Société d'Editions Géographiques, Maritimes et Coloniales, 1888.
———. *Reconnaissance au Maroc, 1883–1884, Ouvrage Illustré.* Paris: Société d'Editions Géographiques, Maritimes et Coloniales, 1934.
———. *Reconnaissance au Maroc; Journal de Route Conforme à l'Edition de 1888 et Augmenté de Fragments Inédits Rédigés par l'Auteur pour son Cousin, François de Bondy.* Paris Société d'Editions Géographiques, Maritimes et Coloniales, 1939.
Gauderoy-Demombynes, Maurice. *Muslim Institutions.* (Trans. from the French by John P. Macgregor.) London: Allen and Unwin, 1950.
Gendre, F. "Tafilalet," *Revue de Géographie Marocaine,* XXVI, Nos. 3–4 (May–August 1942), 43–57.
Harris, Walter B. *Morocco That Was.* London: Blackwood, 1921.
Hart, David M. "Notes on the Rifian Community of Tangier," *The Middle East Journal,* II, No. 2 (Spring 1957), 153–162.
Hitti, Philip K. *History of the Arabs.* London: Macmillan, 1943.
———. *History of the Arabs.* New York: St. Martin's Press, 1956.
International Labour Organisation: International Labour Office. *Year Book of Labour Statistics, 1954.* Geneva: 1955.
———. *Year Book of Labour Statistics, 1956.* Geneva: 1957.
Joly, A. "L'Industrie à Tétouan," *Archives Marocaines,* VIII (1906), 196–329.
———."L'Industrie à Tétouan," *Archives Marocaines,* XI(1907) 361–393.
———. "L'Industrie à Tétouan," *Archives Marocaines,* XI (1909), 80–151.
Joly, Fernand. "Casablanca: Eléments pour une Etude de Géographie Urbaine," *Les Cahiers d'Outre-Mer. Revue de Géographic de Bordeaux et de l'Atlantique,* I, No. 2 (April–June 1948), 119–148.
———. "Les Ait Khebbache de Taouz (Maroc Sud-Oriental)," *Travaux de l'Institut de Recherches Sahariennes,* VII (1951), 129–159.
Kitchen, Helen. *The Press in Africa.* Washington, D.C.: Sloan, 1956.
Laoust, Emil. *Etude sur le Dialecte Berbère des Ntifa.* Paris: Leroux, 1918.
Lehrman, Hal. "Morocco's Jews Enter the 20th Century," *Commentary* (August 1954), 118–126.
Lévi-Provençal, E. *Textes Arabes de l'Ouargha, Dialecte des Jbala.* Paris: Leroux, 1922.
Lévi-Provençal, E., and Colin, G. S. "Morocco: Population, Social and Economic Life, and Religious Life." Pages 590–597 in M. T. Houtsma, *et al.* (eds.), *The Encyclopedia of Islam,* III, London: Luzac, 1936.

Louvignac, V. "Le Monde Berbère et ses Institutions." Pages 275–301 in M. Sagnes (ed.), *Introduction à la Connaissance du Maroc*, Casablanca: Imprimeries Réunies, 1942.

Marçais, W. *Textes Arabes de Tanger*. Paris: Ecole des Langues Orientales Vivantes, 1911.

Mercier, Henry. *Vocabulaire et Textes Berbères dan le Dialecte Berbère des Ait Izdeg*. Rabat: Céré, 1937.

Miege, Jean-Louis. "La Nouvelle Medina de Casablanca: Le Berb Corlotti," *Les Cahiers d'Outre-Mer, Revue de Géographie*, VI, No. 23 (July–September 1953), 244–257.

Montagne, Robert. *Les Berbères et le Makhzen dans le Sud du Maroc. Essai sur la Transformation Politique des Berbères Sedentaires (groupe chliuh)*. Paris: Librairie Felix Alcan, 1930.

_____. "The Power of the Chieftains in Morocco," *Journal of African Administration*, I, No. 3 (July 1949).

Morocco: Office Marocain du Tourisme. *Morocco*. Rabat: n.d.

_____. Imprimerie Officielle, *Bulletin Officiel. Empire Cherifien*. (Since August 1957, *Bulletin Officiel Royaume du Maroc*.) Rabat: 1956–March 1958, *passim*.

Morstin, Henri. "Les Faubourgs Indigènes de Rabat," *Cahiers d'Outre-Mer, Revue de Géographie*, III, No. 9 (January–March 1950), 66–76.

Murdock, George Peter. "Political Moieties." Pages 133–147 in Leonard D. White (ed.), *The State of the Social Sciences*, Chicago: University of Chicago Press, 1955.

Newman, Bernard. *Morocco Today*. London: Hale, 1954. *New York Times*, 1957–1958, *passim*.

"Progress in the Arab States," *The Arab World* (Special Issue, IV, Nos. 2–5). New York: Arab Information Center, February, March, and April 1958.

Renisio, Amédée. *Etude sur les Dialectes Berbères des Beni Iznassen du Rif et des Sanhaja de Srair*. Paris: Leroux, 1932.

Rossano, Jean. "La Colonisation Européene dans le Haouz de Marrakech." *Les Cahiers d'Outre-Mer, Revue de Géoraphie*, VII, No. 28 (October–December 1954), 342–366.

Sandeman, Leonard. "Handbook on Moroccan Labor." Washington, D.C.: U.S. Department of Labor, 1957. (Unpublished manuscript.)

Sarrionandia, Pedro. *Gramática de la Lengua Rifeña*. Tangier: Imprenta Hispanico-Arabiga de la Misión Católica, 1905.

Soualah, Mohammed. *La Société Indigène de l'Afrique du Nord: Algérie, Tunisie, Maroc, Sahara* (3d ed.), vols I and II. Algier, La Typo-Litho and Jules Carbonel, 1946.

Spillman, Georges. *Les Ait Atta du Sahara et la Pacification du Haut Dra*. (Publications de l'Institut des Hautes-Etudes Marocaines, No. 29.) Rabat: Editions Felix Moncho, 1936.

Stuart, Graham. H. *The International City of Tangier*. Stanford, California: Stanford University Press, 1931.

──────. *The International City of Tangier.* (2d ed.) Stanford, California: Stanford University Press, 1955.

Stumme, Hans. *Handbuch des Schilhischen von Tazerwalt.* Leipzig: Heinrich, 1899.

Thibert, J. "Skoura: Etude sur l'Utilisation du Milieu Naturel dans une Oasis du Sud Marocain," *Revue de Géographie Marocaine,* XXXII, Nos. 2, 3, 4 (1948).

Tolliver, Catherine. *Moroccan Horizons.* Casablanca: Les Impressions Edita, 1952.

Le Tourneau, Roger. *Fès Avant le Protectorat; Etude Economique et Sociale d'une Ville de l'Occident Musulman.* (Publications de l'Institut des Hautes-Etudes Marocaines, No. 45.) Casablanca: 1949.

Le Tourneau, Roger, Paye, L., and Guyot, R. "La Corporation des Tanneurs et l'Industrie de la Tannerie à Fès," *Hesperis,* XXXI, No. 1 (1935), 167–240.

"Unemployment and Underemployment in Morocco," American Universities Field Staff, Letter from Charles Gallagher, July 24, 1957.

United Nations. *Non-Self-Governing Territories, Summaries and Analyses of Information Transmitted to the Secretary-General during 1952.* New York: 1953.

──────. *Non-Self-Governing Territories, Summaries and Analyses of Information Transmitted to the Secretary-General during 1955.* New York: 1957.

──────. *Special Study on Education Conditions in Non-Self-Governing Territories, Summaries and Analyses of Information Transmitted to the Secretary-General during 1953.* New York: 1954.

──────. *Special Study on Social Conditions in Non-Self-Governing Territories, Summaries and Analyses of Information Transmitted to the Secretary-General during 1955.* New York: 1956.

──────. Department of Economic and Social Affairs. *Economic Developments in Africa, 1955–1956.* (Supplement to World Economic Survey, E/2984/ST/ECA/46.) New York: 1957.

──────. Statistical Office. *Demographic Yearbook, 1955.* New York: 1955.

──────. *Statistical Yearbook, 1955 (Seventh Issue).* New York: 1955.

United Nations Educational, Scientific, and Cultural Organization. *World Survey of Education: Handbook of Educational Organization and Statistics.* Paris: 1955.

──────: Department of Mass Communication. *World Communication: Press, Radio, Film, Television.* (3d ed.) New York: 1956.

U.S. Department of Commerce: Bureau of Foreign Commerce. *Establishing a Business in French Morocco.* (World Trade

Information Service: Economic Reports, Part I, No. 55-85.) Washington, D.C.: Government Printing Office, 1955.

U.S. Department of Labor: Bureau of Labor Statistics, Division of Foreign Labor Conditions. *Labor Developments Abroad.* Washington, D.C.: Government Printing Office, May 1957 and December 1957.

Warmington, B. H. *The North African Provinces from Diocletian to the Vandal Conquest.* Cambridge: Cambridge University Press, 1954.

Welch, Galbraith. *North African Prelude: The First Seven Thousand Years.* New York: Morrow, 1949.

"A Young Country at Work. Morocco: Goals, Plans and Prospects." The text of the speech of H. E. Dr. El-Mahdy Ben Aboud, Ambassador of Morocco, delivered at the banquet at the Shoreham Hotel on Friday, January 31, 1958, at the Twelfth Annual Conference of the Middle East Institute.

World Health Organization. *WHO Newsletter*, IX, Nos. 11-12 (November-December 1956).

Section II. Political

RECOMMENDED SOURCES

Ashford, Douglas E. *Political Change in Morocco.* Princeton: Princeton University Press, 1961.
Centre d'Etudes Nord-Africaines. *Annuaire de l'Afrique du Nord, 1962,* I. Aix-en-Provence: Centre National de la Recherche Scientifique, 1964.
Centre de Recherches sur l'Afrique Méditerranéenne. *Annuaire de l'Afrique du Nord, 1963,* II. Aix-en-Provence: Centre National de la Recherche Scientifique, 1965.
Lacouture, Jean and Simonne. *Le Maroc à l'épreuve.* Paris: Editions du Seuil, 1958.
Le Tourneau, Roger. *Evolution politique de l'Afrique du Nord musulmane, 1920-1961.* Paris: Librairie Armand Colin, 1962.
Lowenthal, Richard. "China." In Z. Brzezinski (ed.), *Africa and the Communist World.* Stanford: Stanford University Press, 1963, 142-203.
Maghreb, "Où en sont les partis politiques marocains," No. 7, January-February 1965, 19-25.
Marais, Octave. "La Classe dirigeante au Maroc," *Revue Française de Science Politique,* XIV, August 1964, 709-737.
Robert, Jacques. *Monarchie marocaine.* Paris: Librairie Générale de Droit et de Jurisprudence, 1963.
Zartman, I. William. *Destiny of a Dynasty: The Search for Institutions in Morocco's Developing Society.* Columbia: University of South Carolina Press, 1964.

OTHER SOURCES USED

Ashford, Douglas E. "Elections in Morocco: Progress or Confusion," *Middle East Journal,* XV, Winter 1961, 1-15.
──────. *Perspectives of a Moroccan Nationalist.* Totowa, New Jersey: Bedminster Press, 1964.
──────. *Second and Third Generation Elites in the Maghreb.* Washington: U.S. Department of State, 1963.
Barbour, Nevill. "Two Problems in Modern Morocco," *Civilisations,* XI, No. 3, 1961, 265-274.

_____. "Variations of Arab Nationalist Feeling in French North Africa," *Middle East Journal*, VIII, Summer 1954, 308, 309.
Beling, W. A. "Some Implications of the New Constitutional Monarchy in Morocco," *Middle East Journal*, XVIII, Spring 1964, 163-179.
Bernard, Stephane. *Le Conflit franco-marocain, 1943-1956*. Brussels: Editions de l'Institut de Sociologie de l'Université Libre de Bruxelles, 1963.
Buttin, Paul. "La Relève au Maroc des cadres français par les cadres marocains," *Civilisations*, XI, No. 1, 1961, 52-60.
"China, The Arab World and Africa: A Factual Survey 1959-1964." *The Mizan Newsletter*, VI, May 1964.
Confluent (Special Issue: on "La Constitution Marocaine"), No. 27, January 1961.
Daoud, Zakya. "Ahardane revendique un ètat plus berbere," *Jeune Afrique*, No. 211, December 20, 1964, 18-21.
_____. "L'Aïd le plus long," *Jeune Afrique*, No. 230, May 2, 1965, 14, 15.
_____. "Ceux qui restent," *Jeune Afrique*, No. 228, April 18, 1965, 19-22.
_____. "Maroc: une opposition en quête d'avenir," *Jeune Afrique*. No. 209, December 6, 1964, 14-16.
_____. "Pour les français du Maroc c'est plus q'un au revoir," *Jeune Afrique*, No. 226, April 4, 1965, 19-22.
_____. "Rabat: le dialogue à deux prépare l'entente à trois," *Jeune Afrique*, No. 234, May 30, 1965, 21.
Duverger, M. "La Nouvelle constitution marocaine," *Le Monde*, November 30, 1962.
Fage, J. D. *An Introduction to the History of West Africa*. (3d ed.) Cambridge: Cambridge University Press, 1962.
Gallagher, Charles F. "The Death of a Group." (AUFS Reports Service, North Africa Series, X, No. 4.) New York: American Universities Field Staff, 1963.
_____. "The Evolving Moroccan Political Scene: Ben Barka and the National Union." (AUFS Reports Service, North Africa Series, V, No. 5.) New York: American Universities Field Staff, 1959.
_____. "France in Morocco: A Former Colony Lives Amicably with the French." (AUFS Reports Service, North Africa Series, VIII, No. 1.) New York: American Universities Field Staff, 1962.
_____. "The Meanings of the Moroccan Elections." (AUFS Reports Service, North Africa Series, IX, No. 5.) New York: American Universities Field Staff, 1963.
_____. "The Moroccan Constitution: Text and Comment." (AUFS Reports Service, North Africa Series, CFG-2-'63.) New York: American Universities Field Staff, 1963.

———. "The Moroccan Restoration: A Discussion of the Political Pressures That Led King Muhammad V to Assume the Premiership in May 1960." (AUFS Reports Service, North Africa Series, CFG-9-'60.) New York: American Universities Field Staff, 1960.

———. "The Moroccanization of Morocco." (AUFS Reports Service, North Africa Series, CFG-2-'58.) New York: American Universities Field Staff, 1958.

———. "New Laws for Old: The Moroccan Code of Personal Status." (AUFS Reports Service, North Africa Series, V, No. 1.) New York: American Universities Field Staff, 1959.

———. "North African Problems and Prospects, Pt. I: Rural Reform and Revolution." (AUFS Reports Service, North Africa Series, X, No. 2.) New York: American Universities Field Staff, February 1964.

———. "The Peace Corps in the Maghreb." (AUFS Reports Service, North Africa Series, CFG-1-'64.) New York: American Universities Field Staff, 1964.

———. "Toward Constitutional Government in Morocco; A Referendum Endorses the Constitution." (AUFS Reports Service, North Africa Series, CFG-1-'63.) New York: American Universities Field Staff, 1963.

———. *The United States and North Africa: Morocco, Algeria and Tunisia*. Cambridge: Harvard University Press, 1963.

Gellner, Ernest. "From Ibn Khaldun to Karl Marx," *The Political Quarterly*, No. 32, October 1961, 385-392.

———. "Patterns of Rural Rebellion in Morocco: Tribes as Minorities," *Archives Européennes de Sociologie*, III, No. 2, 1962, 297-311.

———. "The Struggle for Morocco's Past," *Middle East Journal*, XV, No. 1, 1961, 79-90.

Gordon, David C. *North Africa's French Legacy, 1954-1962*. (Harvard Middle Eastern Monographs, IX.) Cambridge: Harvard University Press, 1964.

Gravier, Louis. "Maroc: tolérés parce que monarchistes et peu nombreux," *Le Monde Hebdomadaire*, April 15-21, 1965, 5.

Halpern, Manfred. *The Politics of Social Change in the Middle East and North Africa*. Princeton: Princeton University Press, 1963.

Jawad, Kamal. "La Gauche marocaine riposte," *Jeune Afrique*, No. 129, April 8-14, 1963, 6, 7.

———. "Les idées de Guédira," *Jeune Afrique*, No. 128, April 1-7, 1963, 10-13.

Lahlou, Abbés. "La Bourgeoisie, symbole et reflet direct de l'occidentalisation de la société marocaine," Civilisations, XIV, No. 1-2, 1964, 62-80.

Lewis, William H. "Rural Administration in Morocco," *Middle East Journal*, XIV, No. 1, 1960, 45-60.

Mohammed V, S.M. *Le Maroc à l'heure de l'independence*, I. Rabat: Ministère de l'Information et Tourisme, 1957.
Morere, Maurice. *Manuel d'organisation judiciare au Maroc*. Casablanca: Librairie Farraire, 1961.
"The New Constitution of Morocco," *Bulletin of the International Commission of Jurists*, No. 16, July 1963, 28-37.
Ougrour, Jean. "Le Fait berbere: essai de demystification," *Confluent*, No. 23-24, September-October 1962, 617-634.
Poulsson, Erik T. "The Treason Trial in Morocco," *Bulletin of the International Commission of Jurists*, No. 18, March 1964, 26-37.
Recoules, Jean. "Un Aspect du Maroc actuel: le bled sans caïd," *L'Afrique et l'Asie*, No. 40, 1957, 52-54.
———. " 'Siba' au Maroc," *L'Afrique et l'Asie*, No. 51, 1960, 13-19.
Reyner, Anthony S. "Morocco's International Boundaries: A Factual Background," *Journal of Modern African Studies*, I, No. 3, 1963, 313-326.
Rezette, Robert. *Les Partis politiques marocaines.* (2d ed.) Paris: A. Colin, 1955.
Rustow, Dankwart A. "The Politics of the Near East." In Gabriel A. Almond and James E. Coleman (eds.), *The Politics of the Developing Areas*. Princeton: Princeton University Press, 1960, 369-454.
Schaar, Stuart. "King Hassan's Alternatives," *Africa Report*, VIII, August 1963, 7-12.
Shuster, James R. "Bureaucratic Transition in Morocco," *Human Organization*, XXIV, Spring 1965, 53-58.
Sterling, Claire. "Morocco's Troubled Young King," *The Reporter*, June 17, 1965, 21-24.
U.S. Department of State. Bureau of Intelligence and Research. *World Strength of the Communist Party Organizations*. (16th Annual Report.) Washington: 1964.
Von Grunebaum, G. E. "Islam: Essays in the Nature and Growth of a Cultural Tradition," *The American Anthropologist*, LVII, No. 2, Pt. 2 (Memoir No. 81), April 1955.
Yata, Ali. "Way Out of the Crises Possible," *Information Bulletin*, No. 25, November 1964. (Issued by World Marxist Review.)
Zartman, I. William. "Characteristics of Developing Foreign Policies in Former French Africa." (Paper delivered at the International Congress on French-Speaking Africa, August 1964, Washington, D.C.)
———. *Government and Politics in North Africa*. New York: Praeger, 1963.
———. *Morocco: Problems of New Power*. New York: Atherton Press, 1964.
———. "The Sahara—Bridge or Barrier?" *International Conciliation*, No. 541, January 1963.

(Various issues of the following periodicals were also used in the preparation of this section: *Africa Report* [Washington], from January 1963 through June 1965; *L'Afrique et l'Asie* [Paris], from January 1957 through December 1964; *The Christian Science Monitor*, from January 1965 through June 1965; *Confluent* [Rabat], from January 1963 through June 1965; *Jeune Afrique* [Tunis], from January 1963 through June 1965; *Maghreb* [Paris], from January 1964 through June 1965; *Maghreb Digest* [Los Angeles], from January 1964 through June 1965; *Maroc Informations* [Casablanca], from January 1965 through June 1965; *Middle East Journal* [Washington], from January 1958 through December 1964; *Le Monde* [Paris], from January 1962 through June 1965; *La Nation Africaine* [Rabat], from September 1964 through June 1965; *New York Times*, from January 1965 through June 1965; *L'Opinion* [Rabat], from March 1965 through June 1965; and *Le Petit Marocain* [Casablanca], from January 1965 through June 1965.)

RECOMMENDED FURTHER READING

"Amertume à Rabat," *Le Monde* (sélection hebdomadaire), No. 489 (February 27–March 5, 1958), 3.

Balafrej, Ahmed. "Morocco Plans for Independence," *Foreign Affairs*, XXXIV, No. 3 (April 1956).

Cordero Torres, José Maria. "La Independencia de Marruecos," *Cuaderno de Politica Internacional*, No. 25 (January–March 1956), 9–25 and 157–229.

———. "La Independencia de Marruecos," *Cuaderno de Politica Internacional*, No. 26 (April–June 1956), 155–201.

Corval, Pierre. *Le Maroc en Révolution*. Paris: Bibliothèque de l'Homme d'Action, 1956.

"France-Morocco: Joint Declaration; Diplomatic Accord," *American Journal of International Law*, LI (July 1957), 676–683.

Gellner, Ernest. "Independence in the Central High Atlas," *The Middle East Journal*, II, No. 3 (Summer 1957), 237–252.

Hahn, Lorna. "Last Chance in North Africa," *Foreign Affairs*, XXXVI, No. 2 (January 1958), 302–314.

Howe, Marvine. "The Birth of the Moroccan Nation," *The Middle East Journal*, X, No. 1 (Winter 1956).

The Istiqlal (Independence) Party of Morocco. *Morocco Under the Protectorate: Forty Years of French Administration*. New York: Moroccan Office of Information and Documentation, 1953.

Julien, Charles-André. "Morocco: The End of an Era," *Foreign Affairs*, XXXIV, No. 2 (January 1956).

Kirkpatrick, Evron M. *Target, the World: Communist Propaganda Activities in 1955*. New York: Macmillan, 1956.

———. *Year of Crisis: Communist Propaganda Activities in 1956.* New York: Macmillan, 1957.

Landau, Rom. *Mohammed V, King of Morocco.* Rabat: Morocco Publishers, 1957.

———. *Moroccan Drama, 1900–1955.* San Francisco: The American Academy of Asian Studies, 1956.

Lehrman, Hal. "North Africa and the West," *The Reporter*, XVIII, No. 11 (May 29, 1958).

Lewis, William H. "The New Nomadism in North Africa," *The Middle East Journal*, II, No. 3 (Summer 1957), 269–281.

Montagne, Robert. *Révolution au Maroc.* Paris: Editions France-Empire, 1953.

"Morocco Joins the Pressure Group," *The Economist*, CLXXXVI, No. 5977 (March 15, 1958), 922.

Newman, Bernard. *Morocco Today.* London: Hale, 1954.

"North Africa and the Western Mediterranean" (Report of Senator Mike Mansfield to the Committee on Foreign Relations, United States Senate, January 30, 1958). Washington, D.C.: Government Printing Office, 1958.

Rézette, Robert. *Les Partis Politiques Marocains.* (Cahiers de la Fondation Nationale des Sciences Politiques, Partis et Elections, No. 70.) Paris: Librairie Armand Colin, 1955.

"Status of Tangier: Final Declaration and Annexed Protocol of the International Conference of Tangier," *American Journal of International Law*, LI (April 1957), 460–466.

Young, Richard. "The End of American Consular Jurisdiction in Morocco," *American Journal of International Law*, LI, No. 2 (April 1957).

OTHER SOURCES USED

Buttin, Paul. *Le Drame du Maroc.* Paris: Les Editions du Cerf, 1955.

Coon, Carleton. *Caravan, the Story of the Middle East.* New York: Holt, 1951.

"Documentary Background on Recent Political Events in Morocco (June 21 to December 13, 1955)," *Moroccan Affairs*, No. 10 (January 1956).

Al-Istiqlal (Rabat), May and June 1958, *passim*. (French-language weekly of the Istiqlal Party.)

Gallagher, Charles F. *The Moroccanization of Morocco.* Washington, D.C.: American Universities Field Studies, February 1958.

Grandval, Gilbert. *Ma Mission au Maroc.* Paris: Librarie Plon, 1956.

Howe, Marvine. *The Prince and I.* New York: Day, 1955.

Hudson, Manley O. "Rights of United States National in Morocco," *American Journal of International Law*, XLI, No. 1 (January 1953), 8–15.

──────. "The Thirty-First Year of the World Court," *American Journal of International Law*, XLI, No. 1 (January 1953).

Johansen, O. Lund. *World Radio Handbook: Broadcasting—Television, 1957* (11th ed.). Copenhagen: Det Berlingske Bogtrykker, 1957.

Julien, Charles-André. *L'Afrique du Nord en Marche*. Paris: Julliard, 1952.

Lacoutre, Jean. "La Crise Marocaine," *Le Monde* (sélection hebdomadaire), No. 497 (April 17-23, 1958), 2.

Landau, Rom. "Moroccan Profiles: A Nationalist View," *The Middle East Journal*, VII (Winter 1953), 45-57.

──────. *Portrait of Tangier*. London: Hale, 1950.

de Latour, Pierre Boyer. *Vérités sur l'Afrique du Nord*. Paris: Librairie Plon, 1956.

"Makhzen," *Encyclopedia of Islam*, III, 168-170.

The Middle East Journal, "Development of the Quarter: Comment and Chronology" (1954-1957), *passim*.

Middle Eastern Affairs, "Chronology" (1955-1958), *passim*.

"Morocco '54," *Encyclopédie Mensuelle d'Outre-Mer* (Special Issue.) Paris: 1954.

"Morocco Between Two Eras," *The World Today*, XIII, No. 9 (September 1957), 389-401.

New York Times, 1957-1958, *passim*.

──────. "Dashing Moroccan Heir, Moulay Hassan," November 29, 1957.

──────, "France Protests Moroccan Action," March 27, 1958.

──────, "Frenchmen Condemned," March 25, 1958.

──────, "King of Morocco Urges Ifni Peace," December 4, 1957.

──────, "Morocco Appeals for Youth Militia," May 28, 1958.

──────, "Morocco Set Up a Sahara Office," November 13, 1957.

──────, "Planned Economy Seen in Morocco," December 29, 1957.

──────, "Westernmost Arab King, Mohammed V," November 26, 1957.

Parent, Pierre. *The Truth about Morocco*. New York: Moroccan Office of Information and Documentation, 1953.

Rivlin, Benjamin. "Cultural Conflict in French North Africa," *The Annals of the American Academy of Political and Social Sciences*, CCCVI, No. 3 (July 1956), 4-9.

──────. "North Africa Meets the Modern World: Islam and Democracy in Morocco and Tunisia," *Commentary* (October 1956).

El-Saghieb, Khaleb Ibrahim. "The United Nations and Nationalism in Morocco." Unpublished Doctoral dissertation, American University Graduate School. Washington, D.C.: June 1955.

"The Spanish in Morocco: a Retrospect," *The World Today*, XII, No. 8 (August 1956), 313-321.

Sterling, Claire. "Morocco: The Struggle Neither Side Can Win," *The Reporter* (April 13, 1954).

Stevens, Emund. *North African Powder Keg*. New York: Coward-McCann, 1955.

Strasser, Daniel, *Réalitiés et Promesses Sahariennes*. Paris: Encyclopédie d'Outre-Mer, 1956.

Stuart, Graham, H. *The International City of Tangier*. (2d ed.) Stanford, California: Stanford University Press, 1955.

Taillard, T. *Le Nationalisme Marocain*. Paris: Les Editions du Cerf, 1947.

Thornton, Philip. *The Voice of Atlas*. London: Maclehose, 1936.

Time, "The Moslem World: Beyond the Veil," November 11, 1957, 32–36.

Vidal, Frederico Schmidt. "Religious Brotherhoods in Morocco Politics," *Middle East Journal*, IV, No. 4 (Autumn 1950), 427–446.

Welles, Benjamin. "Spain Reported Ready to Yield Protectorate Region to Morocco," *New York Times*, March 21, 1958.

———. "Spain Reports Rout of Sahara Rebels," *New York Times*, January 16, 1958.

———. "Spanish Repulse Raid in Morocco," *New York Times*, November 26, 1957.

Section III. Economic

RECOMMENDED SOURCES

Among the sources consulted in the preparation of this section, the following are recommended as additional reading on the basis of quality and general availability.

International Monetary Fund. *Fifteenth Annual Report on Exchange Restrictions 1964.* Washington: IMF, 1964.

_____. *Twelfth Annual Report on Exchange Restrictions 1961.* Washington: IMF, 1961.

Morocco. Présidence du Conseil. Division de la Coordination Economique et du Plan. Service Central des Statistiques. *Résultats préliminaires due recensement de 1960 (sondage au 1/50ème).* Rabat: Service Central de Statistiques, 1963.

Stewart, Charles F. *The Economy of Morocco 1912-1962.* (Harvard Middle Eastern Monographs XII.) Cambridge: Harvard University Press, 1964.

U.S. Department of Commerce. Bureau of International Commerce. *International Commerce.* (Special Supplement: "A Market for U.S. Products in Morocco"), 1964.

U.S. Department of Labor. Bureau of Labor Statistics. *Labor Law and Practice in Morocco.* (BLS Report No. 282.) Washington: GPO, 1965.

OTHER SOURCES USED

Adie, W. A. C. "Chou En-lai on Safari," *The China Quarterly* (London), No. 18, April-June 1964, 174-194.

American Friends of the Middle East, Inc. *Basic Facts on Morocco.* (Comp., Richard J. Blake.) Washington: AFME, 1964.

Ashford, Douglas E. "Political Aspects of Rural Development in North Africa." (Paper delivered at 18th Annual Conference of the Middle East Institute, Washington, D.C., May 9, 1964.)

_____. *Political Change in Morocco.* Princeton: Princeton University Press, 1961.

Banque du Maroc. *Rapport sur l'exercice 1963.* Rabat: Banque du Maroc, n.d.

Banque Marocaine du Commerce Extérieur. *Rapport sur l'exercice 1963.* N.pl.: n.d.

———. Département d'Etudes and Banque Nationale pour le Développement Economique. *How to Invest in Morocco.* Casablanca: 1962.

Banque Nationale pour le Développement Economique. *Rapport annuel exercice 1963.* Rabat: BNDE, n.d.

Berque, Jacques. "Le Systeme rural du Maghreb." (Paper delivered at 18th Annual Conference of the Middle East Institute, Washington, D.C., May 9, 1964.)

Brunet, Jean. "L'Office National des Irrigations au Maroc, deux ans d'experience." Pages 249–267 in Centre d'Etudes Nord Africaines. *Annuaire de l'Afrique du Nord, 1962,* I. Aix-en-Provence: Centre National de la Recherche Scientifique, 1964.

Carey, Jane Perry Clark, and Carey, Andrew Galbraith. "The Two Developing Worlds of Morocco: A Case Study in Economic Development and Planning," *Middle East Journal,* XVI, Autumn 1962, 457–475.

Morocco. Ministère de l'Economie Nationale et des Finances. *Finances publiques du Maroc,* by M. Champion. Rabat: 1961.

Daoud, Zakya. "Maroc: les partis, les paysans et la terre," *Jeune Afrique,* No. 198, September 1964, 14.

de Sugny, Jacques. "Maroc: le réforme agraire ne peut plus attendre," *Jeune Afrique,* No. 195, August 3, 1964, 14, 15.

Emerson, James P. "Agriculture Development in Morocco" (with special reference to U.S. AID, 1957–1964). Rabat: U.S. AID Mission to Morocco, April 1964 (mimeo.).

"Les Finances publiques marocaines et le plan d'assainissement," *Maghreb,* No. 4, July–August 1964, 21–25.

Gallagher, Charles F. "North African Problems and Prospects, Pt. I: Rural Reform and Revolution." (AUFS Reports Service, North Africa Series, X, No. 2.) New York: American Universities Field Staff, February 1964.

———. "North African Problems and Prospects, Part II: Industrialization and Development." (AUFS Reports Service, North Africa Series, X, No. 3.) New York: American Universities Field Staff, March 1964.

Governmental Affairs Institute. *Morocco.* (Labor Practice Series.) Washington: 1961.

Hance, William A. *The Geography of Modern Africa.* New York: Columbia University Press, 1964.

Les Hommes, la Terre et l'Eau (Bulletin de Liaison et d'Information de l'Office National des Irrigations), No. 6, October 1963; No. 7, March 1964.

International Labour Organisation. International Labour Office. *Labour Survey of North Africa.* Geneva: ILO, 1960.

"Les Investissements etrangers en Afrique du Nord: Maroc," *Maghreb,* No. 4, July–August 1964, 41–49.

"Irrigation Networks are Built to End Water Waste in Morocco," *New York Times*, January 20, 1964, 48.

Jucker-Fleetwood, Erin E. *Money and Finance in Africa.* New York: Praeger, 1964.

Meyer, A. J. "Economic Planning in North Africa." (Paper delivered at 18th Annual Conference of the Middle East Institute, Washington, D.C., May 9, 1964.)

The Middle East and North Africa, 1964-65. London: Europa Publications, 1964.

Mikesell, Marvin W. *Northern Morocco: A Cultural Geography.* (University of California Publications in Geography, XIV.) Berkeley: University of California Press, 1961.

──────. "The Role of Tribal Markets in Morocco," *Geographical Review*, XLVIII, October 1958, 494-511.

Minerals Yearbook 1963, I. Washington: U.S. Department of the Interior, 1964.

Monteil, Vincent. *Morocco.* (Trans., Veronica Hull.) New York: Viking Press, 1964.

Morocco. Cabinet Royal. Délégation Générale la Promotion Nationale et au Plan. Service Central des Statistiques. *Bulletin Mensuel de Statistique*, No. 78, October 1964.

Morocco. Cabinet Royal. Délégation Générale à la Promotion Nationale et au Plan. Division du Plan et les Statistiques. *La Situation economique du Maroc en 1962.* Rabat: Service Central des Statistiques, July 1963.

Morocco. Ministère du Commerce, de l'Industrie, des Mines, de l'Artisanat et de la Marine Marchande. *Guide de l'industriel désirant s'établir au Maroc.* Rabat: 1961.

Morocco. Ministère de l'Economie Nationale et des Finances. *Basic Data on the Economy of Morocco.* Rabat: 1962.

──────. *Ce qu'il faut savoir sur l'economie marocaine.* Rabat: 1962.

──────. Direction des Mines et de la Géologie. *Etat des statistiques des productions des exportations et des ventes locales minières.* N.pl.: n.d.

Morocco. Ministère de l'Economie Nationale et des Finances. Division de la Coordination Economique et du Plan. *Plan quinquennal 1960-1964: le développement industriel.* Rabat: Service Central de Statistiques, 1961.

Morocco. Ministère des Postes, Télégraphes et Téléphones. *Revue des P.T.T.*, No. 5, March 1963.

Morocco. Ministère du Travail et des Questions Sociales. *Le Maroc au travail.* (Edition nouvelle.) Rabat: 1961.

Morocco. Présidence du Conseil. Division de la Coordination Economique et du Plan. Service Central des Statistiques. *Rapport sur l'enquête "investissements: besoins de l'industrie en personnel qualifié."* N.pl.: 1963.

La Nation Africaine (Rabat), December 14, 1964; December 29, 1964.

News of Morocco (Embassy of Morocco, Washington), II, October 1960.

Nicolas-Mourer, H. "Les Collectivités locales dans l'administration territoriale du Royaume du Maroc." In Centre de Recherches sur l'Afrique Méditerranéenne *Annuaire de l'Afrique du Nord, 1963*, II. Aix-en-Provence: Centre National de la Recherche Scientifique, 1965, 129-160.

1963 Pick's Currency Yearbook. New York: Pick, 1963.

Notes d'Information et Statistiques (Banque Centrale des Etats de l'Afrique de l'Ouest) (Paris), No. 100, November 1963.

Oved, Georges. "Economic Development Problems in Morocco," *Tiers-Monde*, July-September 1961.

Stewart, Charles F. "Industrialization in Morocco." In Paul J. Klat (ed.), *Middle East Economic Papers 1957*. (Economic Research Institute, American University of Beirut.) N.pl.: n.d, 89-110.

Taylor, Brian H. "Melting Morocco's Agricultural Iceberg," *Freedom from Hunger Campaign News*, IV, December 1963, 6-9.

U.S. Congress. 88th, 2d Session. House of Representatives. Foreign Affairs Committee. *Hearings on Foreign Assistance Act of 1964*. Washington: GPO, 1964.

U.S. Department of Agriculture. Economic Research Service. *Africa: Indices of Agricultural Production in 28 African Countries*. Washington: USDA, 1964.

_____. *The Agriculture of Morocco: Programs, Progress, Prospects*, by Henrietta M. Holm. (USDA, ERS Foreign 11.) Washington: USDA, 1961.

_____. "Morocco." Washington: USDA, 1963 (mimeo.).

_____. *The 1964 World Agricultural Situation: The 1964 Africa and West Asia Agricultural Situation*, supplement No. 5. Washington: USDA, 1964.

_____. "United States Agricultural Exports to Morocco, 1961, 1962 and 1963." Washington: USDA, 1964 (mimeo.).

_____. "United States Agricultural Imports from Morocco, 1961, 1962, and 1963." Washington: USDA, 1964 (mimeo.).

U.S. Department of Commerce. Bureau of International Commerce. *Basic Data on the Economy of Morocco*. (Overseas Business Reports OBR-63-1.) Washington: 1963.

_____. *Establishing a Business in Morocco*. (Overseas Business Reports OBR 65-17.) Washington: 1965.

U.S. Department of Labor. Bureau of Labor Statistics. *Labor Developments Abroad*. Washington: GPO, 1964.

U.S. International Cooperation Administration. Office of Labor Affairs. *Summary of the Labor Situation in Morocco*. (Prepared by the U.S. Department of Labor. Bureau of Labor Statistics.) Washington: GPO, 1959.

La Vie Economique (Special Number: "Les Travaux Publiques au Maroc") (Casablanca), September 1963.

Wilson, Dick. "China's Economic Relations with Africa," *Race* (London), V, April 1964, 61-72.

Zartman, I. William. "Farming and Land Ownership in Morocco," *Land Economics*, XXXIX, May 1963, 187-198.

———. "Morocco." Chapter II in *Government and Politics in Northern Africa*. New York: Praeger, 1963.

———. *Morocco: Problems of New Power*. New York: Atherton Press, 1964.

(Various issues of the following periodicals were also used in the preparation of this section: *Africa Report* [Washington], from June 1962 through May 1965; *Foreign Agriculture* [U.S. Department of Agriculture], from October 1963 through May 1965; *International Commerce* [U.S. Department of Commerce], from February 1964 through May 1965; *International Financial News Survey* [International Monetary Fund], from January 1962 through May 1965; *International Financial Statistics* [International Monetary Fund], from January 1963 through June 1965; *Jeune Afrique* [Tunis], from June 1962 through May 1965; *Maghreb* [Paris], from January 1964 through May 1965; *Maghreb Digest* [Los Angeles], from January 1963 through May 1965; *Maroc Informations* [Casablanca], from April 1964 through May 1965; *New York Times*, from January 1963 through June 1965; *Le Petit Marocain* [Casablanca], from December 1964 through May 1965; *Statements and Documents* [Moroccan Embassy in Washington], from January 1962 through June 1965; and *La Vie Economique* [Casablanca], from June 1964 through May 1965.)

The following additional sources were used in the preparation of the original Area Handbook for Morocco, published in 1958.

RECOMMENDED FURTHER READING

Chenier, Louis de. *The Present State of the Empire of Morocco*. (Vol. I.) London: Robinson, 1788.

Harris, Walter B., and Cozens-Hardy, W. *Modern Morocco: A Report on Trade Prospects, with Some Geographical and Historical Notes*. London: Adams and Shardlow, 1919.

Landau, Rom. *The Beauty of Morocco*. London: Evans Brothers, 1951.

———. *Invitation to Morocco*. London: Faber and Faber, n.d.

———. *Moroccan Drama, 1900-1955*. San Francisco: The American Academy of Asian Studies, 1956.

Mannin, Ethel. *Moroccan Mosaic*. London: Jarrolds, 1953.

"Morocco," *Encyclopaedia Britannica* (1953 ed.), XV, 808-816.

"Morocco '54," *Encyclopédie Mensuelle d'Outre-Mer* (Special Issue). Paris: 1954.

Newman, Bernard. *Morocco Today*. London: Hale, 1954.

New York Times, "Morocco Plant for General Tire," December 27, 1957.

Sefrioui, Ahmed. *Morocco*. (Hachette World Albums.) Paris: Librairie Hachette, 1956.

Stevens, Edmund. "Moroccans Brand French Cartel Exploiters of North African Economy," *Christian Science Monitor* (January 9, 1953).

———. *North African Powder Keg*. New York: Coward-McCann, 1955.

Tolliver, Catherine. *Moroccan Horizons*. Casablanca: Les Impressions Edita, 1952.

OTHER SOURCES USED

International Monetary Fund. *International Financial News Survey*. Washington, D.C.: February 14, 1958, 258.

Kabbani, Rashid. "Morocco: from Protectorate to Independence, 1912–1956." Unpublished Doctoral dissertation, American University, Graduate School. Washington, D.C.: 1957.

Kerr, Robert. *Morocco After Twenty-Five Years*. London: Murray and Evenden, 1912.

Knight, Melvin M. *Morocco as a French Economic Venture*. New York: Appleton-Century, 1937.

El-Saghieb, Khaleb Ibraham. "The United Nations and Nationalism in Morocco." Unpublished Doctoral dissertation, American University Graduate School. Washington, D.C.: June 1955.

U.S. Department of Commerce. *Foreign Commerce Weekly*, LIX, No. 9 (March 3, 1958).

———: Bureau of Foreign Commerce. *Establishing a Business in French Morocco*. (World Trade Information Service: Economic Reports, Part I, No. 55–85.) Washington, D.C.: Government Printing Office, 1955.

Section IV. National Security

"L'Afrique et ses armées." *Jeune Afrique*, No. 202, October 18, 1964, 20, 21.

American Friends of the Middle East, Inc. *Basic Facts on Morocco*. (Comp., Richard J. Blake.) Washington: AFME, 1964.

Ashford, Douglas E. *Political Change in Morocco*. Princeton: Princeton University Press, 1961.

Barbour, Nevill. *Morocco*. London: Thames and Hudson, 1965.

Kitchen, Helen (ed.). *A Handbook of African Affairs*. New York: Praeger, 1964.

Landau, Rom. *Hassan II, King of Morocco*. London: Allen and Unwin, 1962.

_____. *Mohammed V, King of Morocco*. Rabat: Morocco, 1957.

Maghreb, No. 6, November–December 1964.

Military Review, February 1963.

Monteil, Vincent. *Morocco*. (Trans., Veronica Hull.) New York: Viking Press, 1964.

Morere, Maurice. *Manuel d'organisation judiciarie au Maroc*. Casablanca: Librairie Farraire, 1961.

Schaar, Stuart. "King Hassan's Alternatives," *Africa Report*, VIII, August 1963, 7–12.

Segal, Ronald. *Political Africa: A Who's Who of Personalities and Parties*. London: Stevens, 1961.

Weeks, George. "The Armies of Africa," *Africa Report*, IX, January 1964, 4–21.

Zartman, I. William. *Morocco: Problems of New Power*. New York: Atherton Press, 1964.

(Various issues of the following periodicals were also used in the preparation of this section: *Deadline Data on World Affairs* [New York], from 1962 through June 1965; and *Keesing's Contemporary Archives* [London], from 1955 through June 1965.)

BIBLIOGRAPHY FOR REVISED EDITION

Section I. Social

RECOMMENDED SOURCES

Adam, André. *Casablanca: Essai sur la Transformation de la Societé Marocaine au Contact de l'Occident.* Paris: Editions du Centre National de la Recherche Scientifique, 1968.

──────. "Casablanca: Le Role de la Ville dans la Transformation de la Societé Marocaine," *Maghreb: Etudes et Documents* [Paris], No. 32, March–April 1969, 32–41.

al-Fasi, Allal. *The Independence Movements in Arab North Africa.* Washington: American Council of Learned Societies, 1954.

Arntsen, Andrea, and Ansell, Gladyce W. *Inter-Arab Cooperation and U.S. Policy.* (Technical Paper RAC-TP-396.) McLean, Virginia: Research Analysis Corporation, June 1970.

Ashford, Douglas E. *Political Change in Morocco.* Princeton: Princeton University Press, 1964.

Berque, Jacques. *Structures Sociales du Haut-Atlas.* Paris: Presses Universitaires de France, 1955.

Brown, Leon Carl. "Changing Cultures and New Loyalties in North Africa." Pages 95–106 in William H. Lewis (ed.), *French-Speaking Africa: The Search for Identity.* New York: Walker, 1965.

──────. "The Islamic Reformist Movement in North Africa," *Journal of Modern African Studies* [Cambridge, England], II, No. 1, March 1964, 55–64.

Brown, Leon Carl (ed.). *State and Society in Independent North Africa.* Washington: The Middle East Institute, 1966.

Cerych, Ladislav. *Européens et Marocains, 1930–1956: Sociologie d'une Decolonisation.* Bruges, Belgium: De Tempel, 1964.

Cohen, Amnon. "Allal al-Fasi: His Ideas and His Contribution Towards Morocco's Independence," *Asian and African Studies* [Jerusalem], III, 1967, 121–164.

Couleau, Julien, *La Paysannerie Marocaine.* Paris: Editions du Centre National de la Recherche Scientifique, 1968.

Crapanzo, Vincent, and Kramer, Jane. "Life in a Small Arab Town— A World of Saints and She-Demons," *New York Times Magazine,* June 22, 1969, 14–38.

Gallagher, Charles F. *The United States and North Africa.* Cambridge: Harvard University Press, 1963.

Geertz, Clifford. *Islam Observed: Religious Development in Morocco and Indonesia.* New Haven: Yale University Press, 1968.

Gellner, Ernest. *Saints of the Atlas.* Chicago: University of Chicago Press, 1969.

_____. "Sanctity, Puritanism, Secularisation, and Nationalism in North Africa," *Archives de Sociologie des Religions* [Paris], XV, 1963, 71–86.

_____. "Tribalism and Social Change in North Africa." Pages 107–119 in William H. Lewis (ed.), *French-Speaking Africa: The Search for Identity.* New York: Walker, 1965.

Gibb, H. A. R., and Kramers, J. H. *Shorter Encyclopaedia of Islam.* Ithaca: Cornell University Press, 1953.

Golino, Frank R. *Language and Cultural Identity.* (Foreign Affairs Research Series No. 13699.) Washington: Department of State, March 1, 1971 (mimeo.).

Gordon, David C. *North Africa's French Legacy: 1954–1962.* (Harvard Middle Eastern Monographs, No. 9.) Cambridge: Center for Middle Eastern Studies, Harvard University Press, 1962.

Hagopian, Elaine C. "Morocco: A Case Study in the Structural Basis of Social Integration." Unpublished doctoral dissertation, Boston University, Department of Anthropology, 1962.

Halpern, Manfred. *The Politics of Social Change in the Middle East and North Africa.* Princeton: Princeton University Press, 1965.

Hamilton, Margaret. "French Policy Toward Morocco: 1944–1956." Doctoral dissertation, Columbia University. New York: Columbia University, 1959.

Hitti, Philip K. *Islam, a Way of Life.* Minneapolis: University of Minnesota Press, 1970.

Holt, P. M.; Lambton, Ann K. S.; and Lewis, Bernard (eds.). *The Cambridge History of Islam*, II: The Further Islamic Lands, Islamic Society and Civilization. Cambridge: Cambridge University Press, 1970.

Hurewitz, Jacob C. *Middle East Politics: The Military Dimension.* New York: Praeger, 1969.

International Bank for Reconstruction and Development. *The Economic Development of Morocco.* Baltimore: Johns Hopkins University Press, 1966.

Johnson, Katherine Marshall. *Urban Government for the Prefecture of Casablanca.* (The International Urban Studies of the Institute of Public Administration, No. 7.) New York: Praeger, 1970.

Joshua, Wynfred. *Soviet Penetration into the Middle East.* New York: National Strategy Information Center, 1970.

Julien, Charles-André. *History of North Africa: Tunisia, Algeria, Morocco.* (Trans., John Petrie.) London: Routledge and Kegan Paul, 1970.

Khatibi, Abdelkabir. *Le Roman Maghrebin*. Paris: F. Maspero, 1969.

Kirk, George E. *A Short History of the Middle East*. Washington: Praeger, 1968.

Kramer, Jane. *Honor to the Bride Like the Pigeon That Guards Its Grain Under the Clove Tree*. New York: Farrar, Straus Giroux, 1970.

Laroui, Abdallah. *Cultural Problems and Social Structure: The Campaign for Arabization in Morocco*. (Foreign Affairs Research Series No. 13700.) Washington: Department of State, 1971.

"Les Juifs d'Afrique du Nord: Leur Situation et Leurs Problemes en 1968," *Maghreb: Etudes et Documents* [Paris], No. 27, May–June 1968, 24–36.

Mikesell, Marvin W. *North Morocco: A Cultural Geography*. (University of California Publications in Geography, No. 14.) Berkeley: University of California Press, 1961.

Mountjoy, Allan B. *Africa: A New Geographical Survey*. New York: Praeger, 1967.

Muddathir, Ahmed. *Die Arabische Presse in den Maghreb-Staaten*. Hamburg: Deutsches Institut für Afrika-Forschung, 1966.

Norris, H. T. "New Evidence on the Life of Abdullah B. Yasin and the Origins of the Almoravid Movement," *Journal of African History* [London], XII, No. 2, June 1971, 255–268.

Patai, Raphael. *Golden River to Golden Road: Society, Culture, and Change in the Middle East*. Philadelphia: University of Pennsylvania Press, 1969.

Plum, Werner. *Sozialer Wandel im Maghreb*. (Schriftenreihe des Forschungsinstitutes der Friedrich-Ebert Stiftung, A: Sozialwissenschaftliche Schriften.) Hannover: Verlag für Literatur und Zeitgeschehen, 1967.

Rosen, Lawrence. "I Divorce Thee," *Trans-Action*, VII, No. 8, June 1970, 34–37.

———. "A Moroccan Jewish Community During the Middle Eastern Crisis," *American Scholar*, XXXVII, No. 3, Summer 1968, 435–451.

Shinar, P. "Note on the Socio-economic and Cultural Role of Sufi Brotherhoods and Marabutism in the Modern Maghrib." Pages 272–285 in Lalage Bown and Michael Crowder (eds.), *Proceedings of the First International Congress of Africanists*. Evanston: Northwestern University Press, 1964.

Souriau-Hoebrechts, Christiane. *Le Presse Maghrebine*. Paris: Editions du Centre National de la Recherche Scientifique, 1970.

Spencer, William. "Morocco's Monarchical Balancing Act," *Africa Report*, XV, No. 9, December 1970, 19–21.

Steel, Ronald (ed.). *North Africa*. New York: H. W. Wilson, 1967.

"Urbanisme, Habitat et Ruralisme au Maroc," *Jeune Afrique* [Paris], (Special Edition.) July 1970, 85–96.

Zartman, I. William. "The Moroccan-American Base Negotiations," *Middle East Journal*, XVIII, No. 1, Winter 1964, 27-50.

_____. *Problems of New Power: Morocco*. New York: Atherton Press, 1964.

OTHER SOURCES USED

Abun-Nasr, Jamil M. *The Tijaniyya: A Sufi Order in the Modern World*. (Middle Eastern Monographs, No. 7.) N.pl.: Oxford University Press, 1965.

African Research Bulletin [London] (unpublished mimeo.) December 1970–January 1971, 1902.

Al Amin, Ahmed. "L'Evolution de la Femme et le Problème du Mariage au Maroc," *Présence Africaine* [Paris], No. 68, 1968, 32-52.

American Friends of the Middle East. *Basic Facts on Education in the Middle East-North Africa*. (Prepared for the Mid-East/North Africa Workshop, Nos. 24–25, February 1966.) Washington: 1966.

Annuaire de l'Afrique du Nord, VIII. Paris: Editions du Centre National de la Recherche Scientifique, 1970.

Arab Information Center. *Education in the Arab States*. (Information Papers No. 25, I–XIII.) New York: 1966.

The Arab League: Its Origin, Purposes, Structure and Activities. New York: Arab Information Center, April 1955.

Arberry, A. J. *Sufism: An Account of the Mystics of Islam*. New York: Harper and Row, 1970.

Ayache, Albert. *Le Maroc: Bilan d'une Colonisation*. Paris: Editions Sociales, 1956.

Banque Marocaine du Commerce Exterieur. "The 1968-1972 Five Year Plan," *Monthly Bulletin of Information* [Rabat], No. 91, November 1968, 4-29.

Barbour, Nevill. *Morocco*. New York: Walker, 1965.

Becker, A. S., and Horelick, A. L. *Soviet Policy in the Middle East*. (Rand Abstract 504-FF.) Santa Monica: Rand Corporation, 1970.

Beling, Willard A. "Some Implications of the New Constitutional Monarchy in Morocco," *Middle East Journal*, XVIII, No. 2, Spring 1964, 163-179.

Benkirane, Abdelwahab. "Echanges et cooperation entre le Maroc et les pays socialistes de l'Europe," *Bulletin Economique et Social du Maroc* [Rabat], XXVIII, No. 103, 1966, 49-72.

Bernheim, Nicole. "Revolution Feminine au Maghreb, I: Les Marocaines, Victimes du 'qu'en dira-t-on?'," *Jeune Afrique* [Paris], No. 545, June 15, 1971, 55-59.

Berque, Jacques. "The Rural System of the Maghrib." Pages 192–211 in Leon Carl Brown (ed.), *State and Society in Independent North Africa*. Washington: Middle East Institute, 1966.

Blaque-Belair, L. "North African Literature," *Africa Report*, XV, No. 2, February 1970, 32-34.

Brown, Kenneth. "Research Facilities in Morocco," *Middle East Studies Association Bulletin* [London], IV, No. 3, October 1970, 57-65.

Brown, Leon Carl. "Color in Northern Africa," *Daedalus*, XCVI, No. 2, Spring 1967, 464-482.

Burke, Edmund. "Morocco and the Near East: Reflections on Some Basic Differences," *European Journal of Sociology* [Paris], X, No. 1, 1969, 70-94.

Buy, Jacques. "Bidonville et Ensemble Moderne: Approche Sociologique de Deux Populations de Casablanca," *Bulletin Economique et Social du Maroc* [Rabat], XXVIII, Nos. 101-102, April-September 1966, 71-121.

Cantori, Louis J. *Local Leadership Characteristics of the Istiqlal Party of Morocco.* (Foreign Affairs Research Series No. 13687.) New York: Middle East Institute, Columbia University, 1971.

Cohen, Mark I., and Hahn, Lorna. *Morocco: Old Land, New Nation.* New York: Praeger, 1966.

Couvreun, G. "Presentation du plan quinquennal, 1968-1972," *Revue du Geographique Maroc* [Rabat], No. 14, 1968, 151-162.

Cowan, L. Gray, et al. *Education and Nation-Building in Africa.* New York: Praeger, 1965.

Crawford, R. "Cultural Change and Communication in Morocco," *Human Organization*, XXIV, No. 1, Spring 1965, 73-77.

Dadci, Younes. *Petite Histoire du Cinema Algerien.* Paris: Copedith, n.d.

Durand-Reville, L. "Le Maroc en voie de modernisation," *Revue Politique et Parlamentaire* [Paris], No. 789, May 1968, 47-56.

Engelbracht, Ursel. "Das Erzichungswesen im Marokko," *Orient* [Hamburg], V, No. 66, October 1966, 151-156.

Europa Publications. *Middle East and North Africa, 1970-71.* London: 1970.

_____. *World of Learning, 1970-71.* 21st ed. London: 1971.

"A Frontiersman in the States," *Economist* [London], CCXXII, No. 6442, February 11, 1967, 508.

Gaiser, Willy. *Berbersiedlungen im Sudmarokko.* (Geographisches Institutes der Universitat Tübingen Series.) Tübingen: n.pub., 1968.

Garnier, Jean-Claude. "Marruecos: Adiestramiento y Utilización de las Trabajadoras de Campo en Planificación Familiar," *Estudios de Planificación Familiar* [Bogotá], IV, No. 2, 1970, 175-182.

Geertz, Clifford. "In Search of North Africa," *New York Review of Books*, April 22, 1971, 20-24.

Greenberg, Joseph H. *Studies in African Linguistic Classification.* New Haven: Compass, 1955.

Halstead, John P. *Rebirth of a Nation: The Origins and Rise of Moroccan Nationalism, 1912–1944.* (Harvard Middle Eastern Monographs, No. 18.) Cambridge: Center for Middle Eastern Studies, Harvard University Press, 1967.

Hance, William A. *The Geography of Modern Africa.* New York: Columbia University Press, 1964, 78.

Hart, David M. "Segmentary Systems and the Role of 'Five Fifths' in Tribal Morocco," *Revue de l'Occident Musulmane et de la Mediterranée* [Aix-en-Provence], III, 1967, 65–95.

Hess, John L. "Jews of Morocco Shaken by an Attempted Coup," *New York Times*, July 25, 1971, 11.

Hitti, Philip K. *The Near East in History.* New York: Van Nostrand, 1961.

Hoffman, Bernard G. *The Structure of Traditional Moroccan Society.* The Hague: Mouton, 1967.

Hoffmann, Eleanor. *Realm of the Evening Star.* New York: Chilton Books, 1965.

"How to Help a Fellah," *Atlas*, XII, December 1966, 37–38.

Hurewitz, Jacob C. (ed.) *Soviet-American Rivalry in the Middle East.* New York: Praeger, 1969.

International Planned Parenthood Federation. *Situation Report.* London: October 1969.

Ismael, Tareq Y. *Governments and Politics of the Contemporary Middle East.* Homewood: Dorsey Press, 1970.

Joseph, Roger. "Rituals and Relatives: A Study of the Social Uses of Wealth in Morocco." Unpublished doctoral dissertation, Department of Anthropology, University of California at Los Angeles, 1967.

Khadduri, Majid. *Political Trends in the Arab World.* Baltimore: Johns Hopkins Press, 1970.

Kinsman, James. "New Alignments in the Maghreb," *New Middle East* [London], No. 29, February 1971, 23–27.

Kodjo, Samuel. "Betrachtungen uber einige Aspekte der Hochschulbildung im Afrika: das Beispiel des franzosischsprachigen Afrika," *Kölner Zeitung für Soziologie und Socialpsychologie* [Cologne], December 1969, 587–605.

Kroneberg, Eckart. *Zum Beispiel, Marokko.* Munich: R. Piper, 1970.

Lahlimi, Ahmed. "Quelques reflexions sur les collectivités rurales traditionnelles et leur évolution," *Bulletin Economique et Social du Maroc* [Rabat], XXIX, Nos. 106–107, July–December 1967, 59–84.

Lahlou, Abbès. "La Bourgeoisie: Symbols et Reflect Direct de l'Occidentalisation de la Societé Marocaine," *Civilisations* [Brussels], XIV, Nos. 1 and 2, 1964, 62–84.

Landau, Rom. *The Alaouite Dynasty: Art and Architecture* (mimeo., Moroccan Embassy in Washington).

──────. *Morocco.* New York: G. P. Putnam's Sons, 1967.
Landau, Rom, et al. *Marokko.* Cologne: Verlag M. DuMont Schammberg, 1969.
Lapham, Robert J. "Actitudes, conocimiento, y practica de la planificación familiar en la Llanuara de Said," *Estudios de Planificación Familiar* [Bogotá], No. 58, October 1970, 22-43.
──────. "Social Control in the Sais," *Anthropological Quarterly,* XLII, No. 3, July 1969, 244-262.
Laqueur, Walter Z. *The Struggle for the Middle East.* New York: Macmillan, 1969.
Lazarev, Grigori. "Changement Social et Developpement dans les Campagnes Marocaines," *Bulletin Economique et Social du Maroc* [Rabat], XXX, No. 109, April-June 1968, 19-33.
Le Tourneau, Roger. "North Africa to the Sixteenth Century." Pages 211-237 in P. M. Holt, A. K. S. Lambton, and B. Lewis (eds.), *The Cambridge History of Islam,* II. Cambridge: Cambridge University Press, 1970.
Lewis, William H. "Rural Administration in Morocco," *Middle East Journal,* XIV, No. 2, Winter 1960, 45-60.
MacDonald, Robert W. *The League of Arab States.* Princeton: Princeton University Press, 1965.
Mantran, R. "North Africa in the Sixteenth and Seventeenth Centuries." Pages 238-266 in P. M. Holt, A. K. S. Lambton, and B. Lewis (eds.), *The Cambridge History of Islam,* II. Cambridge: Cambridge University Press, 1970.
"Maroc," *Monde Diplomatique* (Supplement) [Paris], XVII, No. 192, March 25, 1970, No. 192, 34.
"Le Maroc dans la Voie du Developpement et du Progrès," *Monde Diplomatique* [Paris], XVII, No. 192, March 1970, 25-44.
Marouni, Abdallah. *Culture et Enseignement en Algerie et au Maghreb.* Paris: F. Maspero, 1969.
Martensson, Mona. "Attitudes vis-a-vis du Travail Professionnel de les Femmes Marocaines," *Bulletin Economique et Social du Maroc* [Rabat], XXVIII, No. 100, January-March 1966, 133-145.
Masland, John W. *Educational Development in Africa: The Role of United States Assistance.* (Occasional Report No. 4.) New York: Education and World Affairs, 1967.
Maxwell, Gavin. *Lords of the Atlas.* London: Longsman, Green, 1966.
Monteil, Vincent. *Morocco.* New York: Viking Press, 1964.
Moore, Clement Henry. *Politics in North Africa: Algeria, Morocco, Tunisia.* Boston: Little, Brown, 1970.
"Morocco." Pages 845-855 in *Encyclopaedia Britannica,* XV. Chicago: Encyclopaedia Britannica, 1969.
Morocco. Conseil Superieur de la Promotion Nationale et du Plan. *Plan Triennal 1965-67: Travaux.* Rabat: Government of Morocco Press, 1965.

Morocco. General Delegation for National Promotion and Planning. *Three-year Plan, 1965-67: Economic Coordination and Planning Development*. Rabat: n.pub., 1965.

Morocco. Ministère de l'Information. *Maroc, 1969: Synthese*. Rabat: Mohammedia, 1969.

Morocco. Ministère des Affaires Economiques, du Plan et de la Formation des Cadres. *Plan Quinquennal, 1968-1972*. Rabat: n.pub., 1969.

Morocco. Ministère d'Etat. Chargé du Plan et de la Formation des Cadres. Division du Plan et des Statistiques. *La Situation Economique du Maroc en 1968*. Rabat: Government of Morocco Press, May 1969.

Morocco. Ministry of Information. *Le Maroc*. Rabat: Government of *Morocco Press, 1966*.

Morocco. Secretaria del Estado para Planificación. División de Estadística. "Conocimiento, Actitudes y práctica de la planificación familiar en las zonas rurales," *Estudios de Planificación Familiar* [Bogotá], No. 58, October 1970, 1-11.

_____. "Encuesta de actitudes respecto a la planificación familiar en las zonas urbanas," *Estudios de Planificación Familiar* [Bogotá], No. 58, October 1970, 12-21.

Moullard, L. "Les Resources en Eau du Maroc," *Les Hommes, La Terre, L'Eau* [Rabat] (Bulletin de Liaison et d'Information de l'Office Nationale des Irrigations), No. 1, December 1961, 17-34.

Nija'i, Jamilah al. "Achievements and Future Plans of National Union of Moroccan Women," *al-Anba*, Rabat, May 8, 1970. [Translated by U.S. Department of Commerce, Office of Technical Services, Joint Publications Research Service (Washington), JPRS: 50,749, *Translations on Africa*, No. 909, June 16, 1970.]

Noin, Daniel. "Aspects du Sous-Developpement au Maroc," *Annales de Géographie* [Paris], LXXV, No. 410, July-August 1966, 410-431.

_____. "L'Urbanisation du Maroc," *L'Information Geographique* [Paris], March-April 1968, 69-81.

Nouschi, André. "North Africa in the Period of Colonization." Pages 299-326 in P. M. Holt, A. K. S. Lambton, and B. Lewis (eds.), *The Cambridge History of Islam*, II. Cambridge: Cambridge University Press, 1970.

Nutting, Anthony. *The Arabs: A Narrative History from Mohammed to the Present*. New York: Clarkson N. Potter, 1965.

"L'Orientation de Pensée du Maroc Actual à travers les Manuels Scolaires en Langue Arabe," *Maghreb: Etudes et Documents* [Paris], No. 36, November-December 1969, 36-41.

Ortzen, Len (ed. and trans.). *North African Writing*. (African Writers Series, No. 73.) London: Heinemann Educational Books, 1970.

Pascon, P. "Population et Developpement," *Bulletin Economique et Social du Maroc* [Rabat], XXIX, Nos. 104-105, January-June 1967, 27-42.

Pigé, Francois. *Radiodiffusion et Television au Maghreb*. (Etudes Maghrebines Series, No. 6.) Paris: Fondation Nationale des Sciences Politiques, Centre d'Etude des Relations Internationales, 1966.

Press, Richard. "Marrakech: A Traditional City in a Changing Society." (Foreign Affairs Research Series No. 2842; Paper presented at African Studies Association Meeting, October 1965.) Washington: Department of State, 1966.

"Problèmes Frontaliers et Territoriaux au Maghreb," *Maghreb: Etudes et Documents* [Paris], XXXVIII, March–April 1970, 35–41.

"Projects et Problèmes de l'Agriculture Marocaine," *Maghreb: Etudes et Documents* [Paris], XXIV, November–December 1967, 27–33.

Proust, J. *Cost of Public Education in Morocco*. Paris: United Nations Educational, Scientific, and Cultural Organization, International Institute of Educational Planning, 1970.

Raymond, André. "North Africa in the Pre-Colonial Period." Pages 266–298 in P. M. Holt, A. K. S. Lambton, and B. Lewis (eds.), *The Cambridge History of Islam*, II. Cambridge: Cambridge University Press, 1970.

"Recent and Current Dam Work Reviewed," *La Vie Economique*, Rabat, March 26, 1971, 1–3. [Translated by U.S. Department of Commerce, Office of Technical Services, Joint Publications Research Service (Washington), JPRS: 53,153, *Translations on Africa*, No. 1034, May 17, 1971.]

"La Regulations des Naissances au Maghreb," *Maghreb: Etudes et Documents* [Paris], No. 25, January–February 1968, 9–12.

Religious Foundations and Islamic Affairs. Rabat: Ministry of Information, Government of Morocco Press, n.d.

Reports on Population and Family Planning. New York: Population Council, Columbia University, December 1969.

Rosenbloom, Joseph R. "A Note on the Size of the Jewish Communities in the South of Morocco," *Jewish Journal of Sociology* [London], II, December 1966, 209–212.

Rosen, Lawrence. "Moslem-Jewish Relations in a Moroccan City," *International Journal of Middle East Studies* [London] (in press).

———. "The Rope of Satan: Social Relations and Reality Bargaining Among Moroccan Men and Women." Princeton: Institute for Advanced Study, n.d. (mimeo.).

———. "Rural Political Process and National Political Structure in Morocco." In Richard T. Antoun and Iliya Harik (eds.), *Rural Politics and Social Change in the Middle East*. Bloomington: Indiana University Press (forthcoming).

Schaar, Stuart H. *The Mass Media in Morocco*. (Foreign Affairs Research Series No. 6881.) Washington: Department of State, 1968.

Schorger, William D. "The Evolution of Political Forms in a North Moroccan Village," *Anthropological Quarterly*, XLII, No. 3, July 1969, 263–286.

Seddon, J. David. "Social and Economic Change in Northeast Morocco," *Current Anthropology*, XII, No. 2, April 1971, 227-229.

Selosse, Jacques. "Perception du Changement Social par une Population Citadine Marocaine," *Revue Française de Sociologie* [Paris], IV, January–March 1963, 144-158.

Shuster, James R. "Bureaucratic Transition in Morocco," *Human Organization*, XXIV, No. 1, 1965, 53-58.

"Sidi Ahmad Circumcised," *Daily Star* [Beirut], March 11, 1971, 2.

Staniland, Martin. "Frantz Fanon and the African Political Class," *African Affairs* [London], LXVIII, No. 270, January 1969, 4-25.

Statistical Yearbook, 1969. Paris: United Nations Educational, Scientific, and Cultural Organization, 1970.

Sylvester, Anthony. "Report on Morocco," *Contemporary Review* [London], CCXI, No. 1220, September 1967, 124-131.

Troin, J. F. "Aspects Geographique de l'Expansion du Tourisme au Maroc," *Revue de Geographie du Maroc* [Rabat], No. 11, 1967, 3-66.

――――. "Observations sur les Soubkes de la Region d'Azrou et de Khenifra," *Revue de Geographie du Maroc* [Rabat], Nos. 3 and 4, 1963, 109-120.

Trout, Frank E. *Morocco's Saharan Frontiers*. Geneva: Dros, 1969.

U.S. Department of State. *Kingdom of Morocco: Background Notes*. Washington: GPO, November 1969.

U.S. Department of State. Office of the Geographer. *Morocco-Spanish Sahara Boundary*. Washington: GPO, September 14, 1961.

Vaciri, M. "Experience de Modernisation en Milieu Rural Marocain," *Revue Tunisienne de Science Social* [Tunis], December 1968, 121-138.

Vidal, F.S. "Religious Brotherhoods in Moroccan Politics," *Middle East Journal*, IV, No. 4, October 1950, 427-446.

Waterbury, John. *The Commander of the Faithful: The Moroccan Political Elite; A Study in Segmented Politics*. (Modern Middle East Series.) New York: Columbia University Press, 1970.

World Radio-TV Handbook, 1971. (Ed., J. M. Frost) (25th ed.) Hellerup: World Radio-Television Handbook Co., 1971.

(Various issues of the following periodical were also used in the preparation of this section: *Maghreb: Etudes et Documents* [Paris], November 1967–December 1967; and *Maroc Documents* [Rabat], May 1968–March 1969.)

Section II. Political

RECOMMENDED SOURCES

al-Fasi, Allal. *The Independence Movements in Arab North Africa.* Washington: American Council of Learned Societies, 1954.

———. "Party President Addresses Istiqlal National Council," *L'Opinion*, Rabat, March 16, 1971. [Translated by U.S. Department of Commerce, Office of Technical Services, Joint Publications Research Service (Washington), JPRS: 52,905, *Translations on Africa*, No. 1022, April 16, 1971.]

al Kader, Abd. "Disclosures Concerning the Moroccan Communist Party," *Remarques Africaines*, Brussels, April 10, 1971. [Translated by U.S. Department of Commerce, Office of Technical Services, Joint Publications Research Service (Washington), JPRS: 53,286, *Translations on North Africa*, No. 1041, June 4, 1971.]

Ashford, Douglas E. *Perspectives of a Moroccan Nationalist.* Totowa, New Jersey: Bedminster Press, 1964.

———. *Political Change in Morocco.* Princeton: Princeton University Press, 1964.

———. "Politics of Rural Mobilization in North Africa," *Journal of Modern Africa Studies* [London], VII, No. 2, July 1969, 187–202.

Beling, Willard A. "Some Implications of the New Constitutional Monarchy in Morocco," *Middle East Journal*, XVIII, No. 2, Spring 1964, 163–179.

Ben Barka, Mehdi. *Option Revolutionnaire au Maroc.* Paris: François Maspero, 1966.

Bouabid, Abdul Rahim. "The Rules of the Game," *Le Nouvel Observateur* [Paris], July 26, 1970, 16–17.

Cantori, Louis J. *Local Leadership Characteristics of the Istiqlal Party of Morocco.* (Foreign Affairs Research Series No. 13687.) New York: Middle East Institute, Columbia University, 1971.

Cohen, Amnon. "Allal al-Fasi: His Ideas and His Contribution Towards Morocco's Independence," *Asian and African Studies* [Jerusalem], III, 1967, 121–164.

Daniel, Jean. "I Prefer My Country to My Throne," *Le Nouvel Observateur* [Paris], July 6, 1970, 18–20.

Gallagher, Charles F. *Ben Barka and the National Union.* (American Universities Field Staff Reports Service, North Africa Series, V, No. 5.) New York: AUFS, September 1959.

———. *The Meanings of the Moroccan Elections.* (American Universities Field Staff Reports Service, North Africa Series, IX, No. 5.) New York: AUFS, June 1963.

———. *The Moroccanization of Morocco.* (American Universities Field Staff Reports Service, North Africa Series, IV, No. 2.) New York: AUFS, February 1958.

———. *A Moroccan Political Party: The Istiqlal.* (American Universities Field Staff Reports Service, North Africa Series, II, No. 2.) New York: AUFS, July 1956.

———. *New Laws for Old: The Moroccan Code of Personal Status.* (American Universities Field Staff Reports Service, North Africa Series, V, No. 1.) New York: AUFS, June 1959.

———. *North African Crossroads, Part I: The Reign of Muhammad V.* (American Universities Field Staff Reports Service, North Africa Series, VII, No. 2.) New York: AUFS, April 1961.

———. *North African Problems and Prospects, Part III: Language and Identity.* (American Universities Field Staff Reports Service, North Africa Series, X, No. 5.) New York: AUFS, June 1964.

———. *Toward Constitutional Government in Morocco.* (American Universities Field Staff Reports Service, North Africa Series, IX, No. 1.) New York: AUFS, June 1963.

———. *The United States and North Africa.* Cambridge: Harvard University Press, 1963.

Geertz, Clifford. "The Commander of the Faithful: The Moroccan Political Elite; A Study in Segmented Politics (Book Review)," *Middle Eastern Studies* [London], VII, No. 2, May 1971, 251-255.

———. *Islam Observed: Religious Development in Morocco and Indonesia.* New Haven: Yale University Press, 1968.

Gibb, Hamilton A. R. "Constitutional Organization." Pages 5-95 in Majid Khadduri and Herbert J. Liebesny (eds.), *Law in the Middle East, I: Origin and Development of Islamic Law.* Washington: The Middle East Institute, 1955.

Gordon, David C. *North Africa's French Legacy, 1954-1962.* (Harvard Middle Eastern Monographs, No. 9.) Cambridge: Center for Middle Eastern Studies, Harvard University Press, 1962.

Halpern, Manfred. *The Politics of Social Change in the Middle East and North Africa.* Princeton: Princeton University Press, 1965.

Hauptfuhrer, Fred. "King Hassan's Claims to Leadership," *New Middle East* [London], No. 17, February 1970, 29-31.

Johnson, Katherine Marshall. *Urban Government for the Prefecture of Casablanca.* (The International Urban Studies of the Institute of Public Administration, No. 7.) New York: Praeger, 1970.

Kinsman, James. "New Alignments in the Maghreb," *New Middle East* [London], No. 29, February 1971, 23-27.

Laroui, Abdallah. *Cultural Problems and Social Structure: The Campaign for Arabization in Morocco.* (Foreign Affairs Research Series No. 13700.) Washington: Department of State, 1971.

Laws, statutes, etc. of Morocco.
U.S. Department of Commerce. Office of Technical Services. Joint Publication Research Service—JPRS (Washington). The following items are from the JPRS series *Translations on North Africa*.

"Decree No. 1-70-194, 31 July 1970, 'Organic Law on the Constitutional Chamber of the Supreme Court'," *Bulletin Officiel*, Rabat, August 1, 1970. (JPRS: 51,343, Series No. 940, September 10, 1970.)

"Decree No. 1-70-206, 31 July 1970, 'Organic Law Concerning the Makeup and Election of the Chamber of Representatives'," *Bulletin Officiel*, Rabat, August 1, 1970. (JPRS: 51,343, Series No. 940, September 10, 1970.)

"Decree No. 1-71-77, 16 June 1971, 'Creation of Administrative Regions'," *Bulletin Officiel*, Rabat, June 23, 1971. (JPRS: 53,721, Series No. 1055, July 30, 1971.)

"Decree No. 2-69-587, 29 January 1970, 'Creation of a National Institute of Judiciary Studies'," *Bulletin Officiel*, Rabat, February 4, 1970. (JPRS: 50,196, Series No. 882, March 31, 1970.)

Moore, Clement Henry. "The Commander of the Faithful: The Moroccan Political Elite; A Study in Segmented Politics (Book Review)," *American Political Science Review*, LXV, No. 2, June 1971, 570-571.

──────. *Politics in North Africa: Algeria, Morocco, Tunisia*. Boston: Little, Brown, 1970.

Moore, Clement Henry, and Hochschild, Arbie R. "Student Unions in North African Politics," *Daedalus*, XCVII, No. 1, Winter 1968, 20-50.

Morocco. Embassy in Washington. "Address Delivered by His Majesty Hassan II of Morocco on the Occasion of the Eighth Anniversary of His Accession to the Throne, March 3, 1969," *Statements and Documents*, V, No. 11, March 1969, 1-31.

Morocco. Embassy in Washington. "Address Delivered by His Majesty King Hassan II of Morocco on the Occasion of the Tenth Anniversary of His Accession to the Throne, March 3, 1971." Washington: 1971 (mimeo.).

Morocco. Embassy in Washington. "Interview Granted by His Majesty Hassan II to Raymond Tournoux," *Statements and Documents*, V, No. 4, February 1968, n.p.

"Morocco: The Royal Escape," *Africa Confidential* [London], XXII, No. 15, July 23, 1971, 1-4.

Rosen, Lawrence. "Rural Political Process and National Political Struture in Morocco." In Richard T. Antoun and Iliya Harik (eds.), *Rural Politics and Social Change in the Middle East*. Bloomington: Indiana University Press (forthcoming).

Schaar, Stuart. "The Commander of the Faithful: The Moroccan Political Elite; A Study in Segmented Politics (Book Review)," *Middle East Journal*, XXV, No. 1, Winter 1971, 102-103.

Spencer, William. "Morocco's Monarchical Balancing Act," *Africa Report*, XV, No. 9, December 1970, 19-21.

Steel, Ronald (ed.). *North Africa*. New York: H. W. Wilson, 1967.

Waterbury, John. *Commander of the Faithful: The Moroccan Political Elite; A Study in Segmented Politics*. (Modern Middle East Series.) New York: Columbia University Press, 1970.

――――. "Kingdom-Building and the Control of the Opposition in Morocco: The Monarchical Uses of Justice," *Government and Opposition* [London], V, No. 1, Winter 1970, 54-66.

――――. "The Place of the Public Administration and Administrative Elite in the Moroccan Political System." (Paper presented at the Conference on North Africa, Middle East Institute, Columbia University, March 1971.) (mimeo.)

Zartman, I. William. *Destiny of a Dynasty: The Search for Institutions in Morocco's Developing Society*. Columbia: R. L. Bryan, 1964.

――――. *Government and Politics in Northern Africa*. New York: Praeger, 1963.

――――. *Problems of New Power: Morocco*. New York: Atherton Press, 1964.

OTHER SOURCES USED

Adam, André. *Casablanca: Essai sur la Transformation de la Societé Marocaine au Contact de l'Occident*. Paris: Editions du Centre National de la Recherche Scientifique, 1968.

Adam, André, and Maurer, Gerard Louis. "Morocco." Pages 845-855 in *Encyclopaedia Britannica*, XV. Chicago: Encyclopaedia Britannica, 1969.

"And Then There Were Still Four—," *Economist* [London], CCXL, No. 6673, July 17, 1971, 15-16.

Antar, Abou. "Ou Va Le Maroc? Hassan II, Les Grandes Puissances, et Le Maghreb," *Jeune Afrique* [Paris], No. 551, July 27, 1971, 44-45.

Arntsen, Andrea, and Ansell, Gladyce W. *Inter-Arab Cooperation and U.S. Policy*. (Technical Paper RAC-TP-396.) McLean, Virginia: Research Analysis Corporation, June 1970.

Balafrej, Ahmed. "Morocco Plans for Independence," *Foreign Affairs*, XXIV, No. 3, April 1956, 483-489.

Barbour, Nevill. "Spain in Morocco: A Retrospect," *World Today* [London], XXII, No. 8, August 1956, 313-321.

Becker, A. S., and Horelick, A. L. *Soviet Policy in the Middle East*. (Rand Abstract 504-FF.) Santa Monica: Rand Corporation, 1970.

Boulanger, Robert. *Morocco*. Paris: Hachette World Guides, 1966.

Brown, Leon Carl (ed.). *State and Society in Independent North Africa*. Washington: Middle East Institute, 1966.

Charoub, Akin. "Ou Va Le Maroc? Hassan II, L'Armée, L'Opposition, et Le Peuple," *Jeune Afrique* [Paris], No. 551, July 27, 1971, 42–43.

"China, the Arab World, and Africa: A Factual Survey, 1959–1964," *Mizan Newsletter* [London], VI, No. 5, May 1964, 24–26.

Cohen, Mark I., and Hahn, Lorna. *Morocco: Old Land, New Nation*. New York: Praeger, 1966.

Europa Publications. *Middle East and North Africa, 1970–71*. London: 1970.

Field, James A., Jr. *America and the Mediterranean World, 1776–1882*. Princeton: Princeton University Press, 1969.

Fodor, Eugene; Curtis, William; and Glavert, Betty (eds.). *Morocco, 1965–1966*. New York: McKay, 1965.

France. Embassy in Washington. Service de Presse et d'Information. *French Foreign Policy: Official Statements, Speeches and Communiques, 1966–1968*. New York: n.pub., n.d.

"France in North Africa," *Round Table* [London], CLXXXIII, June 1956, 230–235.

"France-Morocco: Joint Declaration; Diplomatic Accord," *American Journal of International Law*, LI, July 1957, 676–683.

Gallagher, Charles F. *France in Morocco: A Former Colony Lives Amicably with the French*. (American Universities Field Staff Reports Service, North Africa Series, VIII, No. 1.) New York: AUFS, September 1962.

──────. *Morocco and Its Neighbors: Morocco and Algeria*. (American Universities Field Staff, North Africa Series, XIII, No. 3.) New York: AUFS, March 1967.

──────. *Morocco and Its Neighbors: Morocco and Mauritania*. (American Universities Field Staff, North Africa Series, XIII, No. 4.) New York: AUFS, April 1967.

──────. *Morocco and Its Neighbors: Morocco and Spain*. (American Universities Field Staff, North Africa Series, XIII, No. 2.) New York: AUFS, March 1967.

──────. *Morocco and Its Neighbors: Morocco and the United States*. (American Universities Field Staff, North Africa Series, XIII, No. 5.) New York: AUFS, May 1967.

Gaudio, Attilio. "L'Opposition au Maroc," *Jeune Afrique* [Paris], No. 548, July 6, 1971, 31–34.

Gibb, Hamilton A. R. "The Heritage of Islam in the Modern World, I," *International Journal of Middle East Studies* [London], I, No. 1, January 1970, 3–17.

──────. "The Heritage of Islam in the Modern World, II," *International Journal of Middle East Studies* [London], I, No. 3, July 1970, 221–237.

Holt, P. M.; Lambton, Ann K. S.; and Lewis, Bernard (eds.). *The Cambridge History of Islam*, II: The Further Islamic Lands, Islamic Society and Civilization. Cambridge: Cambridge University Press, 1970.

Hourani, Albert. *Arabic Thought in the Liberal Age, 1798-1939*. New York: Oxford University Press, 1967.

Hughes, Stephen. "France and Morocco: Deep-Rooted Friendship," *Middle East International* [London], No. 2, May 1971, 26-27.

Irwin, R. W. *The Diplomatic Relations Between the United States and the Barbary Powers, 1776-1816*. Chapel Hill: University of North Carolina Press, 1931.

Julien, Charles-André. "Morocco: The End of an Era," *Foreign Affairs*, XXXIV, No. 2, January 1956, 199-211.

Kanovsky, E. "Arab Economic Unity," *Middle East Journal*, XXI, No. 2, Spring 1967, 213-235.

Khadduri, Majid. *Political Trends in the Arab World*. Baltimore: Johns Hopkins Press, 1970.

Landau, Rom. *Hassan II: King of Morocco*. London: Allen and Unwin, 1962.

Legris, Michel. "Morocco: Treason Came Wearing Yellow," *Le Monde* [Paris], July 22-28, 1971, 1, 3.

Legum, Colin, and Drysdale, John. *Africa Contemporary Record: Annual Survey of Documents, 1969-1970*. London: Africa Research, 1970.

Lehrman, Hal. "North Africa and the West," *Reporter* [Nairobi], XVIII, No. 11, May 29, 1958.

Peaslee, Amos J. (ed.) *Constitutions of Nations*. The Hague: Martinus Nijhoff, 1965.

Reyner, Anthony S. "Morocco's International Boundaries: A Factual Background," *Journal of Modern African Studies* [London], I, No. 3, 1963, 313-326.

Schaar, Stuart. "L'Affaire Ben Barka: The Kidnapping Casts Its Shadow," *Africa Report*, XI, No. 3, March 1966, 37-41.

_____. *The Arms Race and Defense Strategy*. (American Universities Field Staff Reports, North Africa Series, XIII, No. 9.) New York: AUFS, December 1967.

_____. "Hassan's Morocco," *Africa Report*, X, No. 7, July 1965, 6-14.

_____. "King Hassan's Alternatives," *Africa Report*, VIII, No. 8, August 1963, 7-12.

Singh, K. R. "Morocco Since Independence: A Study of Political Cross-Currents," *Afro-Asia and World Affairs* [New Delhi], I, No. 2, January 1964, 120-130.

Spencer, William. *The Land and People of Morocco*. Philadelphia: Lippincott, 1965.

"Status of Tangier: Final Declaration and Annexed Protocol of the International Conference of Tangier," *American Journal of International Law*, LI, April 1957, 460-466.

Sterling, Claire. "Morocco's Troubled Young King," *Reporter* [Nairobi], IV, No. 135, June 17, 1965, 21-24.

Sylvester, Anthony. "Report on Morocco," *Contemporary Review* [London], CCXI, No. 1220, September 1967, 124-131.

Thomas, Frederic C., Jr. "The Peace Corps in Morocco," *Middle East Journal*, XIX, No. 3, Summer 1965, 273-283.

Touval, Saadia. "Africa's Frontiers: Reactions to a Colonial Legacy," *International Affairs* [London], XLII, No. 4, October 1966, 641-654.

Trout, Frank E. *Morocco's Saharan Frontier*. Geneva: Dros, 1969.

U.S. Department of State. *Kingdom of Morocco: Background Notes*. Washington: November 1969.

Veysoglu, Recep. "Scientific and Technological Aspects of Government Personnel and Process in Morocco." Doctoral dissertation, University of Missouri at Kansas City, 1967. Kansas City: University of Missouri at Kansas City, 1967.

Vidal, F. S. "Religious Brotherhoods in Moroccan Politics," *Middle East Journal*, IV, No. 4, October 1950, 427-446.

Wolf, Jean. "Rabat: Le Mutinerie Sanglante," *Jeune Afrique* [Paris], No. 550, July 20, 1971, 21-33.

Yahmed, Bechir Ben. "Rabat: Un Roi, Une Armée, Un Peuple," *Jeune Afrique* [Paris], No. 550, July 20, 1971, 19.

Young, Richard. "The End of American Consular Jurisdiction in Morocco," *American Journal of International Law*, LI, No. 2, April 1957.

Zartman, I. William. "Political Pluralism in Morocco," *Government and Opposition* [London], II, No. 4, July-October 1967, 568-583.

Section III. Economic

RECOMMENDED SOURCES

Banque Marocaine du Commerce Exterieur. *Facts and Figures on Morocco.* (4th and 5th eds.) Casablanca: Imprimeries Reunis, 1969, 1970.
International Bank for Reconstruction and Development. *The Economic Development of Morocco.* Baltimore: Johns Hopkins University Press, 1966.
Morocco. Ministry of Economic Affairs, Planning and the Training of Senior Grades. *Five Year Plan, 1968-72.* 2 vols. Rabat: Government of Morocco Press, 1968.
Nehrt, Lee Charles. *The Political Climate for Foreign Investment with Special Reference to North Africa.* New York: Praeger, 1970.
Stewart, Charles F. *The Economy of Morocco, 1912-1962.* Cambridge: Harvard University Press, 1964.

OTHER SOURCES USED

Banque Marocaine du Commerce Exterieur. "Amended Finance Law for 1968," *Monthly Bulletin of Information* [Rabat], No. 84, April 1968, 1, 24.
———. "The Automobile Industry in Morocco (A Study)," *Bulletin Mensuel d'Information* [Casablanca], No. 107, July-August 1970, 3-27.
———. "The Balance of Payments for 1969," *Bulletin Mensuel d'Information* [Casablanca], No. 103, March 1970, 3-23.
———. "Banking Reform," *Monthly Bulletin of Information* [Rabat], No. 75, May 1967, 1, 2, 11-16.
———. "The Continents in Morocco's Foreign Trade in 1969," *Bulletin Mensuel d'Information* [Casablanca], No. 106, June 1970, 3-23.
———. "Insurance in Morocco," *Monthly Bulletin of Information* [Rabat], No. 93, March 1969, 3-19.
———. "Moroccan Oil Growing," *Bulletin Mensuel d'Information* [Casablanca], No. 101, January 1970, 3-10.
———. "The Role of Communications: Air Transport in Morocco," *Bulletin Mensuel d'Information* [Casablanca], No. 100, November-December 1970, 1-44.

———. "Tourism," *Bulletin Mensuel d'Information* [Casablanca], No. 102, February 1970, 1–21.

———. "Trade Exchanges of Morocco in 1969," *Bulletin Mensuel d'Information* [Casablanca], No. 105, May 1970, 3–24.

"Business Outlook: Morocco," *Business Europe* [Geneva], September 25, 1970, 311.

Chemical Bank New York Trust Company. *International Economic Survey: Morocco*. New York: Chemical Bank New York Trust Company, 1968.

Cherkaoui, Souad. "Le Dette Publique Interieure au Maroc," *Bulletin Economique et Social du Maroc* [Rabat], XXXI, No. 115, October–December 1969, 53–98.

Cohen, Mark I., and Hahn, Lorna. *Morocco: Old Land, New Nation*. New York: Praeger, 1966.

Comité Monetaire de la Zone Franc. *La Zone Franc en 1969*. Paris: 1970.

Commodity Research Bureau. *Commodity Yearbook, 1971*. New York: 1971.

"The Construction of a Highway Network in Morocco," *Road International* [Geneva], LXXIV, September 1969, 15–17.

Europa Publications. *The Middle East and North Africa 1970–71: Morocco*. London: 1970.

First National City Bank of New York. *Morocco: An Economic Study*. New York: 1967.

"Floods May Slow Morocco," *International Commerce*, LXXVI, No. 9, March 2, 1970, 29–31.

Fodor, Eugene, and Curtis, William. *Fodor's Morocco, 1971*. London: Hodder and Stroughton, 1971.

Food and Agriculture Organization. *World Forest Inventory, 1963*. Rome: 1963.

Foster, Phillips W. *Research on Agricultural Development in North Africa*. New York: Agricultural Development Council, 1967.

Gallagher, Charles F. *North African Problems and Prospects, I: Rural Reform and Revolution*. (American Universities Field Staff Reports Service, North Africa Series, X, No. 2.) New York: AUFS, February 1964.

———. *North African Problems and Prospects, II: Industrialization and Development*. (American Universities Field Staff Reports Service, North Africa Series, X, No. 3.) New York: AUFS, March 1964.

International Monetary Fund. *International Financial Statistics*, XXIV, No. 8, August 1971, 240–243.

———. *International Financial Statistics: Supplement to 1967/68 Issues*. Washington: 1968.

———. *Twenty-First Annual Report on Exchange Restrictions*. Washington: 1970.

Investment in Morocco (2d ed.) Rabat: Moroccan Investment Promotion Center, July 1969.

Klein, Carolyn K. "Establishing a Business in Morocco," *Overseas Business Reports*. (OBR 70-51.) Washington: Department of Commerce, Bureau of International Commerce, September 1970.

Marthelot, P. "Histoire et réalité de la modernisation du monde rural au Maroc," *Tiers-Monde* [Paris], II, No. 6, April-June 1961, 137-168.

Minerals Yearbook, 1968. Washington: GPO, 1970.

"Morocco-France Development Projects," *Africa Research Bulletin* [Exeter, England], VIII, No. 6, June 15-July 14, 1971, 2,084.

Morocco. Laws, Statutes, etc.

The Agricultural Investment Code. (Dahir No. 1-69-25 of 25 July 1969.) Rabat: Government of Morocco Press, 1969.

Basic Finance Law of November 9, 1963. (Decree 1-63-326.) Rabat: Government of Morocco Press, 1963.

Constitution (1970). Rabat: Government of Morocco Press, 1970.

Law on Banking and Credit of April 26, 1967. (Decree 1967-68.) Rabat: Government of Morocco Press, 1967.

Loi de Finances pour l'Année 1969. (Dahir No. 1012-68, 31 Decembre 1965.) Rabat: Government of Morocco Press, 1966.

Loi de Finances pour l'Année 1966. (Decret Royal No. 1010-65, 31 December 1965.) Rabat: Government of Morocco Press, 1966.

Morocco. Embassy in Washington. Economic Section. *Economic News from Morocco*. January-February 1971, 26.

Morocco. Ministère d'Etat. Chargé du Plan et de la Formation des Cadres. Division du Plan et des Statistiques. *La Situation Economique du Maroc en 1968*. Rabat: Government of Morocco Press, May 1969.

Production Yearbook, XXIII. Rome: Food and Agriculture Organization, 1970.

Santmyer, Carolee. *Morocco's Agriculture in Brief*. Washington: U.S. Department of Agriculture, 1968.

Stamp, L. Dudley (ed.). *A History of Land Use in Arid Regions*. Paris: United Nations Educational, Scientific and Cultural Organization, 1961.

Statesman's Year Book, 1970-71. London: Macmillan, 1970.

Statistical Yearbook, 1969. New York: United Nations, 1970.

Statistical Yearbook, 1970. New York: United Nations, 1971.

United Nations. *Monthly Bulletin of Statistics*, XXV, No. 7, July 1971.

U.S. Agency for International Development. *Gross National Product: Growth Rates and Trend Data*. Washington: GPO, 1971.

_____. *Selected Economic Data for the Less Developed Countries*. Washington: GPO, 1971.

———. *Spring Review of Land Reform: Land Reform in Hungary, Italy, Yugoslavia—Regional Surveys*, X. Washington: June 1970.

U.S. Department of Agriculture. *Indices of Agricultural Production in Africa and the Near East*. Washington: GPO, 1971, table 1.

U.S. Department of Commerce. Bureau of International Commerce. Africa Division. "Foreign Trade Regulations: Morocco," *Overseas Business Reports* (OBR 68-102.) Washington: GPO, December 1968.

U.S. Department of Commerce. *Morocco*. (Foreign Economic Trends, ET 71-012.) Washington: GPO, 1971.

U.S. Department of Commerce. Office of Technical Services. Joint Publication Research Service—JPRS (Washington). The following items are from the JPRS series *Translations on Africa:*

"COMANAV: Pilot Flotilla and Complete Service," *La Vie Economique*, Rabat, December 12, 1969. (JPRS: 49,696, Series No. 856, 1970.)

"Easing of Retransfer Regulations Relating to Foreign Investment in Morocco," *La Vie Economique*, Rabat, February 6, 1970. (JPRS: 50,301, Series No. 889, April 13, 1970.)

"Eighteen Million Olive Trees in Morocco, but Very Irregular Production," *La Vie Economique*, Rabat, April 24, 1970. (JPRS: 50,563, Series No. 900, May 21, 1970.)

"Jaidi Explains Moroccanization of Business Sector," *Information d'Outre-Mer*, Paris, March 3, 1971. (JPRS: 52,741, Series No. 1013, 1971.)

"Long-Range Sugar Industry Planning," *Moniteur Africain*, Paris, February 19, 1970. (JPRS: 50,076, Series No. 876, 1970.)

"Moroccanization: French Investors Fear Future, Cooperants Frustrated," by Zakya Daoud in *Jeune Afrique*, Paris, April 13 and 20, 1971. (JPRS: 53,819, Series No. 1059, August 13, 1971.)

"Morocco Concluded Total of Twenty-Four Air Agreements," *La Vie Economique*, Rabat, February 20, 1970. (JPRS: 50,196, Series No. 882, 1970.)

"Restoring Confidence in Cooperatives," *La Vie Economique*, Rabat, June 5, 1971. (JPRS: 53,550, Series No. 1049, 1971.)

"Trade with Europe and Socialist State," *Information d'Outre-Mer* Paris, June 3, 1970. (JPRS: 50,856, Series No. 483, 1970.)

U.S. Embassy in Rabat. *Foreign Economic Trends and Their Implications for the United States: Morocco*. (Report No. ET-71-012.) Washington: Department of Commerce, Bureau of International Commerce, February 2, 1971.

———. "Monthly Economic Review," *Airgram*, No. 36, April 1971, 4.

U.S. Tennessee Valley Authority. *Morocco: Role of Fertilizer in Agricultural Development*. Muscle Shoals: 1967.

Verdier, J. M. *Structure Foncieres et Developpement Rural au Maghreb*. Paris: Presses Universitaires de France, 1969.

Yearbook of International Trade Statistics, 1969. New York: United Nations, 1970.

Yearbook of National Accounts Statistics, 1969. New York: United Nations, 1970.

Zartman, I. William. "North Africa and the EEC Negotiations," *Middle East Journal*, XXII, Winter 1968, 1-16.

(Various issues of the following periodicals were also used in the preparation of this section: *Bulletin Mensuel* [Rabat], January 1969-February 1971; *Middle East Economic Digest* [London], January 1967-September 1971; *Monthly Bulletin of Information* [Rabat], January 1966-February 1971; and *Quarterly Economic Review* [London], January 1967-September 1971.)

Section IV. National Security

RECOMMENDED SOURCES

Ashford, Douglas E. "Politics of Rural Mobilization in North Africa," *Journal of Modern African Studies* [London], VII, No. 2, July 1969, 187-202.
Finn, Thomas M., et al. *Morocco: Police Survey Report*. Washington: Agency for International Development, 1966.
Gutteridge, W. "Military in Africa," *African Affairs* [London], LXIX, October 1970, 366-370.
_____. "Why Does an African Army Take Power," *Africa Report*, XV, October 1970, 18-21.
Institute for Strategic Studies. *The Military Balance, 1970-71*. London: 1970.
Moore, Clement Henry. *Politics in North Africa: Algeria, Morocco, Tunisia*. Boston: Little, Brown, 1970.
Spencer, William. "Morocco's Monarchical Balancing Act," *Africa Report*, XV, No. 9, December 1970, 19-21.
Waterbury, John. *Commander of the Faithful: The Moroccan Political Elite: A Study in Segmented Politics*. (Modern Middle East Series.) New York: Columbia University Press, 1970.
_____. "Kingdom-Building and the Control of the Opposition in Morocco: The Monarchical Uses of Justice," *Government and Opposition* [London], V, No. 1, Winter 1970, 54-66.

OTHER SOURCES USED

Ashford, Douglas E. *Political Change in Morocco*. Princeton: Princeton University Press, 1964.
Dupuy, Trevor N., et al. *The Almanac of World Military Power*. Harrisburg: T. N. Dupuy Associates, in association with Slaitspole Books, 1970.
Gordon, David C. *North Africa's French Legacy, 1954-1962*. (Harvard Middle Eastern Monographs, No. 9.) Cambridge: Center for Middle Eastern Studies, Harvard University Press, 1962.
Johnson, Katherine Marshall. *Urban Government for the Prefecture of Casablanca*. (The International Urban Studies of the Institute of Public Administration, No. 7.) New York: Praeger, 1970.

U.S. Department of State. Bureau of Intelligence and Research. *World Strength of the Communist Party Organizations.* Washington: GPO, 1970.

GLOSSARY

ALN (Armée de Liberation Nationale)—Army of National Liberation.
amir al muaminin—Commander of the faithful. Traditional and constitutional title of the king of Morocco in his role as religious head of Moroccan Islamic society.
baraka—The quality of special blessedness or grace characterizing marabouts (q.v.) or other divinely favored individuals in North African Islam.
Berber(s)—The indigenous peoples of Northwest Africa, including Morocco. Word is of Latin origin. In 1971 people of Berber descent continued to be a major element in population, particularly in mountain and rural areas.
bidonville—A shantytown adjoining a municipal area, created by large-scale migration of rural poor to cities.
bilad al makhzan—Arabic expression meaning "land of the central government," referring to those areas of preindependence Morocco where central government control was firmly established; may be seen in transliteration as bled el makhzen and similar variations.
bilad al siba—Arabic expression meaning "land of dissidence," referring to those areas of preindependence Morocco where central government control was not fully or consistently in effect; also seen in transliteration as bled el siba and similar variations.
caid—In modern Morocco, the executive head of a rural constituency in the local government structure; formerly, a rural area chief having wider judicial powers than the postindependence caid. Also, qaid.
casbah—The older, interior area of the non-Europeanized portion of North African cities; anciently, often referring to the central fortification of a settled locality, the citadel.
colon—A French colonial settler in Morocco.
dahir—Royal decree; a law promulgated by the king.
dirham (DH)—Unit of currency; in 1971 DH5.06 equaled US$1 at par value.
EEC—European Economic Community.
FAR (Forces Armées Royales)—Royal Armed Forces.
FDIC (Front pour la Défense des Institutions Constitutionnelles)—Front for the Defense of Constitutional Institutions.

GNP—Gross national product. Equal to gross domestic product plus factor income (mainly investment income) earned by Moroccan nationals residing abroad, less factor income earned by foreign nationals residing in Morocco.

Greater Maghrib—Expression used in Moroccan Constitution to identify area to which the country belongs; may have various political interpretations. *See also* Maghrib.

gross domestic product—The value of the total output of domestically produced goods and services.

habus—Islamic religious endowments; a Moroccan usage. Occurs elsewhere in Islamic countries as *waqf*. Sometimes written *habous*.

IBRD—International Bank for Reconstruction and Development.

IDA—International Development Association.

imam—In general, an Islamic leader who is a recognized authority on Islamic theology and law. Specifically in Morocco, refers to the king as religious head of the society under his title of "commander of the faithful." *See amir al muaminin*.

IMF—International Monetary Fund.

jaysh—Arabic word meaning "army." Occurs in reference to *jaysh* tribes, that is, tribes of preindependence Morocco that performed military service for the sultan in exchange for exemption from taxation. French transliteration: *guich*.

khalif—A successor or substitute. Specifically, in modern Morocco the executive head of one of the municipal wards under a *pasha* (q.v.).

khalifa—A successor or deputy; specifically, the governor-representative of the Moroccan sultan in the Spanish protectorate, 1912–56.

Maghrib—Northwest Africa; traditionally includes Morocco, Algeria, Tunisia, and sometimes Libya; literally, the time or place of sunset, the west.

makhzan—Central government.

mallah—The traditional Jewish residential quarter in towns or cities; French transliteration: *mellah*.

marabout—In North Africa, an Islamic holy man, often a Sufi mystic, teaching at local rural levels and thought to be touched by a special divine blessing; not usually a member of the *ulama* (q.v.).

milk land—Private freehold land, often belonging jointly to several owners.

mission civilisatrice—The French concept of duty, which requires the spread of the knowledge and benefits of French civilization and culture for the advancement of humanity; hence, a form of ideological justification for French colonization.

MP (Mouvement Populaire)—Popular Movement.

mulay—In Morocco, a prenominal title for a descendant of the Prophet Muhammad in the male line, that is, an agnatic *sharif*. Also seen as *moulay*, *mawlay*, and similar variant transliterations.

OAU—Organization of African Unity.
oued—French transliteration of Arabic word for stream or river. Standard English transliteration is *wadi*.
pasha—In modern Morocco, the mayor of a municipal area; formerly, a governor under the sultan.
PCM (Parti Communiste Marocain)—Moroccan Communist Party.
PDC (Parti Démocratique Constitutionnel)—Constitutional Democratic Party.
PDI (Parti Démocratique de l'Indépendance)—Democratic Independence Party.
PLS (Parti de Liberation et Socialisme)—Party of Liberation and Socialism.
PRC—People's Republic of China.
PS (Progrès Social)—Social Progress Party.
PSD (Parti Socialist Démocrate)—Democratic Socialist Party.
PUM (Parti de l'Unité Marocaine)—Party of Moroccan Unity.
ribat—Berber religious retreat or fortress; root word for Rabat, the capital city.
shahadah—Islamic statement of belief: "There is no god but God, and Muhammad is His Prophet."
sharia—The traditional code of Islamic law, both civil and criminal, based on the Islamic scriptures called the Quran.
sharif (pl., *shurfa* or *ashraf*)—A descendant of the Prophet Muhammad; a noble. Used as a title.
shaykh—In modern Morocco, the executive head of one of the rural subareas under a *caid* (*q.v.*). Formerly and loosely, a tribal leader.
UAR—United Arab Republic.
UGTM (Union Générale des Travailleurs Marocains)—Union of Moroccan Workers.
ulama (sing., *alim*)—The body of scholars learned in Muslim theology, philosophy, canon law, and Quranic studies. French transliteration: *ulema*.
UMT (Union Marocain du Travail)—Moroccan Labor Union.
UNDP—United Nations Development Program.
UNFM (Union Nationale des Femmes Marocaines)—National Union of Moroccan Women.
UNFP (Union Nationale des Forces Populaires)—National Union of Popular Forces.
UPFM (Union Progressiste des Femmes Marocaines)—Progressive Union of Moroccan Women.
USA (Union des Syndicats Agricoles)—Federation of Farmers' Unions.
wazir (pl., *wazara*)—A minister of the sultan's court in preindependence Morocco; a vizier.
zawiya (pl., *zawiyiin*)—Literally, in Arabic, "a corner." In Morocco, refers to a religious brotherhood or lodge, possibly led by a *marabout* (*q.v.*). Alternate word: *taifa*.

INDEX

Ababou, Mohammed, Colonel: 187, 188, 189
Abarkash, Hadden: 181
Abbasid dynasty: 35, 37
Abdelkader, Bel Hachemy: 139
Abduh, Muhammad: 94
Mulay Abdulla, Prince: 165
Abdulla, Muhammed ben: 208
administrative divisions (*see also* prefectures; provinces): viii, xiv; defense, 3, 320
Afghani, Jamal al Din al: 94
African relationships (*see also* individual countries; Organization of African Unity): 7, 31, 63–64, 65, 160, 162, 188, 200, 203, 212; trade and communications, 285, 286, 298
Agadir: xiv, 11, 12, 17, 22, 153, 177, 274; economy, 252, 255; history, 39, 46, 62; reconstruction, 231, 232; transport, 281, 282, 283, 284
Agency for International Development (AID, U.S.): 284, 305
agriculture (*see also* irrigation; reform, agrarian): viii, 4–5, 11, 12, 51, 172, 185, 218, 219, 224, 226, 234, 245, 246, 249, 300, 301, 305; credit, 223, 238, 239, 259; education, 125, 126, 127, 132–133, 259; government role, 256–259; and the GDP, 220, 221, 225, 245; labor, ix, 245, 246, 267, 268, 269, 271, 272; mechanization, 5, 218, 258, 298; production, 27, 180, 248, 251–259, 278; tax, 235
Ahardane, Majoub: 181
Ahermoumou: 187, 188
aid, foreign (*see also* credit operations; individual countries; individual international institutions): ix, 5, 68, 195, 206, 207, 210, 211–212, 219, 223, 224, 225, 228, 262, 281, 284, 290, 292, 298, 303–305; military, 65, 68, 195, 200, 207, 211, 310, 315–316
air force: ix, 3, 308, 317, 320
air transport: ix, 223, 277, 284–286; lines, ix, 285–286, 290

Aisha, Lala, princess: 29, 165
Ait Ammar: 22
Al Abid River: 13, 16; hydroelectricity, 261
Al Alam: 146, 148, 149, 185
Al Anba: 149
Al Hoceima: xiv, 11, 177; history, 43, 47, 311; transport, 282, 283, 284
Al Jadida: xiv, 12, 177, 252, 282
Al Kulla al Wataniya. *See* National Front
Al Maghrib al Aqsa: 7
Al Ray al-Amm: 146
Alawite dynasty: 1–2, 7, 40, 41–42, 58, 92, 136, 143, 195, 213
Algeciras Conference/Act (1906): 45–46, 51, 97, 209, 299
Algeria (*see also* National Liberation Front): xiv, 7, 8, 17, 63, 65, 68, 180, 196, 197–200, 202, 205, 206, 269; border dispute, 5, 9, 10, 32, 62, 65, 180, 195, 196, 197, 198, 199, 200, 205, 308, 312, 314; communications with, 8, 277, 281, 282, 283, 286; trade, 265, 296, 298
Allies. *See* World War II
Almohads (1147–1212): 37, 38, 86, 135
Almoravids (1062–1147): 36–37, 135
ALN. *See* Army of National Liberation
Amine, Hachem: 183
amir al muaminin: vii, 2, 31, 61, 85, 213
Anti-Atlas: 7, 8, 11, 14, 16, 49, 72, 76, 305
Aqlam: 137
Arab ethnic group (*see also* Arabians; tribes): 25, 31, 36, 39, 53, 73, 74–76, 79, 90, 178, 189, 213
Arab Israeli War: 68–69, 79
Arab League. *See* League of Arab States
Arab Summit Conference (1964): 201
Arabians (*see also* Arab ethnic group; League of Arab States): 31, 64, 65, 162, 186, 188, 195, 198, 200, 204–205;

387

beduins, 36, 37, 38, 74, 76; invasion and rule, 8, 33–36; Israeli war, 68–69, 79, 195, 204

Arabic language: vii, 1, 34, 36, 52, 71, 72, 73, 74, 76, 82, 83, 84, 94, 97, 101, 120, 121, 122, 123, 126, 127, 132, 133, 134, 142, 143, 159, 160, 162, 185; Arabization, 72, 73, 76, 80, 81, 82, 83, 186; classical, 75, 82, 83, 137, 141, 151; dialects, 75; literature, 138, 139; mass media (see also newspapers; radio), 119, 145, 150, 151, 152

Arabization. See Arabic language

archaeology: 119, 143

architecture: 107, 134, 136, 139–140

armed forces (see also aid; air force; Auxilliary Forces; navy; Royal Armed Forces; Royal Gendarmerie): 62, 66, 158, 192, 216, 307, 309–321; Chief of Staff, 191, 307, 313, 320; civil efforts, 192, 312–315; command, 3, 163, 305; conscription, 314; foreign, 62, 63, 209, 284; materiel, 315–316; officers, 2, 315; training, 310, 315

Army of National Liberation (Armée de Liberation Nationale, ALN): 58, 62, 310, 312, 314, 315

Arslan, Shakib: 53, 54

arts. See architecture; dance music; painting

Association of Andalusian Music: 141

Association of North African Muslim Students: 53

Atlantic Ocean: xiv, 7, 8, 11, 15, 16, 17, 19, 22, 23, 287

Atlas mountains (see also Anti-Atlas; High Atlas; Middle Atlas; Sahara): vii, 7, 12, 15, 16, 19, 20, 21, 25, 32, 246, 251

automobiles: viii, 108, 281–282, 296; assembling: 265, 266, 267, 282, 304

Auxiliary Forces: ix, 3, 308, 324–325

Ayachi Mountains: 13

Aziz, Abdul: 44, 45

Baath Party: 186

Bahnini, Ahmad: 66, 67, 180, 191

bakshish: 111

Balafrej, Ahmed: 52, 54, 55, 192

Bani Wattas: 38, 39, 40

Bank of Morocco: 233, 235, 236, 237, 238, 239, 240, 292, 300

banks and banking: 46, 223, 235–236, 237–239, 240, 241, 242, 280, 292, 301, 303

baraka: 90–91, 92, 93

Basri, Mohammed: 186

Battuta, Ibn (1304–78): 135

Bechar: 10, 197, 312

Bekkai, Embarek: 60, 61, 159

Beling, W.A.: 184

Belkahia, Favid: 141

Ben Arafa, Mohammed, Mulay: 58, 59, 60

Ben Barka, Mehdi: 63, 67–68, 80, 159, 179, 183, 185, 199, 206, 215, 304

Ben Bella, Ahmad, president of Algeria: 199, 206, 312

Ben Bouchte, Mahdi: 171

Benjelloun, Abdulhamid: 138

Ben Jelloun, Ahmad Majid: 192

Ben Sadiq, Mahjub: 182, 183, 184

Ben Youssef University: 132, 145

Benhima, Mohammed: 69

Beni Mellal: xiv, 177, 274, 282

Bennani, Larbi: 155

Bennouna, Mehdi: 150

Berber languages: vii, 72, 73, 74, 76, 120, 142; dialects, 72, 76, 151

Berbers (see also Berber languages; *dahir;* tribes): 1, 8, 25, 71, 73, 74, 75, 76–77, 79, 85, 86, 89, 90, 106, 168, 169, 189, 314; culture, 76, 90, 92, 93, 101, 114, 134, 135, 137, 141, 142, 143; history, 32, 33, 34, 35, 36–39, 40, 41, 42, 53; resistance movements, 48, 57, 58, 59, 62, 63, 310, 311

Berrada, Mohammed: 148, 185

Beth River: 15, 17, 22

bidonvilles: 9, 26, 27, 30, 52, 91, 107

bilad al makhzan: 41, 44, 53, 100, 189

bilad al siba: 41, 44, 53, 100, 189

Bin al Ouidane Dam: 16, 17

birds: 21

birth control: 23–24, 66

birth rate: 9, 24, 83

Bou Arfa: 13, 22, 282

Bou Hamara, pretender: 44, 45

Bou Iblane: 13, 14

Bou Nasser peak: 13, 14

Bouabid, Abdul Rahim: 181, 184, 190, 192

Boulemane: 13

Boumedienne, Houari, president of Algeria: 10, 197–198

boundaries (see also Algeria): xiv, 9–11, 62, 312; war (1963), 64–65, 312
Bourguiba, Habib, president of Tunisia: 200–201
Boutaleb, Abdul Hadi: 171
Brezhnev, Leonid I.: 211
BRPM. See Bureau of Mining Research and Participation
budget (see also defense): 172, 227, 228, 229–235; deficit. See public debt; expenditure, viii, 227, 229, 230, 231, 291–292; local government, 175, 176; receipts (see also tax), 230–235, 287, 288, 290–292
Bureau of Arabization: 83
Bureau of Mining Research and Participation (Bureau de Recherches et de Participations Minieres, BRPM): 263, 264
Byzantine Empire: 33

cabinet. See Council of Ministers
caid: 40, 44, 49, 50, 53, 54, 57, 143, 174, 175, 176
capital punishment: 186, 208, 309, 319
Carthage: 32
Casablanca: viii, xiv, 8, 9, 12, 16, 17, 19, 20, 22, 23, 28, 107, 108, 169, 175, 177, 187, 188, 264, 275; cultural, 72, 91, 95, 97, 124, 128, 129, 131, 132, 133, 140, 141, 144, 154, 270; economy, 236, 242, 253, 255, 262, 272; history, 46, 51, 56; information, 150, 151; population, 24, 25, 26, 71, 77, 79, 107, 111; riots (1952), 57, 146; riots (1965), 66–67, 123, 181, 216, 309; transportation, 277, 282, 283, 284, 285
Casablanca Bloc: 202, 203, 204, 206
Casablanca Conference (1943): 55
casbah: 25, 41
CDG. See Deposit and Investment Fund
censorship: 57, 146, 148, 181, 216
census: (1952), 81; (1960), 24, 25, 81; (1971–72), 219
Center of Experimentation Research and Training: 28, 144
central bank. See Bank of Morocco
central government (see also makhzan): 86, 100, 104
cereals (see also wheat): 245, 251, 252–253, 256, 280, 295, 300

Ceuta: 11, 17, 208; history, 32, 35, 39, 43, 47
Chamber of Councillors: 180
Chaouia: 12, 20, 251
Charibi, Driss: 138
Charter of Public Liberties: 147, 159
chemicals: viii, 264, 266, 267, 296
Cherkaoui, Ahmed: 54
children (see also students): 23, 27, 28, 29, 87, 112, 113; education (see also education), 72, 76, 82, 83, 95, 121, 122, 124, 125, 131
China. See People's Republic of China
Chou En-Lai, prime minister of the People's Republic of China: 212
Christians and Christianity: 87, 89, 95, 96–97, 136; history, 33, 36, 37, 38, 39, 77
Churchill, Winston, prime minister of Great Britain: 55
citrus fruit: viii, 251, 252, 253; export, 5, 277, 284, 293, 297, 298, 299
civil rights (see also Charter of Public Liberties; freedom of expression; religion; suffrage): 57, 60, 89, 160, 161, 162, 163, 169, 171
civil service (see also Morocconization): 4, 29, 66, 122, 123, 166–168, 174, 193, 269
climate: 15, 16–20, 219, 220, 245, 247, 251, 262, 287; drought, 222, 240, 256
coal: 21, 22, 218, 245, 261, 262, 263, 264, 265, 295
coastal plain: 8, 11–12, 20, 25
colons: 49, 52, 56, 110, 248, 250, 253, 256, 300, 301
Comité d'Action Marocaine (CAM). See Moroccan Action Committee
Comité du Maroc. See Committee of Morocco
commerce (see also trade): viii, 26, 172, 221; chambers of, 172; code, 279–280, 286; historic, 41, 43, 46, 51–52; labor, ix, 268, 269, 274
Committee of Morocco: 46
communal councils: 162, 171, 172, 175–176, 184
communes: 173, 174, 175–176
Communists and communism (see also Moroccan Communist Party): 214, 228, relations with countries (see also Cuba; People's Republic of

389

China; Soviet Union), 210–212, 242, 253, 261, 278, 293, 298
conference of Fedala (1956): 61
Congo: 203
Constituent Assembly: 64
constitution, development of: 158–160
Constitution (1962): 67, 158, 159, 160–161, 162, 163, 164, 170, 179, 181, 222, 224, 229
Constitution (1970): 158; amendments, 162–163; civil rights, 85, 95, 162; economy, 222, 224, 229; foreign policy, 5, 7, 162, 212; government, viii, 165–166, 167, 168, 170, 171–172, 173, 179, 190, 214; labor, 273; monarchy, 162, 163–164; promulgation of, 31, 69, 161, 182
Constitutional Council: 159
Constitutional Democratic Party (Parti Democratique Constitutionnel, PDC); 150, 178, 179, 181, 184
construction: 95, 122, 124, 128, 129, 221, 222, 224, 225, 259, 281, 287, 289, 302, 305, 313; housing, 29–30; irrigation dams, 8, 15–16, 17, 224; labor, 268, 272, 273; materials, viii, 265, 266, 267
Consultative Assembly: 63, 159
consumer goods (see also foodstuffs; textiles): 109, 265, 290, 296
Convention of Lalla Marhnia. See Treaty of Lalla Marhnia
cooperatives: 237, 238, 259, 281; handicrafts: 140
copper: 21, 22, 23
Cordova, Kingdom of: 35, 136
corruption: 170, 186, 189, 191, 224, 307
cost of living: 27, 180, 242, 272, 280
Council of Government (Protectorate): 50, 57
Council of Ministers: viii, 3, 159, 163, 165–166, 168, 172, 175, 178, 187, 191–193, 201, 229, 309, 313
coup attempt (1971): 2, 157, 158, 177, 187–188, 307, 319; consequences, 3, 71, 188–190, 224, 236, 320
courts (see also labor; Supreme Court): viii, 162, 168–170, 323; military, 319; religious, 50, 89, 96, 169
crafts: 110, 119, 135, 137, 140, 172, 221, 226, 245, 260, 279
credit operations: 223, 229, 235, 236, 237, 238, 239, 240–242, 278, 288; foreign (see also aid), 229, 233
crime: 171, 309
Cuba: 200, 210, 293
cultural activities (see also architecture; cultural influences; dance; drama; music; painting): 60, 82; history, 37, 38
cultural influences: 91, 107, 108, 116, 120, 135, 142, 169; Arab, 31, 33, 37, 53, 74, 119, 135; French, vii, 1, 7, 52, 71, 80, 82, 94, 101, 137–138, 140, 166, 168, 271; Roman, 33, Spanish, 37, 135; Turkish, 40
Cultural Mission (Mission Universitaire Culturel Fr ncaise, MUCF): 120, 131
currency: 235–237, 239–242
customs duties (see also tariff): 197, 233–235, 300, 302; history, 46

Daddah, Ould, president of Mauritania: 201
dahir: 163, 171, 257, 288, 302, 314, 318–319; Berber (1930), 53–54, 55, 89, 169; historical, 44, 49, 56, 57
Damascus: 34, 35
dams. See irrigation
dance: 136, 142
Dar al Islam: 33
de Gaulle, Charles, president of France: 68, 206
Declaration of the Rights of Man: 161
decrees. See *dahir*
defense (see also armed forces): ix, 3, 60, 197; administrative divisions, 3; budget, 313–314; minister (see also Ministry of Defense), 3
Democratic Independence Party (Parti Démocratique de l'Indépendance, PDI): 56, 61, 178, 181; publication, 146
Democratic Socialist Party (Parti Socialist Democrate, PSD): 66, 180
democratic traditions: 2, 59, 159, 160, 162, 185, 186, 192, 214, 215
Deposit and Investment Fund (Caisse de Dépôt et de Gestion, CDG): 236, 238, 239, 242
derb: 107–108
Description of Africa: 136
desert (see also *hamaidiya;* Sahara): 14, 16, 20

diplomatic relations. *See* foreign relations
dirham: 236, 239, 292-293
disease: vii, 27-28, 273
divorce: 89, 112, 113-114, 151, 169
Dlimi, Ahmad: 67, 68
Douiri, Mohammed: 54
Doukkala: 12, 17, 20
Doukkala, Bouchaib al: 94
Draa River: 7, 10, 11, 14, 16, 17, 22, 25; history, 39, 47, 49
drama: 142
dress: 76, 101, 108, 116-117; military, 317-318
Driss, Abdelaziz ben: 54

Eastern Morocco: 7, 8, 11, 14-15, 22; economy, 252, 255
economy (*see also* agriculture; industry; minerals; trade): viii, 31, 60, 180, 217-218, 219, 245, 287; development (*see also* Five Year Plans; National Development Program), 218, 224-227, 259, 278, 279; government role, 217, 222-224, 230, 256-259, 280-281, 286, 287-288, 298-299, 301
Eddine, Muhammad Khair: 138
education (*see also* Arabic language; schools; technical education; universities): vii; 3, 4, 31, 52, 72, 73, 82, 83, 109, 117, 119-123, 136, 185, 186, 191, 204-205, 226; adult, 134; religious. *See* Quran
Educational Higher Council: 164
Egypt (*see also* United Arab Republic): 45, 75
Eisenhower, Dwight D., president of U.S.A.: 209
elections: 64, 159, 161, 163, 170, 171, 172-173; (1960), 63, 175; (1963), 180; local government (1969), 69, 176; (1970), 31, 69, 184-185
electricity: 26, 52, 260, 261-262, 280, 301; hydroelectricity, 15, 16, 218, 260, 261-262, 298, 305
emergency, state of: 164, 193; (1965-70), 31, 67-69, 147, 148, 161, 164, 181, 182, 185, 191, 236, 309
emigration (*see also* Jews): 9, 23, 80, 97, 269-270
employment (*see also* labor; unemployment): 26, 72, 119, 120, 218, 269, 287

energy (*see also* electricity; coal; petroleum): 221, 222, 226, 228, 242, 259-260, 261-262, 266
English language: 127, 151, 152
Entente Cordiale: 45
Essaouira: 11, 12, 19, 23, 252, 282
Ethiopia: 199
ethnic groups (*see also* Arabian ethnic group; Berbers; Europeans; Jews): 1, 23, 71, 73-81
Europe, relations with (*see also* European Economic Community; individual countries): 42-47, 51, 196, 205-206; trade, 278, 301; transport, 278, 301
European Economic Community (EEC): 5-6, 205-206, 253, 261, 296, 297
Europeans (*see also colons;* French ethnic group; Spanish ethnic group): 80-81, 85, 96, 101, 107, 108, 109, 218, 223, 253, 257, 271, 278, 279, 290
Eurovision: 153-154
exchange. *See* foreign exchange
export (*see also* customs duties): viii, 4, 5, 217, 219, 223, 225, 264, 277, 290, 293-295, 296, 297, 298, 300; agriculture, 245, 254, 255, 298, 299; earnings, viii, 4, 298

family (*see also* children; marriage): 77, 96, 100, 112, 116, 169
family planning: 9, 23, 24, 25, 201
FAR. *See* Royal Armed Forces
Fassi, Allal al: 31, 53, 54, 58, 94, 137, 149, 179, 181, 184, 185, 187, 190, 202
Fatima, Lala, Princess: 117, 165
fauna. *See* wildlife
Faure, Edgar, premier of France: 59
FDIC. *See* Front for the Defense of Constitutional Institutions
Federal Republic of Germany: 206, 269, 270, 285, 295, 296, 301, 302; aid, ix, 303
Federation of Farmers Unions (Union des Syndicats Agricoles, USA): 182
Ferdinand and Isabella of Spain: 38
fertilizer: 296; production, 265, 266, 267; use, 247, 248, 258
Fes: xiv, 17, 19, 22, 28, 153, 177, 178, 216, 274; cultural, 72, 91, 93, 94,

391

97, 132, 135, 140, 141; economy, 250, 251, 279; history, 35, 38, 40, 46, 48, 52, 54, 311, 312; population, 25, 26, 74; transport, 281, 282, 284

Figuig: 10, 46, 62, 312; transport, 281, 282

films: 120, 154–155; foreign, 75, 117, 120, 154

finance (*see also* banks and banking; budget; investment): viii–ix, 225

fishing and fisheries: viii, 245, 254–255, 280; export, 254–255, 277, 283, 293, 297, 298, 299

Five Year Plan (1968–72): 15, 30, 220, 222, 224, 225, 226, 227, 229, 256; aid for, 207, 303, 305; for birth control, 9, 25; education, 125, 128; employment, 269, 270, 277; for industry, 154, 255, 260, 262, 263; tourism, 287, 288, 289; transport, 281, 285

Five Year Plan (1973–77): 224, 225

FLN. *See* National Liberation Front

floods: 15, 16; control, 16, 219, 254, 258, 259

flora. *See* vegetation

folk culture (*see also* religion): 136, 137, 155

folk lore: 119, 137, 138, 143

foodstuffs: viii, 242, 245, 260, 265, 266, 267, 269, 280, 293, 294, 295, 299; inadequacy, 9, 27, 219, 256

Ford Foundation, U.S.A.: 23

foreign aid. *See* aid

foreign exchange: 4, 219, 225, 233, 236, 237, 240, 241, 256, 265, 287, 290, 299; controls, 223, 259, 290, 292–293, 300, 302

foreign relations (*see also* individual countries): 5–6, 31–32, 60, 62, 63, 64, 65–66, 69, 189, 191, 195–196; diplomatic missions, 157, 163, 187, 189, 196, 197, 198, 200, 201, 203, 204, 205, 206, 209, 210–211, 212, 269; history, 41, 42–47; policy, 195–196, 197, 209, 210, 212

forests and forestry: 11, 20–21, 217, 221, 245, 246, 247, 249, 254, 255–256; reforestation, 256, 259

France (*see also* French rule): 62, 63, 67–68, 124, 131, 141, 152, 153, 196, 206–207, 209, 210, 269, 270, 285, 286; aid, ix, 5, 133, 195, 206, 207, 257, 290, 292, 303, 304, 310, 315–316; disputes, 195, 198, 206, 304, 311; history, 41, 42, 43, 45, 46, 47, 55; trade, 277, 284, 293, 295, 296, 297, 299

Franco, Francisco, Generalissimo: 60, 208

Franco—Moroccan Protectorate Treaty of Fes (1912): 46–47, 48, 49, 57, 59, 60

Franco Spanish Treaty (1912): 47

freedom of expression (*see also* censorship; civil rights): 120, 147, 171, 181

French ethnic group (*see also* colons; European ethnic group): 4, 23, 49, 50, 52, 56, 59, 60, 72–73, 80, 121, 131, 167, 255, 271, 279, 292, 309, 311

French language: vii, 1, 52, 72–73, 75, 76, 82, 83, 84, 119, 120, 122, 123, 126, 127, 129, 132, 133, 134, 143; literature, 138, 139; mass media (*see also* newspapers), 145, 146, 150, 151, 152

French rule (1912–56): vii, 1, 2, 12, 26, 31, 45–60, 63, 72, 78, 80, 81, 82, 89, 94, 99, 101, 140, 142, 157, 165, 167, 174, 202, 209, 213, 256, 259, 271, 309, 314; central government. *See* makhzan; economy, 217, 223, 248, 250, 251, 257, 278, 289–290, 299, 300, 301; education, 72, 120, 121, 131, 132, 144; information, 145–146; laws, 89, 168, 169; movement against, 52–60

French Spanish convention (1912): 10

French Spanish-Muslim Association: 54

French University: 120, 131

Front for the Defense of Constitutional Institutions (Front pour la Défense des Institutions Constitutionelles, FDIC): 64, 66, 67, 179, 180, 181, 182; publication, 146

Fundamental Law (1961): 159

Galaoui, Thami al: 48, 50–51, 57, 58, 59, 105

Gara-Djebilet: 10, 198

General Union of Moroccan Students (Union Generale des Etudiants Marocains, UGEM): 184

Germany (*see also* Federal Republic of Germany): 42, 45, 46; World War II, 55
Gibraltar, Strait of: vii, 11, 42, 47, 74, 208, 282
government. *See* central government; local government
grands seigneurs: 105–106
Great Britain: 42, 43, 45, 46, 50, 269, 285, 286, 295, 296
gross domestic product (GDP): viii, 220–222, 225, 229, 240, 242, 245, 259, 277
Grou River: 17, 22
Guédira, Reda: 160, 178, 180, 182, 309
Guercif: city, 282; plain, 14
Guir River: 10, 16, 17

habus (*see also* Ministry of Religious Foundations and Islamic Affairs): 50, 85; land, 249, 250
Hadith: 86
Hafid, Sultan: 46, 47
hajj: 87, 88, 92
hamaidiya: 14, 16
Haouz plain: 12, 16, 17
harbors. *See* ports
Hassan, Sultan (19th C): 44
Hassan II Institute of Agronomy: 133, 144, 168
Hassan II, King: 1–2, 3, 10, 23, 31, 66, 67, 68, 69, 83, 85, 92, 117, 140, 148, 158, 159–160, 161, 164–165, 166, 168, 177, 178, 179, 180, 181, 182, 184, 186, 190–191, 192, 198, 213, 214, 215, 224, 236, 307, 308, 314, 317, 319, 320; coup attempt, 157, 187, 188, 189; education policies, 95, 110, 119, 123, 125; foreign policy, 65, 68, 197, 199, 200–201, 203, 204, 205, 206, 207, 208, 211, 212; Prince, 62, 64, 310, 311, 312
Mulay Hassan, Prince. *See* Hassan II
health (*see also* disease; medical service): vii, 9, 24, 26, 226, 270, 273
High Atlas: 7, 8, 11, 12–14, 21, 22, 48, 72, 113; population, 25, 76
High Commission on Population: 23
High Court: 170
High Plateau: 8, 14, 20
Higher Board of Education: 122, 124
Higher Council of the Magistracy: 164, 170

Higher Council for National Promotion and Planning: 162, 164, 168, 224
hijrah: 86
holidays: 29, 111
holy wars: 39, 42, 88
House of Representatives: viii, 162, 163, 164, 165, 166, 168, 170, 171–172, 180, 184, 185, 193
housing (*see also* bidonvilles; slums): 9, 25, 26, 108, 144, 227, 268, 272, 273, 274, 300; government programs, 28, 29–30; loans, 28, 30
Husayn, king of Jordan: 188

Ibn Abdullah, Idris: 35
Ibn Bajja: 135
Ibn Khaldun: 77
Ibn Nusayr, Musa: 33
Ibn Rushd: 135
Ibn Tashfin, Yusif: 36
Ibn Tufayl: 135
Ibrahim, Abdullah: 181, 184
Id al Fitr: 88
Idris II: 35
Ifni: 10, 22, 207, 208; history, 43, 47, 51, 61, 62; transport, 281, 282
Ifrane: 144, 189
imazighan: 32
import (*see also* customs duties): viii, 218, 219, 222, 223, 233, 236, 245, 264, 277, 284, 290, 293, 294, 295–296, 297, 299–300, 303
Inaouene River: 14, 15, 17, 305
income (*see also* wages): 219, 273; agricultural, 251, 254; per capita, 27, 217, 225
independence: first years, 61–67; gaining of, vii, 10, 50, 59–61, 178, 209, 210, 213, 310
industry (*see also* energy; manufacturing; mining): viii, 11, 26, 31, 51, 80, 172, 185, 219, 221, 222, 224, 226, 259–261, 300; credit, 223, 238, 239; equipment, viii, 296, 299; labor, ix, 80, 245, 246, 268, 269, 271, 274; production, 245, 278
inflation: 27, 240
Institute of Jewish Studies: 96
insurance: 223, 236, 242, 280, 290, 303
International Bank for Reconstruction and Development (IBRD): ix, 224, 236, 239, 281, 302, 303, 305

international commitments (see also individual organizations): ix, 5, 212, 228, 285, 309
International Development Association (IDA): 125, 129
International Financial Statistics (IFS): 240, 242
International Monetary Fund (IMF): 239, 240
investment, capital (see also private sector; state enterprises): 217, 219, 222, 225, 226, 227, 230, 232, 234, 239, 288-289, 290-292, 303; code, 258, 288, 301-302; foreign, 288, 300-302
iron: 295; ore, 10, 21, 22, 198, 245, 262, 263, 265, 312
irrigation (see also construction): 4, 12, 15-16, 17, 25, 52, 218, 219, 223, 224, 225, 227, 246-247, 251, 257, 258, 259, 260, 305, 313
Isla. See National Reform Party
Islam (see also Islamic law; Quran; reform; Shia Islam; Sunni Islam; values and traditions): vii, 53, 71, 85, 86-89, 109-110, 113, 120, 150, 185; brotherhoods (see also marabouts), 86, 93-94; culture (see also cultural influences), 33-36, 37, 137; education, (see also Quran), 121, 126, 134, 136, 145, 151; introduction of, 33-36, 38, 74, 86, 90, 213; popular (see also Sufi Islam, 86, 90-93; spiritual head, vii, 1, 31, 60, 61, 85, 163, 191, 213, 214, 215, 216; and the state, 85, 86, 88, 89, 159, 160, 162, 163, 215
Islamic law: viii, 50, 53, 89, 113, 132, 135, 168-169, 214, 247
Islamic Solidarity Bloc: 195, 212
Islamic Summit Conference (1969): 10, 201, 205
Ismail, Mulay, Sultan (1672-1727): 41, 136, 143, 202
Israel: 71, 78, 200, 201, 204, 206; Arab war, 68-69, 71, 79, 195, 204
Istiqlal Party: 55, 57, 58, 59, 61, 62, 63, 64, 66, 69, 93, 147, 157, 159, 160, 161, 167, 174, 178, 179, 181, 184, 190, 192, 197, 310; irredentist policies, 179, 201, 202; labor/youth movements, 182-184; publications, 137, 146, 147-148, 167, 185

Italy: 206, 286, 295, 296, 305; history, 45, 56

jaysh: 40, 43, 105; land, 249
Jews and Judaism: 1, 9, 24, 26, 36, 68-69, 71, 73, 77-80, 85, 87, 89, 92, 95, 96, 108, 131; anti, 38, 55, 185; emigration, 78, 79, 80, 107; law, 168, 169; Sephardic, 38, 78, 96
journalists and journalism: 137, 145, 216
journals and periodicals (see also newspapers): 120-121, 137, 146, 150; French, 138, political 137; research, 143, 144, 145
judges: 50
judiciary (see also courts): viii, 64, 162, 164, 168-170, 193, 197; French rule, 50, 53, 54
Juin, Alphonse, General: 56-57
justice (see also Islamic law; judiciary; laws and legal codes): viii, 3, 191; military, 318-320
Karaouine University, Fes: 52, 121, 132, 134, 135, 136, 145
Karim, Abdul: 88
Kasba Tadla: 14
Keita, Modibo, president of Mali: 64, 199
Kenitra: xiv, 12, 22, 23, 26, 128, 177, 209; transport, 282, 283, 284
Kharidjites: 34, 35
Khouribga: xiv, 12, 22, 23, 177, 263, 281
king, duties and powers (see also Hassan II; Mohammed V; monarchy): vii, viii, ix, 3, 31, 69, 85, 100, 158, 159, 161, 162, 163-164, 165, 166, 168, 170, 171, 172, 174, 193, 214, 215, 216, 217, 223, 224, 308, 314, 321, 322; succession, 164
Kingdom of Morocco (see also boundaries): location, vii, 7; size, vii, 4, 7
Krim, Abdel: 199
Ksar al Souk: xiv, 177, 275; transport, 281, 282
Kuwait Fund for Arab Economic Development (KFAED): 305

L' Opinion: 148, 149, 185
La Nation Africaine: 147-148, 149
labor (see also wages): ix, 29, 219, 245-246, 266-271; arbitration, 273-

275; code, 271; conditions, 271–273; courts, 169–170, 273; riots, 57, 66, 185, 309, 314; unions. *See* trade unions

Lamrani, Mohammed Karim: 191, 192

land (*see also* reform, agrarian): ownership and tenure, 5, 218, 223, 248, 249–251, 256–257; utilization, 246, 247, 248

languages (*see also* Arabic language; English language; French language; Spanish language): vii, 31, 72, 73, 81–84, 109

Larache: 15, 17, 22, 282; history, 41, 46

Laraki, Ahmed: 69, 186, 187, 190, 207

Latifa, Lala: 165

laws and legal codes (*see also* Islamic law): viii, 89, 168–169, 271; commercial, 279–280, 286; military, 318–319; penal, 95, 319; promulgation, 163, 171

League of Arab States: ix, 5, 57, 63, 195, 199, 200, 202, 204, 212

Leo Africanus. *See* Wazzi

levante: 20

Liberal Independents: 178, 182

libraries: 143, 144–145

Libya: 157, 188, 189, 196, 202, 203, 269, 298

literacy: vii, 83, 120, 134

literature: 135, 136, 137–139

livestock: 245, 248, 254, 257

living standards (*see also* housing; nutrition; sanitation): 9, 27–28, 56, 80, 185

local government: viii, 63, 161, 162, 173–177; finances, 227, 228, 229, 233; history, 40, 44; in the protectorate, 47, 50, 173

Louis XIV, king of France: 41

Loukkos River: 15, 17, 22

Lyautey, Louis, Marshal: 48, 49, 51, 52

Lyazidi, Mohammed: 54, 55, 56

Lycée Lyautev: 131

Madbuh, Mohammed, General: 188, 189

madina: 26, 108, 140, 279

Madrid Conference (1880): 43, 45

Maghrib (*see also* Algeria; Libya; Mauritania; North Africa; Tunisia): 7, 64, 160, 162, 196–197, 198, 201; communications, 283, 284, 286; history, 36; trade, 298

Maghrib Arab Press (MAP): 149, 150–151

makhzan (*see also* central government): French, 47, 48, 49, 50, 53, 56, 93, 105, 169; history, 37, 38, 39, 40, 41, 43, 44, 100, 105, 166, 189; land (*see also* bilad al *makhzan*), 249

Mali: 195, 199, 202, 293

Malikite rite. *See* Sunni Islam

mallah: 26, 78, 108

Mamlaka al Maghribia: 7

Mamora: 21

mandub: 51

manganese: 21, 22, 263, 265, 295, 298

Mansur, Sultan Mulay Ahmad al: 40

manufacturing: viii, 245, 259, 260, 265–266, 294, 301

marabouts: 37, 38, 39, 40, 48, 51, 53, 85, 90, 94, 104, 105, 135; modification of power, 41, 53, 86, 94, 104

Marin Bani: 38

Marinids (1269–1465): 38–39, 41, 135, 143

Marrakech: xiv, 12, 13, 17, 19, 20, 22, 26, 28, 170, 274; administration, 105, 177; cultural, 72, 132, 140, 141, 145; economy, 250, 252, 279; history, 36, 37, 38, 40, 46, 48, 51, 143; population, 26, 79; transport, 281, 282, 283, 284

marriage: 74–75, 89, 100, 112, 113–114, 116, 117, 151, 169; intermarriage, 74, 101

marshland: 11, 12, 247

Mas, Pierre: 146

Masmuda Berbers: 35, 77

Massa River: 16, 17, 22

Mauritania: xiv, 6, 8, 17, 22, 64, 65, 152, 153, 195, 196, 197, 200, 201–202, 206; history, 40; territorial claims in, 10, 201, 202, 203

medical services: vii, 9, 24, 28, 52, 271, 272

Mediterranean Sea: xiv, 7, 11, 15, 17, 22, 287

Meknes: xiv, 15, 17, 21, 22, 25, 26, 177, 274, 310, 311, 315; cultural, 91, 140; economy, 250, 251, 279; history, 40, 143; transport, 281

395

Mekouar, Ahmed: 54
Melilla: 11, 17, 22, 208; history, 39, 43, 47
Meseta: 8
Messouak, Abdulhadi: 187
Middle Atlas: 7, 8, 11, 12–14, 20, 21, 22, 72, 246; history, 49, 310, 311; population, 25, 76, 77
Middle East (*see also* individual countries): 162, 186, 195, 213
migration, internal: 4, 5, 9, 25–26, 27, 52, 78, 91, 106, 107, 110, 111, 259; historic, 7; seasonal, 267, 268
Mikoyan, Anastas I.: 211
military. *See* armed forces
Military Assistance Program (MAP, U.S.): 318
milk land: 249, 250, 251, 301
minerals (*see also* iron; manganese; phosphates; zinc): 8, 21–23, 51, 217, 218, 223, 245, 262, 263, 294; export, 235, 263, 264, 294, 295
mining: viii, 198, 221, 223, 226, 259, 260, 262–265; labor, 272, 273
Ministries of Education: 66, 96, 124, 125, 132, 191, 231, 232
ministries and ministers (*see also* Council of Ministers; individual ministries): 162, 163, 165–166, 170, 191, 231, 232
Ministry of Agriculture and National Development: 125, 127, 191, 231, 232, 295
Ministry of Commerce: 144, 231, 232
Ministry of Culture: 138, 155
Ministry of Defense: 191, 192, 231, 232, 308, 309, 320
Ministry of Finance: 229, 237, 292; minister, 238
Ministry of Information: 146, 149, 154, 192, 231, 232
Ministry of Interior: 2, 3, 28, 144, 174, 175, 186, 189, 191, 192, 270, 308, 320; minister, 3, 147, 173, 176, 324
Ministry of Justice: 96, 167, 191, 231, 232; minister, 170
Ministry of Labor and Social Affairs (*see also* Ministry of Youth and Recreation): 28, 125, 128, 231, 232
Ministry of Public Health: 28, 192, 231, 232
Ministry of Public Works and Communications: 284, 285

Ministry of Religious Foundations and Islamic Affairs: 85, 95, 191
Ministry of Youth and Recreation: 28, 192, 231, 232; (1971), 269, 270, 271, 274
mission civilisatrice: 43, 57, 72, 81–82
Mohammed V Dam: 15, 17
Mohammed V, King (previously Sultan): 2, 31, 51, 54, 55, 57, 60, 63, 64, 147, 149, 159, 164, 165, 167, 177, 178, 200, 213, 309; exile, 2, 58–59, 214; foreign policy, 202, 203, 209; tomb, 92, 140
Mohammed, Sultan (18th C): 41, 136
Mohammed V University. *See* University of Rabat
Mohammedia: 279; transport, 282, 283, 284
Mohammedia Engineering School: 127, 132, 168
monarchy (*see also* king): viii, 1, 2, 61, 99, 100, 163, 184, 189, 195, 203, 204, 208, 212, 214, 216, 217, 307; constitutional, 31, 59, 62, 158, 159–160, 162, 193, 214
Moriscos: 38, 74
Moroccan Action Committee (Comité d'Action Marocaine, CAM): 54, 55
Moroccan Cinematographic Center (Centre Cinematographique Morocain, CCM): 154–155
Moroccan Communist Party (Parti Communiste Marocain, PCM): 57, 58, 160, 177, 181, 182, 184, 187; publications, 147
Moroccan General Library and Archives (Bibliotheque Generale et Archives du Maroc): 145
Moroccan Labor Union (Union Marocain du Travail, UMT): 69, 142, 167, 182, 183, 246, 273, 274
Moroccan League for Fundamental Education and Literacy: 134
Moroccan League for the Protection of Children: 29
Moroccan Muslims: vii, 8, 24
Moroccan National Front: 57
Moroccan National Office for Railroads (Office National des Chemins de Fer Maroc, ONCF): 282
Moroccan Press Association: 147
Moroccan Radio and Television (Radiodiffusion Television Morocain, RTM): 151, 152, 153, 228

Moroccan Shipping Company (Campagnie Marocaine de Navigation, COMANAV): 284
Moroccan Unity Party: 55
Moroccan Worker—Youth (Jeunesse Ouvrière Marocain, JOM): 182, 274
Moroccanization: 206, 246, 248, 270, 303; education, 72, 82; government, 72, 83, 167, 169
mosques: 25, 87, 95, 107, 140; schools. *See* Quran
Mouline, Rashid: 178
Moulouya: history, 35; River, 11, 13, 15, 17, 22; valley, 8, 13, 14, 17, 22, 25, 255
mountains (*see also* individual ranges): vii, 7, 11, 19, 20, 287
MP. *See* Popular Movement
Msoun River: 13, 15
Muhammad, Prophet: 33, 34, 86, 87, 88, 89, 90, 135; descendents (*see also sharif*), 1, 34, 35, 39, 40, 85, 90, 109, 136, 213
Mulay Sidi Mohammed, Crown Prince: 165
museums: 140
music: 136, 141–143
Muslims (*see also* Islam; Moroccan Muslims): vii, 2, 33, 87, 160, 213; history, 38, 39

Naciri, Muhammad al Mekki: 54, 55, 150
Nador: xiv, 11, 15, 17, 22, 265, 274, 282, 305
Nakhla River: 15, 17
names (*see also* titles): 75, 77, 104
narcotics: 308, 323
Nasser, Gamal Abdul, president of United Arab Republic: 205
National Agricultural Credit Bank (Caisse Nationale de Crédit Agricole, CNCA): 237, 238
National Development Program (Promotion Nationale): 29, 259, 269
National Economic Development Bank (Banque Nationale pour le Developpement Economique, BNDE): 237, 238, 239
National Front: 184, 192
National Investment Company (Societé Nationale d'Investissements): 303

National Liberation Front (Front de Liberation Nationale, FLN), Algerian: 62, 198, 199, 206, 311
National Mutual Aid (Entr'Aide Nationale, EAN): 29
National Party: 54
National Reform Party: 55, 178
National Social Security Bank: 29
National Tourist Office: 287–288
National Transport Agency (Office National de Transport, ONT): 281
National Union of Moroccan Students (Union Nationale des Etudiants Marocaines, UNFEM): 183
National Union of Moroccan Women (Union Nationale des Femmes Marocaines, UNFM): 117, 165
National Union of Popular Forces (Union Nationale des Forces Populaires, UNFP): 63, 64, 66, 67, 69, 157, 159, 160, 161, 167, 179, 180, 181, 182, 183, 184, 185, 186, 187, 190, 192; labor/youth movements, 182–184, 274; publications, 137, 146
nationalists and nationalism (*see also* independence): 2, 31, 80, 83, 146, 159, 196, 214, 310; and culture, 137; and education, 121; and Islam, 88, 89, 94, 216; movement, 50, 52–61
navy: ix, 3, 308, 317, 320
news agencies: 149, 150–151
newspapers (*see also* press): 119, 121, 181; Arabic, 146, 148, 149; French, 145, 146, 147, 148, 149
nonalignment: 31, 64, 65–66, 179, 195, 198, 200, 210
North Africa (*see also* Maghrib): 7, 68, 74, 75, 162, 213: history, 31, 32, 33, 310; religion, 90, 93
nutrition: 9

oases: 7, 14, 16, 20, 25, 46
Official Bulletin: 171, 172, 176
official language (*see also* Arabic language): vii, 1, 71
oil, edible: 245, 253, 255, 258, 280, 290, 293, 294, 297
Organization of African Unity (OAU): ix, 5, 195, 197, 199, 200, 201, 212, 312
Ottoman Empire: 31, 40, 41, 42, 213
Ouanoukrim peak: 13

Ouarzazate: 14, 16, 17, 22, 23, 25, 177; transport, 281, 282
Ouezzani, Mohammed Hassan: 53, 54, 56
Oufkir, Mohammed, General: 2–3, 67, 68, 157, 186, 187, 188, 189, 191, 192, 307–308, 313, 320
Oujda: xiv, 15, 17, 22, 26, 62, 153, 177, 262, 274, 312; history, 46; transport, 281, 282, 284
Oum al Rbia River: 12, 16, 17, 22, 25

painting: 140–141
Palestine Liberation Movement: 204, 205
Parliament: 64, 161, 180, 181
Party of Independent Liberals (Parti des Liberaux Independants, PLI): 146
Party of Liberation and Socialism (Parti de Liberation et Socialisme, PLS): 182, 184
Party of Moroccan Unity (Parti de L'Unité Marocaine, PUM): 178
pashas: 40, 44, 49, 50, 53, 54, 174, 175, 176
PCM. See Moroccan Communist Party
PDC. See Constitutional Democratic Party
PDI. See Democratic Independence Party
PDS. See Democratic Socialist Party
penal system (*see also* laws and legal codes): 325
Penon de Velez: 39, 43, 47
People's Republic of China, (PRC): 65, 198, 210, 211, 212, 293, 295, 298
petroleum (*see also* energy): 8, 22, 23, 218, 219, 245, 262, 263, 264–265, 266, 301, 304; imports, viii, 218, 264, 277, 300
Phoenicians: 32, 71, 75
phosphates: viii, 4, 223, 228, 233, 245, 262, 263–264, 266, 267, 277, 283, 284, 298; deposits, 10, 12, 21–22, 218
privates and piracy: 38, 39, 41
Plan of Reforms: 55
Podgorny, Nikolai: 211
police (*see also* Royal Gendarmerie; Sûreté Nationale): ix, 62, 66, 169, 187, 216, 308, 311, 312, 313, 314, 321–325; history, 46, 47
political parties (*see also* individual parties): 159, 160, 161, 162, 173,

177–182, 216; opposition, 1, 23, 157, 160, 176, 179, 180, 181, 182, 184, 185, 186, 190, 208, 246
polygyny: 116
Pompidou, Georges, president of France: 206, 207
Pope Leo X: 136
Popular Credit Bank: 236
Popular Movement (Mouvement Populaire, MP): 54, 63, 64, 178, 179, 181, 182, 184; publication, 146
population (*see also* census): vii, 3, 7, 8–9, 11, 12, 23–26, 185, 219, 256
ports: xiv, 227, 228, 264, 266, 282; air, ix, 2, 284, 285; sea, ix, 11, 12, 283
Portugal: 203, 255; history, 38; rule of Morocco, 39
prefectures (*see also* individual prefectures): viii, xiv, 173, 175, 176–177
press (*see also* newspapers): 27, 75, 83, 119, 145–151, 303; censorship, 57, 121; code, 147, 148; history, 145–146; opposition, 148, 149
prices (*see also* cost of living): 66, 69, 123, 236; controls, 236, 258, 259, 278, 280–281
prime minister, duties: viii, 147, 158, 161, 162, 163, 165–166, 171, 172, 190, 193, 225, 231, 232
prisoners: 325; amnesty, 66, 181, 185; exchange, 65
private sector: 30, 217, 222–223, 225, 227, 263, 266, 286, 288, 290–291, 300, 303; credit, 223, 236, 237, 238, 240–242; foreign, 4, 222, 235, 236, 288; incentives, 278, 288–289, 301–302; land. See land
professionals: ix, 29, 78, 79, 80, 81, 122, 215, 246, 270; associations, 171
Progressive Union of Moroccan Women (Union Progressiste des Femmes Marocaines, UPFM): 182
Prophet. See Muhammed
protectorate. See French rule; Spanish rule
provinces (*see also* individual provinces): viii, xiv, 173, 175, 176–177
public debt (*see also* trade): 227, 229, 233, 236, 242–243, 292; domestic, 235
public sector (*see also* budget; state enterprises): 227–229, 290, 291

publishing (*see also* press): 145, 146, 147
PUM. *See* Party of Moroccan Unity
Qadr, Abdul: 42
Quran: 34, 75, 85, 86, 87, 90, 94, 110, 132, 151, 191, 214; schools, 94, 95, 107, 121, 125–126, 140

Rabat: vii, viii, xiv, 8, 9, 11, 12, 16, 17, 22, 28, 175, 177, 187, 188, 323; cultural, 72, 94, 97, 130, 132, 133, 140, 141, 155; history, 38, 46, 53, 54, 58, 143; information, 146, 150, 151; justice, 169, 170, 274, 319; population, 26, 79; transport, 282, 283, 284, 285
Mulay Rachid, Prince: 165
radio: ix, 75, 83, 97, 117, 119, 120, 142, 150, 151–153, 187, 190; educational, 95, 151–152; international, 151, 152, 153; propaganda: 65
Radio Maroc. *See* Moroccan Radio and Television
Radio Tangier International: 151
Rahman, Sultan Mulay (19th.C): 42
railways: ix, 223, 264, 266, 273, 277, 282–283, 301
Raisuli: 44–45
Ramadan: 87–88, 94–95
Ramadani, Muhammad Tazi Abdelaziz: 155
Rashid, Sultan Mulay (17th.C): 41
Red Crescent: 29
referenda: 160, 162, 163, 170; (1962), 160; (1970), 158, 161, 182, 184–185
reform: 47, 48, 56, 158, 168, 175, 177, 192, 193, 225; agrarian, 81, 224, 256–257, 301; political, 59; religious, 52, 53, 94–95, 135, 214; social, 31, 47, 62, 66, 179
Regency Council: 59
religion (*see also* Christians and Christianity; Islam; reform): vii, 215; freedom of, 85, 95, 162
repatriation of capital: 299; from Morocco, 236, 278, 288, 302; to Morocco, 291, 292
reptiles: 21
research: 28, 143–145, 201; agriculture, 259; drama, 142; education, 124, 125
resident general: 48, 49, 173
Rharb Plain: 8, 12, 15, 17, 20, 23, 251; Sebou project, 305

Rif Massif: 7, 8, 11, 13, 15, 19, 20, 21; cultural, 72, 74; development, 259, 305; history, 32, 45; resistance movements, 48, 59, 62, 63, 310, 311, 315; society, 76, 113
Rifi: 72, 76
riots (*see also* Casablanca; students): Meknes (1956), 311
rivers (*see also* individual rivers): 11, 12, 13, 15–16, 17
roads and highways: ix, 223, 259, 277, 281–282, 312
Roberto, Holden: 203
Roman Empire: 32–33, 143
Roosevelt, Franklin D., president of the U.S.A.: 55, 209
Royal Air Inter (RAI): ix, 285
Royal Air Maroc (RAM): ix, 285, 286, 290, 305
Royal Armed Forces (Forces Armées Royales, FAR): ix, 3, 62, 204, 307, 308, 312–315, 316, 320, 323, 325
Royal Charter. *See* Charter of Public Liberties
Royal Gendarmerie: ix, 3, 308, 320, 323–324
Royal Guard: 308
Royal Military Academy: 189, 310, 315
Royal Military Household: 189
Royal Moroccan Army: 62, 308
rural society: vii, viii, 4, 9, 24, 25, 27, 99, 101, 110, 169, 174, 267, 286; administration, 100, 106; cultural, 75–76, 137; economy, 237, 240, 259, 261, 272, 277, 278; education, 126, 259; politics, 63, 178, 181, 215; population, 71, 77, 218; religion, 85, 91; structure, 101–106

Saad dynasty (1549–1660): 39, 40–41, 136, 143
Sabbagh, Muhammed al: 138–139
Safi: xiv, 17, 22, 26, 177, 252, 264; history, 39; transport, 282, 283
Sahara: 10, 14, 17, 202, 206; Algerian, 8, 9; Atlas, 13, 14; desert, 7; population, 76, 77; pre Sahara, 8, 11, 14; Spanish, xiv, 8, 10–11, 17, 51, 195, 208, 263
Salafiya: 52, 53, 94
salaries. *See* wages
Salé: 38, 41, 177; transport, 282, 284
sand dunes: 11

Sanhaja Berbers: 35, 36, 77
sanitation: 26, 28, 52, 273, 325
Sarho Mountain: 14
School of Mines: 127
schools (*see also* students; teachers; universities): vii, 52, 53, 74, 83, 84, 122, 123–129, 183; public, 83, 119, 123, 128; private, 83, 97, 120, 121, 123, 124, 131, 270
Schumann, Maurice: 207
Sebou River: 11, 12, 13, 14–15, 17, 22; development, 144
security (*see also* police; riots; strikes): 3, 186, 195, 311, 312; crime against, 319
Sefriou, Ahmed: 138
Seguiet al Hamra: 10
Selassie, Haile, emperor of Ethiopia: 65, 199, 312
Senoussi, Abdullah Ben Driss: 94
services, utility: 221, 222, 226, 277, 291; labor, ix, 268, 269, 303
Settat: xiv, 17, 22, 177
settlement patterns: 25
shahadah: 87
sharia. See Islamic law
sharif and Sharifian dynasties: 35, 39–42, 44, 45, 85, 90, 92, 93, 100, 165
Sharifian Office of Phosphates (Office Cherifien des Phosphates, OCP): 263, 298
Sharkawi, Mohammed: 182
Shenab, Muhammed Ben: 143
Shia Islam: 34, 35, 86
shurfa. See *sharif*
sirocco: 20
Siroua: 14
Skhirat Palace: 157, 187, 188, 190
slave trade: 40, 41
slums (*see also* bidonvilles): 5, 99, 268
Social Progress Party (Progres Social, PS): 184
social security: 28–29, 269–270, 271, 273, 274
social welfare (*see also* medical services; social security): 27, 28–30, 313, 317; religious, 95
socialists and socialism: 179, 181, 186, 216
soils: 12, 20
souk: 25, 106, 107, 115, 277, 278–279

Sous Plain: 8, 14, 20, 21, 77, 105, 255; history, 39, 49; River, 17, 22
South Rifian Strait: 14
Soviet Union: 65–66, 68, 195, 198, 202, 210, 211, 262, 293, 303, 305, 316; trade, 263, 264, 284, 296, 298
Spain (*see also* Spanish rule): xiv, 8, 62, 96, 196, 200, 206, 207–208, 269, 277, 285; history, 31, 33, 34, 35, 37, 38, 39, 43, 45, 46, 47, 54, 74, 77, 135, 139; trade, 293, 295, 299
Spanish ethnic group: 97, 309
Spanish language: 134, 151
Spanish rule (1912–56) (*see also* Sahara): vii, 1, 7, 10, 12, 26, 31, 47, 48, 51, 81, 145, 146, 168, 198, 207, 213, 217, 286, 311; movement against, 48, 54–55, 60–61, 62
sports: 112
state enterprises (*see also* public sector): 217, 223, 227, 228, 229, 233, 234, 264, 266, 284
steppes: 14, 19, 25
strikes: 182, 185, 274; right of, 273
students: 119, 120, 123, 169, 189; music, 141; politics/riots, 66–67, 123, 181, 183, 184, 185, 189, 196, 215, 216, 309, 314
suffrage: 64, 160, 171, 172, 175
Sufi Islam: 37, 38, 39
sugar: viii, 245, 253, 258, 266, 267, 280, 304; beet, 253, 256, 295; import, 277, 295, 299
sultan, office and duties: 43–44, 47, 48, 49, 51, 57, 60, 61, 100, 249; succession, 136
Sunni Islam: vii, 34, 35, 39, 86; Malikite rite, 36, 37, 51, 89
Supreme Court: viii, 78, 164, 170, 171, 319; Constitutional Chamber, 163, 170, 173
Sûreté Nationale: ix, 3, 67, 308, 309, 321–323, 325
Syria: 196, 199, 200, 205

Tadla Plain: 12, 13, 16, 17, 25, 251
Tafilalt Plain: 16, 17, 25; history, 36, 39, 40
Tamazight: 72, 76, 151
Tan Tan: xiv, 282
Tangier: xiv, 11, 17, 20, 22, 26, 97, 170, 177, 274, 286, 302; cultural, 72, 140; history, 32, 39, 41, 42, 45, 47, 48, 51, 54, 56, 61; information, 150,

151, 153; transport, 277, 281, 282, 283, 284, 285

Tarfaya: xiv, 10, 61, 177, 281, 282

tariff (*see also* customs duties): 300; preferential, 225, 297; protection, 223

Tashilhit: 72, 76, 151

tax: 80, 223, 229, 233–235; excise, 233; history, 43, 44, 50, 100; incentives, 222, 259, 288, 302; religious, 87

Taza: xiv, 14, 177; city, 14, 15, 282; cultural, 72; history, 33, 38, 48, 311, 312

Taza Pass: 8, 12, 13, 14

Tazi, Muhammad: 137

teachers (*see also* universities): vii, 72, 83, 120, 121, 122, 123, 125, 126, 128, 129–131; foreign, 125, 130, 144, 205, 207, 270; training, 123, 125, 129–130

technical education (*see also* agriculture): 66, 119, 120, 123, 124, 125, 127–128, 134, 144, 270, 274, 314; civil service, 168, 225

telecommunications (*see also* newspapers; radio; television): ix, 31, 217, 223, 226, 286, 304

television: ix, 119, 120, 150, 153–154, 187; educational: 95, 152

Tell Region: 8

Teniet al Sassi: 10

Tensift River: 12, 16, 17, 22

Tessaout River: 16, 17

Tetouan: xiv, 11, 15, 17, 22, 26, 151, 177, 274, 282; cultural, 72, 132, 145; history, 39, 48, 51, 54, 311

Tetuán. *See* Tetouan

textiles: viii, 225, 260, 265, 266, 267, 272, 296

Thawat al Haq: 137

theater: 142–143

Tichka Pass: 13

timber: 51

Tindouf: 10, 68, 197, 312

titles: 40, 88, 91, 104

Tlemcen: 40, 42; conference and treaty, 197

topography (*see also* mountains; rivers): vii, 7

Torres, Abdel: 54, 55, 178

Toubkal, peak: 13

tourists and tourism: 4, 8, 23, 110, 218, 219, 222, 224, 225, 226, 245, 277, 278, 281, 282, 284, 286–289, 290, 301, 305, 309, 314

trade (*see also* commerce; export; import): 226, 277, 280–281, 290, 293, 300, 303; balance/deficit, 277, 278, 289–290, 299, 305; barter, 261; domestic, 277, 278–279, 280; foreign, 206, 212, 223, 228, 277, 278, 294, 296–298, 299–300

trade unions: 67, 69, 150, 168, 172, 181, 182–183, 184, 185, 216, 246, 273–275

transport (*see also* air transport; railways; roads and highways): ix, 12, 31, 51, 217, 221, 223, 224, 226, 228, 238, 242, 256, 277, 280, 290, 291, 303, 305; labor, ix, 268, 269, 273; sea, 283–284

treaties and agreements (*see also* individual treaties; international commitments): 41, 45, 163–164, 197, 198, 199, 200, 201, 205, 208, 209, 212, 285, 293, 297, 302, 310

Treaty of Fes (1969): 10

Treaty of Lalla Marhnia (1845): 10, 45

Treaty of Marrakech (1787): 41

Treaty of Meknes (1836): 42

tribes (*see also* Arabs; Berbers): 38, 71, 73, 76, 99, 100, 101–106, 110, 111, 112, 113, 174, 178, 257, 262, 311; nomad, 254

Tripolitania: 45

Tumart, Mohammed bin: 37

Tunisia: 7, 65, 196, 197, 200–201, 205, 298; history, 32, 33, 35, 43; transport, 277, 283, 286

UGTM. *See* Union of Moroccan Workers

ulama: 38, 47, 52, 58, 82, 85, 93, 95, 165

Umayyad dynasty: 34, 35, 36, 139

UMT. *See* Moroccan Labor Union

unemployment and under employment: ix, 3–4, 9, 27, 29, 66, 84, 109, 110, 123, 180, 182, 185, 186, 216, 219, 246, 259, 266, 269, 313

UNFP. *See* National Union of Popular Forces

Union of Moroccan Workers (Union Generale des Travailleurs Marocains, UGTM): 183, 185, 246, 273

United Arab Republic: 63, 68, 196, 199, 200, 202, 204, 205, 206, 293
United Nations: ix, 5, 24, 25, 60, 68, 144, 195, 200, 202, 203, 209, 210, 212, 224, 255; Development Program, 125, 224, 225, 305; Economic Commission for Africa, 197; Law of the Sea, 208
United States of America: 41, 42, 43, 45, 46, 50, 55, 65, 153, 195, 200, 208–210, 263, 285, 286; aid, ix, 5, 68, 210, 284, 303, 304–305, 316, 318; bases, 63, 209, 284; food program, 228, 259, 269, 304; trade, 298, 296, 297, 301, 302
universities (*see also* individual universities): 52, 132–134, 169, 183; graduates, 4, 315; teachers, 124, 134
University of Rabat: 28, 119, 130, 132, 133, 144, 145
urban society: vii, viii, 4, 5, 9, 11, 23, 26, 27, 52, 99, 101, 140, 153, 154, 169, 174, 261, 286; cultural, 75, 76; economy, 277, 278, 279; education, 122, 124; politics, 63, 66, 178, 215, 216; population, 77, 80, 96, 107; structure, 106–112

values and traditions: 160, 169; Arab/Islamic, 137, 149, 215; educational, 109–110; political, 213–216; social, 112, 116–117
Vandals, 33
vegetation (*see also* forests and forestry): 11, 12–13
vehicles. *See* automobiles
Villa Sanjurjo. *See* Al Hoceima

Voice of America: 153
Voice of Morocco: 151

wages: 69, 185, 274, 292, 302; civil service, 168, 222; controls, 236; military, 316–317, 320; minimum, 272, 273–274; tax, 235
water supply: 251, 280; agricultural. *See* irrigation; urban, 15, 16, 26
wazir: 44, 50, 166
Wazzani, Mohammed: 182
Wazzi, Hassan Ibn Mohammed al: 135–136
West Germany. *See* Federal Republic of Germany
wheat: 245, 248, 252, 280–281; import, viii, 219, 277, 281, 290
wildlife: 21
Wilhelm II, Kaiser: 45
women: 23, 24, 27, 29, 74, 76, 87, 91, 92, 95, 96, 106, 112, 113, 114, 115, 116–117; associations, 117, 182; education, 96, 128
World Bank. *See* International Bank for Reconstruction and Development
World War II: 55–56, 256, 310, 314

Yata, Ali: 181, 182, 184
Yazghi, Mohammed: 185, 186
Youssoufia: 22, 263, 283
youth (*see also* students): 215, 216, 226; movements, 182–184
Yusif, Mulay: 47

Zanata Berbers: 35, 36, 38, 77
zinc: 198, 263, 265, 295, 298
Ziz River: 7, 16, 17, 22

PUBLISHED AREA HANDBOOKS

550-65	Afghanistan	550-41	Korea, Republic of
550-98	Albania	550-58	Laos
550-44	Algeria	550-24	Lebanon
550-59	Angola	550-38	Liberia
550-73	Argentina	550-85	Libya
550-20	Brazil	550-45	Malaysia
550-61	Burma	550-76	Mongolia
550-83	Burundi	550-49	Morocco
550-50	Cambodia	550-64	Mozambique
550-96	Ceylon	550-35	Nepal (with Sikkim and Bhutan)
550-26	Colombia		
550-60	Communist China	550-88	Nicaragua
550-91	Congo (Brazzaville)	550-157	Nigeria
550-67	Congo (Kinshasa)	550-94	Oceania
550-90	Costa Rica	550-48	Pakistan
		550-156	Paraguay
550-152	Cuba		
550-22	Cyprus	550-92	Peripheral States of the Arabian Peninsula
550-158	Czechoslovakia		
550-54	Dominican Republic	550-42	Peru
550-52	Ecuador	550-72	Philippines, Republic of
		550-84	Rwanda
550-150	El Salvador	550-51	Saudi Arabia
550-28	Ethiopia		
550-29	Germany	550-70	Senegal
550-153	Ghana	550-86	Somalia
550-87	Greece	550-93	South Africa, Republic of
		550-95	Soviet Union
550-78	Guatemala	550-27	Sudan
550-82	Guyana		
550-151	Honduras	550-47	Syria
550-21	India	550-62	Tanzania
550-154	Indian Ocean Territories	550-53	Thailand
		550-89	Tunisia
550-39	Indonesia	550-80	Turkey
550-68	Iran		
550-31	Iraq	550-74	Uganda
550-25	Israel	550-43	United Arab Republic
550-30	Japan	550-97	Uruguay
		550-71	Venezuela
550-34	Jordan	550-57	Vietnam, North
550-56	Kenya		
550-81	Korea, North	550-55	Vietnam, South
		550-75	Zambia

www.ingramcontent.com/pod-product-compliance
Lightning Source LLC
Chambersburg PA
CBHW030213170426
43201CB00006B/77